The Life Cycle of Corporate Governance

Corporate Governance in the New Global Economy

Series Editors: Kevin Keasey
Leeds Permanent Building Society Professor of Financial Services and Director, International Institute of Banking and Financial Services, Leeds University Business School, UK
Steve Thompson
Professor of Strategic Management, Nottingham University Business School, UK
Mike Wright
Professor of Financial Studies and Director, Centre for Management Buy-out Research, Nottingham University Business School, UK

For a list of all Edward Elgar published titles visit our site on the World Wide Web at
www.e-elgar.com

The Life Cycle of Corporate Governance

Edited by

Igor Filatotchev

Professor of International Strategic Management, Department of Management, King's College London, UK

and

Mike Wright

Professor of Financial Studies and Director of the Centre for Management Buy-out Research, Nottingham University Business School, UK and Visiting Professor, Erasmus University Rotterdam, The Netherlands

CORPORATE GOVERNANCE IN THE NEW GLOBAL ECONOMY

An Elgar Reference Collection
Cheltenham, UK • Northampton, MA, USA

Published by
Edward Elgar Publishing Limited
Glensanda House
Montpellier Parade
Cheltenham
Glos GL50 1UA
UK

Edward Elgar Publishing, Inc.
136 West Street
Suite 202
Northampton
Massachusetts 01060
USA

A catalogue record for this book
is available from the British Library

ISBN 1 84542 214 7

Typeset by Manton Typesetters, Louth, Lincolnshire, UK.
Printed and bound in Great Britain by MPG Books Ltd, Bodmin, Cornwall.

Contents

Contributors

Mufit Arberk, Management Centre, University of Bradford, UK

Ian Colville, School of Management, University of Bath, UK

R. Dino, University of Connecticut, USA

Susanne Espenlaub, Manchester School of Accounting and Finance, University of Manchester, UK

Igor Filatotchev, King's College, University of London, UK

Carles Gispert, University Autonoma Barcelona, Spain

Marc Goergen, Manchester School of Management, UMIST, UK and European Corporate Governance Institute, Belgium

Michelle Haynes, Nottingham University Business School, UK

James C. Hayton, Department of Management and Human Resources, College of Business, Utah State University, USA

Derek C. Jones, Department of Economics, Hamilton College, USA

Abe de Jong, Erasmus University Rotterdam, The Netherlands

Rezaul Kabir, Tilburg University, The Netherlands

Arif Khurshed, Manchester School of Accounting and Finance, University of Manchester, UK

David Laing, Robert Gordon University, Aberdeen, UK

Michael Lubatkin, School of Business, University of Connecticut, USA and Ecole de Management de Lyon, France

Colin Mayer, Said Business School, Oxford University, UK

Niels Mygind, Center for East European Studies, Copenhagen Business School, Denmark

Annie Pye, School of Management, University of Bath, UK

Luc Renneboog, Department of Finance and CentER for Economic Research, Tilburg University, The Netherlands

Bill Schulze, Weatherhead School of Management, Case Western Reserve University, Cleveland, USA

Steve Thompson, Nottingham University Business School, UK

Steve Toms, School of Management, University of York, UK

Charlie Weir, Robert Gordon University, Aberdeen, UK

Mike Wright, Centre for Management Buy-out Research, Nottingham University Business School, UK and Erasmus University Rotterdam, The Netherlands

Shaker A. Zahra, Babson College, Wellesley, USA

[1]

The corporate governance life cycle

Igor Filatotchev and Mike Wright

Introduction

The last decade has witnessed an explosion in both policy and research attention devoted to corporate governance. Corporate failures and regulatory initiatives have placed corporate governance systems under closer scrutiny than ever. High-profile corporate scandals such as Maxwell in the UK and Enron in the USA have given substantial influence to these developments. Starting with the Cadbury Report in the UK (Cadbury, 1992) there has been an international diffusion of codes and recommendations (see Demirag et al., 2000 for a review). This geographical spread has not been restricted to countries with Anglo-American corporate governance systems.

Emphasis has been placed on the monitoring and control dimensions of governance. Indeed the Cadbury Report's terms of reference were specifically restricted to financial or accountability aspects. Both policy and research attention has thus been focused on the roles of non-executive directors and the functioning of boards, disclosure practices, companies' relationships with auditors, executive remuneration issues and the roles of institutional investors (Short et al., 1999).

Much of this attention has been focused on large mature companies, with samples typically based on the largest FTSE listed corporations in the UK and the Fortune 500 in the USA. Many of these firms operate in relatively stable or 'low velocity' environments. From a theoretical point of view, much research effort has been underpinned by an agency perspective (Hart, 1995).

These developments have given rise to an overly narrow perspective on corporate governance. Corporate governance is both about ensuring accountability of management in order to minimize downside risks to shareholders and about enabling management to exercise enterprise in order to enable shareholders to benefit from the upside potential of firms (Keasey and Wright, 1993; Tricker, 1984). This distinction has sometimes been referred to as the conformance and performance aspects of corporate governance. We suggest, therefore, that there is a need to extend our understanding of governance issues beyond the narrow confines of economics and finance perspectives to embrace both learning and knowledge dimensions as well as contextual issues.

From a resource-based perspective, a firm's corporate governance system per se may not be a source of sustained competitive advantage but some firms may be much more skilled at implementing common governance devices and these skills may be heterogeneously distributed across firms. Implementing the correct governance in a given situation may help firms to realize the benefits of the resources they control through incentivizing and/or monitoring management to undertake the relevant actions. Governance choices may impact both the creation of rents from the use of valuable, rare, costly to imitate, and non-substitutable resources as well as their appropriation (Coff, 1999). Managers may be able to appropriate a disproportionate share of the rents a firm generates from an agency perspective. On the other hand, adequate compensation for their firm-specific investments may serve to reduce agency conflicts and be in the interests of equity holders (Castanias and Helfat, 2001). Similarly, boards may be more effective where they involve the recruitment of skilled directors who can help a firm fully realize its potential for generating economic rents rather than the appointment of the CEO's cronies or of outsiders focused on minimizing agency conflicts between a firm and its equity holders. This suggests that there may be important differences between the structure and functioning of a board designed to minimize agency costs, and a board designed to maximize a firm's rent generating potential (Barney et al., 2001).

Corporate governance issues have typically been focused on large firms with diffuse ownership; they are also important for younger founder-managed firms, particularly for those reaching a point in their development when they begin to face constraints on their ability to realize growth opportunities. The agency-based corporate governance lens may be applied to these threshold firms since it is at this point that issues arise surrounding the pressures on founders to cede control if their firms are to grow. Yet at the same time these firms need to find the resources and knowledge to enable them to grow.

Gedajlovic et al. (2004) extend an agency perspective on governance to suggest that the particular blend of incentives, authority relations and norms of legitimacy in founder firms interacts with the external environment to affect the nature and pace of learning and capability development. Founder–manager governance becomes less adept at dealing with the environments that become more munificent, complex and stable as firms develop. They suggest that governance needs to change first to overcome these problems as a prerequisite for dealing with the need to change a firm's resources, processes, values and culture. In contrast, Zahra and Filatotchev (2004) suggest that a knowledge-based view offers a more realistic and dynamic insight into the relationships that pervade threshold firms' governance systems. At the threshold stage, the resource and knowledge roles of governance may be particularly important for increasing strategic flexibility and ensuring long-term growth and survival. When the entrepreneurial firm matures and its management becomes more professionalized, changes in its ownership structure and the growing importance of external stakeholders may shift the balance towards the monitoring and control functions of governance systems, as suggested by agency research. Zahra and Filatotchev argue that corporate governance systems and organizational learning are interdependent, and in some cases may substitute or complement each other. A knowledge-based analysis of governance recognizes the importance of strategic context and the relevance of different types of knowledge at different stages of the firm's life cycle.

This debate suggests the notion of a number of firm life-cycle stages where different forms of corporate governance may be needed. Corporate governance may thus need to be viewed as a dynamic system that may change as firms evolve over these stages. The firm's evolution is accompanied by changes in ownership structure, board composition, the degree of founder involvement and so on. The balance of the accountability and enterprise roles of the various governance elements may change over this life cycle from establishment, growth, maturity and decline. For example, the knowledge contribution of boards may be more important in growing entrepreneurial firms than in firms facing more mature markets.

These arguments suggest that the firm's strategic dynamics and corporate governance changes are interlinked, and the firm's life cycle may go hand in hand with dramatic shifts in its governance system. Figure 1.1 provides a summary of this complex, time-dependent interrelationship, best envisaged as two interacting continua with the extreme cases of narrow and extensive organizational resource base at either end of the vertical axis and of high and limited accountability of managers to external shareholders at either end of the horizontal.

As Figure 1.1 shows, changes in organizational development stages are accompanied by different combinations of resource diversity and accountability, and these combinations

		Transparency/Accountability	
	Narrow	**Limited**	**High**
		Quadrant 1	*Quadrant 2*
		Small family businesses	'Threshold firms'
		Start-ups	Initial public offerings(IPOs)
Organizational resource base		University spin-offs	
	Extensive		
		Quadrant 4	*Quadrant 3*
		Declining organizations	Mature listed firms
		Public-to-private buy-outs	

Figure 1.1   Organizational and corporate governance dynamics

define the strategic positioning of an individual firm with respect to its environment. In the early stages of the life cycle (Quadrant 1), the entrepreneurial firm has a narrow resource base. It is, as a rule, owned and controlled by a tightly knit group of founder–managers and/or family investors, and the level of managerial accountability to external shareholders is rather low.

However, as the firm grows following its market expansion strategy and new opportunities, its governance system begins to change. In order to access external resources and expertise that may fuel and support this growth, the firm opens up its governance system to emerging external investors, such as 'business angels' and venture capital firms. At this stage, the balance between resources and accountability starts to shift towards greater transparency and increasing monitoring and control by these emerging external providers of resources. An initial public offering (IPO) (Quadrant 2) represents a dramatic shift from an entrepreneurial firm to a 'professional' firm with a fully developed governance system. This shift in accountability widens the firm's access to the vast pool of financial resources of the stock market. This stage is followed by an expansion of the firm's resources base as it matures and exploits strategic opportunities (Quadrant 3).

Quadrant 4 represents a final stage in our resource-governance cycle. At this stage, the firm may have exhausted its growth opportunities in the focal industry and over-diversified into related and unrelated industries (Hitt et al., 2003). As a result, its governance system may have become less transparent, and incentive alignment between managers and external shareholders looser. Managerial drive for ever-increasing expansion and diversification leads to performance deterioration and loss in shareholder value. Despite a substantial inherited resource base, an opaque and inefficient governance system cannot prevent managerial opportunism or arrest organizational decline (Filatotchev and Toms, 2003). In a turnaround situation, governance itself may turn into a driver of further decline by imposing serious financial constraints on the organization that erode its resource base (Toms and Filatotchev, 2004). The only viable strategic alternative at this stage may be to take a public company private. In terms of Figure 1.1, this would complete the firm's governance life cycle. Restructuring of a declining organization or following a public to private buy-out may result in a reinvigoration of the life cycle as more transparent incentive and governance mechanisms are introduced in the form of increased managerial equity, monitoring by private equity firms and a commitment to service debt (Jensen, 1993; Thompson and Wright, 1995). As such, the organization may narrow the scope of its activities and move back towards the other quadrants.

By focusing on resource-accountability issues, this framework may be a useful heuristic lens to analyse various content and context aspects of the corporate governance life cycle. First, it may help to understand factors that affect the balance between the possible functions of corporate governance. Agency research is predominantly focused on the monitoring and control functions of the corporate governance mechanisms. The resource dependence and strategic change perspectives have suggested that, in addition to control functions, corporate governance factors may also play service/resource and strategic roles in the decision-making process (Pfeffer, 1972; Zahra and Pearce, 1989), especially when the firm is in a crucial transition phase such as the IPO (Daily and Dalton, 1992). For example, the links that independent directors have with the firm's environment can be used to obtain the financial resources needed for growth, as well as important information and strategic expertise (Golden and Zajac, 2001). Institutional investors involved in a focal firm also may be an important support mechanism by providing access to financial resources when needed (Filatotchev and Toms, 2003).

Figure 1.1 informs our understanding of governance dynamics and the changing roles of governance factors when the firm evolves along its life cycle. As noted earlier, the 'threshold' stages of the firm's evolution, resource and knowledge roles of governance may be particularly important for increasing strategic flexibility and ensuring a long-term focus on growth and survival. When the entrepreneurial firm matures and its management becomes more 'professionalized', changes in its ownership structure and the growing importance of external stakeholders may shift the balance towards the monitoring and control functions of governance systems, as suggested by agency research. When the firm enters the stages of maturity and decline, the resource and strategy roles of corporate governance may once again become important (Toms and Filatotchev, 2004). The top management team and outside investors, therefore, have to find the right balance between the multiple functions that corporate governance may perform in the evolving firm.

Second, the research framework presented in Figure 1.1 may be extended beyond the simple emphasis on firm-level aspects and mechanisms to encompass more general industrial and institutional changes in a particular country. Deregulation, for example, may impact both the resource base and governance characteristics of firms such as in the utilities and transport sectors in many countries, and define a new phase in their life cycle. Similarly, institutional changes such as the development of a market for corporate control may change the extent of managerial accountability even if other, firm-level, governance factors do not change. This framework suggests that the firm's strategy and governance life cycles should not be analysed separately from economic and institutional dynamics in a particular country.

The chapters in this book examine the various life-cycle stages of firms. The first eight chapters examine corporate governance and life-cycle stages in general. The next four chapters consider the corporate governance life cycle in different industrial and institutional contexts. These contributions are reviewed in the following two sections. The subsequent section considers crucial governance issues relating to the transition between stages. Finally, some conclusions are drawn.

Governance and Life-cycle Stages

Mayer (Chapter 2) examines the role of venture capital and changes in corporate governance over the different stages of venture growth. This involves a transition from personal to business angel, to venture capital (VC) to stock market finance and a gradual broadening of the investor base. Control moves from the entrepreneur to single outside investors who are active managers, to financial institutions who use intermediary VC firms to screen and manage their investments, to stock markets with largely passive investors. As such, VC is just one stage in a gradual transition from tight ownership and control by founders and families to widely held shareholdings. The VC helps bridge that transition by providing intermediation between investors and firms. As such, it is an institutional form for which there will be an enduring need. The notion of venture capital may vary between institutional environments. A VC firm performs a fundamental intermediary role in the UK and the USA that few other institutions undertake. While there may be a continuing need for VC type institutions within the context of Anglo-American market economies, their function and significance may endure in other forms elsewhere. For example, in many countries the VC firm is little more than a subsidiary form that allows a bank to invest in higher-risk activities. Mayer suggests that there is no single best form of high-tech financing, and the most important function that regulation can perform is to encourage institutional experimentation and innovation.

As environmental and organizational complexities grow, different knowledge and skills are needed to effectively manage the entrepreneurial and administrative challenges, and the founder's knowledge that has been accumulated in the past may create a cognitive barrier to effective strategic responses to changing circumstances (Daily and Dalton, 1992). This situation presents a threshold for early-stage firms. To cross this threshold these firms need to cede control to professional managers. Zahra and Hayton (Chapter 3) shed light on this issue by examining how board composition varies from the start-up (years 1–5) to the adolescent stage (years 6–8) of the organizational life cycle and how board composition influences the innovative and financial performance of high-technology new ventures. Innovation enables new ventures to position their products differently from the competition and achieve profits that reward entrepreneurs for their willingness to take risks. They apply organizational life-cycle and resource-dependence theories in examining 416 US high-technology new ventures and find that significant shifts occur in board composition as new ventures move from the start-up to the adolescent stage. Changes in board composition reflect the strategic challenges and contingencies new ventures face in their operations. Different board composition variables influence the innovative and financial performance of new ventures differently in the start-up versus adolescent stages. The representation of outside directors on the board increases significantly as firms mature and boards in adolescent firms show greater diversity in their educational and functional backgrounds than those that govern start-up firms.

Using an agency-theoretic lens and insights drawn from the behavioural economics and family business literatures, Schulze, Lubatkin and Dino (Chapter 4) develop hypotheses concerning the effect of dispersion of ownership on the use of debt by private family-owned and family-managed firms. From a field study of 1464 family firms they find that, during periods of market growth, the relationship between the use of debt and the dispersion of ownership among directors at family firms can be graphed as a U-shaped curve. They argue that just as the separation of ownership and control in widely held firms drives a wedge between the interests of principal and agent, the dispersion of ownership in family-held firms drives a wedge between the interests of those who lead a firm and other family owners. Their arguments suggest that, contrary to the tenets of conventional agency research, inside ownership and board oversight do not efficiently resolve the problems experienced by private, family-owned and -managed firms.

As Figure 1.1 suggests, an IPO represents the first major shift in the firm's life cycle. Although expanding, the resource base of the firm is still relatively narrow, but emergent external investors demand an increase in managerial accountability in exchange for their support. Considerable attention has been focused on the principal–agent problem between VC and entrepreneurs. VC-backed IPOs may in fact suffer from two sets of agency costs which are related to principal–agent and principal–principal relationships between the founders and members of the VC syndicate. As a result, new governance arrangements may need to be introduced to mitigate the agency costs associated with VC involvement in IPO firms. Filatotchev, Wright and Arberk (Chapter 5) examine the development of effective boards in VC-backed IPOs. Using a unique sample of 293 entrepreneurial IPOs in the UK, they show that VC syndicates invest in relatively more risky firms. VC-backed IPOs have more independent boards than IPOs with no VC involvement, with board independence being higher in syndicated VC-backed firms. They also find that single VCs team up with industry partners, whereas in syndicated IPOs there is a higher equity presence of passive private equity firms investing alongside VC firms.

Espenlaub, Goergen and Khurshed (Chapter 6) take a step further along the firm's governance life cycle and explore possible governance effects of lock-in arrangements after the IPO. These agreements form an important contractual context that defines ownership structure during the first few months after flotation since they require that (some) pre-IPO shareholders refrain from selling some or all of the shares they retained at the IPO during a certain, pre-specified period. Using a sample of IPOs issued in the UK during 1992–98, they investigate whether VC backing of the IPO, and the existence, types and characteristics of agreements used by VC backers to lock in their retained shareholdings, has any systematic association with the corresponding features of the lock-in agreements of company directors and other pre-IPO shareholders. The authors argue that lock-in arrangements serve a number of governance functions that may not be solved by traditional governance arrangements such as board characteristics and other control systems. These functions may be related to such issues as the information asymmetry associated with a fast-growing firm or the need to retain key managerial talent. The chapter's analysis sheds light on the question whether the presence of VC backing and the lock-in agreements of VCs act as strategic complements or substitutes to the lock-in agreements of the directors and other shareholders. The authors also document the retained post-IPO share ownership of directors, VCs and other shareholders, and examine the associations between retained ownership, on the one hand, and the presence of VC backing and the existence and contractual characteristics of the lock-in agreements of VCs, directors and other shareholders, on the other.

Poor long-run performance post-IPO may arise from the agency problems caused when ownership by the original shareholders is diluted in the IPO. Goergen and Renneboog (Chapter 7) examine ownership retention in a sample of German and UK IPOs covering the period 1981–88, the determinants of ownership retention and its impact on IPO long-term performance. First, they study ownership retention by pre-IPO shareholders over a period of six years following the flotation. They find that this is a function of four factors: total risk, growth rate of assets, involvement of the founder, and the existence of non-voting shares. This suggests that results obtained from studies on corporate performance and ownership that have assumed ownership to be exogenous may suffer from serious econometric biases. They also provide evidence on whether the poor long-run performance of IPOs is due to the reduction in the holdings of the pre-IPO shareholders. Using recently developed econometric estimation techniques, which do not suffer from omitted-variable bias, they find that long-run performance and ownership are unrelated. They find that poor long-term performance of IPOs cannot be explained by the observed dilution of ownership by the original shareholders after the IPO and possible agency conflicts caused by this dilution.

Considerable research attention has been devoted to the role of corporate governance in mature firms. Johnson (1996) reviewed studies that examine corporate refocusing, while a number of studies focusing specifically on the determinants of divestment have identified the role of corporate governance factors (Hoskisson et al., 1994; Haynes et al., 2000, 2003). However, attention to the role of incentives for managers in this work has been problematical. Murphy (1997) suggests that conventional size-based remuneration and non-pecuniary benefits of executive employment would tend to generate an incentive to build and maintain corporate empires. If the modern economy requires large firms to divest non-core activities, as Jensen (1993) and others have argued, the shareholder–principals need to provide alternative incentives. These are most obviously supplied in the form of share-based compensation. Haynes, Thompson and Wright (Chapter 8) extend previous work on the determinants of divestment in mature firms. Their chapter presents the first attempt to test for the importance of share-based incentives in motivating managers to take non-preferred downsizing decisions. Agency theory suggests that options are a cost-effective form of providing high-powered incentives (Sadler, 1999). They construct a series of share-based measures aimed at combining the incentive effects of actual share ownership with the wealth-augmenting effect of share price appreciation on the stock of options held by executives. Using a sample of 158 of the top 500 listed firms in the UK, they show that share-based incentives are indeed associated with divestment activity over the period 1985–93 and suggest they might be necessary to persuade managers to take downsizing decisions that might otherwise harm their pecuniary and non-pecuniary well-being.

Toms and Filatotchev (Chapter 9) develop a theoretical model of strategic corporate turnaround integrating governance and associated financial arrangements. Inclusion of the latter elements reinforces the earlier model developed by Robbins and Pearce (1992), which places retrenchment at the centre of the turnaround process. Unlike Robbins and Pearce, their model suggests that in certain conditions retrenchment may be prevented by hard financial constraints. While some turnaround researchers suggest that retrenchment strategies involving the sale of critical assets might be detrimental as a result of trading short-run survival for longer-run strategic advantage (Barker and Mone, 1994), the model presented by Toms and Filatotchev suggests a more complex story. First, retrenchment is an integral part of the turnaround process according to a rational decision-making model with financial and governance constraints. The supporting empirical case of the cotton textile industry confirms retrenchment to be a necessary condition for subsequent turnaround. Second, they show that asset sales are not always discretionary and the governance arrangements may prevent such disposals. This problem is less likely to occur in multi-product firms where managers are more likely to be able to redeploy resources from one sector to another, but this may only be possible where managers avoid investment in highly specific assets with associated high levels of fixed cost. Their arguments point to a stark choice for management. Management either have to commit themselves to high fixed-cost sunk investments and pay the price in the event of a crisis, or they avoid them and thereby avoid crisis, but instead fail to achieve competitive advantage and only receive the normal profit levels at the given stage of the business cycle.

Mature listed corporations may face shortcomings in their corporate governance system that mean that they do not adapt to changed environmental circumstances. For example, they may fail to exit from sectors with limited positive net present value projects and have substantial free cash flow (Jensen, 1993). Taking a corporation private leads to changes in its corporate governance mechanisms aimed at reducing agency costs and increasing the upside incentives for management. Public-to-private buy-outs typically involve significantly increased equity holding by management, concentrated equity holding by private equity firms who also become active investors through their board positions, specification of reporting requirements and other conditions in the corporate charter (shareholders' agreement) by the private equity firm that constrain management, and the pressure to service debt (Thompson and Wright, 1995). Weir, Laing and Wright (Chapter 10) investigate the factors that influence the decision to change the status of a publicly quoted company to that of a private company. The mechanisms identified in the Cadbury Code would be expected to mitigate the agency problems associated with weak internal governance. An independent board pursuing shareholders' interests is indicative of effective internal monitoring. Thus boards with a greater proportion of non-executive directors as suggested by the Cadbury Code may be expected to be more effective monitors. Similarly, boards that separate the posts of chief executive officer and chairman will be better able to influence decisions. Therefore duality is less likely to be present in firms going private. More effective external monitoring will occur as institutional shareholdings increase and the free-rider problem is overcome. Alternatively, public-to-private (PTP) transactions may be driven by the incentives for management to obtain substantial financial gains as they increase their shareholding post-PTP. Using a matched sample of firms that go private and those that do not, they find that firms that go private are more likely to have higher CEO ownership and higher institutional ownership. In relation to their board structures, firms going private tend to have more duality but there is no statistical difference in the proportion of non-executive directors. They do not show signs of having excess free cash flows, but there is some evidence of lower growth opportunities. They do not find that firms going private experience a greater threat of hostile acquisition. Their results are consistent with incentive and monitoring explanations of going private. Calculation of the probability of going private shows that incentive effects are stronger than the monitoring effects.

Industrial and Institutional Life Cycles

The firm life cycle needs to be viewed as taking place within the life cycle of the market environment in which the firm is operating and, more broadly, the institutional life cycle of the country in which the firm is located. Developed market economies may typically be considered to be stable but may be subject over long periods of time to significant institutional changes. Toms and Wright (Chapter 11) adopt a systemic view and compare two countries whose systems are often linked closely in the governance literature but which in fact have marked differences. They examine why American and British firms adopted diversification strategies and multi-divisional structures in the middle of the twentieth century and why this strategy and structure was reversed towards the end. To explain this change they develop a theoretical framework that links the firm resource base, corporate governance arrangements, and the impact on entrepreneurial activity, managerial behaviour and business performance. Adoption of the American model by British firms is found to have been very partial in the 1950–80 period. This meant that British firms were more easily able to adjust to capital market pressures to reduce diversification after 1980. In particular, their greater use of management buy-outs was an effective vehicle for this restructuring. In the USA, cheap debt and greater scrutiny from the capital markets was a threat to the model of managerial entrenchment that evolved up to 1980. Unlike in the UK, the role of the leveraged buy-out (LBO) was more temporary and ultimately mitigated by parent-to-parent subsidiary transfers creating opportunities for managerial re-entrenchment through financial and corporate restructuring.

In addition to major economic and political developments over time, the last decade or so has seen the development of the life cycle of an important institutional change in relation to corporate governance codes. From an absence of specific corporate governance codes save those enshrined in company law, these codes have developed in the UK over time to become more refined and comprehensive. From an initial narrow focus on accountability (Cadbury, 1992) they have developed to cover specific recommendations on the determination of executive remuneration (Greenbury, 1995), to recommendations regarding business performance (Hampel, 1998), to the Combined Code (Committee on Corporate Governance, 1998), through a review of company law (Company Law Review Steering Committee, 1999) and a consultative document on directors' remuneration (DTI, 1999), guidance relating to the implementation of the Combined Code relating to internal control (Turnbull, 1999), a report on the role of institutional investors (Myners, 2001), more detailed recommendations on the role of non-executive directors (Higgs, 2003) and the role of internal audit (Smith, 2003), and a revised Combined Code of Practice in 2003 (FRC, 2003) (for discussion see Short et al., 1999, 2000). Similar developments are also occurring internationally.

Pye and Colville's chapter (Chapter 12) keys into this theme of changes in corporate governance and the environment facing enterprises in the specific UK context relating to changes in what happens at board level in a sample of large UK organizations which are classically described as at a mature stage in their life cycle. Based on two studies conducted in 1987 and 2001, Pye and Colville examine the changing environmental context in which boards of directors and their firms now operate compared to over a decade earlier. Pye and Colville broaden the scope of conceptual analysis beyond agency theory to develop an integrated analysis of processes of interaction in making sense of boards and their sense-making. This approach considers not just what boards do but also how and why they do it. They suggest that the governance life cycle is affected not just by the state of maturity of a corporation but is also influenced by managers' mindsets and their cultural heritage. A consequence is that the role of boards is perhaps to 'interrupt' the organizational life cycle – changing direction in some way rather than progressing on to the next stage of development or metamorphosis. They find that it is the relationship between chairman and CEO around which board culture (r)evolves and that this is the key to director effectiveness. A macro–micro tension arises here in that greater reliance on codes of conduct encourages more to happen 'off stage', which works against the drive for greater openness and transparency.

Corporate governance factors found to be important in one specific governance system may not be generalizable into other systems. Country-specific features may be highly relevant. Gispert et al. (Chapter 13) investigate whether international differences in corporate governance systems affect firm performance. They construct a firm-level panel database of a sample of matched industrial companies listed on the stock exchanges in Belgium, the Netherlands and the UK. The UK is an example of the market-based model and comes under the Common Law family with the strongest protection of shareholders and creditors (La Porta et al., 1998). Belgium is an example of French Civil Law family which is characterized by relatively weak investor protection and corporate law enforcement. In between the UK and Belgium is the Netherlands, which falls under the German Civil Law system, having somewhat stronger protection of creditors. Share ownership is not as dispersed (concentrated) as in the UK (Belgium). In particular, they investigate whether differences in two key aspects of a corporate governance mechanism, that is control concentration and board structure, affect firm performance. They include governance characteristics that are present in all three countries as well as characteristics that are unique to one of the three countries. The two-tier corporate board structure is the norm in the Netherlands while one-tier boards are typical in Belgium and the UK. They find significant cross-country differences in board size, board composition, and ownership structure of listed firms. The average board size and the proportion of non-executives in Belgian firms is larger than that of the Netherlands and the UK. Ownership concentration is the highest in Belgium and the lowest in the UK. These common features do not have similar cross-country relationships with corporate performance. Their analysis of stock returns, for example, shows that financial institutional investors only have a significant impact in the UK, which is positive. Specific corporate governance features of a country play an important role in determining corporate performance relative to the common characteristics. For example, for each of the three performance measures used, a significantly negative impact of so-called holding companies is found in Belgium. This characteristic is unique to the Belgian setting.

Emerging markets may be particularly dynamic. For example, transition economies emerging from central planning face marked shifts in their institutional life cycle as policies are introduced to create a market economy through enacting wide-ranging property rights and corporate reporting legislation as well as to transfer enterprises from the state to the private sector. These changes may trigger a dynamic period of adjustment as the governance, and particularly ownership features, attempt to adapt to the new environment. Jones and Mygind (Chapter 14) show that the governance cycle for transitional countries reflects some specific characteristics, for example privatization often produces specific initial ownership structures, with an unusually high proportion of insider, especially employee, ownership. Subsequently pressures for restructuring produce strong impulses for ownership changes. There is limited possibility for external finance because of the embryonic development of the banking system and the capital markets during early transition. The governance cycle is also influenced by specific features of the institutional, cultural and economic environment in a country. The varying importance of these factors is expected to produce differences in key features of ownership cycles such as the speed at which particular ownership changes occur. They examine the ownership cycle in three Baltic countries through a series of transition matrices showing both starting and final ownership configurations for sample enterprises and simultaneously providing information on changes in concentration for the largest single owner. In spite of important differences in institutional development, especially concerning the privatization process, they find that governance cycles are broadly similar in all countries. Employee ownership is rapidly fading and mainly being succeeded by managerial ownership. There are changes back and forth between manager and domestic external ownership, while foreign ownership is quite stable. Ownership concentration is mostly increasing after privatization, which included diversification both to employees and external owners. Since ownership diversification did not sit well with the slow development of the institutional framework, as expected, they find a subsequent concentration of ownership on managers, external domestic and foreign owners. However, there are also important differences across countries. The adjustment of ownership structures is faster in Estonia and this can be explained by the relatively fast pace of institutional change and evolution of important governance institutions, including tough bankruptcy legislation and advances in the financial system.

The Governance Transition Process between Stages

Daily and Dalton (1992) have focused attention on the professionalization problems faced by the emerging founder-managed firm; this is not the only threshold in the life cycle of the firm. Each transition between the stages of a firm's life cycle may be conceived as representing a threshold that needs to be surmounted. A key issue faced by firms concerns how they pass through the threshold from one stage in their life cycle to the next and how corporate governance mechanisms adapt to facilitate or hinder this process.

An important aspect of this issue concerns the extent to which firms are able to adapt their governance mechanisms in a very flexible manner or whether there is significant path dependence. An interesting approach is adopted by Lynall et al. (2003), who consider agency, resource dependence, institutional, and social network theories to show how board composition and, consequently, firm performance are a reflection of both the firm's life-cycle stage and the relative power of the CEO and external financiers at the time of founding. They argue that boards are subject to path dependence, and, thus, board composition is likely to persist over time.

High-tech ventures being spun off from universities provide interesting examples of very early-stage thresholds faced by new ventures. Vohora et al. (2004) identify four critical junctures in the development of these spin-offs: opportunity recognition, entrepreneurial commitment, credibility to customers and financiers, and sustainability. The nature of governance may need to change quite significantly over these stages of development to enable the venture to overcome the critical junctures. Ucbasaran et al. (2003) have shown that an important part of the development process of a venture is the entry and exit of team members. In spin-offs from universities, the initial opportunity recognition and entrepreneurial commitment phases may require the academic entrepreneur to be supplemented by an external, surrogate entrepreneur with the requisite commercial and industrial skills (Franklin et al., 2001). Post-doctoral students may have an important technical role to play. The university's technology transfer office may also have an important governance role in shaping the establishment of the venture and creating a legal entity. Initial governance issues here concern the initial allocation of equity holdings by these parties and their influence in the development of the business. At the later credibility and sustainability phases, there may be a need for more formal governance mechanisms with the entry of non-executive directors, commercial managers, external investors and so on. Academic and surrogate entrepreneurs, university technology transfer officers and post-doctoral students may exit the venture at the entrepreneurial commitment, credibility and sustainability phases owing to conflicts regarding the future direction of the venture (especially as ventures typically require reorientation as the feasible route to market becomes clearer) or because their skills cease to be valuable. These entries and exits raise important governance issues in terms of how changes in the equity holdings are negotiated, the selection of new equity holders and the replacement of existing equity holders. For example, at the earlier stages of the venture major differences arising because of the different objectives and understanding of market factors between academic and surrogate entrepreneurs may only be resolved by the exit. Similarly, while there may have to be entry of individuals with generalist market-related skills in order to overcome the juncture of credibility, the existing parties need to recognize this need and be able to act on it. To what extent can these changes be resolved by the power that comes from the size of an individual's equity holding or to what extent and when do other governance mechanisms become more important? Further research is required to examine the process by which these changes are facilitated.

The succession process in family-owned firms raises important governance issues. Several studies have examined the mechanisms and structures that can be utilized by family firm owners seeking to transfer family firm ownership and management control to the next generation of family members (Morris et al., 1997). This is an important issue as only about one-quarter of family businesses are estimated naturally to possess the blend of skills and capabilities needed to transfer their business to the next generation (Lansberg, 1999). Many of the factors impeding the transfer of family firms to the next generation are influenced by the complex intertwining of family, ownership and management systems that exist in family firms (Ward, 1987; Neubauer and Lank, 1998). There may be irreconcilable family differences between owners of family firms, and an internal transfer of ownership within the dominant family group owning the business cannot be achieved. Few studies focus on the transfer of majority share ownership in former family businesses to individuals who are not related to the original family firm owners (Bachkaniwala et al., 2001; Birley and Westhead, 1993; Bleackley et al., 1996). A management buy-out (MBO) provides one means of realizing the family's investment in the firm as well as allowing its continued independent ownership and ethos, yet there may be important information asymmetries between the vendor family and the incumbent non-family management that can affect the nature of succession of this form (Howorth et al., 2004). Where information is shared equally between the vendors and the MBO team, both sides are likely to co-operate closely through the negotiation process with a joint commitment to the firm's future and a continuing relationship facilitate knowledge transfer and improved post-deal performance. Alternatively, in a stereotypical patriarchal family firm, with a commitment to the future of the firm, vendors may take an autocratic approach in negotiations, which the MBO team go along with. Where there is little trust or relationship between the parties or where it breaks down during negotiations, negotiations tend to be competitive. The MBO team may have more information, usually because they are more involved in the day-to-day running of the firm, and thus tend to dominate the deal process. Conflict post-MBO is likely as the true value becomes apparent. The vendor may have little further involvement in the firm while performance may improve with increased managerial motivation.

Initial public offerings (IPOs) of entrepreneurial firms present a unique context for studying young, fast-growing organizations that are undergoing dramatic change (Welbourne and Andrews, 1996). This transitory stage of the firm's life-cycle development is often equated with the 're-birth' or 're-start' of organizations (Finkle, 1998: 6). Daily and Dalton (1992:

25–6) indicate that at this threshold stage the firm is 'at (or near) the point of transition from entrepreneurial to professional management. This transition appears to be inevitable as the firm outgrows the expertise and resources of the entrepreneur-founder.' In moving from private to public ownership, IPO firms offer their stock to the public market for the first time. The associated transition from 'entrepreneurial' to 'professional' management (Daily and Dalton, 1992) requires a substantial effort, particularly on the part of the company's top management team, existing investors and advisers, to prepare the IPO firm for the scrutiny of the regulator and investment community and, more specifically, to establish a corporate governance system that will comply with the regulator's guidelines, such as the UK Listing Authority's Combined Code on Corporate Governance. Despite its growing importance for both academic and business communities, the process of corporate governance development in these threshold firms is not well understood. More specifically, very little is known about the factors affecting particular governance characteristics of this type of firm, such as the selection and incentives of non-executive directors (Daily and Dalton, 1992).

Previous research on the corporate governance problems of IPOs has increasingly drawn on agency theory (e.g. Beatty and Zajac, 1994) and upper echelon research (e.g. Filatotchev and Bishop, 2002) to generate a body of conceptual and empirical studies that are focused on various organizational outcomes associated with board structural characteristics and the allocation of ownership and control rights after the issue. Some authors have emphasized the governance role of large external shareholders in general and VC firms in particular (e.g. Megginson and Weiss, 1991) in restraining the self-serving behaviour of decision makers in the IPO firm. This research, however, does not provide the answer to a related and equally important question – what factors determine *ex ante* board selection and ownership structure of the IPO firm in the first place?

A growing number of studies in the strategy area (e.g. Beatty and Zajac, 1994) and entrepreneurship research (e.g. Daily and Dalton, 1992) stress that, in the context of IPOs, the governance system may be an endogenous mechanism that is closely related to the IPO founder team's (TMT – Top Management Team's) characteristics and distribution of power within the organization (Filatotchev and Bishop, 2002). Being at an early stage of the firm's corporate governance life cycle, the IPO provides a unique context for the analysis of the board development process. More specifically, IPO research may help to shed light on a number of relatively underresearched issues that Pettigrew (1992: 176) raised in his study on managerial elites, such as: why do boards look the way they do? How are particular constellations of human resource assets on the board defined and built up? How does TMT power affect the control relationships between team members and the board? These questions, however, extend discussion beyond the relatively narrow boundaries of agency theory; and a growing number of studies suggest that an agency framework should be used in conjunction with complementary theories in examining governance-related issues, including behavioural and socio-cognitive research.

At the opposite end of the spectrum of the firm's life-cycle stages is the situation of organizational decline, and an important issue is related to governance transitions from maturity to decline. Research on business strategies in crisis situations has grown considerably in recent years, and a number of studies suggest that governance factors will interact with other firms' strategic characteristics to enable or constrain effective managerial response in crisis situations. These relationships are encapsulated in the notion of the organization's 'strategic flexibility', defined as 'a firm's ability to respond to various demands from dynamic competitive environments' (Sanchez, 1995: 138). Strategic flexibility depends jointly on the inherent flexibility of resources available to the firm and on the abilities of managers and their incentives to develop effective restructuring strategies in the short and long run. Previous research has recognized that organizational diversity factors such as product diversification, vertical integration, a multi-plant structure and so on are likely to promote strategic flexibility and impact positively on the strategic options available to managers in a crisis situation. For example, specialization strategies by product or market are more likely to be associated with non-fungible, task-specific assets. On the other hand greater diversity in products, production equipment and managerial hierarchy facilitates portfolio, financial and organizational restructuring (Hoskisson et al., 1994). However, organizational diversity may be a necessary but not sufficient condition of a higher strategic flexibility. Learning how to adapt an organization to its environment rests largely with the firm's leaders whose knowledge and skills determine an organization's ability to leverage and exploit its resources (Sanchez, 1995). Previous research associated strategic flexibility with managerial characteristics such as cognitive abilities, risk-taking, entrepreneurial orientation and so on (see Hitt et al., 2003, for a discussion). However, the impact of general corporate governance factors on strategic flexibility of the organization remains largely unexplored.

As acknowledged in a number of previous studies, when managers fail to respond to the adverse effects of rapid economic and social change and an actual or anticipated resource depletion, effective corporate governance can significantly influence organizational capacity to change in terms of managerial ability and willingness to undertake restructuring (Hoskisson et al., 1994; Zahra and Pearce, 1989). While the general literature on strategic restructuring has accommodated this paradigm and achieved significant results, the effects of corporate governance mechanisms on managerial decisions and firm survival in an environment of industrial decline are relatively underresearched. Filatotchev and Toms (2003), for example, focus on broader governance factors such as ownership structure and board characteristics in their empirical investigation of the cotton textile industry in the UK. They found that board diversity and institutional share ownership were important factors that helped a number of firms in a declining industry to survive. In a more recent study, Toms and Filatotchev (2004) use institutional theory and argue that a firm's governance life cycle lags behind its strategic development, and this lag is defined, among other factors, by the institutional constraints and membership in various networks. These authors show that governance factors may constrain the firm's strategic flexibility, in particular in a business turnaround situation.

Agency theory has been predominantly used as a tool to analyse management and leverage buy-outs of listed firms in mature sectors with few investment opportunities. Here the pressure to service debt, the introduction of active investors and significant equity stakes for management may lead to a greater search for profitable opportunities and the elimination of free cash flow. The chapter by Weir et al. presented here (Chapter 10) indicates that the evidence for free cash flow argument for buy-outs is weak and suggests that buy-outs of listed companies may be quite heterogeneous since management may perceive opportunities for gains that cannot be realized if the firm remains listed. A potential problem is that while commitment to the firm may increase if the management invest further amounts of their own cash to purchase the shares acquired in a PTP, the increased leverage that typically accompanies a PTP may mean that management can increase their equity stake without increasing their financial commitment to the business and may indeed allow management to liquidate some of their wealth. This may mean that the effects on performance are not as strong as expected.

Similarly, Wright et al. (2000, 2001) identified scope for buy-outs of listed entrepreneurial companies that may require a reinvigoration of entrepreneurial talent and/or enhanced monitoring. These 'busted techs' may require quite different managerial incentives and monitoring from the more traditional efficiency-oriented buy-outs. Importantly, they may also require a different complementarity between the skills of management, the skills of the private equity investor and the nature of financing. Wright et al. (2000, 2001) suggest that traditional buy-outs that involve efforts to enhance efficiency require management that respond to enhance financial incentives and private equity firms with financial monitoring skills. They also suggest, however, that where public-to-private transactions involve scope for entrepreneurial activity and innovation, there is a need for management with an entrepreneurial mindset, private equity investors that possess more specific industry skills and a more flexible financing structure with lower leverage that allows the venture scope to invest in more uncertain activities. These differences, therefore, have implications for the composition of boards in these ventures and the recruitment of managers that are as yet not well understood. To what extent, for example, are boards of directors in PTPs changed to bring in executive and non-executive directors with the skills to grow as well a restructure a business? To what extent do those fairly common PTPs where the management already have a significant equity stake lead to the release of entrepreneurial activities that were constrained by the stock market or simply the entrenchment of that management?

Conclusions

The chapters presented in this volume show that corporate governance is important at different parts of the life cycle of firms and organizations, not just in respect of mature firms where most research attention has hitherto been focused. As the chapters in this book show, there is a clear imbalance in the amount of research devoted to corporate governance at the different stages in the life cycle of firms. We have identified different roles for corporate governance but as yet there is no framework that convincingly integrates how these different roles relate to the different stages in the life cycle. There is a need for more research that examines the process by which firms change their governance mechanisms as they pass through these thresholds. It is our hope that the chapters presented here will provide a stimulus to this potentially exciting new research agenda.

References

Bachkaniwala, D., Wright, M. and Ram, M. (2001), 'Succession in South Asian businesses in the UK', *International Small Business Journal*, **19**(4): 15–27.

Barker III, V.L. and Mone, M.A. (1994), 'Retrenchment: Cause of turnaround or consequence of decline?', *Strategic Management Journal*, **15**: 395–405.

Barney, J., Wright, M. and Ketchen, D. (2001), 'The RBV of the firm: ten years after 1991', *Journal of Management*, **27**: 625–41.

Beatty, R.P. and Zajac, E. (1994), 'Managerial incentives, monitoring, and risk bearing: a study of executive compensation, ownership, and board structure in initial public offerings', *Administrative Science Quarterly*, **39**: 313–35.

Birley, S. and Westhead, P. (1993), 'The owner–manager's exit route', in H. Klandt (ed.), *Entrepreneurship and Business Development*, Aldershot: Gower, 123–40.

Bleackley, M., Hay, M., Wright, M. and Robbie, K. (1996), 'Entrepreneurial attitudes to venture capital investment realization: evidence from the UK and France', *Entrepreneurship and Regional Development*, **8**: 37–55.

Cadbury A. (1992), *Report of the Committee on the Financial Aspects of Corporate Governance*, London: Gee Publishing.

Castanias, R. and Helfat, C. (2001), 'The managerial rents model: theory and empirical analysis', *Journal of Management*, **27**: 661–78.

Coff, R. (1999), 'When competitive advantage doesn't lead to performance: the resource-based view and stakeholder bargaining power', *Organization Science*, **10**(2): 119–33.

Committee on Corporate Governance (1998), *The Combined Code*, London Stock Exchange Limited, London: Gee Publishing.

Company Law Review Steering Committee (1999), *Modern Company Law for a Competitive Economy: The Strategic Framework*. London: DTI.

Daily, C. and Dalton, D. (1992), 'The relationship between governance structure and corporate performance in entrepreneurial firms', *Journal of Business Venturing*, **7**: 375–86.

Demirag, I., Sudarsanam, S. and Wright, M. (2000), 'Corporate governance: overview and research agenda', *British Accounting Review*, **32**: 341–54.

Department of Trade and Industry (1999), *Directors' Remuneration: A Consultative Document*, London: DTI.

Filatotchev, I. and Bishop, K. (2002), 'Board composition, share ownership and "underpricing" of UK IPO firms', *Strategic Management Journal*, **28**: 941–55.

Filatotchev, I. and Toms, S. (2003), 'Corporate governance, strategy and survival in a declining industry: a study of UK cotton textile companies', *Journal of Management Studies*, **40**(4): 895–920.

Financial Reporting Council (2003), *Revised Combined Code*, London: FRC.

Finkle, T.A. (1998), 'The relationship between boards of directors and initial public offerings in the biotechnology industry', *Entrepreneurship Theory and Practice*, **22**: 5–29.

Franklin, S., Wright, M. and Lockett, A. (2001), 'Academic and surrogate entrepreneurs in university spin-out companies', *Journal of Technology Transfer*, **26**(1–2): 127–41.

Gedajlovic, E., Lubatkin, M. and Schulze, W. (2004), 'Crossing the threshold from founder management to professional management: a governance perspective', *Journal of Management Studies*, **41**: 899–912.

Golden, B.R. and Zajac, E. (2001), 'When will boards influence strategy? Inclination × power = strategic change', *Strategic Management Journal*, **22**: 1087–111.

Greenbury, R. (1995), *Directors' Remuneration: Report of a Study Group Chaired by Sir Richard Greenbury*, London: Gee Publishing.

Hampel, R. (1998), *Committee on Corporate Governance: Final Report*, London: Gee Publishing.

Hart, O. (1995), 'Corporate governance: some theory and implications', *Economic Journal*, **105**: 678–89.

Haynes, M., Thompson, S. and Wright, M. (2000), 'The determinants of corporate divestment in the UK', *International Journal of Industrial Organization*, **18**, 1201–22.

Haynes, M., Thompson, S. and Wright, M. (2003), 'Divestment in the UK: a panel data study', *Journal of Economic Behavior and Organization*, **52**: 147–66

Higgs, D. (2003), *Review of the Role and Effectiveness of Non-executive Directors*, London: DTI.

Hitt, M.A., Ireland, R.D. and Hoskisson, R.E. (2003), *Strategic Management. Competitiveness and Globalization*, Minneapolis and New York: West Publishing Company.

Hoskisson, R.E., Johnson, R.A. and Moesel, D.D. (1994), 'Corporate divestiture intensity in restructuring firms: effects of governance, strategy and performance', *Academy of Management Journal*, **37**: 1207–51.

Howorth, C., Westhead, P. and Wright, M. (2004), 'Management buy-outs of family owned firms: asymmetric information and the family–management dyad', *Journal of Business Venturing*, **19**(4): 509–34.

Jensen, M.C. (1993), 'The modern industrial revolution, exit and the failure of internal control systems', *Journal of Finance*, **48**(3): 831–80.

Johnson, R. (1996), 'Antecedents and outcomes of corporate refocusing', *Journal of Management*, **22**: 439–83.

Keasey, K. and Wright, M. (1993), 'Corporate governance: issues and concerns', *Accounting and Business Research*, **23**: 301–13.

Lansberg, I. (1999), *Succeeding Generations: Realizing the Dream of Families in Business*, Boston: Harvard Business School Press.

La Porta, R., Lopez-De-Silanes, F., Shleifer, A. and Vishny, R. (1998), 'Law and finance', *Journal of Political Economy*, **106**: 1113–55.

Lynall, M., Golden, B.R. and Hillman, A. (2003), 'Board composition from adolescence to maturity: a multi-theoretic view', *Academy of Management Review*, **28**: 416–31.

Megginson, W.L. and Weiss, K.A. (1991), 'Venture capitalist certification in initial public offerings', *Journal of Finance*, **96**: 879–903.

Morris, M.H., Williams, R.O., Allen, J.A. and Avila, R.A. (1997), 'Correlates of success in family business transitions', *Journal of Business Venturing*, **12**(5): 341–422.

Murphy, K.J. (1997), 'Executive compensation and the modern industrial revolution', *International Journal of Industrial Organization*, **15**(4): 413–532.

Myners, P. (2001), *Review of Institutional Investment in the UK*, London: UK Treasury.

Neubauer, F. and Lank, A.G. (1998), *The Family Business: Its Governance for Sustainability*, London: Macmillan Press.

Pettigrew, A.M. (1992), 'On studying managerial elites', *Strategic Management Journal*, **13**: 163–82.

Pfeffer, J. (1972), 'Size and composition of corporate boards of directors: the organization and its environment', *Administrative Science Quarterly*, **17**: 218–22.

Robbins, K.D. and Pearce, J.A. (1992), 'Turnaround: Retrenchment and recovery', *Strategic Management Journal*, **13**(4): 287–309.

Sadler, G. (1999), 'Executive compensation and share options in UK quoted companies', unpublished PhD thesis, University of Warwick.

Sanchez, R. (1995), 'Strategic flexibility in product competition', *Strategic Management Journal*, **16**: 135–59.

Short, H., Keasey, K., Wright, M. and Hull, A. (1999), 'Corporate governance: from accountability to enterprise', *Accounting and Business Research*, **29**: 337–52.

Short, H., Keasey, K. and Wright, M. (2000), 'Corporate governance: accountability versus enterprise', *Hume Papers on Public Policy*, **8**(1): 70–91.

Smith, Sir R. (2003), *Audit Committees: Combined Code guidance*, London: Financial Reporting Council.

Thompson, S. and Wright, M. (1995), 'Corporate governance: the role of restructuring transactions', *Economic Journal*, **105**: 690–703.

Toms, S. and Filatotchev, I. (2004), 'Corporate governance, business strategy and the dynamics of networks: a theoretical model and application to the British cotton industry, 1830–1980', *Organization Studies*, **25**: 629–52.

Tricker, R. (1984), *Corporate Governance*, Burlington, VT: Gower.

Turnbull, N. (1999), *Internal Control: Guidance for Directors of Listed Companies Incorporated in the UK: Consultation Draft*, London: ICAEW.

Ucbasaran, D., Lockett, A., Wright, M. and Westhead, P. (2003), 'Entrepreneurial founder teams: factors associated with member entry and exit', *Entrepreneurship Theory and Practice*, **28**(2): 107–28.

Vohora, A., Wright, M. and Lockett, A. (2004), 'Critical junctures in the development of university high-tech spinout companies', *Research Policy*, **33**: 147–74.

Ward, J.L. (1987), *Keeping the Family Business Healthy: How to Plan for Continued Growth, Profitability, and Family Leadership*, San Fransisco, CA: Jossey-Bass.

Welbourne, T.M. and Andrews, A.O. (1996), 'Predicting the performance of initial public offering: should human research management be in the equation?' *Academy of Management Journal*, **39**: 891–919.

Wright, M., Hoskisson, R.E. and Busenitz, L.W. (2001), 'Firm rebirth: buy-outs as facilitators of strategic growth and entrepreneurship', *Academy of Maanagement Executive*, **15**(1): 111–25.

Wright, M., Hoskisson, R.E., Busenitz, L.W. and Dial, J. (2000), 'Entrepreneurial growth through privatization: the upside of management buy-outs', *Academy of Management Review*, **25**(3): 591–601.

Zahra, S.A. and Pearce, J.A. (1989), 'Boards of directors and corporate financial performance: a review and integrative model', *Journal of Management*, **15**: 291–334.

Zahra, S.A. and Filatotchev, I. (2004), 'Governance of the entrepreneurial threshold firm: a knowledge based perspective', *Journal of Management Studies*, **41**: 885–98.

[2]
Venture capital and the corporate governance life cycle

Colin Mayer

1. Introduction

The dominant paradigm among law and finance academics and the most influential policy prescription is that investor protection is key to financial development and economic growth (La Porta et al., 1997, 1998). This policy has risen to the fore in international agencies such as the OECD and the World Bank as well as among governments around the world.

The basis for this assertion is that investor protection is critical to the willingness of minority investors to participate in the financing of corporations. In the absence of adequate protection, minority investors are exposed to self-interest of large shareholders and markets are dominated by these shareholdings. Participation by outside investors is then discouraged, and the development of financial systems is stunted. Furthermore, investment in some companies and industries is particularly dependent on external finance. The growth of these firms and industries is therefore impeded and economic development suffers.

The policy prescription is therefore straightforward. Strengthen investor protection and financial development will follow. This will promote external finance, which will accelerate economic growth.

This emphasis on investor protection takes several different forms. It stresses the importance of bank regulation and the protection of depositors through prudential supervision. It points to sound regulation of non-bank financial institutions, such as pension funds, life assurance firms and mutual funds. It takes the form of creditor protection and the establishment of insolvency procedures that preserve creditor rights and priorities. And it concerns the rights of shareholders to vote on corporate policies, to dismiss management and to litigate against injustices.

It is not difficult to see failures in financial markets that justify regulation. At the very least, they are prone to imperfect information that exposes investors to incompetence and bad management. More seriously, investors are at risk of fraud, which pervades financial markets more than any other because of the ease of perpetrating it, the difficulty of detecting and the frequent impossibility of prosecuting for it successfully even when disclosed. Furthermore, regulation can readily be justified by threats to financial systems as well as to individual investors.

The pre-eminence of investor protection pervades most current financial market policy proposals. For example, the response in the USA to financial irregularities is to introduce legislation that strengthens accounting standards, increases directors' fiduciary responsibilities, imposes larger penalties for corporate governance failures and encourages whistleblowing by insiders. Conflicts of interest are to be discouraged by raising barriers between different institutional activities, such as analysis and broking.

Nowhere is this policy more evident than in the context of European corporate governance and takeovers. Speakers at a recent debate in the Oxford Union – the debating chamber of Oxford University – argued that the culture of British business is fundamentally different from the USA and that Enron could not happen in the UK. There is less use of stock options as a form of executive remuneration and there is a less rule-based system of accounting, which means that US style accounting scandals could not happen in Britain. For example, directors of British companies have had to sign off their accounts as being a true and fair representation of the financial condition of their firms for a long time. The implication of this is that the British system of corporate governance, of accounting, regulation and doing business is inherently superior to that in the USA.

This is the latest twist in a debate that has been raging for decades if not the best part of a century about the comparative merits of different financial systems and forms of corporate governance. One officer of a German Great Bank observed in the early part of the last century that: 'In Germany our banks are largely responsible for the development of the Empire, having fostered and built up its industries. ... To them, more than any other agency may be credited the splendid results thus far realized.'

In the last ten years, we have seen the Japanese system held up as the model, with Japanese banks posed to take over US industry. Then as the Japanese bubble burst and the economy went into recession the only model that the Japanese economy seemed to exemplify was that of crony capitalism.

As the bubble drifted from Japan to the USA, Japan was replaced by the USA as the role model. Until recently, the exhortation was to adopt US Generally Accepted Accounting Principles (GAAP) as fast as possible and in preference to International Accounting Standards. The USA was viewed as the engine of entrepreneurship and the new economy, and the rest of us were plagued by sclerosis. But as its high-tech, Internet bubble turned to bust, the USA has been viewed as exemplifying the excesses of capitalism, the problems of paying executives with options, the home of accounting manipulations and the breeding ground of conflicts of interests between auditors, managers, credit rating agencies, analysts, brokers, investment banks, not to mention between government and business.

That is how the UK rose to the fore. It has come to be seen as providing an appropriate balance between unrestrained capitalism of the USA and the private benefit systems of Continental Europe and the Far East. It supposedly has good accounting standards, it has led the way through the Cadbury Committee of establishing codes of good corporate governance conduct and it has well-functioning markets in corporate control. Of course, the new-found glory of British corporate governance will last just as long as the British economy performs tolerably well and can therefore be expected to end very shortly.

What can be learnt from this volatile history of the rising and waning fortunes of different corporate governance systems? The first lesson is that there is a widely held view that there exists an El Dorado of corporate governance and, second, that this system of corporate governance is generally applicable to all economies and to all firms. It is this second assertion that is considered here in the context of the life-cycle development of firms.

2.   The Financing of Entrepreneurial Firms

The development of high-tech firms involves several phases (see Figure 2.1). The first is the seed stage, when a concept has still to be proven and developed. The second is the start-up phase, when products are developed and initial marketing takes place. The firm may be a year old or younger at this stage. The third is the early-stage development, when the firm is expanding and producing but may well remain unprofitable; it is often less than five years old at this stage. During the fourth stage of expansion it might go public after six months or a year.

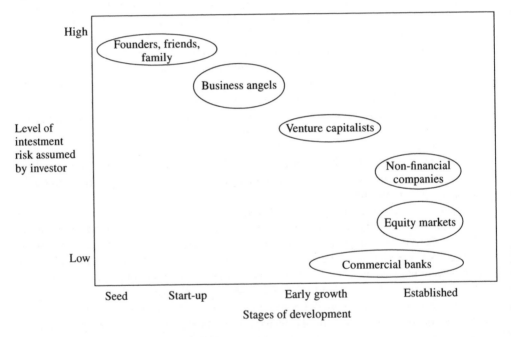

Source: Van Osnabrugge and Robinson (2000).

Figure 2.1   The development and financing of entrepreneurial firms

The initial development almost invariably comes from savings and relatives. Initial external equity financing does not generally come from venture capital firms but from business angels. In the USA, it is estimated that the venture capital industry invested around $5 billion in 1998 in 1000 early-stage firms. In comparison, business angels (wealthy or reasonably wealthy private investors) were estimated to invest $15 billion annually in 60 000 early-stage firms. In the UK, it is estimated that about 5 per cent of small firms receive business angel support as against 1 per cent receiving venture capital finance.

What accounts for the different contribution of business angels and venture capitalists to start-up financing? Evidence from detailed comparisons of the way in which venture capitalists and business angels operate suggests that venture capitalists are highly rule-based, using careful screening of applicants and due diligence (Van Osnabrugge and Robinson, 2000; Ehrlich et al., 1994). Business angels place more emphasis on *ex post* involvement in investments to reduce risks, such as their ability to contribute to the management of the business. Venture capitalists therefore act like institutions following principal–agent relations of limiting risks through monitoring. That is not surprising given that, at least in the UK, they are frequently subsidiaries of institutions, such as pension funds. Business angels are more actively involved in the subsequent management of activities, exerting more direct control.

From the outset, venture capitalists are focused on exit, business angels much less so. Venture capitalists in general look for rates of return of between 30 and 40 per cent, business angels in the UK between 20 and 30 per cent. Initial public offerings (IPOs) are the preferred route of exit for investors, since they yield the highest return, but they are not the most common. It is estimated that fewer than one in a thousand new ventures have an IPO. However, entrepreneurs are much more optimistic than this record would warrant. One study estimated that 70 per cent of new technology firms believed that a public stock offering was 'highly likely' or 'probable' (Freear et al., 1991). Trade sales are the most common exit route of business angels, accounting for over 40 per cent of exits, followed by sales of shares to other shareholders and sales to third parties. IPOs account for just over 10 per cent of business angel exits.

In the USA, around 25 per cent of venture capital funds are invested in early-stage firms. In the UK, start-up and early-stage investments also accounted for around a quarter of venture capital investments in 1984 but this had fallen to a figure of around 4 per cent by the end of the 1990s. MBOs and MBIs (management buy-outs and management buy-ins) have substituted for start-up financing increasing from 20 per cent to 70 per cent of UK funds' investment.

An important reason for the greater success of US venture capital in funding start-up businesses is the structure of the US industry. Venture capital comprises two parties (see Figure 2.2): the limited partners which are the institutional and individual investors, and the general partners which are the venture capital firms investing in individual companies and entrepreneurs. The general partners manage portfolios of companies and are frequently

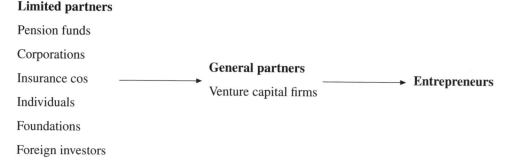

Limited partners

Pension funds

Corporations

General partners

Insurance cos ──────────▶ **Entrepreneurs**

Venture capital firms

Individuals

Foundations

Foreign investors

Figure 2.2   The structure of the US venture capital industry

successful entrepreneurs themselves who want to manage larger portfolios of investments. They therefore provide intermediate technical expertise between the investing institutions on the one hand and the entrepreneurs on the other. Venture capital industries in other countries, including the UK, frequently lack the pool of entrepreneurial scientists on which to draw to provide this intermediary function.

The picture that emerges is that the financing of new high-tech firms is highly reliant on own funds, families and friends. Once these are exhausted, external equity initially comes from private investors who are actively involved in the management of the investment. Venture capitalists come in at a later-stage, acting more at arm's-length than business angels and seeking higher returns over short periods. A small fraction of the most successful firms are floated on stock markets; most are sold as trade sales and sales to other investors. Much venture capital finance in particular in the UK is not associated with funding new investments but management buy-outs.

To understand high-tech finance, it is therefore important to appreciate it as being intimately connected to the control of firms (Figure 2.3). The transition from personal to business angel to venture capital to stock market finance involves a gradual broadening of the investor base. This moves rapidly from the entrepreneur to single outside investors who are active managers, to financial institutions who use intermediary venture capital firms to screen and manage their investments, to stock markets with largely passive investors.

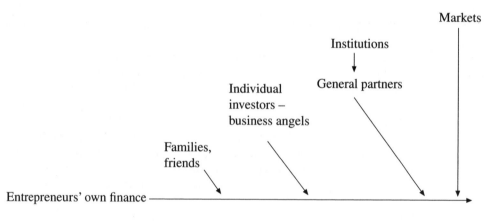

Figure 2.3   Stages of entrepreneurial finance

The financing of Amazon.com illustrates this (see Table 2.1). The firm was initially funded out of Jeff Bezos's own savings and some borrowings. The family then invested a quarter of a million dollars. Two business angels then came in, followed by a larger business angel syndicate. There was a further small family investment followed by a substantial venture capital injection of $8 million. A year later the firm went public with an IPO of $49 million.

The pattern of evolving control persists after firms have gone to the stock market. Stock market listings are important, not only in subjecting firms to the discipline of the takeover market but also in providing them with the opportunity of expanding through acquisitions themselves.

Table 2.1   The financing of Amazon.com (1994–99)

Time line	Price/share	Sources of funds
1994 – July to Nov.	$0.001	*Founder*: Jeff Bezos starts Amazon.com with $10 000, borrows $44 000
1995 – Febr. to July	$0.1717	*Family*: Founder's father and mother invest $245 500
1995 – Aug. to Dec.	$0.1287–0.3333	*Business angels*: Two angels invest $54 408
1995/6 – Dec. to May	$0.3333	*Business angels*: Twenty angels invest $937 000
1996 – May	$0.3333	*Family*: Founder's siblings invest $20 000
1996 – June	$2.3417	*Venture capitalists*: Two venture capital funds invest $8 million
1997 – May	$18	*IPO*: 3 million shares issued raising $49.1 million
1997/8 – Dec. to May	$52.11	*Bond issue*: $326 million bond issue

Source: Smith and Kiholm (2000).

In summary, what distinguishes the growth of high-technology firms is the rapidly evolving patterns of control and financing. VC is just one stage in a gradual transition from tight ownership and control by founders and families to widely held shareholdings. The VC is an institutional mechanism of bridging that transition by providing intermediation between investors and firms through limited and general partnerships. As such, it is an institutional form for which, in one way or another, there will be an enduring need. The current malaise of the VC industry may persist for some time, so long as financial markets remain depressed, but while technological developments continue to demand the creation of new start-up companies, there will be an important role for VC firms to perform.

3.   Venture Capital outside the USA and UK

The above characterizes the VC industry in the USA and UK. Until the recent downturn, there had also been a marked growth in VC activity elsewhere in Europe. Bottazzi and Da Rin (2002) report that funds raised in Europe trebled over the two years 1997–99 from €8 billion to €25 billion. Some of the fastest growth has occurred in Continental Europe. Bottazzi and Da Rin (2002) report that by the end of the 1990s venture capital investments in Belgium and Sweden represented approximately the same share of GDP as those in the UK, having started from much lower bases at the beginning of the 1990s. Vittols (2000) reports that venture capital in Germany has more than doubled since 1996 from DM6.1 billion to DM13.8 billion in 1999. Early-stage financing has more than doubled as a proportion of total venture capital from 14 per cent in 1996 to 31 per cent in 1999.

While VC grew rapidly in many countries until the end of the 1990s, the nature and structure of VC varies appreciably across countries. First, while, as described above, VC firms generally take the form of limited partnerships, that does not apply everywhere. In Japan, for example, all VC funds are joint stock companies, often affiliates of banks and securities companies. In Germany about a quarter of VC funds are listed companies (AGs). Second, while VC finance is closely associated with convertible debt in the USA, that again does not apply universally. In Germany and Japan for example, equity is the dominant form of investment.

Third, there are significant differences across countries in the sources of finance for VC firms. As noted above, VC finance in the UK and USA is closely associated with pension funds, life assurance companies and other institutional investors. Elsewhere, banks are frequently a major source of finance for VC firms. For example, they are the dominant source in Germany and Japan. In some countries, notably Israel, corporations, in particular US corporations, have been an important source of finance.

Fourth, there are substantial variations in the activities in which VC firms are engaged. This is most clearly seen in terms of stages of finance. It has already been noted that there is a pronounced difference in stage of finance between the UK and the USA, with much VC finance in the UK now being associated with management buy-outs, buy-ins and later-stage development. There is a remarkably close similarity in stage of finance between Germany and the UK, despite the frequently cited differences in their financial systems. Elsewhere, VC firms are much more focused on early-stage investments in Israel and in much later stages in Japan.

There are also significant differences in VCs' sector focus. While biotechnology and life sciences receive a substantial level of attention in many countries, a much larger fraction of VC firms in, for example, Israel and Japan invest in information technology and software. In contrast, in Germany and the UK, the chemical and manufacturing sectors receive more attention.

One interesting feature of these differences is that there appears to be a significant relation between sources of finance of VC firms in different countries and the investment activities in which they are engaged. In particular, banks and pension-funds-backed VC firms tend to invest in later-stage activities, whereas VC firms relying on private individual investors favour early-stage activities. Industry and privately backed funds are focused towards information technology, software and electronics, while pension-funds-backed VC firms invest in manufacturing sectors.

Why are there these pronounced differences in supposedly similar financial institutions across countries? There are several possible explanations. First, the function performed by VC firms in the UK and the USA may be performed by other institutions elsewhere. VC firms play a role in providing a link between dispersed, arm's-length investors and actively involved monitors of corporate activities. These are activities that are sometimes associated with banks in countries with close relations between banks and firms – the supposed bank-oriented financial systems. The observation that VC firms are bank funded in these countries is consistent with the notion that they are essentially subsidiaries of banks that engage in comparatively high-risk investments. The requirement for distinct intermediation between institutional investors may be more pressing in Anglo-American style financial systems where there are more arm's-length relations between investors and firms.

A second explanation for the international differences is that the demand for entrepreneurial finance varies across countries. A range of factors, such as the educational and cultural environment and taxation, affect the type as well as the level of entrepreneurship. For example, the emphasis on IT and software in Israel reflects the needs of the military for defence-related procurement. The provision of finance to management buy-out and buy-in teams in the UK is a product of a stronger culture to acquire control of existing firms than to establish new companies.

One influence on the demand for entrepreneurship is the degree to which high-tech activities are undertaken within large corporations. The low levels of VC funding for electronics and semiconductors in Japan is clearly not a reflection of a weakness in these sectors but of a tendency for this activity to be undertaken in large corporations.

Therefore the term VC refers to quite different activities in different countries. What passes as a VC firm in one country might be quite different from that in another. The VC industry has to be considered within the context of the financial and corporate institutional structure within which it operates. In many countries the VC firm is little more than a subsidiary form that allows a bank to invest in higher-risk activities and to provide higher-powered incentives to its employees than in the remainder of its business. A shift into and out of VC firms in these countries is little more than a rebalancing of bank portfolios between different industries. In contrast, as previously described, a VC firm performs a fundamental intermediary role in the UK and USA that few other institutions undertake. While there may therefore be a continuing need for VC type institutions within the context of Anglo-American market economies, their function and significance may endure in other forms elsewhere.

4.   Market Failures and the Role of the State

One of the traditional ways in which the state has intervened in high-tech financing has been by creating specific financial institutions to perform this function. For example, throughout the 1960s there was a perception that the German economy was suffering from an 'equity gap'. The response of the German government was to encourage the formation of a new institution, the Deutsche Wagnisfinanzierungsgesellschaft (WFG), in 1975 devoted to the financing of young enterprises. In an excellent study, Becker and Hellmann (2003) document the development and performance of the WFG. The ownership, investment strategy, performance and subsequent developments of the WFG can be summarized as follows.

Ownership. Twenty-nine German banks founded the WFG with a government guarantee of 75 per cent of any losses that the banks might incur. The board of the WFG comprised representatives from industry and government, and scientists and consultants.

Investment strategy. The WFG initially focused on early-stage investment in particular in manufacturing and information technology. The criteria for selecting investments were the degree of innovation of products and processes, their potential markets, the quality of entrepreneurs and the shortage of alternative sources of finance. The WFG took minority equity stakes, granted the entrepreneur a buy-back right over the equity and took no control rights. It offered entrepreneurs standardized contracts with essentially uniformity of pricing.

Performance. The performance of the WFG was disastrous. It made losses in each of its first nine years. Most of the firms it supported recorded net losses at exit and bankruptcies accounted for a high proportion of exits. In contrast to evidence from US VC-backed firms, entrepreneurs were ashamed to admit that the WFG had a stake in their firm.

Subsequent developments. In 1984, the WFG underwent a fundamental transformation involving a liquidation of the old firm and the creation of a new one. The government exited and the government representatives resigned from the board. The WFG refocused its attention away from start-ups to later-stage financing and shifted its hiring policy away from people with technological to business experience. In 1988, the new WFG was in turn disbanded and the portfolio was taken over by Deutsche Bank and one small bank.

It is interesting to contrast this case with a similar British organization, the Industrial and Commercial Finance Corporation (ICFC).[1]

Ownership. ICFC was set up in the UK in 1945 to fill what was known as the Macmillan gap (the failure of the City to supply long-term finance to small and medium-sized firms). It was owned by the UK clearing banks and the Bank of England but created in the face of considerable opposition from the banks, which regarded it as a competitive threat rather than a complementary institution.

Investment strategy. ICFC focused on small manufacturing companies in their early development stage. It undertook active screening and monitoring of borrowers. Unusually for British clearing banks, its loan officers had a high degree of technical competence and displayed a high degree of commitment to long-term lending. ICFC took equity stakes but did not have direct representation on the boards of firms.

Performance. Following losses in its first three years to 1948, ICFC made substantial profits in every year subsequently. The number of its investments went up by a factor of ten between 1954 and 1984 and investments by ICFC were regarded as signals of quality certification.

Subsequent developments. In 1983 ICFC was consolidated in the 3i group. Its investments became increasingly concentrated on venture capital. Initially it focused on start-ups, early-stage and development capital. By the beginning of the 1990s, it became by far the largest provider of venture capital in the UK. Increasingly, however, its investments focused on management buy-outs and buy-ins and the repositioning of its activities contributed significantly to the switch in aggregate UK venture capital from early-stage in the mid-1980s to MBOs and MBIs by the end of the 1990s.

The markedly different performance of the WFG and ICFC cannot be readily attributed to their origins or ownership structure. Both were formed in response to a financing gap and both had (reluctant) banks as their owners. Neither can the supply of entrepreneurs be cited as a fundamental difference between the UK and Germany. The post-war British culture has been regarded as particularly anti-commercial. The UK has a creditor-oriented bankruptcy system and a strong bankruptcy stigma. For much of the period there were prohibitively high rates of personal taxation in the UK. However, where the two institutions differed was in the involvement of the banks and the government. In many respects ICFC had the characteristics of a US VC partnership: lenders with technical expertise intermediating between investors on one side and companies on the other. The banks were kept at a distance by the presence of the Bank of England and there was no government involvement in ICFC or 3i. In contrast, the WFG could not disentangle itself from the banks or the government.

This suggests that if the establishment of new financial institutions is the approach taken to solving market failures, then considerable effort is required in the design of these institutions. However, it is not the route that is in general favoured today and it is not the one that most European governments are following. Instead, there is a greater emphasis in government policy on promoting the functioning of markets rather than substituting for them. How can governments promote the financing of high-tech activities? Regulation is the current panacea for all market ills. If markets are not functioning, it must be a consequence of inadequate or inappropriate regulation.

There is in particular a considerable emphasis at present on minority investor protection and corporate governance. These are regarded as being fundamental to the successful operation of markets and the excesses of the high-tech boom and new economy are presented as justification for them. While there is much truth in this, considerable care is required in designing regulatory policy towards financial systems.

The regulation of the high-tech sector illustrates this well. While the UK and the USA are generally classified under similar common law systems, there are actually pronounced differences between the two countries in their approach to the regulation of non-bank financial institutions, such as pension funds and fund managers. One of the important contributors to the development of venture capital in the USA was the relaxation of the 'prudent man' rule on pension funds at the end of the 1970s. This stimulated a substantial expansion in investment in VC activities during the 1980s. US regulation emphasizes the importance of disclosure of information to investors, auditing of the behaviour of institutions and the imposition of penalties, in the event of failure being uncovered.

In the UK, investor protection has relied more heavily on public compensation schemes and the imposition of detailed conduct of business rules. For example, to protect pensioners from the types of losses that were incurred in pension fund scandals during the 1990s, rules were imposed that encouraged pension funds to invest heavily in government securities. These had the effect of discouraging investment in more risky investments such as VC funds.

US regulation therefore promotes private contracting; UK regulation relies more heavily on public contracting. Private contracting systems do not require institutions to amass capital before they are allowed to transact. They do not presume that there is a single best way of transacting business and they do not seek to impose common rules of conduct. Instead, they allow institutions and investors to choose how to organize their business and where to invest. If malpractice is uncovered, then there is a significant probability that it will be uncovered through auditing and penalized through the courts.

A critical question that this comparison raises is the extent to which reliance should be placed on public versus private contracting to provide protection in non-bank financial institutions. The advantage of private over public contracting is that it does not prejudge what is acceptable. It allows for a greater degree of diversity of institutional form. It permits institutions to adapt more rapidly in the face of changing requirements of both investors and firms. This has therefore made it easier for institutions to respond to the changing financing and control needs of high-technology firms in the USA than in the UK.

On the other hand, it relies on 'caveat emptor' and in general provides investors with less protection than public contracting schemes. As recent experience has illustrated, it places considerable emphasis on private agents, such as analysts, accountants and auditors, to collect and process information. It relies on the courts to enforce contracts. All of these are better developed in the USA than elsewhere and it is questionable therefore whether the US model is the appropriate one for elsewhere.

5. Conclusion

To conclude, this chapter has argued that the development of high-tech firms does raise particular financing needs that the emergence of venture capital firms and business angels were designed to meet. In particular, the characteristic feature of high-tech firms is the rapid evolution from tight ownership and control by entrepreneurs and families to outside participation by dispersed investors. Business angels and venture capitalists play a critical role in that evolution.

It has been argued that venture capitalists have to be considered within the context of the wider structure of financial systems. Their function, financing and form differ appreciably across countries. This in part reflects different entrepreneurial needs in different countries and the greater tendency for high-tech activities to be performed within large companies in some countries than others. However, it also results from the existence of financial institutions that perform functions similar to VC firms. The requirement for the VC transformation function between investors and firms is therefore more pressing in some countries than others.

Finally, this chapter has considered public policies towards the development of high-tech financing. The design of financial institutions to perform these functions is complex and has gone out of favour as the failures of government alongside those of markets are more widely appreciated. Instead, regulation is the flavour of the month. But even here care is required in designing policy. A central feature of high-tech financing is its diversity across time and country. There is not a single best form and the most important function that regulation can perform is to encourage institutional experimentation and innovation. 'Let many financiers boom' might be a motto that should be inscribed on every policy maker's heart.

Note

1.   For an excellent history of the firm and its successor organization, see Coopey and Clarke (1995).

References

Becker, R. and Hellmann, T. (2003), 'The genesis of venture capital: lessons from the German experience', in C. Keuschnigg and V. Kanniainen (eds), *Venture Capital, Entrepreneurship, and Public Policy*, Boston: MIT Press.

Bottazzi, L. and Da Rin, M. (2002), 'Venture capital in Europe and the financing of innovative companies', *Economic Policy*, **34**: 229–62.

Coopey, R. and Clarke, D. (1995), *3i – Fifty Years Investing in Industry*, Oxford: Oxford University Press.

Ehrlich, S., De Noble, A., Moore, T. and Weaver, R. (1994), 'After the cash arrives: a comparative study of venture capital and private investor involvement in entrepreneurial firms', *Journal of Business Venturing*, **9**: 67–82.

Freear, J., Sohl, J. and Wetzel, W. (1991), 'Raising venture capital to finance growth', *Frontiers of Entrepreneurship Research*, Wellesley, MA: Babson College.

La Porta, R., Lopez-De-Silanes, F., Shleifer, A. and Vishny, R. (1997), 'Legal determinants of external finance', *Journal of Finance*, **52**(3): 1131–50.

La Porta, R., Lopez-De-Silanes, F., Shleifer, A. and Vishny, R. (1998), 'Law and finance', *Journal of Political Economy*, **106**: 1113–55.

Smith, R. and Kiholm, J. (2000), *Entrepreneurial Finance*, New York: Wiley.

Van Osnabrugge, M. and Robinson, R. (2000), *Angel Investing*, San Fransisco, CA: Jossey-Bass.

Vittols, S. (2000), 'Frankfurt's Neuer Market and the IPO explosion: is Germany on the road to Silicon Valley yet?' mimeo, Wissenschaftszentrum Berlin für Sozialforschung.

[3]

Organizational life-cycle transitions and their consequences for the governance of entrepreneurial firms: an analysis of start-up and adolescent high-technology new ventures

Shaker A. Zahra and James C. Hayton

Introduction

Research on corporate governance has grown rapidly over the past two decades, reflecting the important role it plays in determining organizational performance. Despite the growth and sophistication, major gaps exist in this research. Governance researchers have primarily studied large companies while ignoring younger entrepreneurial firms (Daily et al., 2002) that play a major role in creating jobs, promoting economic growth, and developing and introducing new technologies. Yet entrepreneurial companies face unique challenges in acquiring the resources needed to support and sustain their operations. They also face significantly different strategic issues from those of more well-established companies, highlighting a need to understand how new ventures' governance systems might influence their performance.

Another shortcoming of the literature is its failure to document the shifts that might occur in a company's governance system over time. The OLC (organizational life-cycle) theory suggests that companies undergo major strategic shifts in their goals, organizational structures and decision-making processes (Adzies, 1979; Churchill and Lewis, 1983; Kimberly and Evanisko, 1981; Miller and Friesen, 1984). Companies also face different strategic challenges as they move from one phase of their OLC to the next (Drazin and Kazanjian,

1990; Lester and Parnell, 1999; Smith et al., 1985; Quinn and Cameron, 1983), requiring changes in the way boards of directors are composed. While some prior research has explored governance issues in smaller and even younger firms (Castaldi and Wortman, 1984; Daily and Dalton, 1992b; Fiegener et al., 2000; Ford, 1988), little attention has been given to the potential transitions that take place over the course of the OLC. Zahra and Pearce (1989) have drawn attention the need to understand the implications of the changes in the OLC on governance variables and company performance.

In this chapter, we empirically examine the effect of select governance variables, primarily boards of directors, on the performance of high-technology new ventures. New ventures, companies eight years or younger, face the daunting task of assembling resources quickly while seeking to achieve legitimacy. The resource dependence theory (Pfeffer and Salancik, 1978) posits that under these conditions, the board of directors could play an important role in acquiring the resources (including knowledge) necessary for successful company performance.

The study focuses on the innovative and financial dimensions of company performance. Our focus on innovative outcomes stems from the fact that high-technology new ventures are the creators of change in their respective industries and the champions of radical innovation. In these ventures, senior management's attention and organizational resources are likely to be dedicated to ensuring successful and continuous innovation (Zahra and Bogner, 2000). Our focus on financial performance is understandable; entrepreneurs usually establish new firms primarily to create wealth.

This chapter reports the results of an empirical study that examines the effect of board composition on the innovative and financial performance of entrepreneurial companies at two points of their OLC: start-up and adolescence. A vast body of research has yielded contradictory results on the effect of board composition on performance in large, established and publicly held companies (Zahra and Pearce, 1989). We currently know little about the effect of board composition on entrepreneurial firms' performance at the start-up versus the adolescent stages of their OLC. The analyses reported in this chapter capture the significant shifts that new ventures may experience as they become more established. The analyses apply the OLC and resource dependence theories to link board composition variables to new ventures' innovative and financial performance.

Theory and Hypotheses

High-technology new ventures face serious challenges early on in their OLC. In the start-up phase, they have to achieve legitimacy with their various stakeholders in order to overcome the liability of newness and acquire the resources necessary to support their operations by extracting important resources from different groups, sometimes less expensively than the going market rates. High-technology new ventures also compete in dynamic environments where innovations diffuse rapidly, making it imperative for these firms to move quickly to exploit their discoveries. Also, organizational skills become obsolete quickly because of these environmental changes. Consequently, new firms must rapidly assemble the resources (including knowledge) and capabilities necessary to respond to persistent environmental dynamism.

High-technology new ventures often suffer from serious imbalances in their expertise where the founders and other leaders enjoy strong technical expertise but may not possess the required marketing, distribution and production skills. Such shortages may limit new ventures' ability to survive or expand their operations. In a dynamic environment, new ventures also need information about their competitors and customers. This is an area where the board can provide useful insights, which will allow new ventures to craft effective strategies that improve their financial performance. This information can also stimulate innovation in the firm's products, processes and administrative systems. The specific benefits a new venture gains from its boards may change over the course of the various stages of the OLC, as discussed next.

The OLC and key organizational transitions

The OLC theory suggests that companies undergo predictable transitions over the course of their evolution. These transitions usually reflect industry and competitive shifts, the companies' own actions, and changes in the resource base of the firm. While many new start-ups fail within a few years of their birth, some will survive and reach the adolescent stage (Bantel, 1998). The OLC theory also posits that marked shifts occur in the strategic focus, management, structure and organization and functional priorities as companies move from the start-up to the adolescent stage of the OLC. These changes are summarized in Table 3.1.

As Table 3.1 indicates, whereas start-ups focus on achieving legitimacy in their markets in order to acquire the resources necessary to develop a viable niche, adolescent firms focus

Table 3.1   Comparison of the key characteristics of start-up versus adolescent firms

Dimensions	Start-up phase	Adolescent phase
Strategic focus	• Legitimacy • Developing a viable niche • Gaining access to resources	• Funding growth • Product line expansion
Management	• Single owner or limited team • Centralized	• Bigger management team • Professionalization of management • More diffused power base
Structure and organization	• Simple and organic	• More formalized • Greater role differentiation
Functional focus	• Innovation • Engineering • Manufacturing	• Marketing • Administration
Organizational size	• Smaller	• Bigger

more on funding their product line expansion as a means of achieving sales growth. Therefore, management's attention shifts from a focus on innovation, engineering and manufacturing as primary challenges in the start-up phase to stressing marketing and distribution in the adolescent stage of the OLC.

Parallel to these changes, the OLC theory suggests that companies experience considerable shifts in their management and structures as they move from the start-up to the adolescent stage. Companies often expand their top management teams and differentiate the various roles senior managers play. Companies also hire new employees who have strong functional skills and empower them to make decisions. These changes make the organizational structure less centralized, aiming to increase responsiveness to the market. Adolescent companies also place greater emphasis on the formal analysis of their markets and competition, seeking new customers for their products. These changes increase the formality of the decision-making process in adolescent firms.

Resource dependence theory (Pfeffer and Salancik, 1978) argues that, under conditions of uncertainty and scarcity, companies will develop internal systems that reflect the external contingencies they face. For instance, companies will have boards of directors that will enable them to manage key sources of uncertainty, as shown by Pearce and Zahra (1992). Boards serve as an important bridge between the firm and its external environment. Therefore companies will pay attention to the effective composition of their boards in order to deal with the challenges they face in the start-up versus adolescent stages of the OLC. Following the resource dependence theory, we expect the composition of the board to differ markedly between the start-up and adolescent stages of the OLC. Further, different board composition variables will influence performance quite differently in these two stages.

Board composition and the OLC stages

As our preceding discussion suggests, in the start-up stage of the OLC, the primary strategic focus of a new venture centers on establishing organizational legitimacy, developing a viable market niche, and obtaining the various resources needed to survive and grow. The venture will also be smaller, more centralized and dominated by a technical orientation among its senior managers (e.g. focus on engineering). About five years into their existence, new firms are expected to have entered the adolescent stage of their OLC (Bantel, 1998). This stage is characterized by an emphasis on growth and the expansion of these firms' product lines. As firms expand and grow, their management structures become more complex, mirroring their increasingly complex environmental challenges. With this larger, more diverse management structure comes greater formalization and differentiation and firms become more dominated by strong administrative and marketing orientations.

The changes just described suggest that the founders are less likely to remain CEOs as their high-technology new ventures reach their adolescence. As firms approach this stage of the OLC, they also experience a significant shift toward a strong market orientation. These firms will also become increasingly internally differentiated and dominated by an administrative focus where the size of the top management team and the board is expected to increase. This suggests the following hypotheses:

Hypothesis 1: Firms will have the founders as CEOs in the start-up stage more than adolescent firms.

Hypothesis 2: Adolescent firms will have a larger top management team than start-up firms.

Hypothesis 3: Adolescent firms will have a larger board than start-up firms.

Firms that seek to grow by introducing new product lines or exploiting new markets need to broaden their network and exploit their social capital (e.g. Shane and Stuart, 2002). They also have to increase the received independence and monitoring power of the board, consistent with the needs of their shareholders (Zahra and Pearce, 1989). This often means adding more outside directors to the board. Outside directors are not employees or managers of the firm and are not consultants to the firm's managers or lawyers representing the firm. Therefore, concurrent with the expansion of the board, we expect that there will be proportionally more outside directors. This suggests the following hypothesis.

Hypothesis 4: The proportion of outsider representation on the board of directors will be greater for adolescent firms than for start-up firms.

As firms move from the start-up to the adolescent stage of the OLC, they achieve a measure of legitimacy and financial success. This should allow them to attract more traditional sources of financing. Venture capitalists tend to focus on the potentially high level of returns obtained from funding high-risk start-ups rather than established firms. Further, while the board is expected to increase in size as the firm grows, it is unlikely that venture capitalists will be added to the board. Rather, outside directors with diverse skills in marketing, distribution and finance are more likely to be added. Therefore, we expect that the proportion of venture capitalists represented on the board will decrease as the firm reaches adolescence. This leads to the following hypothesis:

Hypothesis 5: The proportion of venture capitalists on boards of directors will be lower for adolescent firms than for start-up firms.

In response to the growing complexity of their external environment, there is a stronger focus on administrative issues, and a strategic orientation towards expansion and growth. Adolescent firms are expected to increase the role differentiation of their various senior managers. Board diversity increases because of the addition of members with administrative, finance and marketing expertise to supplement the existing technical expertise. Further, board diversity should rise as board members with links to different industries are added to the firm to key external resource providers and new networks of knowledge and capabilities. This suggests the following hypotheses:

Hypothesis 6: The functional diversity of boards of directors will be greater for adolescent firms than start-up firms.

Hypothesis 7: The educational diversity of boards of directors will be greater for adolescent firms than start-up firms.

In addition to changes in the composition of the board noted above, it is anticipated that the relationship between key board composition variables and firm innovative and financial performance will also change as the firm moves from the start-up to the adolescent stage of the OLC. These changing relationships are discussed next.

Board composition and new venture performance

In high-technology new ventures, the board plays a key role in establishing a firm's legitimacy and connecting it to important strategic networks. Furthermore, board characteristics can significantly influence the firm's access to new knowledge, as well as the internal processing of knowledge through decision making. Board composition is also expected to influence a firm's innovative and financial performance by promoting the acquisition and integration of needed resources, knowledge and capabilities from the firm's external environment.

From the resource dependence theory, important board characteristics include CEO duality (i.e. when the CEO is also the chairman of the board); the proportion of board members who are also founders; the proportion of outside directors; the proportion of venture capitalists on the board; and the diversity of functional and educational backgrounds of board members. The relative significance of board composition variables for innovative and financial performance is expected to change as the firm moves from the start-up to the adolescent stage of the OLC.

CEO DUALITY

CEO duality has frequently been cited as an undesirable characteristic from the perspective of shareholders (Daily et al., 2002; Finkelstein and D'Aveni, 1994). When the CEO is also the chairman of the board of directors, the board is less independent and therefore cannot effectively monitor the activities of senior managers. Similarly, while the resource dependence theory suggests that the board is an important mechanism for control over sources of uncertainty in the firm's external environment (Pearce and Zahra, 1992; Pfeffer and Salancik, 1978), CEO duality may limit the board's decision-making scope and capabilities. However, separating the chairman and CEO positions creates an additional set of social and human capital that positively influences the firm's resource acquisition capacity, possibly improving its performance.

The influence of CEO duality on company performance is also expected to change over the OLC stage. Specifically, the centralization of power and decision-making authority supports unity of command and clarity of purpose, which may improve firm performance (Finkelstein and D'Aveni, 1994). In the case of start-ups, which usually struggle to establish their legitimacy and reach profitability, centralization of power and unity of command can be supportive of innovative and financial performance. However, as the firm reaches the adolescent stage of the OLC, firm performance will have reached a sustainable level and therefore the risk of CEO entrenchment increases. Thus CEO duality can have a dysfunctional effect on the firm's risk-taking propensity, reducing its willingness to innovate.

Zahra et al. (2000) report that for a sample of 231 established manufacturing firms (average age 33 years), the separation of CEO and chairman roles is positively associated with entrepreneurship. Thus, while duality is beneficial early in the OLC, it may be dysfunctional for performance later as a firm develops. Indeed, it has also been observed that the impact of the CEO on company performance may decrease as firms grow larger and more complex (e.g. Norburn and Birley, 1988). Therefore, as firms develop and reach the adolescent stage of the OLC, CEO duality will not have as much effect on innovative and financial performance outcomes. These observations suggest the following hypotheses:

Hypothesis 8a: CEO duality will be positively associated with innovative performance in start-up high-technology new ventures, but not in adolescent new ventures.

Hypothesis 8b: CEO duality will be positively associated with financial performance in start-up high-technology new ventures, but not in adolescent new ventures.

FOUNDERS ON THE BOARD

A second board characteristic that can be expected to influence the firm's innovative and financial performance is the presence of the founder and members of the founding team on the board. Having the founder serve on the board implies greater monitoring and alignment of the interests of management with those of the founder–owners. There is mixed evidence on the effect of founders on the board on firm performance (e.g. Daily and Dalton, 1992a, b; Krause, 1988). However, over time, founders of successful firms may become conservative and increasingly unaware of changing competitive forces (Ranft and O'Neill, 2001). Their prior successes lead to a myopia that can inhibit the entrepreneurial spirit that was the original source of their new ventures' competitive advantage (Miller, 1991).

Early in the OLC, the proportion of members of the founding team on the board can improve innovation and financial performance. However, from the resource dependence theory, as the firm moves to face new challenges in the adolescent stage of the OLC, founder representation on the board can increasingly limit the board's influence on firm performance. As long as the founding team exerts control over board activities, the board's impact on resource recognition and acquisition will remain limited. The greater the proportion of the founding team serving on the board, the higher the chances of organizational myopia and less responsiveness to the firm's external environment in the adolescent stage of the OLC. This suggests the following hypotheses:

Hypothesis 9a: The proportion of founders on the board of directors will be positively associated with innovative performance of high-technology new ventures in the start-up stage, but not in the adolescent stage.

Hypothesis 9b: The proportion of founders on the board of directors will be positively associated with the financial performance of high-technology new ventures in the start-up stage, but not in the adolescent stage.

OUTSIDE DIRECTOR REPRESENTATION

The extent to which the board consists of outside or inside directors has received considerable attention in previous research (Daily et al., 2002). It is widely assumed that the proportion of outside directors will positively influence firm performance because it increases board independence and monitoring of executives (Zahra and Pearce, 1989), forcing managers to pursue strategies that maximize profits in the interest of the owners. However, the empirical evidence for this positive influence of outside directors has been mixed (Zahra and Pearce, 1989). One explanation is that the effectiveness of outside directors is moderated by their willingness and ability to perform the monitoring role. Zahra et al. (2000) find that the extent of outside directors' stock ownership, a proxy for directors' incentives, is positively associated with their willingness to support entrepreneurship.

In addition to the important monitoring role of outside directors, they connect the firm to various external networks and serve as boundary spanners between the firm and its industry, customers and suppliers. From the resource dependence theory, outside directors can enhance a firm's ability to influence or control vitally important resources (Pearce and Zahra, 1992). By bringing new sets of knowledge, experience and social capital to the firm, outside directors increase the number of potential linkages available through the board. Outside directors can also enhance the capacity of the board to influence resource acquisition and control and promote financial performance (Zahra et al., 2000). While the type of resources that a firm seeks may change over the OLC, new high-technology firms pursuing entrepreneurial strategies will continue to be dependent on external sources for new technological and market knowledge. Therefore, the board's boundary-spanning role is important at all stages of the OLC. Thus we suggest the following hypotheses:

Hypothesis 10a: The proportion of outside directors on the board will be positively associated with innovative performance in both start-up and adolescent new ventures.

Hypothesis 10b: The proportion of outside directors on the board will be positively associated with financial performance in both start-up and adolescent new ventures.

VENTURE CAPITAL INVOLVEMENT

Venture capitalist involvement on the board of directors is important from a resource dependence theory point of view. It signals a firm's potential viability (Shane and Stuart, 2002) and brings important social capital that connects the firm with the networks necessary for resource acquisition early in a firm's life (Aldrich and Zimmer, 1986; Stuart et al., 1999). Venture capitalists also help the firm to acquire the necessary administrative and marketing skills in the start-up phase that will support their survival until they internalize these capabilities in the adolescent stage of the OLC. Venture capitalist involvement also signals that a firm has survived the rigorous due diligence process and won prized financial backing. Such signals enhance the ability of the start-ups to acquire other necessary resources, including human capital, suppliers and customers. Shane and Stuart (2002) empirically show that links with venture capitalists significantly increase the probability that a firm will issue an initial public offering of stock, indicating that investors can play a major role in the success of new ventures.

The innovative and financial performance of start-up firms is dependent upon their ability to attract critical resources. However, over time the information asymmetries associated with new start-ups decrease, as potential stakeholders become more aware of these firms' capabilities. For example, as firms build a track record of successful performance, investors pay increasing attention to this as a signal rather than the mere presence or absence of venture capitalists on the board. Similarly, as the firm expands its board and builds marketing and distribution capabilities, the role venture capitalists play in connecting the firm to its external networks is likely to decline. Therefore, we suggest the following hypotheses:

Hypothesis 11a: The proportion of venture capitalists on the board of directors will be positively associated with innovative performance in start-up new ventures but not adolescent firms.

Hypothesis 11b: The proportion of venture capitalists on the board of directors will be positively associated with financial performance in start-up new ventures but not adolescent firms.

BOARD FUNCTIONAL AND EDUCATIONAL DIVERSITY

The human capital available to high-technology new ventures has been found to be associated with important organizational outcomes such as survival, growth and financial performance (e.g. Chandler and Hanks, 1994; Deeds et al., 1997). The breadth of human capital at the level of the board determines the pool of cognitive resources available for effective problem identification, formulation and exploration (e.g. Bantel and Jackson, 1989). There is empirical support for the proposition that individual characteristics such as education, intelligence and cognitive style are associated with both the creativity (e.g. Oldham and Cummings, 1996; Woodman and Schoenfeldt, 1989) and receptivity to innovative ideas (e.g. Kimberly and Evanisko, 1981; Rogers and Shoemaker, 1971). Therefore, diversity increases the openness of the board to new sources of information, expanding the search for new resources to support firm growth.

In a study of 199 banks in the USA, Bantel and Jackson (1989) found that the level of innovation was positively associated with top management teams that are more educated and more heterogeneous with respect to their functional backgrounds. Wiersema and Bantel (1992) also found that the top management team's level of education in general, their level of education in scientific disciplines and the diversity in terms of educational specialization were all positively and significantly associated with the propensity to change corporate strategy. Strategic flexibility, in turn, can contribute to the innovative performance of firms (e.g. Lumpkin and Dess, 1996).

From resource dependence theory, the breadth of functional backgrounds and educational experiences at the level of the board is expected to be positively associated with the breadth and quality of social networks to which directors are connected (e.g. Certo et al., 2001). The greater the functional and educational diversity of the board, the wider and more diverse the range of new knowledge and capabilities the firm can access. The firm's connections to various external sources of knowledge are especially important at the start-up stage of the OLC, when legitimacy and critical resources are necessary to sustain the new firm. Further, as the firm moves to the adolescent stage of the OLC, the types of resources shift to those that support the sustained growth and expansion of product lines. Therefore, in both stages of the OLC we expect that access to external knowledge is important. This access is facilitated by the human capital diversity of the board. This discussion suggests the following hypotheses:

Hypothesis 12a: The functional diversity of the board of directors is positively associated with innovative performance for both start-ups and adolescent firms.

Hypothesis 12b: The functional diversity of the board of directors is positively associated with the financial performance of both start-ups and adolescent firms.

Hypothesis 13a: The educational diversity of the board of directors is positively associated with innovative performance for both start-ups and adolescent firms.

Hypothesis 13b: The educational diversity of the board of directors is positively associated with the financial performance of both start-ups and adolescent firms.

Methods

Sample and data

The data for this study were obtained via a mail survey that was sent to the highest-ranking executive in 1700 new ventures (defined as companies eight years or younger) operating in 11 industries. Names and addresses were obtained from trade associations, state business directories, and company websites. Complete responses were obtained from 419 new ventures, providing a response rate of 24.6 percent. In order to assess the reliability of the responses to survey items, a second questionnaire was sent to another senior executive in each of the responding firms. The second survey yielded 103 responses and the inter-rater reliability between the two responding executives on items used in this chapter was $r = 0.69$ ($p<0.001$).

We assessed non-response bias by comparing respondents with non-responding firms on age, size (assets and employees), location, and industry type (low versus high technology). There were no significant differences between these two groups. The mean age of the ventures in the sample is 4.2 years (s.d. = 2.8) and the mean number of employees is 29 (s.d. = 44.67). There were 293 start-ups with an average age of 2.9 years. The remaining 126 firms were in their adolescent stage of the OLC, averaging 7.1 years.

Single source bias was assessed using factor analysis to determine if a single methods factor existed in the survey responses we received. The analysis yielded multiple significant factors, none of which explained more than 25 percent of the variance. This indicated that method bias was not a problem in this study.

Measures

Data used in this chapter are a part of the larger survey mentioned earlier. We used the following variables to measure a company's board composition:

a   A dummy variable was created to reflect whether the CEO was also a founder of the firm.
b   A second dummy variable was created to indicate if the CEO was also the chair, reflecting CEO duality (Finkelstein and D'Aveni, 1994).
c   The ratio of the founding team to the total size of the board was used to measure the representation of the founders on the board of directors.
d   The size of the board was a count of the total number of directors, including the board chairman (Zahra and Pearce, 1989).
e   The ratio of outside (non-executive) directors to total board size was used to indicate the proportion of outsiders on the board (Zahra, 1996).

  f   The size of the top management team was indicated by the number of executives at or
        above the level of vice president (Bantel and Jackson, 1989).
  g   Board functional and educational diversity were assessed using Blau's (1977) index of
        heterogeneity: $(1 - E\ p_i^2)$, where p was the proportion of group members in each
        category, and i was the number of different categories. Functional diversity was assessed
        in terms of technical versus non-technical roles. Educational diversity was assessed in
        terms of formal education in science, business and/or the humanities (Bantel and Jackson,
        1989).

CONTROL VARIABLES

Three variables expected to influence firm performance were included in the analysis to
control for their effects. We controlled for new ventures' size by the log of the firm's full-
time employees (Zahra et al., 2000). We also controlled for past performance, measured by
return on assets (Zahra et al., 2000). We controlled for industry-level effects on innovation
and financial performance by including dummy variables for the four-digit SIC of the 11
industries represented in this study (using 10 dummy variables).

INNOVATIVE PERFORMANCE

Innovative performance was assessed in three ways. The first was R&D expenditures divided
by sales, using data obtained from the survey data and secondary sources. R&D intensity was
an indicator of a firm's commitment to innovation (Zahra, 1996). The second was the number
of new product announcements obtained from Lexis-Nexus and verified by the survey data.
The third was a scale measure of a firm's commitment to entrepreneurship using eight items
from Miller (1983), reflecting senior managers' overall assessment of firm innovation.

FINANCIAL PERFORMANCE

We measured firm financial performance using both return on assets (ROA) and return on
equity (ROE), employing data from various secondary sources (e.g. trade associations and
company websites).

Analysis and Results

Overall differences in organizational and board variables

Table 3.2 reports the means for multiple variables that have been used to determine the
differences between ventures in the start-up versus adolescent stages of the OLC. Initially, a
two-group discriminant analysis was performed and the results were significant ($p<0.001$).
Following discriminant analysis, t-tests identified the sources of significant differences
between start-up and adolescent ventures. Table 3.2 shows that adolescent ventures had
more formal structures and had standardized their operations more than start-ups, as indicated by the OLC theory (Kazanjian and Drazin, 1990).

   Table 3.2 also shows that 92 percent of the start-ups had their founders serving as CEOs
as compared to 71 percent of adolescent firms. The differences between the two groups were
significant ($p<0.001$), supporting Hypothesis 1. The top management team of start-up busi-

Table 3.2   Organizational changes between start-up and adolescent stages of the OLC

Variables	Start-up phase (< 5 years)	Adolescent phase (6–8 years)	F
Standardization	2.7	3.9	11.03***
Formalization	2.6	3.4	7.11***
CEO is founder (Yes = 1)	0.92	0.71	23.11***
Size of top management team	2.19	4.83	16.09***
Board size	4.1	6.7	7.95***
Outsiders on board (%)	56	66	5.39**
VC on board (%)	19	15	2.01
Board functional diversity	0.34	0.59	6.27**
Board educational diversity	0.51	0.73	4.51**

Note: *** $p<0.001$; ** $p<0.01$.

nesses was also smaller than in adolescent ventures, supporting the OLC theory. In fact, adolescent firms had twice the number of top management team members than start-up ventures. The differences were statistically significant ($p<0.001$), supporting Hypothesis 2. In support of Hypothesis 3, we found that board size also increased from 4.1 among start-ups to 6.7 among adolescent ventures. The differences were statistically significant ($p<0.001$). Fifty-six percent of start-up board members were outsiders compared to 66 percent of the total membership of adolescent companies' boards and the differences were statistically significant ($p<0.01$). However, there were no significant differences in the representation of venture capitalists on boards. Venture capitalists represented 19 percent of the membership of boards among start-ups as compared to only 15 percent in adolescent companies. These results did not support Hypothesis 5.

The last two items in Table 3.2 focused on board functional and educational diversity. In both cases, diversity measures increased as firms moved from the start-up to adolescent stage of the OLC. In support of Hypothesis 6, board functional diversity was significantly smaller in start-ups as compared to adolescent firms ($p<0.01$). Finally, in support of Hypothesis 7, adolescent ventures had more diverse boards than start-ups in terms of educational background, and the differences were statistically significant ($p<0.01$). Overall, the data supported all but one of our hypotheses concerning the potential differences in board characteristics as firms moved from the start-up to adolescent stage of the OLC.

Entrepreneurial companies' governance and innovation

We also investigated the effect of board composition variables on three measures of innovative performance: R&D spending as a percentage of their sales (Zahra and Bogner, 2000), the total number of new products announced over a three-year period following the data collection, and Miller's (1983) entrepreneurship index. Separate analyses were conducted for firms in the start-up versus the adolescent stages of the OLC. The results using these three measures appear in Tables 3.3, 3.4 and 3.5, respectively.

Table 3.3   Regression results for R&D spending

Variables	Start-up phase	Adolescent phase
CEO duality	0.12	0.04
% of founding team on board	0.21*	0.29**
% outsiders on board	0.07	−0.03
% VC on board	0.18*	−0.02
Board functional diversity	0.10	0.10
Board educational diversity	0.29**	0.28*
Company size (log assets)	0.19*	0.15†
Adjusted R Squared	0.13***	0.19***

Notes:
*** $p<0.001$; ** $p<0.01$; * $p<0.05$; † $p<0.10$.

17 dummy variables were included in the analyses. All variables were standardized before performing regression analyses.

Table 3.4   Regression results for number of new products introductions

Variables	Start-up phase	Adolescent phase
CEO duality	0.17*	−0.09
% of founding team on board	0.28**	0.18*
% outsiders on board	0.03	0.07
% VC on board	−0.09	−0.02
Board functional diversity	0.11	0.20*
Board educational diversity	0.23*	0.27**
Company size (log assets)	0.15†	0.13†
Adjusted R squared	0.15***	0.18***

Notes:
*** $p<0.001$; ** $p<0.01$; * $p<0.05$; † $p<0.10$.

17 dummy variables were included in the analyses. All variables were standardized before performing regression analyses.

R&D SPENDING

Focusing on R&D spending, Table 3.3 shows that the regression model for the start-up phase was significant ($p<0.001$), explaining 13 percent of variance. The regression model for the adolescent phase of the OLC was also significant ($p<0.001$), explaining 19 percent of the variance. Contrary to Hypothesis 8a, CEO duality was not significantly associated with R&D spending at either stage of the OLC. The percentage of the founding team on the board was significant in the start-up (beta = 0.21; $p<0.05$) and adolescent stages (beta = 0.29;

Table 3.5 Regression results for focus on entrepreneurship

Variables	Start-up phase	Adolescent phase
CEO duality	0.26*	−0.02
% of founding team on board	0.20*	0.09
% outsiders on board	0.03	0.07
% VC on board	−0.09	−0.02
Board functional diversity	0.19*	0.20*
Board educational diversity	0.25*	0.15†
Company size (log assets)	0.19*	0.07
Adjusted R squared	0.21***	0.13*

Notes:
*** $p<0.001$; ** $p<0.01$; * $p<0.05$; † $p<0.10$.

17 dummy variables were included in the analyses. All variables were standardized before performing regression analyses.

$p<0.01$), which partially supported Hypothesis 9a with respect to start-up firms, but not adolescent firms. The effect of outside directors on the board was positive and insignificant in the start-up phase; it was negative and insignificant in the adolescent stage. Thus there was no support for Hypothesis 10a with respect to R&D spending. In support of Hypothesis 11a, having venture capitalists on the board was positive only in the start-up phase of the OLC ($p<0.05$). As hypothesized, the effect of venture capitalists' representation on the board was negative and insignificant in the adolescent stage. Contrary to Hypothesis 12a, the effect of board functional diversity on R&D spending was not significant in either the start-up or the adolescent phases of the OLC. Conversely, the educational diversity of the board was positively associated with R&D spending in the start-up ($p<0.01$) and adolescent stages ($p<0.05$). Thus Hypothesis 13a was supported.

NUMBER OF NEW PRODUCTS

Table 3.4 presents the results for the effect of boards of directors on new ventures' number of new products introduced over a period of three years. The regression model for the start-up phase was significant ($p<0.001$), explaining 15 percent of the variance. The model was also significant for the adolescent stage of the new venture life cycle ($p<0.001$), explaining 18 percent of variance.

Table 3.4 also revealed significant differences in the way that independent variables influenced the number of new products introduced. CEO duality was positive and significant ($p<0.05$) in the start-up phase, but was negative and insignificant in the adolescent stage. Thus, in contrast to innovation measured by R&D expenditures, the data supported Hypothesis 8a when the number of new products was used to capture innovation. Having members of the founding team on the board was positively associated with the number of new products in the start-up ($p<0.01$) and adolescent stages of the OLC ($p<0.05$). These results partially supported Hypothesis 9a as well as the results reported earlier for innovation measured as R&D expenditures.

Outsiders' board membership had a positive effect in the start-up and adolescent stages of the OLC, but betas were insignificant. Thus there was no support for Hypothesis 10a using R&D spending. The representation of venture capitalists on the board had a negative but insignificant effect across the two phases of the OLC. Therefore, contradicting previous findings for R&D expenditures, we did not find support for Hypothesis 11a when innovation was measured by new products. Functional diversity had a positive but insignificant coefficient in the start-up phase of the OLC, but it had a positive and significant effect in the adolescent stage ($p<0.05$). This partially supported Hypothesis 12a. Board educational diversity had positive coefficients in the start-up ($p<0.05$) and adolescent stage ($p<0.01$) of the OLC.

ENTREPRENEURSHIP

Table 3.5 presents the results for the entrepreneurship index. The two regression models were significant for the start-up phase ($p<0.001$) and the adolescent stage of the OLC ($p<0.05$). The model for the start-up explained 21 percent of the variance, whereas the same model explained 13 percent of the variance in the adolescent stage. CEO duality had a positive and significant effect ($p<0.05$) in the start-up stage but had a negative and insignificant effect in the adolescent stage of the OLC. These results supported Hypothesis 8a. In support of Hypothesis 9a, representation of the founding team on the board also had a positive effect on entrepreneurship ($p<0.05$) in the start-up phase and a positive but insignificant effect in the adolescent phase.

Next, outsiders' representation on the board had a positive but insignificant beta with entrepreneurship in the start-up and adolescent phases of the OLC. The results did not support Hypothesis 10a; this was also true with other measures of innovative performance. The representation of venture capitalists had a negative but insignificant effect on entrepreneurship in the start-up and adolescent stages of the OLC. Therefore, for entrepreneurship, we found no support for Hypothesis 11a, and overall we found only weak support for the hypothesized relationship between venture capital involvement on the board and R&D spending. Board functional diversity had a positive effect in the start-up and adolescent stages of the OLC (both at $p<0.05$). Thus, in contrast to the previous indicators, we found some evidence of the hypothesized relationship between functional diversity and innovation. However, across the three indicators, we found only weak support for this relationship. Finally, board educational diversity was significant in the start-up phase ($p<0.05$), and marginally significant in the adolescent stage of the OLC ($p<0.10$). Overall, these results supported Hypothesis 13a. Table 3.6 summarizes the support for the hypotheses on the relationship between board characteristics and the innovative performance of start-up and adolescent new ventures.

The effect of governance on new ventures' financial performance

Multiple regression analysis examined the effect of board composition variables (controlling for other variables) on new ventures' performance. Tables 3.7 and 3.8 present the results for ROA and ROE, respectively. This section summarizes the results.

Table 3.6   Summary of results for hypotheses relating board characteristics to innovation

Hypotheses	R&D/sales	New products	Entrepreneurship
H8a: CEO duality will be positively associated with innovative performance in start-up high-technology ventures, but not in adolescent ventures.	n/s	* (start-up)	*(start-up)
H9a: The proportion of founders on the board of directors will be positively associated with innovative performance of high-technology firms in the start-up stage, but not in the adolescent stage.	**	**	*(start-up)
H10a: The proportion of outside directors on the board will be positively associated with innovative performance in both start-up and adolescent firms.	n/s	n/s	n/s
H11a: The proportion of venture capitalists on the board of directors will be positively associated with innovative performance in start-up ventures but not adolescent firms.	*(start-up)	n/s	n/s
H12a: The functional diversity of the board of directors is positively associated with innovative performance for both start-ups and adolescent firms.	n/s	* (adolescent)	**
H13a: The educational diversity of the board of directors is positively associated with innovative performance for both start-ups and adolescent firms	**	**	**

Notes: ** significant result for both stages of firm development; * (firm growth stage) result significant only for the growth stage shown; 'n/s' not supported; 'a' result significant at $p<0.10$.

Table 3.7   Regression results for return on assets (ROA)

Variables	Start-up phase	Adolescent phase
CEO duality	–0.16*	–0.22*
% of founding team on board	0.18*	0.19*
% outsiders on board	0.08	0.09
% VC on board	0.05	0.17*
Board functional diversity	0.11	0.29**
Board educational diversity	0.12	0.11
Company size (log assets)	–0.09	–0.07
Adjusted R squared	0.18***	0.15***

Notes:
*** $p<0.001$; ** $p<0.01$; * $p<0.05$.

17 dummy variables were included in the analyses. All variables were standardized before performing regression analyses.

Table 3.8   Regression results for return on equity (ROE)

Variables	Start-up phase	Adolescent phase
CEO duality	0.21*	–0.09
% of founding team on board	–0.11	0.14†
% outsiders on board	0.04	0.13
% VC on board	0.14†	0.02
Board functional diversity	0.15†	0.20**
Board educational diversity	0.10	0.19*
Company size (log assets)	0.04	0.03
Adjusted R Squared	0.16**	0.19***

Notes:
*** $p<0.001$; ** $p<0.01$; * $p<0.05$; † $p<0.10$.

17 dummy variables were included in the analyses. All variables were standardized before performing regression analyses.

RETURN ON ASSETS (ROA)

Table 3.7 shows that the regression model for ROA for both the start-up and adolescent phases of the OLC was significant ($p<0.001$). The model explained 18 percent of the variance in ROA in the start-up phase, compared to 15 percent in the adolescent stage of the OLC. CEO duality had a negative and significant effect in the start-up and adolescent phases of the OLC ($p<0.05$). This was in the opposite direction from that proposed in Hypothesis 8b. The representation of the founding team on the firm's board had a positive and significant effect on ROA ($p<0.05$) in both the start-up and adolescent phases. This provided partial support for Hypothesis 9b with respect to ROA of the OLC. Though positive, outsiders' representation on the board was not significant in the start-up and adolescent phases, failing to support Hypothesis 10b. Having venture capitalists on the board was positively associated with ROA in the adolescent phase ($p<0.05$), but lacked significance in the start-up phase. Thus the results did not support Hypothesis 11b.

The level of functional diversity was positively associated with ROA for start-up and adolescent firms. However, this relationship was only significant for adolescent firms ($p<0.01$), partially supporting Hypothesis 12b. Finally, although educational diversity was also positively associated with ROA, it was not significant for firms at either the start-up or adolescent stages of the OLC, failing to support Hypothesis 13b.

RETURN ON EQUITY (ROE)

Table 3.8 presents the results for the effect of board composition variables on ROE. The regression model for the start-up phase was significant ($p<0.01$), explaining 16 percent of the variance. The model for the adolescent stage of the OLC was also significant ($p<0.001$), explaining 19 percent of variance in ROE. CEO duality was significant and positively associated with ROE in the start-up phase ($p<0.05$), but negative and insignificant in the adolescent stage. Thus, in contrast to ROA, we found support for Hypothesis 8b. The representation of the founding team on the board had a negative but insignificant effect on ROE in the start-up phase of OLC, but had a positive marginal effect in the adolescent stage ($p<0.10$). These results did not support Hypothesis 9b, which received only marginal support for start-ups but not adolescent firms.

Having outside directors on the board was positively, but not significantly, associated with ROE, in both the start-up and adolescent stages of the OLC. There was no support for Hypothesis 10b. Having venture capitalists on the board was marginally and positively significant in the start-up phase ($p<0.10$), but not significant in the adolescent phase of the OLC. Overall, analyses using ROE provided support for Hypothesis 11b. Board functional diversity was marginally and positively significant in the start-up phase ($p<0.10$) and was significant and positive in the adolescent stage of OLC ($p<0.01$). These results supported Hypothesis 12b. Board educational diversity had a positive but insignificant effect in the start-up stage and positive and significant ($p<0.05$) in the adolescent stage of the OLC, partially supporting Hypothesis 13b. To ensure clarity, the results for the hypotheses on the relationship between board characteristics and financial performance across stages of development are summarized in Table 3.9.

Discussion

This study has examined the effect of board composition on a company's innovative and financial performance in the start-up versus adolescent stages of the OLC. Grounded in the OLC and resource dependence theories, the results lead to three conclusions. The first is that young entrepreneurial companies experience major changes in the composition of their boards as they reach adolescence. While founders continue to play a key role in leading their companies, they become less likely to occupy the position of CEO (see Table 3.2). However,

Table 3.9   Summary of results for hypotheses relating board characteristics to measures of financial performance

Hypotheses	ROA	ROE
H8b: CEO duality will be positively associated with financial performance in start-up high-technology ventures, but not in adolescent ventures.	**[b]	*(start-up)
H9b: The proportion of founders on the board of directors will be positively associated with financial performance of high-technology firms in the start-up stage, but not in the adolescent stage.	**	*(adolescent)[a]
H10b: The proportion of outside directors on the board will be positively associated with financial performance in both start-up and adolescent firms.	n/s	n/s
H11b: The proportion of venture capitalists on the board of directors will be positively associated with financial performance in start-up ventures but not adolescent firms.	*(adolescent)	*(start-up)[a]
H12b: The functional diversity of the board of directors is positively associated with financial performance for both start-up and adolescent firms.	*(adolescent)	**[a]
H13b: The educational diversity of the board of directors is positively associated with financial performance for both start-up and adolescent firms.	n/s	*(adolescent)

Notes: ** indicates significant result for both stages of firm development; * (firm growth stage) indicates that result significant only for the growth stage shown; n/s means that relationship is not supported; [a] means that the results are significant at $p < 0.10$; [b] means that the relationship is opposite to expectations.

founders' influence does not decline as companies reach the adolescent stage of the OLC (Tables 3.3–3.8). Founders often surround themselves with a larger top management team in order to deal with the growing complexity of their operations. The board grows also in size, reflecting the need to co-opt new stakeholders within and outside the organization, which is supporting the resource dependence theory (Pfeffer and Salancik, 1978).

The results also show that as companies reach adolescence, the representation of outside directors on the board increases significantly. Boards also show greater diversity in their educational and functional backgrounds than those that govern start-up firms. The resource dependence theory suggests that the growing diversity of the board composition responds to the need to manage the multiple, new and complex challenges that new ventures encounter in their markets and industries. Board functional and educational diversity gives companies a larger pool of expertise to address these growing challenges. Larger boards also connect entrepreneurial companies with multiple external stakeholders and garner support for their various operations (Pfeffer and Salancik, 1978; Pearce and Zahra, 1992).

The second conclusion to be drawn from the study is that different board composition variables influence innovative performance at the start-up versus the adolescent stages of the OLC. In particular, CEO duality enhances innovative performance among start-ups but not in adolescent firms. This is in line with the proposition that CEO duality increases unity of command (Finkelstein and D'Aveni, 1994), clarity of purpose and an innovative orientation in young firms. The fact that this relationship becomes non-significant as the firm grows is also consistent with prior findings on the importance of separating the CEO and board chair positions as the firm enters the adolescent phase of the OLC (e.g. Zahra et al., 2000). Interestingly, support for this conclusion comes from output (e.g. new products) rather than input (i.e. R&D spending) measures of innovative performance.

The results also show that the percentage of the founding team serving on the board is conducive to higher R&D spending and new product introductions at both the start-up and adolescent stages of the OLC. This finding contradicts the argument that some founders become insensitive to changing technological and competitive conditions, possibly increasing organizational myopia as the firm evolves (Ranft and O'Neill, 2001). Our results suggest that founders understand the need to support R&D as a means of creating value. Insiders, in general, might be better disposed to understand and support innovative and risky ventures (Zahra, 1996). The exception to this general trend in our data is seen when entrepreneurship is considered, where a proportion of the founders on the board is not significant among adolescent firms.

Next, the effect of outside directors serving on the board on innovative performance is not statistically significant, using the R&D spending, new product introduction and entrepreneurship measures. These results support the notion that inside directors might be better positioned to promote innovation (Zahra, 1996). Insiders have the experience, first-hand knowledge and appreciation of the various challenges the company faces. They are also better positioned to evaluate various innovative ventures. Alternatively, we need to consider outsiders' willingness and ability before we can fully understand their contributions to firm performance (Zahra et al., 2000).

The effect of venture capitalists serving on the board on a company's innovative performance appears to be minimal. Perhaps venture capitalists are more interested in protecting their investments and harvesting the venture than improving its long-term innovative performance. Venture capitalists, therefore, may play a control role rather than becoming intimately involved in promoting innovation. This perspective is supported by the fact that the input side of innovative performance (i.e. R&D investments) is positively associated with venture capitalist involvement at the start-up stage of the OLC.

Functional and educational diversity of board members appears to play an important role in enhancing innovation. While not uniform, the results support the previous studies that document a positive effect for diversity of the top management team on innovative perform-ance (e.g. Bantel and Jackson, 1989; Wiersema and Bantel, 1992). Diverse boards provide important information that can stimulate innovation and promote entrepreneurial activities. We have proposed that for innovative performance, functional and educational diversity is important across both stages of the firm's OLC. Our results show that for these innovative outcomes, both board educational and functional diversity have a significant effect.

A third and final contribution of the chapter is to show how board composition variables might influence new venture financial performance. Examining Tables 3.7 and 3.8 reveals that board variables do not have a uniform effect on ROA and ROE. CEO duality has a negative effect on ROA in the start-up and adolescent phases of the OLC, indicating that consolidation of power in the hands of the CEO can harm performance. However, CEO duality is positively related to ROE in the start-up stage only where the new venture might benefit from the unity of command that might exist in its leadership (Finkelstein and D'Aveni, 1994). As with previous studies of CEO duality, this study finds mixed results. The results are also sensitive to the performance measure used and the OLC stage examined.

The presence of the founding team on a new venture's board is associated with higher ROA in both the start-up and adolescent stages of the OLC. As with the effect of founders on innovative performance, their influence on financial performance continues as the firm develops. These results contradict previous findings suggesting that founder entrenchment often leads to myopia that inhibits firm performance (Ranft and O'Neill, 2001). Our results indicate that entrepreneurial companies might benefit from the experience, wisdom and first-hand knowledge of their founding managers who serve on the board. However, it is also possible that superior performance leads to longer tenure for founders on the board of directors. Thus, as long as the firm is financially successful, the founders remain on the board. When performance is poor or below expectations, then founders are less likely to retain their influential positions on their companies' boards.

The representation of venture capitalists on the board has a limited effect on a company's financial performance; it is positive and significant only in the adolescent stage of the OLC, using ROA as the primary performance measure. It also has a positive but marginally significant effect on ROE in the start-up phase of the OLC. Our results show that venture capitalists keep management honest but may not add significantly to a company's financial performance.

It is also noteworthy that board functional diversity gains importance as the firm reaches adolescence. Functional diversity is significantly and positively associated with ROA and ROE only in the adolescent stage of the OLC. Perhaps this diversity allows companies to capitalize on a vast reservoir of experience that exists among their senior managers, espe-cially as the firm expands its product offerings and considers new market segments. Thus, as the literature cited earlier indicates, this relationship is understandable because as firms mature they often require a broad range of functional expertise. Board educational diversity becomes important for gaining higher ROE as the company reaches adolescence, as this diversity promotes strategic variety and enables the company to conceive and pursue new market opportunities and achieve higher ROE.

In general, the results on the influence of board characteristics on financial performance of high-technology start-ups and adolescent ventures are more mixed than those for innovative performance. There are two possible reasons for this. First, while financial performance is positively associated with innovative performance, especially in high-technology companies, there tends to be a time lag of several years between innovation and profitability (e.g. Zahra and Covin, 1995). Second, our study has not considered different types of high-technology industries. Knowledge trajectories, product development cycles and the innovation–profitability time lags vary significantly from one sector to another. Future research should consider analyzing separate groups of firms based on the type of industry in which they compete.

Limitations

The results should be interpreted with caution given that the study has focused only on high-technology industries and made no distinction between the various segments of those industries. We have also examined only two different stages of the OLC: start-up and adolescent. There are other phases for the OLC (e.g. Hanks et al., 1994) and the changes that might take place in governance over the phases of the OLC also deserve attention. Further, we have examined only US companies whose experiences may not generalize to other countries. Our data collection was made when high-technology new ventures were highly valued by the market at large, possibly influencing these ventures' ability to survive and achieve superior performance. Finally, our study has overlooked the different types of new ventures (e.g. lifestyle) and their corresponding goals. These variables can significantly influence new ventures' financial performance.

Managerial implications

The results should encourage new venture founders, owners and managers to recognize that the board composition should be revisited as their companies become established. Board composition variables that influence performance positively at one stage of the OLC may have the opposite effect at other stages. Consequently, it is essential to create a mechanism by which board composition is evaluated, and changes are made based on the strategic challenges facing the company and the demands of the OLC.

A second issue to consider as the venture moves across the stages of the OLC is whether founders should remain active in the business. Contrary to some recent arguments, we find evidence to support the need for the continued involvement of founders on the board in order to stimulate entrepreneurial and innovative performance.

Managers and founders also need to evaluate the diversity of their boards in terms of educational and functional backgrounds. As our results make clear, these two variables can influence the financial and innovative performance of new ventures. Given that these new ventures seek to create wealth through innovation, senior managers should thoroughly examine their directors' educational backgrounds and skills in order to ensure diversity.

Finally, in this study, CEO duality emerges as a double-edged sword. While some CEOs may want also to serve as the board chair to ensure unity of command and set the direction for their firms as they develop, this practice might backfire because there are not enough checks and balances in the governance system. CEOs who want to hold the title of the chair should realize that this may have an adverse effect on how their companies perform financially.

Implications for future research

The results show a need for more research on governance systems in entrepreneurial companies. New firms are the source of economic and technological progress. Therefore, understanding the variables that affect their performance is a worthwhile research issue. Future studies should consider how different entrepreneurial ventures also vary in their goals and governance practices.

Research should also examine the processes boards use to make decisions and how these processes change over the course of the OLC. This study has ignored these processes. Decision processes make a significant difference to the speed and quality of the resultant decisions. Consequently, it is important to document the processes by which boards make decisions and how these processes change over the various stages of the OLC.

It is important also to consider ownership structure and how this might affect the composition of the board and, in turn, firm innovative and financial performance. This study has explored whether members of the founding team are represented or hold leadership positions on the board. Future studies should delve more deeply into how ownership structure affects these choices and, in turn, how these choices influence performance. New ventures usually have financial and ownership structures that differ considerably from those that exist in established public companies. Consequently, prior findings on the effect of ownership structures on financial performance (e.g. Zahra et al., 2000) may not generalize to new ventures. It is important also to examine the governance structures of non-US new ventures and how these structures might influence their performance differently in different high-technology industries over the different stages of the OLC.

Conclusion

Little research has been conducted on the governance systems of new ventures, especially those that compete in high-technology industries. Less is known about the changes in new ventures' governance systems over the various stages of the OLC. The study reported in this chapter shows that major changes occur in board composition as new ventures move from the start-up to the adolescent stage of the OLC and these changes might influence key indicators of innovative and financial performance differently. Future studies should examine board processes and how they evolve over the course of the new ventures' OLC.

References

Adizes, I. (1979), 'Organizational passages: diagnosing and treating life cycle problems in organizations', *Organizational Dynamics*, **8**: 3–24.

Aldrich, H.E. and Zimmer, C. (1986), 'Entrepreneurship through social networks', in D.L. Sexton and R.W. Smilor (eds), *The Art and Science of Entrepreneurship*, Cambridge, MA: Ballinger, pp. 3–23.

Bantel, K.A. (1998), 'Technology-based, "adolescent" firm configurations: strategy identification, context, and performance', *Journal of Business Venturing*, **13**(3): 205–34.

Bantel, K.A. and Jackson, S.E. (1989), 'Top Management and innovations in banking: does the composition of the top team make a difference?', *Strategic Management Journal*, 10: 107–25.

Blau, P. (1977), *Inequality and Heterogeneity*, New York: The Free Press.

Castaldi, R. and Wortman, M. (1984), 'Boards of directors in small corporations: an untapped resource', *American Journal of Small Business*, **9**(2): 1–10.

Certo, S.T., Daily, C.M. and Dalton, D.R. (2001), 'Signaling firm value through board structure: an investigation of initial public offerings', *Entrepreneurship Theory & Practice*, **26**(2): 33–50.

Chandler, G.N. and Hanks, S.H. (1994), 'Market attractiveness, resource-based capabilities, venture strategies, and venture performance', *Journal of Business Venturing*, **9**: 331–49.

Churchill, N. and Lewis, V. (1983), 'The five stages of small business growth', *Harvard Business Review*, **61**: May–June, 30–50.

Daily, C.M. and Dalton, D.R. (1992a), 'The relationship between governance structure and corporate performance in entrepreneurial firms', *Journal of Business Venturing*, **7**: 375–86.

Daily, C.M. and Dalton, D.R. (1992b), 'Financial performance of founder-managed versus professionally managed small corporations', *Journal of Small Business Management*, **30**(2): 25–34.

Daily, C.M. and Dalton, D.R. (1993), 'Board of directors leadership and structure: control and performance implications', *Entrepreneurship: Theory & Practice*, **17**(3): 65–81.

Daily, C.M., McDougall, P.P., Covin, J.G. and Dalton, D.R. (2002), 'Governance and strategic leadership in entrepreneurial firms', *Journal of Management*, **28**(3): 387–412.

Deeds, D.L., DeCarolis, D. and Coombs, J.E. (1997), 'The impact of firm specific capabilities on the amount of capital raised in an initial public offering: evidence from the biotechnology industry', *Journal of Business Venturing*, **12**: 31–46.

Drazin, R. and Kazanjian, R.K. (1990), 'A reanalysis of Miller and Friesen's life cycle data', *Strategic Management Journal*, **11**: 319–25.

Fiegener, M.K., Brown, B.M., Dreux IV, D.R. and Dennis, W.J., Jr (2000), 'The adoption of outside boards by small private US firms', *Entrepreneurship and Regional Development*, **12**(4): 291–310.

Finkelstein, S. and D'Aveni, R.A. (1994), 'CEO duality as a double-edged sword: how boards of directors balance entrenchment avoidance and unity of command', *Academy of Management Journal*, **37**(5): 1079–108.

Ford, R.H. (1988), 'Outside directors and the privately owned firm: are they necessary?', *Entrepreneurship Theory & Practice*, **13**(1): 49–57.

Hanks, S.H., Watson, C.J., Jansen, E. and Chandler, G.N. (1994), 'Tightening the life-cycle construct: a taxonomic study of growth stage configurations in high-technology organizations', *Entrepreneurship Theory & Practice*, **18**(2): 5–29.

Kazanjian, R.K. and Drazin, R. (1990), 'A state-contingent model of design and growth for technology based new ventures', *Journal of Business Venturing*, **5**(3): 137–50.

Kimberly, J.R. and Evanisko, M.J. (1981), 'Organizational innovation: the influence of individual, organizational, and contextual factors on hospital adoption of technological and administrative innovations', *Academy of Management Journal*, **24**(4): 689–713.

Krause, D.S. (1988), 'Corporate control', *Journal of Political Economy*, **73**(2): 110–20.

Lester, D. and Parnell, J. (1999), 'A strategic interpretation of organizational life cycle', *The Journal of Applied Management and Entrepreneurship*, **5**(1): 14–32.

Lumpkin, G.T. and Dess, G.G. (1996), 'Clarifying the entrepreneurial orientation construct and linking it to performance', *Academy of Management Review*, **21**(1): 135–73.

Miller, D. (1983), 'The correlates of entrepreneurship in three types of firms', *Management Science*, **29**(7): 770–92.

Miller, D. (1991), 'Stale in the saddle: CEO tenure and the match between organization and environment', *Management Science*, **37**(1): 34–52.

Miller, D. and Friesen, P. (1984), 'A longitudinal study of the corporate life cycle', *Management Science*, **30**: 1161–83.

Norburn, D. and Birley, S. (1988), 'The top management team and corporate performance', *Strategic Management Journal*, **9**: 225–37.

Oldham, G.R. and Cummings, A. (1996), 'Employee creativity: personal and contextual factors at work', *Academy of Management Journal*, **39**(3): 607–34.

Pearce, J.A. II and Zahra, S.A. (1992), 'Board composition from a strategic contingency perspective', *Journal of Management Studies*, **29**(4): 411–38.

Pfeffer, J. and Salancik, G.R. (1978), *The External Control of Organizations: A Resource of Dependence Perspective*, New York: Harper and Row.

Quinn, R. and Cameron, K. (1983), 'Organizational life cycles and shifting criteria of effectiveness: some preliminary evidence', *Management Science*, **29**: 33–51.

Ranft, A.L. and O'Neill, H.M. (2001), 'Board composition and high flying founders: hints of trouble to come?', *Academy of Management Executive*, **15**(1): 126–38.

Shane, S. and Stuart, T. (2002), 'Organizational endowments and the performance of university start-ups', *Management Science*, **48**(1): 154–70.

Smith, K., Mitchell, T. and Summer, C. (1985), 'Top management priorities in different stages of the organizational life cycle', *Academy of Management Journal*, **28**: 799–820.

Stuart, S., Huang, H. and Hybels, R. (1999), 'Interorganizational endorsements and the performance of entrepreneurial ventures', *Administrative Science Quarterly*, **44**: 315–49.

Wiersema, M.F. and Bantel, K.A. (1992), 'Top management team demography and corporate strategic change', *Academy of Management Journal*, **35**(1): 91–121.

Woodman, R.W. and Schoenfeldt, L.F. (1989), 'Individual differences in creativity: An interactionist perspective', in J.A. Glover, R.R. Ronning and C.R. Reynolds (eds), *Handbook of Creativity*, New York: Plenum, pp. 77–98.

Zahra, S.A. (1996), 'Governance, ownership, and corporate entrepreneurship: the moderating impact of industry technological opportunities', *Academy of Management Journal*, **39**(6): 1713–35.

Zahra, S.A. and Bogner, W.C. (2000), 'Technology strategy and software new ventures' performance: exploring the moderating effect of the competitive environment', *Journal of Business Venturing*, **15**(2): 135–73.

Zahra, S.A. and Covin, J.G. (1995), 'Contextual influences on the corporate entrepreneurship–performance relationship: a longitudinal analysis', *Journal of Business Venturing*, **10**(1): 43–58.

Zahra, S.A., Neubaum, D.O. and Huse, M. (2000), 'Entrepreneurship in medium-size companies: exploring the effects of ownership and governance systems', *Journal of Management*, **26**(5): 947–76.

Zahra, S.A. and Pearce, J.A. (1989), 'Boards of directors and corporate financial performance: a review and integrative model', *Journal of Management*, **15**(2): 291–334.

[4]

Exploring the agency consequences of ownership dispersion among the directors of private family firms*

Bill Schulze, Michael Lubatkin and R. Dino

The principal–agent model has had a profound influence on corporate governance theory (Jensen, 1998). A central premise of this theory is that management decisions are strongly influenced by the ownership status of each decision maker who serves on a corporation's board of directors. The agency positions of outside owners and owner–managers differ. Outside owners prefer growth-oriented risk taking because they benefit solely from the appreciation of shareholder value. They are also indifferent to the level of risk that is specific to any particular investment made by a given firm because they can reduce that risk by holding diversified portfolios. Owners who manage a private firm, in contrast, define its value in terms of utility, and so they will undertake risks that are commensurate with their preferences for certain outcomes. These outcomes not only include financial and non-financial benefits, but also the utility generated by the ability to exercise authority, dictate strategy and choose which investments the firm will undertake.

Should an owner–manager relinquish equity to outside owners, the agency theory prediction is that changes in the incentives facing the owner–manager will cause the firm's value to decline. Specifically, because inside owners would now bear only a fraction of the cost of the benefits they receive, they have incentive to act opportunistically and make decisions that promote their self-regarding interests as opposed to the interests of outside shareholders (Demsetz, 1973; Jensen and Meckling, 1976; Fama and Jensen, 1983a). In this way, fractional ownership creates agency problems: it gives inside owners incentive to free-ride on outside owners' equity and to favor consumption over investment.

But what if there are no outside shareholders and firm equity is instead distributed among family members? Will fractional ownership create agency problems, as the conventional agency model implies, or do family relationships promote the within-group alignment of

* First published in *Academy of Management Journal*, June 2003, **46**(2): 179–94. Reprinted with permission of the Copyright Clearance Centre and Academy of Management.

ownership interests and encourage investment? This and other questions about the govern-ance of private family firms has been largely glossed over in the management literature, yet family firms account for 40 to 60 percent of US gross national product and employ upwards of 80 percent of the workforce (Gomez-Mejia et al., 2001). Answers to these questions can enrich corporate governance theory, which heretofore has focused primarily on public firms and the challenge of aligning insider goals with those of outside investors (Morck et al., 1988; Wright et al., 1996), while overlooking private firms and the challenge of achieving within-group goal alignment.

In this study, we examine how ownership dispersion among family directors influences a firm's use of debt in 1464 medium-sized, private, family-owned and -managed firms; the average firm in our sample had annual sales of $36 million, had 182 employees, and had been in business for 49 years. Our thesis is that both market conditions and the dispersion of ownership influence the agency position of individual directors in such a way that they are more willing to use debt and bear the attendant risk it poses to their individual wealth when (1) market growth rates are high and (2) control rests in the hands of a controlling owner or with a coalition of minority shareholders rather than being more equally dispersed. Consist-ent with our hypotheses, our finding is that the relationship between a family firm's use of debt and the dispersion of ownership among its directors forms a U-shaped function when market growth is high, but not when market growth is low.

Governance Efficiencies in the Family Firm

Agency costs arise whenever ownership and control are separated. Agency theorists, begin-ning with Fama and Jensen (1983a, 1985), have long presumed that family governance minimizes these costs. For example, the need to monitor family agent conduct is reduced because familiarity and the intimate knowledge gained from long association facilitate communication and promote cooperation among family owners and family agents. Fama and Jensen noted that 'family members have many dimensions of exchange with one another over a long horizon that lead to advantages in monitoring and disciplining family-related decision agents' (1983b: 306). The need to incur bonding costs is also reduced because family ties link them to a kinship network that is characterized by norms of reciprocity, strong social ties, a shared identity and a common history (Ouchi, 1980). Kinship thus tempers self-interest – and the conflict it can cause – by fostering loyalty and commitment to the family and the firm.

Self-interest is further tempered by parental altruism. This trait, which economists model as a utility function in which the welfare of individuals is positively linked to the welfare of others (Becker, 1981; Lunati, 1997), compels parents to be generous to their children. It also encourages family members to be considerate of one another and to care for each other in time of need, even to the point of sacrifice. The result, Fama and Jensen concluded, is that 'special relations with other decision agents allow agency problems to be controlled without separation of the management and control decisions' (1983b: 306).

Altruism and kinship offset some of the inefficiencies in risk bearing that otherwise accompany private ownership. All else being the same, private ownership limits access to capital, forcing a private, family-owned and -managed firm to rely on internal sources to fund investments. The fact that most of their wealth is invested in the firm also tends to make private firm owners reluctant to use debt. Should the owners be linked to the same kinship network, however, their individual calculus for framing investment decisions changes. Specifically, altruism and kinship can make them more willing to use debt and bear the threat it poses to their individual wealth, because they temper their self-interest with concern for the welfare of the family and firm. Altruism and kinship thus make family directors more willing to use debt to fund investment and pursue growth than agency theorists would predict, especially when market conditions are promising. The assumption that ownership will remain within the family also gives family directors incentive to make investments that will benefit the next generation of owners. This long-term perspective, combined with the type of deep knowledge that family directors acquire from lifelong involvement in the principal industry of their family firm, makes them better able to evaluate risk and make strategic investments (Kang, 1999).

It is tempting to conclude that family ownership and management naturally minimize agency costs while giving family directors the incentive to make investment decisions that serve the best interests of a firm and family. However, this positive portrait is at odds with evidence suggesting that these firms are 'plagued by conflicts' that can cause them to flounder, if not fail (Levinson, 1971: 90) and that they are vulnerable to a form of inertia that can paralyze decision making and threaten firm survival (Meyer and Zucker, 1989).

This positive portrait is also at odds with the recent study by Schulze et al. (2001), who found indirect support for the thesis that altruism has a dark side. Although it can temper self-interest and engender loyalty, commitment and a long-term perspective, altruism can also alter the incentive structure of a firm so that some of the agency benefits gained are offset by free-riding and other agency problems. For example, altruism can create a sense of entitlement among family members by encouraging CEOs (usually a parent and/or head of household of the controlling family) to use the firm's resources to provide family members with employment, perquisites and privileges that they would not otherwise receive. Altruism can also bias CEOs' perceptions of their employed children, which hampers their ability to monitor and discipline them. The result, Schulze and colleagues concluded, is that family-owner management does not necessarily minimize the agency cost of fractional ownership and, in some cases, can exacerbate it.

We expand this argument in the following sections. Our thesis is that just as the separation of ownership from control in widely held firms drives a wedge between the interests of principal and agent, the dispersion of ownership in family-held firms drives a wedge between the interests of those who lead a firm – and often own a controlling interest – and other family owners. We begin by proposing that, contrary to the tenets of agency theory, inside ownership and board oversight do not efficiently resolve the agency problems experienced by private, family-owned and -managed firms. Drawing on behavioral economics theory, we then explain how private ownership and family management can combine to raise the agency costs of fractional ownership, and thereby influence family director conduct and a firm's use of debt.

The Governance Effects of Private Ownership and Family Management

According to the principal–agent model, inside ownership and board oversight efficiently resolve the conflicts caused by fractional ownership because: (1) ownership aligns inside owners' risk preferences with those of outsiders while increasing communication and co-operation among them; (2) liquid markets limit the cost of board conflict by making it possible for disputing parties to buy or sell shares at a market-determined price; and (3) voting generates economically efficient outcomes since it reflects the proportionate distribution of risk and reward among a firm's owners (e.g. Alchian and Woodward, 1988; Fama and Jensen, 1983a; Jensen, 1998; Jensen and Smith, 1985). We argue in this section that none of these three governance mechanisms operates as theorized when firms are privately owned and family managed.

First, the agency theory assumption that increased inside ownership aligns owner preferences implies that individuals are economically rational wealth maximizers. In contrast, behavioral economists, such as O'Donoghue and Rabin (2000) and Thaler and Shefrin (1981), have argued that individuals are motivated by an idiosyncratic set of preferences – some economic and some non-economic in character, and some self-regarding (egoistic) and some other-regarding (altruistic) – and are driven to maximize the utility they gain from each. Taken together, these assertions suggest that goal alignment within any board would be difficult to attain and sustain. Further, they suggest that conflicts of interest arise because resource constraints prevent board members from maximizing their different types of preferences simultaneously. For example, actions taken to promote wealth can prevent actions taken to promote leisure, while actions motivated by self-interest can prevent actions taken to promote the welfare of others.

Unlike public firms, which can rely on external governance mechanisms to minimize the adverse effects of these internal conflicts, family firms cannot do so because private ownership isolates them from the discipline that external markets provide. Moreover, altruism hampers the ability of a family firm's principal owner (who is usually the CEO) to use internal governance mechanisms like monitoring to minimize internal conflicts and the agency threats they engender (Schulze et al., 2001). Field study findings concur: family-firm CEOs tend to rely on informal monitoring and control mechanisms (Daily and Dollinger, 1992; Geeraerts, 1984) and are notorious for avoiding disciplinary issues that might have repercussions for familial relations both inside and outside the firms (Meyer and Zucker, 1989; Ward, 1987). In sum, whereas the agency theory assumption is that ownership and monitoring efficiently align shareholder interests in public firms, behavioral economic perspectives suggest that ownership can have the opposite effect when firms are private and family-managed.

Second, agency theory also suggests that market liquidity, and hence the ability to exit a firm at low cost, limits the potential cost of settling conflicts of interests among the directors of public firms, because those who disagree with the majority opinion can simply sell their shares at the current market price and exit the firm. Of course, this claim rests on the assumption that the only transaction cost that matters is the cost of selling equity. Behavioral agency theorists, such as Wiseman and Gomez-Mejia (1998), would take exception to this statement. According to their theory, which melds insights from prospect theory with agency theory, insiders face a number of non-economic exit costs, including the value of the firm-specific knowledge, experience and social networks that they accumulated while employed in the firm's upper-management ranks, as well as the emotional costs associated with a change in status, the possible relocation of the family and so on.

Family-member inside directors arguably face higher exit costs. There are no liquid markets for their stock. Even if there were, exiting the firm would still mean forgoing certain rights, perquisites and other privileges that generally come with being employed by one's family (Schulze et al., 2001). Moreover, exiting might not only entail forgoing (or at least reducing) the share one expects to inherit in the firm and/or the family's estate, but also forgoing or reducing benefits that might accrue from continued close association with the firm and family (Holtz-Eakin et al., 1993). Finally, and perhaps most importantly, leaving a family firm entails significant emotional costs associated with lost intimacy, reduced status, breaking familial expectations and, in some cases, a severing of family ties (Gersick et al., 1997).

Thus, if market liquidity (along with monitoring and voting) is necessary for an efficient resolution of conflicts among members of a board of directors, then higher exit costs should make board conflict resolution more costly in family firms. High exit costs, therefore, tend to lock insider directors into a firm, thereby making the conflicts that arise more persistent and a convergence of interests more difficult to achieve. Thus, we again infer that a different set of incentives is at play among inside family directors (those who are both directors and employees), a situation that affects board conduct in ways that extant agency models do not predict.

Finally, agency theorists assert that although inside and outside owners of public firms may have differences that defy consensus, voting assures that the preferences of the risk-neutral majority will prevail. Of course, this assertion relies on the assumption that board members carry out their fiduciary responsibilities and that the independence of outsiders is not compromised by the influence of insiders. This is not always the case (e.g. Finkelstein and Hambrick, 1996). CEOs, by virtue of their professional and political ties as well as the authority of their office, can make both inside and (some) outside directors beholden to them (Kroll et al., 1993). Also, the boards of some firms, especially those with widely distributed ownership and without large-block owners, may appoint outsiders who are not vigilant in monitoring and/or fail to exercise their fiduciary authority over insiders (Walsh and Seward, 1990). Thus entrenchment threatens the autonomy of such a board and undermines the effectiveness of its oversight. Family firms are particularly vulnerable to voting imperfections and entrenchment. The CEO of a family firm generally wields power that is disproportionate to his or her share of ownership; this disproportionate power stems from familial sources (for instance, status as the head of the family), hierarchical sources (such as status as the head of the firm), and (because the firm is privately held) freedom from the oversight and discipline provided by the market for corporate control and other sources of external governance. Not surprisingly, family-firm CEOs tend to be entrenched; their average tenure of 24 years (Beckhard and Dyer, 1983) is twice that observed in widely held firms (Hambrick and Fukutomi, 1991: 736). Further, family firms tend to have small boards of directors (there was an average of four members per board in the sample used in this study, whereas experts recommend seven or more), and they tend to appoint directors who are friends of the CEO and/or happen to have a fiduciary relationship with the firm (such as their attorneys and accountants), further compromising director autonomy and board vigilance (Ford, 1988; Gersick et al., 1997; Nash, 1988; Ward and Handy, 1988).

In sum, the combined influence of private ownership and family management results in a web of incentives that undermine a family firm's governance and raise the agency cost of fractional ownership. In the next section, we explain how ownership dispersion influences director conduct and family firms' use of debt.

The Effects of Ownership Dispersion at Family Firms

Whereas the boards of public firms consist of inside and outside directors, a family firm's board consists of a principal owner (who is usually, but not always, the founder and CEO) and minority shareholders (who tend to be members of the nuclear and/or extended family and are often, but not always, employed by the firm). Family-firm ownership tends to get dispersed in a somewhat episodic and 'stepwise' fashion over a relatively long period of time, with shares usually passed from parent to child around the time of the principal owner's retirement and/or death.

While patterns of ownership dispersion vary, ranging from primogeniture (in which leadership and control of the voting stock passes to the firstborn) to coparcenary (in which offspring receive relatively equal shares), the tendency in the USA is to grant the most shares to the chief executive, and more shares to offspring who are employed by the firm than to those who are not. (Testing for confirmation, we found the first tendency held true in all the cases in which we could identify the occupation of a firm's principal shareholder, and the second tendency held true for the preponderance of the 1464 family firms represented in this sample.)

The ownership of a family firm generally passes through three broad stages of dispersion (Gersick et al., 1997): controlling owner, in which most shares are held by the founder, or in the case of later generations, by a single individual; the sibling partnership, in which relatively equal proportions of ownership are held by members of a single generation; and the cousin consortium, in which ownership is further fractionalized as it is passed on to include third and later generations. Although the conflicts that accompany each stage differ, the agency model that we describe below explains the conduct indigenous to each.

Controlling owner

As we previously noted, in the principal–agent model, owners who manage a private (family or non-family) firm define its value in terms of their personal utility. Thus they have powerful incentives to pursue options that they perceive as best and to bear the associated risks to the point where the marginal benefit received is offset by the threat the risks pose to their personal wealth (Jensen and Meckling, 1976). Proponents of behavioral agency theory (e.g. Wiseman and Gomez-Mejia, 1998) have refined that insight, arguing that the amount of risk that these owners are willing to bear is based, at least in part, on how they frame their expectations. For example, the owner–managers of private firms should have incentive to invest when they expect conditions in their firms' markets to grow, but not when they expect market growth to decline or slow. Lacking access to the equity markets, however, their ability to invest is limited by the availability of internally generated funds (Casson, 1999) – unless, of course they take on or increase debt. It follows that the owner–managers of private firms will be more willing to use debt, and more willing to bear the threat it poses to their individual wealth, during periods of high market growth than they will during periods of decline or low market growth.

We posit that parental altruism causes owners to pursue first-best actions when a private firm is family owned and is managed by a controlling owner.[1] Altruism is a trait that positively links the controlling owner's welfare, as head of the family, to that of other family members (Schulze et al., 2001). Altruism thus compels the controlling owner to consider the needs of the firm and each family member when defining her or his first-best options (for instance, it may make the controlling owner more willing to pursue investments with longer-term payoffs). Over time, however, the economic incentive to do what maximizes personal utility can blur the controlling owner's perception of what is best for the firm or family; self-interest and the firm's and family's best interests may be viewed as one and the same in what we might call the 'what's good for GM' phenomenon. For instance, age may cause the controlling owner to avoid investments that other family members favor because he or she views the investments as too risky or as personally threatening – in the case, perhaps, of their requiring the controlling owner to learn new skills. Conflicts of interest can therefore arise that give family members reason to question the extent to which they can rely on the controlling owner to make decisions that they deem as being in the family's best interests. The family members thus have incentives to monitor the controlling owner and incur other agency costs in an effort to assure that their best interests are being served.

Moreover, family members and controlling owners face different sets of incentives, and thus hold different views of what investments are best. For example, like their counterparts in public firms, family-member employees of family-owned and -managed firms bear only a fraction of the risk associated with an investment decision but, unlike their counterparts, are able to enjoy a disproportionate share of the benefits owing to their family status. They are also likely to feel entitled to these benefits since, as family members, they believe that they own *de facto* options in the firms, or a residual but legitimate claim on them in the form of an inheritance at a future date (Holtz-Eakin et al., 1993; Stark and Falk, 1998).

This sense of entitlement has two important agency consequences. First, it can cause employed family members and their prospective heirs to become fiscally conservative, if not loss-averse, since added risk threatens the value of their anticipated inheritance. Put differently, an endowment effect (Wiseman and Gomez-Mejia, 1998) engenders loss aversion by altering their risk–return calculus. Second, when the sense of entitlement is coupled with high exit costs and the perception that the potential cost of exiting a firm exceeds the expected value of other opportunities, hopeful family heirs can become locked into a dependent relationship with the firm. This makes it possible for a state of 'double moral hazard' (Gupta and Romano, 1998) or 'owner opportunism' (Perrow, 1986) to develop in which the controlling owner has the power, and perhaps the incentive, to unilaterally change his or her estate plans, thereby placing family members' claims to the firm at risk.[2]

Although double moral hazard ordinarily gives agents incentives to invest resources in monitoring a principal's conduct, family members' ability to influence a controlling family owner is constrained by both their minority (or even non-shareholder) status and the added authority controlling owners have by virtue of being the heads of the family households and, in many cases, the founders of the firms. These constraints, combined with the risk that the controlling owner may undertake investments that other family members do not view as best, gives these family members incentive to prefer consumption to investment, and to do so (in the form of pecuniary and non-pecuniary benefits) at rates that are high relative to their ownership stakes. Consumption, of course, precludes alternative uses for the funds that are consumed.

The net result is a pattern of incentives that is the reverse of that theorized to exist at widely held public firms. Whereas fractional ownership at widely held public firms gives insiders incentives to free-ride on the outside owners' equity, we argue that it gives family insiders (family-member directors and employees) incentives to free-ride on the controlling owner's equity. Controlling owners are likely to recognize that (some) family members are free-riding on their (*qua* the family's) holdings. And, although altruism and the repercussions that disciplinary actions might have for family relations compel the controlling owners to accept this free-riding, they also give them incentive to be wary of the investment decisions that the family insiders might recommend. Thus, although we anticipate that the controlling owners of family firms, and especially founders, will initially have strong incentive to use debt to fund investments that they think are the best, we argue in the next section that their ability (and willingness to do so) will decline as the percentage of ownership held by loss-averse, consumption-oriented family members increases.

Sibling partnership

The agency dynamics during the sibling partnership stage become more problematic. As in the controlling owner stage, the principal shareholder (that is, the largest shareholder) in a sibling partnership is likely to serve as the CEO, to control the largest single block of ownership, and, by virtue of his or her office, to continue to wield influence that is disproportionate to ownership share. And, like a founder, the principal shareholder can be expected to fulfill a quasi-family-leader role, using the firm's resources to promote family welfare and to favor the reinvestment of earnings over the consumption of those earnings via dividends and other payments (Gersick et al., 1997). Yet, typically, the principal shareholder in a sibling partnership is neither the founder of the family firm nor the biological head of the family and, lacking that authority and influence over the siblings, is less able to obtain – whether by cooperation, co-option or edict – the support of the other family directors for making investments and pursuing the opportunities that he or she believes to be the best options.

In addition, and in line with both the family business literature (Gersick et al., 1997) and economic theory about altruism, all sibling partners are also likely to be more concerned about their own welfare and that of their immediate families than they will be about each other's welfare. (According to this theory, a parent's concern for her or his children tends to be stronger than the children's concern for the parent (Stark and Falk, 1998), and altruistic ties among members of a nuclear family tend to be stronger than those among members of an extended family (Becker, 1981)). Thus agency conditions in sibling partnerships resemble those in the controlling owner stage, with sibling partners having incentives to use a family firm's resources to maximize their own utility; acting on these incentives can, again, engender double moral hazard problems and conflict between the sibling partners.

The risk of intrafamily conflict is further exacerbated as families age. Siblings who were once able to forge an effective partnership may find it torn apart as resource constraints force them to make hard decisions about dividend payout policy (to fund college tuitions, for instance) and/or the involvement of their adult children in the firm's operations. The risk of intrafirm conflict also rises if ownership is distributed somewhat equally among a principal shareholder and sibling partners. In this scenario, one loss-averse sibling can prevent others from putting a firm's resources to their desired (first-best) use. Consequently, we would expect sibling partners to have the incentive to engage in various political maneuvers, like vote swapping and 'hostage taking', actions that might cause a series of compromises, ill-will, and second-best decisions about growth, investments in new technology and so on.

The result could be a state of paralysis in which no one sibling is willing to bear added risk or use debt to pursue opportunities that others believe are best. Thus, whereas the principal–agent model assumption is that increased ownership aligns the interests of rival parties, we posit that increased ownership dispersion among sibling partnerships will engender misalignment and loss aversion. Put differently, the increased concern for their own children, the added pressure from outside family directors (and in-laws) to sustain or enhance the rate of dividend payout, and the ageing siblings' increasing reluctance to bear risk can cause a firm to reduce its use of debt, even when market conditions are perceived as favorable, and to get bogged down in the types of conflict that cause many family firms to flounder or fail (Levinson, 1971).

Cousin consortium

Finally, we expect that the agency position of a principal and the minority owners will become more aligned in a family firm's cousin consortium stage. By the time the firm enters this stage, ownership has become more dispersed, or fractionalized, and it is less likely that a single individual owns a controlling or majority interest in the firm. This situation increases the degree of relative influence that each family director has on the future value of his or her claim on the firm, thereby mitigating the double moral hazard problem that characterized owner control and sibling partnership. Inside directors, it follows, should be less concerned with consumption and more concerned about the future value of their estates and how that value will be affected by any future dilution of ownership. The end result is an increase in the alignment of interest that exists among board members and, hence, reduced agency costs.

In the cousin consortium stage of a family firm, ownership has likely passed to members of the extended family, the majority of whom are not employed by the firm. All things being the same, these outside family members are less 'overinvested' in the firm and, so, they should have risk preferences that are more akin to those of institutional investors and others who invest in public firms. We therefore anticipate that cousin consortiums' managers are both more willing to use debt to pursue their objectives and, because of the dispersion of ownership, more able (and more likely) to bear that risk.

It remains true, however, that because these firms are private (there is no liquid market for their shares), outside family owners can benefit from growth in earnings (through the payout of dividends), but not from growth in valuation. Consequently, during this ownership stage, most outside family shareholders will continue to favor consumption, while insiders (whose combined equity holdings usually represent the majority) will continue to favor investment owing to their concern about the effect of further dilution on the value of their estates. Thus the primary challenge facing the cousin consortium boards of family firms is to invest in growth while maintaining a dividend level that satisfies outside family owners (Gersick et al., 1997).

In summary, we anticipate that the dispersion of ownership that characterizes the cousin consortium stage engenders a coalition in which ownership brings the interests of the inside family directors into alignment. We do not expect that this alignment will be as stable as it is for widely held public firms, because ownership is not as dispersed and the problems of market liquidity and exit costs remain. Nevertheless, we posit that for family firms in the cousin consortium stage, the greater the ownership dispersion (and the smaller the average shareholding), the more likely their boards will be to favor growth and, in the absence of the ability to issue equity or cut dividends, the more likely they will be to risk the use of debt to fund growth.

Hypotheses

Taken together, our arguments support Morck and his coauthors' (1988) conjecture that dispersion of ownership has a significant influence on board conduct. By extending their arguments to the domain of private family-owned and -managed firms, we hypothesize that family boards will be more willing to use debt when ownership is either concentrated in the hands of a controlling owner or dispersed into the hands of many owners (as in a cousin consortium), and less willing to use debt when ownership is split into relatively equal proportions (as in a sibling partnership). Stated formally:

Hypothesis 1. The relationship between a family firm's use of debt and the dispersion of its ownership can be graphed as a U-shaped curve.

In line with behavioral agency theory, we anticipate that a board's willingness to use debt varies with growth conditions in a family firm's market. All else being the same, we predict that family firms will increase borrowing during periods of high growth and, because of their dependence on internal cash flows and limited access to external capital markets, will reduce it during periods of low growth (Wright et al., 1996). Accordingly, we tested our hypotheses under conditions of both high and low market growth rates, positing that the relationships stated in Hypothesis 1 will be supported during periods of high growth, but not during periods of low growth.

Hypothesis 2. The relationship between a family firm's use of debt and the dispersion of its ownership is moderated by the growth rate of the firm's market.

Methods

Sample

Reliable information on family firms is extremely difficult to obtain (Wortman, 1994). Public information is unreliable because most family firms are privately held and have no legal obligation to disclose information. Government documents and Dunn and Bradstreet are also of little use because family-managed firms are not listed as a separate category of business organization. Finally, it is difficult for researchers to collect primary data or to target selected groups of family-managed firms for study because there is no reliable way to identify family firms *a priori* (Daily and Dollinger, 1993). Consequently, researchers are forced to rely on self-reported data, sample from a broad population, and identify family-managed firms *ex post* (Daily and Dollinger, 1992, 1993; Handler, 1989).

We field-tested our hypotheses using data from one of the largest and most comprehensive surveys ever conducted on family firms (Gersick et al., 1997), a 1995 survey of American family businesses that was designed and administered by the Arthur Andersen Center for Family Business. Since all of the firms in the sample were privately held, and the data were confidential and proprietary, we were unable to establish their reliability independently. Andersen's statisticians assured us, however, that they were reliable and representative of the population. While the use of secondary data can limit generalizability, Ilgen (1986) and Sackett and Larsen (1990: 435) pointed out that representativeness is less of a concern when a sample typifies the relevant population and the research question concerns whether the hypothesized effects can occur, as opposed to concerning the frequency or strength of observed effects. The Arthur Andersen data are well suited to this task because the survey was designed to obtain 'reliable benchmarks' about American family businesses (Arthur Andersen & Co., 1995: 3).

Before we mailed the survey to the chief executives of 37 304 privately held US family businesses, we had the items in this survey reviewed by a focus group of family business owners and pilot-tested it on a hold-out sample. A single mailing yielded 3860 responses within one month; this constitutes a response rate of 10.3 percent, which is comparable to 'the 10–12 percent rate typical for studies which target executives in upper echelons' (Geletkanycz, 1997: 622; Hambrick et al., 1993; Koch and McGrath, 1996) or chief executives in small to mid-sized firms (MacDougall and Robinson, 1990).

Because of the *a priori* selection problems, Andersen survey respondents ranged from 'mom and pop' proprietorships to large family-managed corporations. We therefore applied a number of *ex post* screening criteria to the data. First, we deleted 334 partnerships and proprietorships because different laws and tax policies influence their governance. Second, we dropped 1650 cases because data about firm ownership and/or board composition were missing, and we dropped another 209 because some information about the other 13 variables included in the regression analyses was missing. (We tested and found no differences in the use of debt or in the mean values of our model's independent variables between cases that included data about ownership or board composition and those that did not.) Finally, by deleting 203 firms that had $5 million or less in sales, we excluded 'lifestyle firms' (small firms that might be operated mainly for the purpose of 'income substitution' [Allen and Panian, 1982]); firms whose use of debt might be biased by their receiving subsidies;[3] and others for which growth might not be a strategic objective (see, for example, Rubenson and Gupta, 1996 and Carland et al., 1984, who also excluded these types of firms from samples, arguing that growth may not be among their strategic objectives). Larger firms are less likely to be operated in this manner since the demands of managing them mitigate a family's or a family CEO's primary motive for suppressing growth – to more easily maintain managerial and ownership control (Daily and Dollinger, 1992; Whisler, 1988). Thus the final sample consisted of 1464 firms. Our average firm had annual sales of $36 million, had 182 employees, and had been in business for 49 years.

Variables

DEPENDENT VARIABLE

We used debt as the dependent variable. As we previously discussed, the ownership structure of privately owned firms, unlike that of their public counterparts, does not allow for unrestricted risk bearing via the issue of common stock. Capital investment is thus limited to that which can be supported by internally generated funds and the shareholders' willingness to bear the risk that debt poses to their individual wealth (Casson, 1999). Although private ownership thus engenders fiscal conservatism, all else being the same, we deduce from a behavioral agency view that directors are willing to incur debt to pursue the investments that they perceive to be the best ones, particularly when the directors expect their firm's market to grow.

Our variable measuring debt is a six-level indicator of a firm's debt-to-equity ratio (from 1 to 6, codings were 'no debt,' '1–25%,' '26–50%,' '50–100%,' '101–200%,' and 'over 200%'). The mean debt-to-equity ratio among our sample group of mature firms was 2.57, which interpolates to about 18 percent. The measure was self-reported and, as is the case with virtually all privately held firms, objective measures were not available. However, performance measures reported by executives have been shown to be reliable (Nayyar, 1992; Tan and Litschert, 1994), particularly when reported on anonymous surveys (Dillman, 1978; Nunnally, 1978). The impact of common method bias, which arises when a common method (such as a survey) is used to gather data about both independent and dependent variables, should also be less here than it might be for other types of studies because social desirability and other sources of bias are diminished when variables are demographic, descriptive and/or non-affective, as are most of our variables (Crampton and Wagner, 1994).

COVARIATES

We included nine covariates to reduce variance that would be extraneous to the research question or that might confound interpretation: firm size, firm age, multiple family ownership, number of family employees, exports as a percentage of sales, information technology intensity, CEO tenure, average board tenure, board size, family ownership goal, and ownership held by the board. Each covariate is described and its use is justified in the Appendix.

INDEPENDENT VARIABLE

The mean percentage of shares controlled by the boards of the firms in our sample was 90 percent, and the largest shareholder controlled an average 52 percent of the votes (the largest shareholder was a sole owner in 18 percent of the cases). In contrast, the second through the fifth largest shareholders on the family-firm boards controlled, on the average, 25, 8, 3 and 1 percent of the votes. Interestingly, the remaining members about whom we had information (that is, the sixth through the eighth largest shareholders) together controlled barely half of 1 percent of the votes. Moreover, extreme variance in the shares held by these board members was indicated by standard deviations that ranged to values up to ten times the size of the mean. This distribution is not a surprise, given that only 166 firms in the sample had six or more board members, and 107 had seven or more. Following Tabachnick and Fidell (1989), we therefore dropped these observations in our primary analyses of Hypotheses 1 and 2 and based our calculation of the independent variable, balance of voting power, on the total shares held by the five largest shareholders who served on a board. We also tested the sensitivity of our results by adding the shares held by the sixth largest shareholder, then the seventh, and then the eighth to the calculation and repeating our tests; results are reported below.

Balance of voting power was calculated as the sum of the squares of the minority board members' percentage share of votes divided by the square of the largest shareholder's percentage share of the votes. The sum of squares is used here like the Herfindal index, which economists use to describe the distribution of market share among industry participants: the sum of squares captures the effects of different distributions of ownership. Higher values are associated with increased power held by individual shareholders, and lower values, with a more equal, and/or more diffuse dispersion of power on a board.[4] The balance of voting power variable therefore captures the variance associated with changes in the dispersion of ownership that would not appear if the ratio were computed using a simple sum of each director's shareholdings. Values of 1:1 or less indicated the distribution of ownership favored the largest shareholder, and values higher than this indicated that the dispersion of ownership favored the minority shareholders. The dispersion of ownership favored the largest shareholder in 73 percent of our cases and favored minority shareholders in the remaining 27 percent of the cases.

MODERATOR

We used a dummy variable, industry sales growth, to test the proposition that investor expectations influence a family firm's use of debt. Since the industry categories identified in the Andersen survey do not correspond directly to SIC-based industry classifications, we coded industry sales growth 1 if the mean of the reported growth in sales for the industry category was greater than the median ratio for all industry categories, and we coded the variable 0 if mean growth was below the median. Although coarse-grained, this measure distinguishes industries that enjoyed high levels of sales growth during this period (for instance, manufacturing and telecommunications) from those that did not. Further, we were unable to employ financial statistics derived from SIC-based data for control purposes since such data include information from large, widely held businesses whose markets and capital structures differ markedly from those of family firms.

Results

Table 4.1 reports descriptive statistics (unstandardized) and Pearson correlations, and Tables 4.2 and 4.3 report the results for all regression analyses. The change in explained variance

Table 4.1   Descriptive statistics and correlations[a]

A		B	C	D	E	F	G	H	I	J	K	L	M	N	O	P
1.	Debt	2.56	1.45													
2.	Firm size	37.44	121.71	0.18												
3.	Firm age	48.98	27.00	−0.02	0.10											
4.	Multiple family ownership	0.91	0.29	0.05	−0.03	0.01										
5.	Number of family-member employees	3.43	2.03	0.02	0.09	0.01	0.07									
6.	Exports as a percentage of sales	1.51	0.82	0.01	0.07	0.01	0.00	−0.03								
7.	Information technology intensity	3.07	0.92	0.08	0.17	0.06	0.03	0.00	0.06							
8.	Industry sales growth	0.52	0.50	0.04	−0.02	0.08	−0.01	0.02	0.24	−0.02						
9.	Ownership held by board	89.62	19.61	0.01	−0.15	−0.16	0.08	−0.07	−0.09	−0.02	−0.06					
10.	CEO tenure	2.45	1.13	−0.08	−0.07	−0.10	0.02	0.09	−0.03	−0.05	0.00	0.01				
11.	Average board tenure	17.52	7.75	−0.11	−0.06	0.13	−0.03	0.06	−0.10	−0.02	0.00	0.08	0.13			
12.	Board size	3.98	1.75	0.04	0.21	0.22	−0.05	0.25	0.08	0.04	0.08	−0.23	−0.04	−0.20		
13.	Family ownership goal	0.68	0.47	−0.03	−0.03	−0.04	0.07	−0.04	−0.05	0.04	−0.09	0.12	0.01	0.03	−0.09	
14.	Balance of voting power	0.70	0.81	−0.01	0.02	0.08	−0.14	0.27	−0.03	0.01	0.02	0.00	−0.11	0.06	0.23	−0.03

Legend:

A – Variables	B – Mean	C – s.d.	D – 1	E – 2	F – 3	G – 4	H – 5
1 – 6	J – 7	K – 8	L – 9	M – 10	N – 11	O – 12	P – 13

Note: [a] *n* = 1464. Correlations larger than 0.04 are significant at *p* = 0.05.

Table 4.2   Results of full-sample regression analyses for debt

A	B	C	E	D
Covariates				
Firm size	0.17(***)	0.17(***)	0.17(***)	0.17(***)
Firm age	-0.03	-0.03	-0.03	-0.03
Multiple family ownership	0.06(*)	0.05(*)	0.05(*)	0.05(*)
Number of family-member employees	0.02	0.02	0.03	0.02
Exports as a percentage of sates	-0.02	-0.02	-0.02	-0.02
Information technology intensity	0.05(*)	0.05(*)	0.05(*)	0.05(*)
Ownership held by board	0.04	0.04	0.04	0.04
CEO tenure	-0.06(*)	-0.07(*)	-0.06(*)	-0.07(*)
Average board tenure	-0.09(***)	-0.09(***)	-0.09(***)	-0.09(***)
Board size	-0.01	-0.01	-0.01	-0.01
Family ownership goal	-0.03	-0.03	-0.03	-0.03
Industry sales growth	0.06(*)	0.06(*)	-0.01	0.06(*)
Predictors				
Balance of voting power		-0.04	0.05	-0.04
Balance of voting power squared Interactions		0.03	0.08	0.03
Balance of voting power × industry sales growth			-0.14(**)	-0.01
Balance of voting power squared × industry sales growth			0.02(***)	
R^2	0.05			
Adjusted R^2		0.05	0.06	0.05
F	7.17(***)	6.23(***)	6.19(***)	5.84(***)
F		0.36	10.99(***)	0.10
n	1464	1464	1464	1464

Legend: A – Variables

Note: (*) $p = 0.05$; (**) $p = 0.01$; (***) $p = 0.001$.

Table 4.3   Results of subsample regression analyses for debt

A	B	C	D	E	F	G
Covariates						
Firm size	0.17(***)	0.17(***)	0.17(***)	0.17(***)	0.17(***)	0.17(***)
Firm age	-0.05	-0.05	-0.05	-0.01	-0.01	-0.01
Multiple family ownership	0.08(*)	0.08(*)	0.07(*)	0.04	0.03	0.04
Number of family-member employees	0.02	0.02	0.03	0.02	0.02	0.02
Exports as a percentage of sales	-0.03	-0.03	-0.03	-0.01	-0.01	-0.01
Information technology intensity	0.08(*)	0.08(*)	0.08(*)	0.02	0.02	0.02
Ownership held by board	0.02	0.02	0.02	0.06	0.06	0.06
CEO tenure	-0.06	-0.06	-0.06	-0.07	-0.07	-0.07
Average board tenure	-0.10(**)	-0.09(**)	-0.09(**)	-0.08(*)	-0.08(*)	-0.08(*)
Board size	-0.03	-0.03	-0.05	0.01	0.01	0.01
Family ownership goal	-0.05	-0.05	-0.05	0.01	-0.01	-0.01
Predictors						
Balance of voting power		-0.02	-0.12(*)		-0.01	0.03
Balance of voting power squared			0.13(**)			-0.05
R^2	0.05	0.06	0.06		0.04	0.04
Adjusted R^2				0.04		
F	4.48(***)	4.13(***)	4.31(***)	3.52(***)	3.26(***)	3.05(***)
F		0.25	6.54(**)		0.77	0.35
n	764	764	764	700	700	700

Legend:
A – Variable   B – Model 2: High industry growth   C – Model 2: High industry growth   D – Model 2: High industry growth
E – Model 3: Low industry growth   F – Model 3: Low industry growth   G – Model 3: Low industry growth

Note: (*) $p = 0.05$; (**) $p = 0.01$; (***) $p = 0.001$.

(*F*) associated with the covariate set ranges from 3.52 ($p = 0.001$) to 7.17 ($p = 0.000$), and the *F*-statistic associated with the set of hypothesized variables, after hierarchically adjusting for covariates, ranges from 6.54 ($p = 0.01$) to 10.99 ($p = 0.000$).[5] Hypothesis 1 was tested in both the full sample (Table 4.2) and in the two-industry (high and low industry growth) subsamples (Table 4.3). We used only the full sample to test Hypothesis 2.

We used moderated hierarchical polynomial regression analysis to confirm that industry sales growth does, indeed, influence a family-owned and -managed firm's use of debt. In model 1 (Table 4.2), centered variables (and their product terms) were entered hierarchically for both the balance of voting power and its square, and then, in the next step, the products of the independent variable and its square with industry sales growth were entered. As one would expect if the hypothesized relationships were non-linear and moderated, the product of balance of voting power and industry sales growth ($p = 0.009$) was negatively associated with the use of debt, while the product of balance of voting power squared with industry sales growth was positively associated with the use of debt ($p = 0.001$). The significance of the product terms indicates support for Hypothesis 2. In addition, and consistent with Hypothesis 1, the negative value of the first coefficient, combined with the positive sign of its square, suggests that the relationship is positively U-shaped over the relevant range.

We then tested the sensitivity of these results by using the three alternative calculations of balance of voting power previously mentioned to test Hypotheses 1 and 2. All results (available on request) were correctly signed, and although their significance levels weakened incrementally as shareholders were added to the calculation, balance of voting power ($p = 0.08$) – but not its square – became marginally insignificant when calculated using information from all eight shareholders. Given the extreme variance associated with the addition of this information to the computation of the variable (previously discussed and reported), we concluded the results were not highly sensitive to its computation.

Results of the subgroup analysis (Table 4.3, models 2 and 3) lend further support to the hypotheses. The balance of voting power variable and its square are significant ($p = 0.03$ and $p = 0.01$, respectively) and correctly signed when industry sales growth is high, and they are insignificant when industry sales growth is low.

Discussion and Conclusion

Family firms constitute over 80 percent of all business organizations in the USA and are the dominant form of economic enterprise throughout the world (La Porta et al., 1999), yet over two-thirds of first-generation family firms do not survive to a second generation of family ownership (Gersick et al., 1997). Understanding how the agency positions of the controlling owner and the minority shareholders influence the conduct of family firms is a small step toward understanding why many fail. In this chapter, we drew from behavioral and economic theories to argue that the incentives facing the directors of privately held, family-managed firms are different from those facing the directors of widely held public firms. Whereas ownership is expected to align incentives in public firms, we found that how ownership is dispersed among the various family owners of a privately held firm affects such decisions as the use of debt. Our findings are therefore not only consistent with Morck and his colleagues' (1988) conjecture, but also suggest that the principal–agent model requires modification before being applied to family firms. Furthermore, our findings about the moderating influence of industry growth are also consistent with the views of behavioral agency theorists such as Wiseman and Gomez-Mejia (1998), who pointed out that the amount of risk that owners will bear is a function of how they frame their expectations in terms of opportunities.

Our story identifies two interesting *de facto* reversals of incentives, patterns that diverge from predictions based on the conventional agency model. First, we argue that, whereas 'blockholding' in widely held public firms reduces the risk that insiders will free-ride on outside owners' equity, controlling ownership in a family firm (the counterpart of block-holding in public firms) can give family-member firm employees and directors the incentive to free-ride on the controlling owner's equity. Second, we argued that, whereas the outside shareholders in widely held public firms have the incentive to promote investment and growth-oriented risk taking, dispersion of ownership can give outside shareholders at private family firms the incentive to favor consumption. This story is also interesting from a theoretical perspective, since it identifies at least one population in which information about ownership dispersion, as well as ownership concentration, is needed to predict director (and board) conduct.

Results from our field study of 1464 family firms support our hypotheses that their use of debt has a curvilinear (U-shaped) relationship to the dispersion of ownership among voting members of their boards of directors, particularly during periods of market expansion. The non-linear relationship suggests that family firms are most vulnerable to conflict, and least willing to bear added risk, when ownership is split in relatively equal proportions. Interestingly, the fact that this distribution appeared in only 22 percent of our sample firms suggests that most family firm owners may take such risk into consideration when making their estate plans. This speculation is consistent with the views of Gersick and his coauthors (1997), who noted that successful sibling partnerships are rare because they are so difficult to manage and recommended that founders and controlling owners settle their estates in a manner that prevents the development of sibling partnerships.

The purpose of our empirical tests, however, was to lend credibility to our theory, not to confirm its validity or determine the strengths of its effects. Indeed, we cannot claim that our tests were confirmatory since we used cross-sectional data and relied upon survey data gathered for other purposes. However, we think these tests lend credibility to our theory since the firms represented by the Andersen survey are typical of a population of firms that is rarely studied and whose data are difficult (and quite expensive) to obtain (Gersick et al., 1997: 25; Sackett and Larsen, 1990). The size of our sample also gave us sufficient power to detect small effects and yet conclude with a high degree of confidence that these results are not the product of chance. Although some of the measures are coarser than we would have liked (for example, balance of voting power was computed from a simple sort of shareholdings by size, which captured only the average effects of ownership dispersion and its specific effects), that coarseness also lends a conservative bias to the analysis, since coarse measures deflate variance and the likelihood of obtaining significant results (Hunter and Schmidt, 1990). The fact that we obtained significant results, despite the type of measures used and the presence of nine control variables, suggests that these results are robust. Future research must, however, address these weaknesses through use of more appropriate survey research methodology and finer-grained measures.

The effect of ownership dispersion on goal alignment within family-firm boards is a complex issue, and this study investigates only one of its aspects. Future studies might examine the relationship between minority shareholder influence and the dispersion of ownership among minority members. We suspect that a relatively equal distribution of ownership among fewer minority owners promotes a more stable coalition that would be more able to influence firm conduct. Future studies might also examine whether the severity of the double moral hazard problem varies with ownership stage. We suspect that this problem is more likely to manifest itself under a controlling owner than under a sibling partnership. We also suspect that this problem may be more common when family firms are owned by more than one family than when different branches of the same family compete on the boards and for the firms' resources. Future studies might examine whether our hypotheses apply without modification to family-controlled public firms. At what level of ownership and control might the controlling owners' concern for family welfare start to generate agency costs for outside shareholders? Are double agency problems, or the allegiance of a CEO to both stockholders and family, more problematic in public owner-controlled firms (like Microsoft), sibling partnerships (such as Wal-Mart), or cousin consortiums (like the Ford Motor Company)? And what is the effect of family ownership on the outside owners' agency costs? (The recent proxy fight at Hewlett-Packard over a proposed merger with Compaq Computer is one case germane to this question.)

These and other interesting questions that can enrich corporate governance theory remain. Our study represents an early attempt to pinpoint the dynamics of ownership and control in family firms. By showing that the dispersion of ownership influences family firms' use of debt, we provided a long overdue response to Morck and colleagues' (1988) call for research, while at the same time revealing information about an economically important population of firms that has been largely neglected by researchers.

Acknowledgments

We would like to thank Jack Veiga and the anonymous reviewers for their encouragement and critique of earlier versions of this chapter. Survey data were provided courtesy of the Arthur Andersen Center for Family Business. The support of the H.R. Horvitz Family Foundation and of the Family Business Programs at the Weatherhead School of Management, Case Western Reserve University, and the School of Business at the University of Connecticut is also acknowledged.

Notes

1. First-best actions maximize a principal's expected utility subject to the constraint that an agent receives his or her reservation utility (the utility the agent could receive by redeploying resources to their best alternative use).
2. Witness the now famous case of the former Playboy model, Anna Nicole Smith, who inherited $475 million (reduced on legal appeal to $88 million) after a brief marriage to a septuagenarian husband, much to his children's dismay.
3. For example, 95 percent of all loans guaranteed by the Small Business Administration go to firms

with fewer than 50 employees (Small Business Administration, 2002), a statistic that characterizes the firms in this sample that had less than $5 million in annual sales.
4. For example, a change in minority ownership dispersion from 25:25 to 20:20:10 will cause the
value of the numerator to fall from 1250 to 900.
5. Overall, the regression models explain from 5 to 6 percent of the variance in our dependent
variable. These small effect sizes are likely the result in part (1) of the high heterogeneity the
sample contained by virtue of its very large and diverse representation of firms and industries and
(2) of the categorical nature of the dependent variable. Cohen and Cohen (1980) noted, however,
that an advantage of large samples is that they give analysts the ability to detect small effects with
a high degree of confidence. Kraemer and Thiemann (1987: 105) estimated that the reliability or
power of a sample to detect observed effect sizes is 0.80.

References

Alchian, A.A. and Woodward, S. (1988), 'The firm is dead: long live the firm: a review of Oliver E.
Williamson's *The economic institutions of capitalism*', *Journal of Economic Literature*, **26**: 65–79.
Allen, M.P. and Panian, S.K. (1982), 'Power, performance, and succession in the large corporation',
Administrative Science Quarterly, **27**: 538–47.
Arthur Andersen & Co. (1995), *American Family Business Survey*, St Charles, IL: Arthur Andersen
Center for Family Business.
Becker, G.S. (1981), *A Treatise on the Family*, Cambridge, MA: Harvard University Press.
Beckhard, R. and Dyer, W.G., Jr (1983), 'Managing continuity in the family owned business',
Organizational Dynamics, **12**(1): 5–12.
Carland, J.W., Hoy, F., Boulton, W. and Carland, J.A.C. (1984), 'Differentiating entrepreneurs from
small business owners: a conceptualization', *Academy of Management Review*, **9**: 354–9.
Casson, M. (1999), 'The economics of the family firm', *Scandinavian Economic History Review*,
47(1): 10–23.
Cohen, J. and Cohen, P. (1983), *Applied multiple regression/correlation analysis for the behavioral
sciences*, Hillsdale, NJ: Erlbaum.
Crampton, S.M. and Wagner, J.A. (1994), 'Percept–percept inflation in microorganizational research:
an investigation of prevalence and effect', *Journal of Applied Psychology*, **79**: 67–76.
Daily, C.M. and Dollinger, M.J. (1992), 'An empirical examination of ownership structure in family
and professionally-managed firms', *Family Business Review*, **5**(2): 117–36.
Daily, C.M. and Dollinger, M.J. (1993), 'Alternative methods for identifying family vs. nonfamily
managed small businesses', *Journal of Small Business Management*, **31**(2): 79–90.
Demsetz, H. (1973), 'Industry structure, market rivalry, and public policy', *Journal of Law and
Economics*, **16**: 1–10.
Dillman, D.A. (1978), *Mail and Telephone Surveys: The Total Design Method*, New York: Wiley.
Fama, E. and Jensen, M.C. (1983a), 'Agency problems and residual claims', *Journal of Law and
Economics*, **26**: 325–44.
Fama, E. and Jensen, M.C. (1983b), 'Separation of ownership and control', *Journal of Law and
Economics*, **26**: 301–25.
Fama, E. and Jensen, M.C. (1985), 'Organizational forms and investment decisions', *Journal of
Financial Economics*, **14**: 101–19.
Finkelstein, S. and Hambrick, D.C. (1990), 'Top management team tenure and organizational out-
comes: the moderating role of managerial discretion', *Administrative Science Quarterly*, **35**: 484–
503.
Finkelstein, S. and Hambrick, D.C. (1996), *Strategic Leadership: Top Executives and their Effects on
Organizations*, St Paul: West.
Ford, R.H. (1988), 'Outside directors and privately-held firms: are they necessary?', *Entrepreneurship
Theory and Practice*, **13**(1): 49–57.

Geeraerts, G. (1984), 'The effect of ownership on the organization structure in small firms', *Administrative Science Quarterly*, **29**: 232–7.

Geletkanycz, M.A. (1997), 'The salience of "culture's consequences": the effect of cultural values on top executive commitment to the status quo', *Strategic Management Journal*, **18**: 615–34.

Gersick, K.E., Davis, J.A., Hampton, M.M. and Lansberg, I. (1997), *Generation to Generation: Life Cycles of the Family Business*, Boston: Harvard Business School Press.

Gomez-Mejia, L., Nuñez-Nickel, M. and Gutierrez, I. (2001), 'The role of family ties in agency contracts', *Academy of Management Journal*, **44**: 81–95.

Gupta, S. and Romano, R.E. (1998), 'Monitoring the principal with multiple agents', *Rand Journal of Economics*, **29**: 427–42.

Hambrick, D.C. and Fukutomi, G.D.S. (1991), 'The seasons of a CEO's tenure', *Academy of Management Review*, **16**: 719–42.

Hambrick, D.C., Geletkanycz, M.A. and Fredrickson, J.A. (1993), 'Top executive commitment to the status quo: some tests of its determinants', *Strategic Management Journal*, **14**: 401–18.

Handler, W.C. (1989), 'Methodological issues and considerations in studying family business', *Family Business Review*, **1**(4): 257–76.

Holtz-Eakin, D., Joulfian, D. and Rosen, H.S. (1993), 'The Carnegie conjecture: some empirical evidence', *Quarterly Journal of Economics*, **108**: 413–35.

Hunter, J.E. and Schmidt, F.L. (1990), *Methods of Meta-analysis: Connecting Error and Bias in Research Findings*, Newbury Park, CA: Sage.

Ilgen, D.R. (1986), 'Laboratory research: a question of when, not if', in E.A. Locke (ed.), *Generalizing from Laboratory to Field Settings*, Lexington, MA: Heath, pp. 257–67.

Jensen, M.C. (1998), 'Self-interest, altruism, incentives, and agency', in M.C. Jensen (ed.), *Foundations of Organizational Strategy*, Cambridge, MA: Harvard University Press, pp. 39–50.

Jensen, M.C. and Meckling, W.H. (1976), 'Theory of the firm: managerial behavior, agency costs, and ownership structure', *Journal of Financial Economics*, **3**: 305–60.

Jensen, M.C. and Smith, C.L. (1985), 'Stockholder, manager and creditor interests: applications of agency theory', in E.I. Altman & M.G. Subrahmanyam (eds), *Recent Advances in Corporate Finance*, Homewood, IL: Irwin, pp. 95–131.

Kang, D. (1999), 'Ownership structure and corporate dividend policy: how large block family owners increase dividend payout and achieve superior firm performance', Harvard Business School working paper number 99-032, Boston.

Koch, M.J. and McGrath, R.G. (1996), 'Improving labor productivity: human resource management policies do matter', *Strategic Management Journal*, **17**: 335–54.

Kraemer, H.C. and Theimann, S. (1987), *How Many Subjects: Statistical Power Analysis in Research*, Newbury Park, CA: Sage.

Kroll, M., Wright, P. and Theerathorn, P. (1993), 'Whose interests do top managers pursue? An examination of acquisition performance and CEO rewards', *Journal of Business Research*, **26**: 133–48.

La Porta, R., Lopez-de-Silanes, F. and Shleifer, A. (1999), 'Corporate ownership around the world', *Journal of Finance*, **54**: 471–517.

Levinson, H. (1971), 'Conflicts that plague family business', *Harvard Business Review*, **49**(2): 90–98.

Lunati, M.T. (1997), *Ethical Issues in Economics: From Altruism to Cooperation to Equity*, London: Macmillan.

MacDougall, P. and Robinson, R.B. (1990), 'New venture strategies: an empirical identification of eight "archetypes" of competitive strategies for entry', *Strategic Management Journal*, **11**: 447–68.

Meyer, M. and Zucker, L.G. (1989), *Permanently Failing Organizations*, Newbury Park, CA: Sage.

Morck, R., Shleifer, A. and Vishny, R.W. (1988), 'Management ownership and market valuation: an empirical analysis', *Journal of Financial Economics*, **20**: 293–315.

Nash, J.M. (1988), 'Boards of privately-held companies: their responsibility and structure', *Family Business Review*, **1**(3): 263–369.

Nayyar, P.R. (1992), 'On the measurement of service diversification strategy: evidence from large U.S. service firms', *Strategic Management Journal*, **13**: 219–35.

Nunnally, J.C. (1978), *Psychometric Theory*, New York: McGraw-Hill.

O'Donoghue, T. and Rabin, M. (2000), 'The economics of immediate gratification', *Journal of Behavioral Decision Making*, **13**: 233–50.

Ouchi, W.G. (1980), 'Markets, bureaucracies, and clans', *Administrative Science Quarterly*, **25**: 129–41.

Perrow, C. (1986), *Complex Organizations*, New York: Random House.

Rubenson, G.C. and Gupta, A.K. (1996), 'The initial succession: a contingency model of founder tenure', *Entrepreneurship Theory and Practice*, **21**(2): 21–35.

Sackett, P.R. and Larsen, J.R., Jr (1990), 'Research strategies and tactics in industrial organization psychology', in M.D. Dunnette and L.M. Hough (eds), *Handbook of industrial and organization psychology*, Palo Alto, CA: Consulting Psychologists Press, pp. 419–90.

Schulze, W.S., Lubatkin, M.H., Dino, R.N. and Buchholtz, A.K. (2001), 'Agency relationships in family firms: theory and evidence', *Organization Science*, **12**: 99–116.

Small Business Administration (2002), 'SBA loan programs', Document number 507, http://asbdc.ualr.edu/fod/fo7.htm.

Stark, O. and Falk, I. (1998), 'Transfers, empathy formation, and reverse transfers', *American Economic Review*, **88**: 271–6.

Tabachnick, B.G. and Fidell, L.S. (1989), *Using Multivariate Statistics*, Cambridge, MA: Harper & Row.

Tan, J.J. and Litschert, R.J. (1994), 'Environment–strategy relationship and its performance implications: an empirical study of the Chinese electronics industry', *Strategic Management Journal*, **15**: 1–20.

Thaler, R.H. and Shefrin, H.M. (1981), 'An economic theory of self-control', *Journal of Political Economy*, **89**: 392–406.

Walsh, J.P. and Seward, J.K. (1990), 'On the efficiency of internal and external control mechanisms', *Academy of Management Review*, **15**: 421–58.

Ward, J.L. (1987), *Keeping the Family Business Healthy: How to Plan for Continuous Growth, Profitability, and Family Leadership*, San Francisco: Jossey-Bass.

Ward, J.L. and Handy, J.L. (1988), 'A survey of board practices', *Family Business Review*, **1**(3): 298–308.

Whisler, T.L. (1988), 'The role of the board in threshold firms', *Family Business Review*, **1**(3): 309–21.

Wiseman, R.M. and Gomez-Mejia, L.R. (1998), 'A behavioral agency model of managerial risk taking', *Academy of Management Review*, **23**: 133–53.

Wortman, M.S., Jr. (1994), 'Theoretical foundations for family-owned business: a conceptual and research-based paradigm', *Family Business Review*, **7**(1): 3–27.

Wright, P., Ferris, S.P., Sarin, A. and Awasthi, V. (1996), 'Impact of corporate insider, blockholder, and institutional equity ownership on firm risk taking', *Academy of Management Journal*, **39**: 441–65.

Appendix

Nine covariates were included to reduce extraneous or confounding variance. Firm size was total firm sales logarithmically transformed to correct for its skewed distribution. Firm age was calibrated in years. Age may be linked to performance via a self-selection bias; older firms existed in this sample simply because they were successful. Multiple family ownership was a dummy variable (0/1) that adjusted for the influence of multiple families owning at least 15 percent of a firm's stock. We also controlled for the number of family-member employees since employment risk rises as families become dependent on a firm for their livelihood. The mean number of family employees for our sample was 3.51; the range was 1–24. Exports as a percentage of sales was a five-level indicator ranging from 'zero' through 'over 50 percent.' In general, firms with export sales report a higher level of indebtedness because they use bank letters of credit and other types of debt instruments to facilitate payment from international customers. Variance in performance and agency conditions linked to information technology intensity was controlled by using this item: 'How important are investments in information technology for the accomplishment of your future goals?' (1 = 'not important,' 4 = 'very important').

We also controlled for CEO tenure, average board tenure and board size. A large body of managerial research indicates that long CEO tenure is generally detrimental to firm performance (Finkelstein and Hambrick, 1990). Individual risk tolerance falls with age, and cognitive processes rigidify. For example, Hambrick and Fukutomi (1991) observed that as managers age, they tend to receive narrower and more filtered information, acquire task knowledge more slowly, lose interest in routine tasks as repetition leads to tedium, and increase their commitment to the status quo (Hambrick et al., 1993). The negative effects of age and tenure on both cognitive diversity and risk tolerance are exacerbated by group processes (Finkelstein and Hambrick, 1996: 124–30). The Andersen survey from which we drew data measured CEO tenure with a five-level variable with responses ranging from '11 or more years until retirement' to 'semiretired.' We found that this indirect measure of tenure correlated with other indirect measures of tenure available from the survey. For example, the bivariate correlation between CEO tenure and CEO age was high ($r = 0.62$, $p = 0.001$), particularly given that scaling differences naturally deflated the correlation between the two variables. Also, the mean age of the CEOs (54 years) and the mean age of the heirs-apparent at the time of this designation (38 years) differed, as we expected, by about one generation. Like Finkelstein and Hambrick (1990), we measured average board tenure as the average of the years members had served and controlled for variance in the number of board members across firms with a count indicating board size. The mean board size in this sample was 3.98, and the standard deviation was 1.74. An item that asked the respondents to rate the likelihood that their families would retain control of the sampled firms in the foreseeable future, family ownership goal, controlled for variance in the strategic directions of these family firms. Lastly, we measured ownership held by board as the percentage of a firm's shares held by members of its board of directors.

[5]

Venture capitalists, syndication and governance in initial public offerings

Igor Filatotchev, Mike Wright and Mufit Arberk

Introduction

Increasing attention has been devoted to firms' decision to go public. Much of this research focuses on the extent of underpricing (Megginson and Weiss, 1991; Brav and Gompers, 1997; Gompers and Lerner, 1999). The role of venture capital firms (VCs) in initial public offerings (IPOs) has been examined with respect to signaling and certification of the quality of a private company (Gompers and Lerner, 1999), yet VCs may have an important governance role in IPOs. Governance issues in relation to IPOs have mainly been addressed in terms of changes in the distribution of ownership rights. In contrast, there is little research on more specific governance characteristics, although Certo (2003) provides a theoretical analysis of the role of boards of directors in IPOs. There is also growing recognition that a significant proportion of VC investments involve syndicates of VC firms. While this literature has tended so far to focus on the motives for syndication (Lockett and Wright, 2001; Brander et al., 2002; Kanniainen and Keuschnigg, 2000; Sorenson and Stuart, 2002) and the impact VC involvement may have on IPO short- and long-term performance (e.g. Barry et al., 1990; Megginson and Weiss, 1991; Lerner, 1994; Gompers, 1995), a neglected issue concerns the implications of syndication for the governance of VC-backed firms during and after the IPO process.

This chapter provides a novel extension to previous work in three ways. First, we argue that VC-backed IPOs suffer from two sets of agency costs which are related to principal–agent and principal–principal relationships. The former arise between the VC firm and the investee in risky investments with asymmetric information. The latter arise between the members of the VC syndicate. Second, we provide empirical evidence on corporate governance characteristics of VC involvement in IPOs, notably in terms of board structures and share ownership, both between VC-backed and non-VC-backed IPOs and between those IPOs with only one VC investor and cases where there is a syndicate of VC and other investors. Third, we examine the extent of syndication outside the VC industry by both single VCs and syndicates of VCs, notably with respect to industrial partners and later-stage private equity firms. This extension of syndication outside the VC sector may make important contributions to accessing and assessing information for the monitoring of VC investments. Fourth, to verify our conceptual framework, we use a unique dataset of 293 entrepreneurial IPOs in the UK (e.g. IPOs in which the original founders retain equity stakes and board positions) during the period of 1999–2002.

This chapter is structured as follows. The next section outlines the conceptual framework adopted. This is followed by a description of the data sources, variable definitions and research methodology. The third section presents the results. Conclusions are drawn in a final section.

Conceptual Framework

We base our arguments on the corporate finance and agency literatures that address the governance problems of IPOs and suggest that VC involvement in entrepreneurial IPOs is more likely when a fast-growing firm represents a risky investment, and traditional sources of finance are not available. To safeguard their investment from the first-tier agency problem arising from potential founders' opportunism, venture capitalists introduce corporate governance arrangements and create more diverse and independent boards than IPOs without VC backing. Another way of dealing with the uncertainties associated with risky IPOs is to syndicate the investment. However, syndication itself may create a second-tier agency problem associated with opportunistic behavior of the syndicate members. Again, we suggest that corporate governance factors may be used to mitigate possible agency costs. The following sections develop these arguments further and generate a number of testable hypotheses.

VC-backed IPOs

The development from a private company to a public company involves the professionalization of management and corporate governance. The establishment of a corporate governance system is necessary to comply with regulators' codes of conduct. The establishment of an efficient board may be especially important in both offsetting the lack of experience of entrepreneurs and providing independent judgement to mitigate entrenchment behavior by incumbent management (Filatotchev and Bishop, 2002). These arguments suggest that internal organizational capacity, such as accumulated knowledge, decision-making ability, resources and so on, no longer meets the demands associated with emergent prospects for growth, and some external help and support are urgently needed by the fast-growing firm.

In the UK, VC firms may invest in both high-risk early-stage ventures as well as management buy-outs. As far as entrepreneurial IPOs are concerned, we expect that VCs would be involved in firms with a higher degree of uncertainty. Amit et al. (1990) show that entrepreneurs may seek to involve venture capital firms in order to share the risks associated with new ventures. Venture capital firms, as opposed to private equity firms investing in later-stage transactions, are likely to possess skills to add value to riskier ventures where internal resources (both in terms of human capital of the entrepreneur and financial resources) are inadequate to take advantage of growth opportunities (Lockett et al., 2002). Entrepreneurs in lower-risk ventures and/or those with highly capable entrepreneurs are likely to find less need for venture capital involvement. In a world of asymmetric information, specialist VCs may possess the expertise necessary to reduce idiosyncratic information-based market failures in risky sectors that are difficult to assess and monitor by other financiers (Amit et al., 1998). However, within these riskier sectors where VCs are expected to focus, they are likely to prefer projects with relatively low costs of selection and monitoring. Hence:

Hypothesis 1a: Venture capital firms' involvement is more likely in higher-risk IPOs.

In a syndication, two or more venture capital firms come together to take an equity stake in an investment. Syndication is an important and widespread part of the venture capital industry. The percentage of investments syndicated in the UK venture capital market rose in 1999 to 27 percent after having fallen for several years. This was followed by a sharp fall in 2000 and 2001 to only 13.1 percent and 13.6 percent, respectively, as venture capital firms moved away from the high tech sector following the collapse of the dot.com boom. By 2002, the more uncertain investment environment appears to have been associated with a further sharp increase with 26.5 percent of investments being syndicated (EVCA, 2003). Venture capital firms typically undertake repeat syndication over time with a network of partners (Bygrave, 1987, 1988; Chiplin et al., 1997).

Each syndicate usually contains a lead firm and one or more non-lead firms, with an individual venture capital firm playing both roles over time, depending on the particular deal. Each syndicate is temporary in nature. The financing structure is constructed specifically for that transaction, with possible staging of additional finance to enable the investee to develop towards a subsequent flotation or sale to a third party. This limited longevity of the syndicated investments may create agency problems associated with opportunistic behavior of some members of the syndicate, information asymmetries and other aspects of what has become known in the agency research literature as the 'principal–principal' relationship (Young et al., 2002).

Syndicated investments may be riskier than stand-alone ventures (Brander et al., 2002). A fully diversified portfolio is more difficult for VC firms than for institutional investors who invest in listed stock because of the presence of large *ex ante* asymmetric information in VC investment decisions, which are compounded by the illiquidity of VC investments which makes mistakes difficult to rectify *ex post* through divestment (Sahlman, 1990; Lockett and Wright, 2001). From a traditional finance perspective, syndication thus may be undertaken as a means of risk sharing through portfolio diversification as it permits VCs to invest in more portfolio companies than would otherwise be possible (Cumming, 2003; Zacharakis, 2002). Hence:

Hypothesis 1b: IPOs backed by syndicates of VCs are more likely to be riskier than IPOs backed by single VCs.

Corporate governance in IPO firms: from principal–agent to principal–principal perspectives

If VC capital firms invest in high-risk entrepreneurial IPOs, they should take measures to safeguard their investment from founders' opportunism. Therefore VC firms may have a particularly important role to play in corporate governance because in a young firm they have specialist monitoring skills and knowledge (Wright and Robbie, 1998). VC firms have substantial decision rights in their investee firms associated with contractual constraints on managerial discretion (Sahlman, 1990). These special control rights are likely to end at the time of the IPO. VC firms also perform important service and resource acquisition functions (Gorman and Sahlman, 1989; Barry et al., 1990) including the recruitment of high-caliber external directors (Black and Gilson, 1998).

Lock-in/lock-up arrangements constrain VC investors to remain as major owners of the firm following IPO (Brav and Gompers, 1997). VC firms may compensate for their relative loss of control by strengthening board independence. VC firms may provide an effective counterbalance to insiders' power and board independence may be used to perform their monitoring and strategic functions. VC firms may attempt to motivate external board members to provide better monitoring by encouraging them to take an equity stake in the firm. VC firms are major shareholders prior to the IPO and retain significant proportions of their holdings after the firm comes to market (Megginson and Weiss, 1991). As VC firms are important providers of managerial oversight, their incentives to develop an efficient board may be expected to be high during and after the IPO when the need for oversight is great.

A number of studies in the entrepreneurship and small business literature suggest that rapidly growing new firms quickly outgrow the founder's managerial capacity (see, for example, Willard et al., 1992, for a discussion). Unless the founders are replaced or supplemented by 'professional' management, their continuing involvement in general management activities may be decreasingly valuable or even detrimental to a company's success (Jayraman et al., 2000). As environmental and organizational complexities grow, different knowledge and skills are needed to effectively manage the entrepreneurial and administrative challenges, and the founder's knowledge that has been accumulated in the past may create a cognitive barrier to effective strategic responses to changing circumstances (Daily and Dalton, 1992). In the context of IPOs, a reduction in founders' share ownership subsequent to flotation may reduce their incentives to learn and apply their knowledge to the benefit of the newly created public firm and its external shareholders (Jain, 2001; Sapienza and Gupta, 1994; Schulze et al., 2003).

These arguments strongly point to the possibility that the corporate governance development process in the IPO firm may be used strategically, as a means to develop further and supplement existing knowledge and experience of the original entrepreneurs by externally generated knowledge and experience. For example, outside non-executive directors serving on the focal firm's board, or 'received interlocks', may be an important channel for the interfirm exchange of strategic information and knowledge (Geletkanycz and Hambrick, 1997).

In both agency and strategic restructuring research there is growing recognition that the company's board structure, characteristics and processes may influence strategic choices and a variety of organizational outcomes (Dalton et al., 1999; Zahra and Pearce, 1989).

From the agency perspective, the critical functions of the board are to monitor and evaluate decisions made by CEOs and other top management team members in terms of company performance and protection of shareholders' value. The effectiveness of these monitoring and control functions is usually related to structural factors such as the proportion of outsiders on the board, CEO/chairman roles held jointly or separately and so on (see Shivdasani, 1993 for a review). However, IPO firms are not typically firms with free cash flow, and, therefore, agency problems are not as prevalent among these organizations (Certo et al., 2001).

The institutional theory and resource dependence perspectives suggest that, in addition to control functions, the creation of a board of directors is an important way in which organizations attempt to co-opt important external constituencies and gain access to valuable, scarce information to enhance the survival of the firm. Therefore board development in general, and recruitment of experienced independent directors in particular, may be undertaken by founders and investors in the IPO firm in an attempt to make the organization isomorphic with the changing institutional environment. Thus the process of searching and recruiting experienced and well-connected non-executive members of board may be systematically related to external legitimacy.

IPO studies have increasingly recognized that large-block investors such as industry partners and venture capitalists may have a strong impact on the process of corporate governance development because they gain detailed knowledge and substantial decision-making rights in the IPO firms that they finance (Gorman and Sahlman, 1989; Lerner, 1994; Gompers and Lerner, 1999). In particular, VC firms impose contractual restraints on managerial discretion, including the use of staged investment, an enforceable nexus of security covenants, and the option to replace the entrepreneur as manager unless key investment objectives are met (see Megginson and Weiss, 1991, for a discussion). Since these special rights end at the time of an IPO, when the need for oversight is particularly great, outside investors may compensate for a relative loss of control by strengthening other governance mechanisms, such as the IPO firm's board (Black and Gilson, 1998). Brav and Gompers (1997), for example, found that VC firms stay on the board of directors long after the IPO, and they put management structures in place that affect the firm's strategic decisions in the long run.

Research from a resource dependence perspective has emphasized that outside investors play a crucial role in providing the firm with the resources needed to survive and function efficiently (Pfeffer, 1972; Oswald and Jahera, 1991). IPO research has also suggested that outside institutional shareholders may provide a young firm with vital support (Mello and Parsons, 1998). Among large external shareholders, VC firms perform particularly important resource and service functions by connecting the firms in their portfolio with management service providers (management consulting firms, lawyers and so on) and assisting management-thin entrepreneurial firms in locating and recruiting high-caliber independent directors (Gorman and Sahlman, 1989; Barry et al., 1990; Schefczyk and Gerpott, 2001). In his analysis of VC-funded biotechnology firms in the USA, Lerner (1994) found that the number of board members increases with each round of VC investment, from a mean of four in the first round to just under six in the fourth and later rounds. Filatotchev and Toms (2003) have presented evidence suggesting that the resource and strategy functions of large institutional investors are facilitated by an increase in board diversity approximated by external interlocks of the focal firm's independent directors. Bearing in mind that the IPO firms are generally resource-poor, fast-growing companies, it is likely that large shareholders may try to secure a board position or encourage managers/founders to use board diversity as a channel to access required resources.

This research suggests that the governance characteristics of the IPO firm may be an effective counterbalance to potential agency conflicts associated with founders' ownership dilution and subsequent misalignment of their financial incentives. Such factors as independent board members, separation between the roles of CEO and chairman, increase in institutional shareholding and so on can be effective tools used by VC firms to circumvent founders' opportunism and to deal with the problems associated with information asymmetries. In addition, diverse boards and the presence of large-block shareholders may provide the IPO firm with legitimacy and the resources necessary to support its fast growth (Filatotchev and Lam, 2002). This discussion suggests the following hypothesis:

Hypothesis 2a: IPOs backed by a VC investor are more likely to be associated with the development of an independent board than are IPOs not backed by a VC investor.

Venture capital syndicates involve the sharing of formal decision-making powers among the syndicate members. This relationship creates a second tier of horizontal agency costs in addition to the traditional investee–investor agency relationship. The lower the level of cooperation among syndicate members, the greater the levels of relational risk and hence the associated agency costs. The origins of the agency costs in the syndicate may arise from the diverse objectives of members and the time-consuming nature of coordination.

Agency theorists define this complex relationship between multiple principals as a 'principal–principal' agency problem (Young et al., 2002) as opposed to the principal–agent problem within the conventional Bearle–Means framework that is focused on separation of ownership and control within the context of diffused share ownership and hired managers. As a result, the primary agency problem in this context is not the failure of professional managers to satisfy the objectives of diffuse shareholders, but rather the opportunistic behavior of the controlling shareholders.

Earlier game theory research moved the 'principal–principal' agency relationship into the context of repeated but time-constrained transactions. For example, Axelrod (1984) suggests that, within a framework of competing game models, a tit-for-tat strategy was superior in a multiple play game and led to continued cooperation, so long as the number of plays was indeterminate. Once a final play is set, defection at the last or next to last play was the dominant strategy.

These agency problems can in principle be addressed in a number of ways. Venture capital firms typically take equity stakes in their investees as they seek their return primarily through a capital gain. Equity stakes in syndicates provide for *ex ante* deterrents to opportunism by the partners. The presence of a syndicate is likely to reduce the equity remaining in the hands of founder managers. Shared equity ownership in VC syndicates may bring benefits of higher levels of trust and knowledge acquisition (Beamish and Banks, 1987), as well as mutual forbearance and stability (Mjoen and Tallman, 1997) that provides an effective remedy to partners' opportunism (Das and Teng, 1998).

However, lead venture capital firms that typically have the task of identifying the deal and coordinating the syndicate may seek a larger equity stake as a means of obtaining a greater return in recognition of this effort (Wright and Lockett, 2003), especially if the main motive for syndication is risk spreading (Lockett and Wright, 1999, 2001). In such circumstances, the non-lead members of syndicates may suffer a severe informational disadvantage in relation to the syndicate lead. The investment agreement between the syndicate members may be an important contractual device setting the boundaries of the behavior of the syndicate partners and providing an *ex post* deterrent to opportunism (Das and Teng, 1998). While contracts may specify rights of access to information, board membership rights and so on, the ability of contracts to foster certainty of cooperation may be questionable because of the problems associated with the complexity of contracting. Similarly, the problems associated with enforcing contracts through legal measures may mean that non-legal sanctions are used extensively to get the parties to act in accordance with the terms of the investment agreement.

The anticipation of future gains from cooperation (Cable and Shane, 1997) means that it is in the interests of the lead venture capital firm not to mislead syndicate partners in sharing information because of the potentially damaging impact on reputation and lack of willingness to reciprocate future deals (Norton and Tenenbaum, 1993; Wright and Lockett, 2004). The repeated interaction between syndicate members during the course of the investment (and also in different deals) can lead to high levels of trust as syndicate members come to know how partners will behave (Lockett and Wright, 1999). As venture capital industries are typically small, close-knit communities, in which investment executives from different firms know one another, this scope for building trust and reputations is enhanced (Black and Gilson, 1998).

Another possibility to reduce the extent of 'principal–principal' agency costs in a syndicated IPO is to use the young firm's governance system as a mechanism for 'arbitrage' between the potentially diverse objectives of syndicate partners. Previous research has identified important governance functions of ownership structure and board characteristics of the IPO firm as a means to reduce agency costs associated with possible opportunism of founding shareholders (e.g. Filatotchev and Bishop, 2002; Gompers, 1995). In the next section we extend this research and suggest that the IPO's internal governance arrangements may also be used, if not to eliminate, at least reduce potential conflicts of interest between the lead VC and other members of the syndicate.

Building on these arguments, we suggest that governance characteristics may also be used by members of the IPO syndicate to mitigate the potential problems associated with information asymmetries and potential opportunism within the syndicate itself. An independent chairman, for example, may also perform the functions of an 'arbiter' who should reconcile potentially diverse interests of the members. The backdrop nature of the syndicate contract and the importance of reputation introduce the importance of the independent board as a mechanism for ensuring the proper functioning of the syndicate. Board membership by syndicate members may enhance transparency in decision making and thus cooperation. Contractual control structures may be rendered less important as decisions are made on the basis of discussion between the parties rather than by imposing the division of power prescribed by the formal control structure. This may be more feasible where syndicates are small, and indeed the mean size of a VC syndicate in the UK is two to three members (Wright and Lockett, 2003). This may be more of a problem with large syndicates. Skilled lead venture capital firms may also be less reliant on the other syndicate members for specialist information (Admati and Pfleiderer, 1994). In such cases, lead investors may be more likely than non-leads to be board members and to exert more frequent hands-on influence over investees (Wright and Lockett, 2003). The development of an independent board may, therefore, be important in ensuring that the syndicate functions effectively. Non-lead syndicate members may seek the appointment of a non-executive chair and the presence of more non-executive directors than would be the case in a single VC-backed venture. Hence:

Hypothesis 2b: IPOs backed by syndicates of VCs are more likely to develop independent boards than are IPOs backed by single VCs.

Syndication of venture-capital investments and syndicate partners

The above arguments are based on agency aspects of IPO syndication. In addition, a resource-based perspective on syndication suggests that it provides a way to better assess the information provided by potential portfolio companies (Lerner, 1994). This will be especially important for projects where VC managers do not have sufficient skills to distinguish between high- or low-quality proposals in specialist areas (Brander et al., 2002). Syndication can also bring specialized resources for the *ex post* management of investments (Brander et al., 2002). By syndicating deals, VC firms are able to increase the portfolio they can optimally manage through resource sharing (Kanniainen and Keuschnigg, 2000; Jääskeläinen et al., 2002). VC firms can access more information by syndicating with other reputable VC firms. However, in specialist areas, VC firms may seek to syndicate with industrial partners. These industrial partners may have more specialist knowledge than either the VC firm itself or other VCs. This knowledge can be important in evaluating the initial investment, in post-investment management and in providing an eventual exit route. Hence:

Hypothesis 3a: IPOs backed by single VCs are more likely to involve investment with industry partners than are IPOs backed by syndicates of VCs.

As the firm develops, there may be a need to access further significant funds. The initial VC backer may have the specialist market-based skills but need to access further funds to diversify the risk associated with scaling up the operation. As VC funds are typically small, they may seek to syndicate deals that are large relative to their fund size. Lockett and Wright (2001) have shown that the dominant motive to syndicate deals for members of the BVCA in the UK, which include both VC and private equity firms, is spreading financial risk through risk sharing. The largest proportion of funds invested by these firms is in later-stage investments. VC syndicates may therefore also syndicate with private equity firms that specialize in later-stage ventures. Hence:

Hypothesis 3b: IPOs backed by syndicates of VCs are more likely also to involve investment with private equity firms that specialize in later-stage ventures than are IPOs backed by single VCs.

Data and Methodology

To construct a sample of entrepreneurial IPOs, a multi-stage data collection procedure has been used. First, we compiled a list of all IPOs that have been floated on the London Stock Exchange (LSE) and the Alternative Investment Market (AIM) from 1 January 1999 to 30 September 2002. Our primary list of IPOs was obtained from the London Stock Exchange New Issues files. Further information was provided by the AIM Market Statistics publications. From the original list of 631 IPOs we excluded re-admissions and transfers from the main market to AIM. We also excluded flotations of unit and investment trusts, since they have very specific governance characteristics. At the second stage, we excluded all IPOs that represented de-mergers, equity carve-outs, reverse take-overs and equity reorganizations. Investment and acquisition vehicles were also excluded since their governance systems are extremely simplified, and their boards resemble investment committees of private equity firms. We included in the final sample spin-offs from existing entrepreneurial firms, but only if the founders of the parent company were also the founders of the IPO firm. Finally, we included flotations of management buy-outs/management buy-ins (MBO/MBI), but only when the lead managers of a buy-out were also involved with the IPO firm. Wright et al. (2000), for example, suggest that MBO/MBIs represent an entrepreneurial transformation of the whole (or part) of an existing business, which justifies their inclusion in our sample. After these selection steps, the final sample included 293 entrepreneurial IPOs, and for each firm we were able to identify the original founders or leaders of a buy-out team. Our main variables of interest were obtained from information provided in the IPO listing prospectuses, which contain detailed information on the career histories and pre- and post-IPO ownership of managing officers and other board members. The IPO prospectuses were obtained from the 'Global Access' database which provides comprehensive coverage of companies' files for publicly quoted firms in the UK. The missing listing prospectuses were collected directly from the firms and/or their advisers by sending written requests. The IPO-related stock market data were obtained from the London Stock Exchange Share Monitoring Service and Datastream.

Board interests were measured in terms of the percentage of the total number of ordinary shares retained by founders, executive and non-executive board members after the IPO as reported in the listing prospectus. In addition, from the 'substantial share interests' section of the prospectus, we obtained information on share ownership of founders who were not board members. In addition to the share ownership stakes mentioned in the 'Directors' interests' section of the prospectus, the three ownership variables for each group of board members also included shareholdings whose voting rights have been effectively controlled by the directors through various trusts, as well as stakes owned by outside firms that were controlled by the directors. The latter allowed us to account for an ownership pyramid effect that may increase directors' voting power beyond the limits of their immediate retained share ownership.

IPO studies have increasingly recognized that venture capitalists may have a strong impact on the process of corporate governance development because they gain a detailed knowledge and substantial decision-making rights in the IPO firms that they finance (Barry et al., 1990; Jain, 2001; Sapienza and Gupta, 1994). In particular, VC firms impose contractual restraints on managerial discretion, including the use of staged investment, an enforceable nexus of security covenants, and the option to replace the entrepreneur as manager unless key investment objectives are met (see Zacharakis, 2002, for a discussion). Since these special rights end at the time of an IPO, when the need for oversight is particularly great, outside investors may compensate for a relative loss of control by strengthening other governance mechanisms, such as the IPO firm's board. Barry et al. (1990), Lerner (1994), Steier and Greenwood (2000) and others suggest a knowledge-based framework to analyze venture capitalists' involvement in the entrepreneurial firm according to which VCs act as 'brokers', linking founders with external pools of knowledge and expertise. To account for possible effects of VC firms on governance developments in the IPO firm, a 'VC involvement' variable was measured in terms of the percentage of the total number of ordinary shares retained by venture capitalists after the IPO. Venture capital firms were identified from the *British Venture Capital Association 2000/2001 Directory, 2000 Pratt's Guide to Venture Capital Sources* and *2000/2001 Venture Capital Report Guide to Venture Capital in the UK* (see Lerner, 1994, for a discussion of these sources of information). The 'VC involvement' variable also included share ownership of venture capital trusts (VCTs) that are managed by established VC firms. VCTs are smaller, specialist funds that are normally set up for tax purposes by the larger players in the UK venture industry.

We used logit regression analysis for the whole sample. T-tests were used for a subsample of VC-backed IPOs as the size of this subsample restricted our ability to use multivariate analysis. To prevent the occurrence of spurious correlation in the Logit regression analysis, several controls were used.

Previous research acknowledges the importance of firm size and age in terms of their effects on organizational outcomes, including performance (Amit et al., 1990; Mikkelson et al., 1997). The IPO's size was measured in terms of the logarithm of the firm's capitalization at the offer price, and age was measured by the number of years between the firm's founding date and its IPO date.

Although firm-specific factors are traditionally considered as the major drivers of strategic change according to the resource-based view (Barney, 2001), a growing body of research suggests that organizational outcomes may also be influenced by external, industry-level factors (see Mauri and Michaels, 1998, for discussion). To control for possible industry effects, four sector dummies were used for non-cyclical consumer products (SIC code 40), cyclical services (SIC code 50), financial sector (SIC code 80), and information technology (SIC code 80) firms, with remaining firms being used as a control. Finally, we introduced two proxies for 'riskiness' of the IPO: scaled risk = number of years of performance; high-risk dummy = 1 if only one year of performance.

Results

Table 5.1 reports the results of logistic regressions that were used to examine the relationship between risk variables and the likelihood of VC involvement (Table 5.3). All the models were well specified. The initial model (Model 1) shows that VC-backed IPOs were significantly more likely to be older and larger and to be in cyclical services and computers and software sectors. VC-backed IPOs were significantly less likely to have taken place in 2000. Model 2 introduces a variable for the presence of profits in the year prior to the IPO, but this

Table 5.1   Logit regression analysis of VC involvement in the IPO

	Model 1	Model 2	Model 3
Age	0.035*	0.039*	0.032[†]
Log (capitalization)	1.12***	1.14***	1.15***
1999	−0.33	−0.36	−0.41
2000	−0.87*	−0.89*	−1.01*
2001	−0.55	−0.61	−0.74
Cyclical services	1.10*	1.11*	1.21*
Non-cyclical services	0.56	0.55	0.64
Financial services	−0.28	−0.24	−0.22
Computers and software	1.07*	1.12*	1.21*
Internet	−0.44	−0.44	−0.43
Profits, year 1		0.00	0.00
Scaled risk			1.02*
High-risk dummy			1.94*
−2Loglikelihood	275.397	272.74	267.74
Nagelkerke R^2	0.20	0.20	0.22

Notes:
[†]$p \leq 0.10$; * $p \leq 0.05$; *** $p \leq 0.001$; scaled risk = number of years of performance; high-risk dummy = 1 if only one year of performance.

variable was not significant. In Model 3, two further risk measures are introduced. Both scaled risk as measured by the number of years of pre-IPO performance available and high risk as measured by the availability of only one year's data are positive and significant at the 5 percent level. These findings provide some support for Hypothesis 1a that VC firms are more likely to be involved in high-risk IPOs.

Table 5.2 examines sample differences between syndicated and single VC-backed IPOs. Using univariate statistical tests, we were unable to detect any statistically significant differences between those firms where there was a syndicate of VCs and those firms with only one VC in age of the firm and assets. Syndicated VC-backed IPOs were also not significantly larger than those IPOs with a single VC in terms of market capitalization (Table 5.2). However, there were significant differences in terms of average sales and pre-tax profits over three years before the flotation between these two groups of firms where we were able to obtain three years of pre-IPO data. These findings are consistent with our arguments suggesting that the extent of VC involvement intensifies with an increase in firm-level risk, as suggested by Hypothesis 1b.

There were some notable significant differences between VC-backed IPOs and the non VC-backed IPOs in the sample in terms of governance characteristics (Table 5.3a). Board size was significantly larger in VC-backed IPOs and these firms also had a significantly larger percentage of non-executive directors on the board. In contrast, non-VC backed IPOs were significantly more likely to have greater shares of founders' and executives' retained ownership following IPO. There were no significant differences between the two groups of

Table 5.2 VC syndication: company characteristics and performance

	VC-syndicated IPOs $N = 27$	Single VC IPOs $N = 45$
Log (capitalization)	1.73	1.69
	(0.62)	(0.69)
Age	7.88	9.35
	(8.20)	(8.49)
Net assets, £ millions	4.19	4.26
	(8.21)	(5.11)
Fixed assets, £ millions	8.24	13.04
	(16.58)	(41.24)
Sales, £ millions (average for last three years)[a]	6.08	42.01**
	(12.32)	(134.78)
Pre-tax profits, £ millions (average for last three years)[a]	–0.91	1.30*
	(2.06)	(5.52)

Notes:
[a] Subsamples of 20 VC-syndicated and 30 single VC-backed IPOs which had three years of performance data. Standard deviations in parentheses. Second column reports results of t-test of mean differences; * $p \leq 0.05$; ** $p \leq 0.01$.

firms in terms of the percentage of cases where the founder was CEO or chairman, the percentage of cases where there was a non-executive chairman, the percentage of cases where the CEO and chairman were separate and the extent of non-executive share ownership. These findings provide mixed support for Hypothesis 2a.

As Table 5.3b clearly indicates, venture capital syndication is associated with further increase of board independence. Syndicated VC-backed IPOs had a significantly larger percentage of non-executive directors on the board compared to single VC IPOs. A significantly larger percentage of these firms had a non-executive chairman and separate CEO and chairman. In contrast, single VC-backed IPOs were significantly more likely to have greater shares of founders' and executives' retained ownership following IPO. There were no significant differences between the two groups of firms in terms of the percentage of cases where the founder was CEO or chairman, and board size. These findings provide support for Hypothesis 2b that syndicated VC investments are more likely to develop independent boards.

There were no significant differences between the two samples in respect of the value and size of the lead VC's portfolio of investments. The mean value of the lead VC's portfolio in syndicated deals was £1.43 billion (standard deviation £1.44 billion) while in single VC-backed firms it was £1.06 billion (standard deviation £1.33 billion). The mean size of the lead VC's portfolio in syndicated deals was £3.79 billion (standard deviation £3.49 billion) while in single VC-backed firms it was £3.16 billion (standard deviation £3.96 billion).

However, significant differences between syndicated VC-backed IPOs and single VC-backed IPOs were identified in terms of a number of ownership and governance characteristics. Share ownership by VCs before the IPO in syndicated deals was weakly significantly

Table 5.3a Governance characteristics: VC-backed and non-VC-backed IPOs

	VC-backed IPOs $N = 72$	Non-VC-backed IPOs $N = 222$
Board size, sample average.	6.40	5.72**
	(1.51)	(1.58)
Non-executive chairman, % of subsample	0.66	0.61
	(0.47)	(0.48)
% of non-executives on board, sample average	0.46	0.31*
	(0.15)	(0.13)
Chairman and CEO separate, % of subsample	0.82	0.84
	(0.38)	(0.36)
Founders' retained share ownership, % of total	24.93	34.27***
	(18.13)	(21.80)
Executives' retained share ownership, % of total	22.60	36.12***
	(19.23)	(22.40)

Notes:
Standard deviations in parentheses. Second column reports results of *t*-test of mean differences, * $p \leq 0.05$; ** $p \leq 0.01$; *** $p \leq 0.001$

Table 5.3b Governance characteristics: VC-syndicated and single VC-backed IPOs

	VC-syndicated IPOs $N = 27$	Single VC IPOs $N = 45$
Board size, sample average	6.70	6.22
	(1.53)	(1.49)
Non-executive chairman, % of subsample	0.81	0.57*
	(0.39)	(0.49)
% of non-executives on board, sample average	0.51	0.42*
	(0.15)	(0.14)
Chairman and CEO separate, % of subsample	0.96	0.73*
	(0.19)	(0.44)
Founders' retained share ownership, % of total	16.25	30.14***
	(12.22)	(19.19)
Executives' retained share ownership, % of total	13.95	27.78**
	(12.94)	(20.60)

Notes:
Standard deviations in parentheses. Second column reports results of *t*-test of mean differences; * $p \leq 0.05$; ** $p \leq 0.01$; *** $p \leq 0.001$.

Table 5.4   Syndication and ownership

	VC-syndicated IPOs N = 27	Single VC IPOs N = 45
VCs		
Number of VC firms before IPO	3.14	1.0***
	(1.65)	
Share ownership of VC before IPO	27.53	17.86[†]
	(22.82)	(16.99)
Retained share ownership of VC after IPO	27.76	11.95***
	(13.91)	(9.35)
Number of VC firms after IPO	2.57	0.84***
	(1.98)	(0.36)
Private equity firms		
Number of other private equity firms before IPO	1.63	0.62**
	(1.46)	(0.87)
Share ownership of other private equity firms before IPO	11.91	4.75**
	(9.88)	(7.91)
Number of other private equity firms after IPO	1.92	1.02*
	(1.77)	(1.45)
Retained share ownership of other private equity firms after IPO	12.61	7.42[†]
	(12.95)	(11.66)
Industry partners		
Number of industry partners before IPO	0.42	0.53
	(0.60)	(0.80)
Share ownership of industry partners before IPO	2.38	6.41
	(3.44)	(13.81)
Number of industry partners after IPO	0.44	0.42
	(0.64)	(0.72)
Retained share ownership of industry partners after IPO	4.05	3.77
	(10.02)	(8.74)

Notes:
Subsample averages. Standard deviations in parentheses. Second column reports results of t-test of mean differences, $^{†}p \leq 0.10$; $* p \leq 0.05$; $** p \leq 0.01$; $*** p \leq 0.001$.

higher than that for single VC-backed deals (Table 5.4). There was a strongly significant difference between the two groups of firm in mean share ownership by VCs after the IPO. It appears that mean retained ownership after IPO changes little in syndicated deals but falls sharply in single VC-backed deals. The mean number of VCs in the syndicate before and after the IPO was 3.14 and 2.58 respectively, which indicates that only a minority of VC firms used IPO as an exit route.

Although the number of industry partners and the share these parties held before IPO was greater for IPOs with single VCs than those funded by syndicates of VCs, the differences were not statistically significant. Hence Hypothesis 3a is not supported. These findings may suggest that there is less need for the specialist skills of industrial partners in syndicated VC investments because there is a greater need for risk spreading in these cases. Where there is a need for specialist industry skills, the difference between IPOs funded by single and syndicated VCs is less clear cut.

It is also clear that syndicated VC-backed deals had a significantly higher number of other private equity investors as well as significantly higher share ownership by these investors, both before and after the IPO, than is the case in single VC-backed firms (Table 5.4). These findings provide support for Hypothesis 3b.

Discussion and Conclusions

Using a unique sample of 293 entrepreneurial IPOs in the UK, this chapter has examined the development of effective boards in VC-backed initial public offerings. Our analysis has made a novel contribution to the understanding of corporate governance in IPO firms and to the nature and operation of syndicated VC investments.

We have argued that VC-backed IPOs experience two sets of agency costs which are related to principal–agent and principal–principal relationships between the founders and members of the VC syndicate. The probability of VC backing is positively associated with risk proxies and contextual factors (high-tech industry, age and size and so on) (Hypothesis 1a). A first-tier agency problem, relating to information asymmetries in high-risk ventures between the founders and external investors, is resolved by syndication. Our evidence shows that VC syndicates invest in relatively more risky firms (Hypothesis 1b). From a governance perspective, VC involvement is associated with more independent boards. VC-backed IPOs have more independent boards than IPOs with no VC involvement (Hypothesis 2a).

A second tier of agency problem arises between the lead and non-lead members of a VC syndicate. The resolution of this agency problem is associated with even higher board independence (Hypothesis 2b). At the same time, founders' retained share ownership is at its lowest in VC-syndicated IPOs. These results are consistent with the assumption that these governance factors are used to mitigate agency costs associated with VC involvement in IPO firms.

Our analysis also identified that the syndication of investments may extend beyond the sharing of investments among a group of VC firms. First, we find single VCs teaming up with industry partners, which may be a sign of knowledge acquisition from the outside VC industry (Hypothesis 3a). This aspect of syndication may be especially important where there is a need to reduce the risk associated with investment in risky early-stage ventures. In contrast, we also find that in syndicated IPOs there is a higher equity presence of passive private equity firms investing alongside VC firms (Hypothesis 3b). As these passive private equity firms are less likely to have specialist industry and monitoring skills, this aspect may be associated more with the risk-sharing hypothesis for syndication.

This study is associated with a number of potential limitations. First, our analysis is focused on IPOs in the period 1999 to 2002. Although we have included a number of 'hot'

IPOs in our sample, the vast majority of firms have been floated during the period of increasing investors' conservatism, and this may have had a systematic impact on IPO governance characteristics. An extension of our sample by including earlier IPOs may help to verify the generalizability of our results. Second, our main variables of interests were collected from listing prospectuses and subsequent annual reports, and very little is known about pre-IPO governance effects of VC firms. Third, the design of our sample included firms that have been successfully floated, which introduces a certain selection bias toward more successful firms. Although this sample selection is in line with previous studies, some authors point out that findings might be biased in studying only firms which went public, instead of all firms which could have conceivably gone public during the sample time period. Therefore there is a need to take into account a potential 'survivor bias' (e.g. Stuart et al., 1999; Higgins and Gulati, 2003).

The findings of the study suggest a number of areas for further research. First, our analysis has focused on governance in VC-backed IPOs in the UK. There is growing recognition that governance and the operation of VC firms may depend on the institutional environment (Jeng and Wells, 2000; Black and Gilson, 1998). Further research might usefully extend our analysis of the role of syndicates to other institutional contexts, such as countries associated with network-based corporate governance systems (La Porta et al., 1997). Second, we did not explore specifically how the VC teams and boards changed from founding until going public. There are commonly several rounds of financing between a firm's founding and IPO, with each new financing round resulting in some changes to the team and board. An obvious extension to this current research would be to explore how the extent of board independence and ownership structure change over time; how different team/board characteristics attract external backers at each round; and vice versa.

Finally, an IPO is not the final stage in the corporate governance life cycle. In a dynamic perspective, corporate governance factors may be affected by strategic choices and outcomes, and the choice of the various governance options could be associated with changes in organizational strategy and firm performance (Dalton et al., 1999). For example, board diversity may be driven by the organization's growing needs for managing the important external elements of the environment that are related to changes in the organization's size and diversity (Provan, 1980; Pfeffer, 1972). Therefore the post-IPO evolution of the firm's governance system is a key research issue.

References

Admati, A. and P. Pfleiderer (1994), 'Robust financial contracting and the role of venture capitalists', *Journal of Finance*, **49**: 371–402.

Amit, R., L. Glosten and E. Muller (1990), 'Entrepreneurial ability, venture investments, and risk sharing', *Management Science*, **36**: 1232–45.

Amit, R., J. Brander and C. Zott (1998), 'Why do venture capital firms exist? Theory and Canadian evidence', *Journal of Business Venturing*, **13**: 441–66.

Axelrod, R. (1984), *The Evolution of Cooperation*, New York: Basic Books.

Barney J.B. (2003), 'Resource-based theories of competitive advantage: a ten-year retrospective on the resource-based view', *Journal of Management*, **27**(6): 643–50.

Barry, C., C. Muscarella, J. Peavy and M. Vetsuypens (1990), 'The role of venture capitalists in the creation of a public company', *Journal of Financial Economics*, **27**: 447–71.

Beamish, P. and J. Banks (1987), 'Equity joint ventures and the theory of the multinational enterprise', *Journal of International Business Studies*, **18**(2): 1–16.

Black, B. and R. Gilson (1998), 'Venture capital and the structure of capital markets: banks versus stock markets', *Journal of Financial Economics*, **47**(3): 243–78.

Brander, J., R. Amit and W. Antweiler (2002), 'Venture capital syndication: improved venture selection vs. the value added hypothesis', *Journal of Economics and Management Strategy*, **11**(3): 422–51.

Brav, A. and P. Gompers (1997), 'Myth or reality? the long-run underperformance of IPOs: Evidence from venture and non-venture capital backed companies', *Journal of Finance*, **52**: 1791–821.

Bygrave, W. (1987), 'Syndicated investments by venture capital firms: a networking perspective', *Journal of Business Venturing*, **2**: 139–54.

Bygrave, W. (1988), 'The structure of investment networks in the venture capital industry', *Journal of Business Venturing*, **3**: 137–57

Cable, D. and S. Shane (1997), 'A prisoner's dilemma approach to entrepreneur–venture capitalist relationships', *Academy of Management Review*, **22**(1): 142–76.

Certo, T.S., J. Covin, C. Daily and D. Dalton (2001), 'Wealth and the effects of founder management among IPO-stage new ventures', *Strategic Management Journal*, **22**: 641–58.

Certo, T. (2003), 'Influencing IPO investors with prestige: signaling with board structures', *Academy of Management Review*, **28**: 432–46.

Chiplin, B., K. Robbie and M. Wright (1997), 'The syndication of venture capital deals: Buy-outs and buy-ins', in Reynolds, P. et al. (eds), *Frontiers of Entrepreneurship Research 1997*, Wellesley, MA: Babson College.

Cumming, D.J. (2003), 'The determinants of venture capital portfolio size: empirical evidence', mimeo, University of New South Wales, Australia.

Daily, C. and D. Dalton (1992), 'The relationship between governance structure and corporate performance in entrepreneurial firms', *Journal of Business Venturing*, **7**: 375–86.

Dalton, D.R., C. Daily, J. Johnson and A. Ellstrand (1999), 'Number of directors and financial performance: a meta-analysis', *Academy of Management Journal*, **42**: 674–86.

Das, T.K. and B.-S. Teng (1998), 'Between trust and control: developing confidence in partner cooperation in alliances', *Academy of Management Review*, **23**(3): 491–512.

EVCA (2003), *EVCA Yearbook 2003*, European Venture Capital Association: Zaventem.

Filatotchev, I. and K. Bishop (2002), 'Board composition, share ownership and "underpricing" of UK IPO firms', *Strategic Management Journal*, **28**: 941–55.

Filatotchev, I. and M. Lam (2002), 'Behind the myth of IPOs', *Professional Investor*, March, pp. 9–12.

Filatotchev, I. and S. Toms (2003), 'Corporate governance, strategy and survival in a declining industry: a study of UK cotton textile companies', *Journal of Management Studies*, **40**(4): 895–920.

Geletkanycz, M.A. and D. Hambrick (1997), 'The external ties of top executives: implications for strategic choice and performance', *Administrative Science Quarterly*, **42**: 654–81.

Gompers, P. (1995), 'Optimal investment, monitoring, and the staging of venture capital', *Journal of Finance*, **50**(5): 1461–89.

Gompers, P. and J. Lerner (1999), *The Venture Capital Cycle*, New York: Wiley

Gorman, M. and W. Sahlman (1989), 'What do venture capitalists do?', *Journal of Business Venturing*, **4**: 231–48.

Higgins, M.C. and R. Gulati (2003), 'Getting off to a good start: the effects of upper echelon affiliations on underwriter prestige', *Organization Science*, **14**(3): 244–63.

Jääskeläinen, M., M. Maula and T. Seppä (2002), 'The optimal portfolio of start-up firms in venture capital finance: the moderating effect of syndication and an empirical test', paper presented at the Babson Kaufmann Entrepreneurship Conference 2002, Boulder, CO.

Jain, B.A. (2001), 'Predictors of performance of venture capital-backed organizations', *Journal of Business Research*, **52**: 223–33.

Jayraman, N., A. Khorana and E. Nelling (2000), 'CEO founder status and firm financial performance', *Strategic Management Journal*, **21**: 1215–24.

Jeng, L. and P. Wells (2000), 'The determinants of venture capital funding: evidence across countries', *Journal of Corporate Finance*, **6**: 241–89.

Kanniainen, V. and C. Keuschnigg (2000), 'The optimal portfolio of start-up firms in venture capital finance', *CESifo Working Paper Series* No. 381.

La Porta, R., F. Lopez-De-Silanes, A. Shleifer and R. Vishny (1997), 'Legal determinants of external finance', *Journal of Finance*, **52**(3): 1131–50.

Lerner, J. (1994), 'The syndication of venture capital investments', *Financial Management*, **23**(3): 16–27.

Lockett, A. and M. Wright (1999), 'The syndication of private equity: evidence from the UK', *Venture Capital*, **1**(4): 303–24.

Lockett, A. and M. Wright (2001), 'The syndication of venture capital investments', *OMEGA: The International Journal of Management Science*, **29**: 375–90.

Lockett, A., G. Murray and M. Wright (2002), 'Do venture capital firms in the UK still have a bias against technology ventures?', *Research Policy*, **31**: 1009–30.

Mauri, A.J. and M. Michaels (1998), 'Firm and industry effects within strategic management: an empirical examination', *Strategic Management Journal*, **19**: 211–19.

Megginson, W. and K. Weiss (1991), 'Venture capitalist certification in IPOs', *Journal of Finance*, **96**: 879–903.

Mello, A.S. and J.E. Parsons (1998), 'Going public and the ownership structure of the firm', *Journal of Financial Economics*, **49**: 79–109.

Mikkelson, W.H, M. Partch and K. Shah (1997), 'Ownership and operating performance of companies that go public', *Journal of Financial Economics*, **44**: 281–307.

Mjoen, H. and S. Tallman (1997), 'Control and performance in international joint ventures', *Organization Science*, **8**(3): 257–74.

Norton, E. and B. Tenenbaum (1993), 'The effects of venture capitalists' characteristics on the structure of a venture capital deal', *Journal of Small Business Management*, **31**: 32–41.

Oswald, S.L. and J.S. Jahera (1991), 'The influence of ownership on performance: an empirical study', *Strategic Management Journal*, **12**: 321–6.

Pfeffer, J. (1972), 'Size and composition of corporate boards of directors: the organization and its environment', *Administrative Science Quarterly*, **17**: 218–22.

Provan, K. (1980), 'Board power and organizational efficiency among human service agencies', *Academy of Management Journal*, **23**: 221–36.

Sahlman, W.A. (1990), 'The structure and governance of venture capital organizations', *Journal of Financial Economics*, **27**: 473–521.

Sapienza, H.J. and A. Gupta (1994), 'Impact of agency risks and task uncertainty on venture capitalist–CEO interaction', *Academy of Management Journal*, **37**: 1618–32.

Schefczyk, M. and T.J. Gerpott (2001), 'Qualifications and turnover of managers and venture capital-financed firm performance', *Journal of Business Venturing*, **16**: 145–63.

Schulze, W.S., M. Lubatkin and R. Dino (2003), 'Exploring the agency consequences of ownership dispersion among the directors of private family firms', *Academy of Management Journal*, **46**: 179–94.

Shivdasani, A. (1993), 'Board composition, ownership structure, and hostile takeovers', *Journal of Accounting and Economics*, **16**: 167–98.

Sorenson, O. and T.E. Stuart (2002), 'Syndication networks and the spatial distribution of venture capital investments', *American Journal of Sociology*, **107**: 216–30.

Steier, L. and R. Greenwood (2000), 'Entrepreneurship and the evolution of angel financial networks', *Organization Studies*, **21**: 163–92.

Stuart, T.E., H. Hoang and R. Hybels (1999), 'Interorganizational endorsements and the performance of entrepreneurial ventures', *Administrative Science Quarterly*, **44**: 315–49.

Willard, G.E., D. Krueger and H. Feeser (1992), 'In order to grow, must the founder go?: a comparison of performance between founder and non-founder managed high-growth manufacturing firms', *Journal of Business Venturing*, **7**: 181–94.

Wright, M. and K. Robbie (1998), 'Venture capital and private equity: a review and synthesis', *Journal of Business, Finance and Accounting*, **25**(5) & (6): 521–70.

Wright, M. and A. Lockett (2003), 'The structure and management of alliances: syndication in the venture capital industry', *Journal of Management Studies*, **40**(8): 2073–104.

Wright, M., R. Hoskisson, L. Busenitz and J. Dial (2000), 'Entrepreneurial growth through privatization: the upside of management buyouts', *Academy of Management Review*, **25**(3): 591–601.

Young, M.N., M. Peng, D. Ahlstrom and G. Bruton (2002), 'Governing the corporation in emerging economies: a principal–principal perspective', in *Best Paper Proceedings*, Academy of Management Annual Meeting, August, Denver, CO.

Zacharakis, A. (2002), 'Business risk, investment risk, and syndication of venture capital deals', paper presented at the August 2002 Academy of Management Meeting, Denver, CO.

Zahra, S.A. and J. Pearce (1989), 'Boards of directors and corporate financial performance: a review and integrative model', *Journal of Management*, **15**: 291–334.

[6]

Governance implications of locked-in venture capitalists (VCs) and founder owners in newly floated UK companies[1]

Susanne Espenlaub, Marc Goergen and Arif Khurshed

I. Introduction

Much of the corporate governance literature focuses on the role and impact of the corporate board and ownership structure in relatively mature, listed companies. In this chapter, we examine the impact of a contractual governance mechanism that appears to play an important role at an early stage of the corporate and governance life cycle, the flotation, or going-public stage, when companies first list on a stock exchange and raise external equity finance through a share issue, a so-called initial public offering (IPO). Previous literature on the corporate governance of IPO companies has examined how companies adapt their control and governance systems in the run-up to the IPO to limit or resolve the informational and agency problems arising at this stage of the life cycle. These studies typically focus on the composition of the board and on ownership structure (e.g. Goergen, 1998 and Filatotchev and Bishop, 2002).

By contrast, the governance mechanism under investigation here takes the form of a contractual agreement between the existing shareholders of the issuing company and the underwriter(s) to the issue. These so-called lock-in agreements (also known in the USA and elsewhere as 'lock-*up* agreements') form part of the underwriting agreement, and extracts of the underwriting agreement, including details of the lock-in clauses, are usually reproduced in the IPO prospectus. Lock-in agreements prohibit the directors and often other major shareholders from selling their shares in the immediate aftermarket following the IPO.[2]

Lock-in agreements in IPOs have only recently become the focus of academic attention, and to date relatively little is known on their precise role in the governance of the underwriting relationship, the relationship between existing inside shareholders and outside IPO investors, and the governance of the corporation more generally.

The empirical literature has identified a number of interesting stylized facts on lock-in agreements. First, there appears to be substantial variation across countries in terms of their regulation. For example, there are no mandatory minimum lock-in periods in the USA[3] and UK[4] markets, whereas the 'new markets' of Continental Europe (the EuroNMs) have certain minimum lock-in contracts (for more details on the regulation of the EuroNMs, see Goergen et al., 2003).

Second, irrespective of the country and regulations, most IPO companies carry lock-in agreements that tend to be longer than the minimum length required by regulators. Further, the length of these agreements tends to differ across countries. For example, in the USA, the lock-in agreements are quite standardized at 180 days after the IPO.[5] In comparison, the lengths of lock-in agreements in Europe are more variable and differ from country to country. For example, preliminary evidence for the UK (based on a subsample of lock-in agreements) suggests that lock-in periods are typically substantially longer and in some cases as long as three years after the IPO (see Espenlaub et al., 2001). The present study indicates that the average lock-in period for IPOs issued in the UK between 1992 and 1998 is around 14 months. For the new markets of Germany and France the lock-in agreements are usually 300 days long and in some cases these can be as long as three years after the IPO (see Goergen et al., 2004). Third, the structure of these lock-in agreements also varies across countries. For example, the lock-in agreements in the USA and Continental Europe have a clear-cut expiry date whereas in the UK the expiry date is frequently relative to a corporate event such as the publication of the preliminary results or the annual report. Finally, some studies on the USA have found a negative share price reaction on the day of lock-in expiry. This result, however, has not been confirmed for UK lock-in agreements (see Espenlaub et al., 2001).

Existing research suggests that lock-in contracts serve to resolve some of the informational and agency problems at the IPO stage. There are few formal theoretical models of lock-in agreements, and most rationales for lock-ins are developed informally, focusing on their role in mitigating the problems and costs of information asymmetries between informed insiders and uninformed IPO investors, given that such asymmetries are particularly pronounced at the IPO stage. By preventing the initial shareholders from selling further shares for a specified period, lock-in agreements reduce the opportunity and incentives of the existing shareholders to cash in on any information withheld or misrepresented at the IPO stage.

Another rationale for lock-in clauses centres on their role in reducing agency problems arising from the dilution, through the IPO, of the existing shareholders' ownership, which reduces their incentives to maximize firm value (or shareholder wealth). The lock-in agreement serves to reduce the resulting conflict of interests between the old (pre-IPO) and the new shareholders by preventing further ownership dilution for a specified period. This in turn limits the (further) deterioration of the existing shareholders' incentives and the divergence of the old and new shareholders' objectives.

A further related aspect of IPOs that has attracted growing academic attention is the impact of venture capital (VC) backing on IPOs. Jain and Kini (2000) find that VC involvement improves the survival profile of IPO issuers. They also assert that VCs have the ability to influence not only the managerial decisions of the firm but also the external market participants such as the sponsors, analysts and institutional shareholders. This suggests that VCs assume a certification role that may in turn mitigate problems of asymmetric information or agency.

In this chapter, we bring together the two aspects of IPOs discussed above. Our first objective is to investigate to what extent the initial owners of IPO companies lock themselves in. Then we analyse whether the backing of the IPO by venture capitalists, and venture-capital backers' agreement to lock in their shares after the IPO, have a systematic effect on (or association with) the lock-in agreements of directors and other pre-IPO shareholders, in terms of the existence and contractual characteristics of their agreements. Specifically, we examine whether venture capital backing and lock-ins result in shorter or longer lock-in periods for the other initial owners, or whether they increase or reduce the locked-in proportion of the shareholdings of the directors and the other initial owners. The analysis is intended to shed light on the question whether the presence of a VC, and the existence and nature of the VCs' lock-in agreements, act as strategic complements or substitutes to the lock-in agreements of the directors and other pre-IPO shareholders. Some preliminary findings (Espenlaub et al., 2003; Goergen et al., 2003) indicate that director and VC lock-in agreements differ systematically, with the directors typically being locked in for longer. However, we know of no in-depth examination of the existence and contractual characteristics of VC lock-ins either in isolation or in relation to the agreements of company directors and other pre-IPO shareholders. We also document the retained post-IPO share ownership of directors, VCs and other shareholders, and examine the associations between retained ownership, on one hand, and the presence of VC backing and the existence and contractual aspects of the lock-in agreements of VCs, directors and other shareholders, on the other.

The rest of the chapter is organized as follows. In Section II we survey the small body of related literature on lock-in agreements. Section III describes the data used in this study. The research issue and the results of our descriptive analysis are presented and discussed in Section IV, and the chapter concludes with a summary of our findings, a discussion of the limitations of our analysis and suggestions for future research in Section V.

II. Survey of the Literature

A formal signalling model of lock-in agreements was developed by Courteau (1995). She extends Leland and Pyle's (1977) signalling model and includes the length of the lock-in period as a signal of firm value. She shows that the length of the lock-in period is a signalling mechanism that complements ownership retention. Her results also show that, depending on the information structure of the IPO firm, the insiders may prefer to lock in for a period of time which is longer than the minimum required by listing regulations.

Brav and Gompers (2003) suggest three explanations for the existence of lock-in agreements. First, they act as a signal of quality of the IPO firm; second, they act as a commitment device to reduce moral hazard problems; and third, they provide a means to the underwriters to extract additional compensation from the issuing firms. However, they find support only for their commitment hypothesis.

Brau et al. (2003) revisit the signalling explanation of lock-ins and extend the work of Brav and Gompers (BG) into a formal model with explicit assumptions and testable predictions. Like Courteau, their model of lock-ins is also in the spirit of Leland and Pyle. Brau et al. evaluate BG evidence against signalling and find it unconvincing. In fact they show that BG empirical evidence lends more support to a signalling model rather than a commitment explanation. Finally Brau et al. test the predictions of their signalling model and find support for their prediction that lock-ins will be longer when the IPO firm has low transparency.

To date, there is only a very small body of literature that examines the impact of VC backing of the IPO on the contractual features of the lock-in agreements, in terms of the existence or absence of lock-in agreements, the lengths of the specified lock-in periods, and the percentage of shares locked in. With the exception of Espenlaub et al. (2003) and Goergen et al. (2004), who use UK and Continental European data, respectively, all these prior studies employ data for US IPOs.

Bradley et al. (2001) study a sample of 2693 US IPOs that went public between 1988 and 1997. They find that the average lock-in period is 224 days, with 75 per cent of their sample firms having a lock-in of exactly 180 days. They further look at the percentage of shares locked in at the time of the IPO and find that for more than 75 per cent of their sample firms the number of locked-in shares exceeds the number of unlocked shares. They partition their sample into VC-backed IPOs and those that are not. Similar to BG, they find that the VC-backed firms have a slightly larger percentage of shares locked in than non-VC-backed firms and that the length of lock-in periods for VC-backed firms (192 days) is much smaller than that for non-VC-backed firms (249 days).

Field and Hanka (2001) report for a sample of 1948 US IPOs that the directors are almost always locked in. They partition their sample into firms with VC backing and those without. They discover that in VC-backed firms non-executives hold more shares and executives fewer shares than in firms without VC financing. The ownership structure of firms with corporate shareholders is similar to that with VCs. However, during the year after the IPO, VCs sell on average 29 per cent (median of 17 per cent) of their holdings as compared to other corporate shareholders that sell only an average of 20 per cent (median of 0).

While all of the above papers focus on US lock-in agreements, there are a few that study the lock-in agreements in Europe. Espenlaub et al. (2001) focus on the characteristics of UK lock-in agreements. Using a sample of 188 firms that went public on the London Stock Exchange (LSE) during 1992–98, they report that the lock-in contracts of LSE-listed firms are much more complex, varied and diverse than US contracts.

Goergen et al. (2003) study the ownership structures and lock-in agreements on the German and French new markets.[6] They report that, contrary to the UK and the USA, firms going public on the French and German new markets are subject to compulsory lock-ins. However, about a third of French firms and half of the German firms have lock-in periods that go beyond the regulatory requirements. Looking at the role of VCs in these IPOs, the authors report that a higher proportion of French firms are backed by VCs, and that French VCs sell a smaller fraction of their holdings at the time of the IPO. They further show that for the German IPOs about two thirds of the VC lock-in agreements follow the minimum legal period of six months. The equivalent figure for the French IPOs is only one fifth. Another interesting difference is that, while in Germany all VCs are locked in, more than one third of the French VCs are not locked in. Running multivariate regressions, the study finds that, for both French and German IPOs, lock-in periods tend to be shorter for the VCs than for the other shareholders of VC-backed firms. Executive directors have the longest lock-in periods, followed by non-executives directors.

In Germany, regulation prescribes a minimum lock-in period of six months covering all the shares, so there is no variation in the percentage of shares locked in. In France, the initial shareholders of firms have a choice between a minimum lock-in period of six months, covering all of the shares held by the old shareholders immediately after the IPO, and a lock-in period of one year, covering only 80 percent of their shares. Hence, for France, there is some degree of interdependence between the percentage locked in and the duration of the lock-in. Goergen et al.'s (2003) results from a multinomial logit model suggest that VCs are not likely to be subject to lock-ins that are more stringent than the two minimum legal contracts. Executives of VC-backed firms are more likely to be locked in with 100 per cent of their shares for six months than with 80 per cent of their shares for one year. Based on these results, the authors argue that, although the French regulator offers two *a priori* equivalent options, these are not perceived to be equal by the initial shareholders. The minimum lock-in covering 100 per cent of the shares for six months is perceived to be less stringent than that of one year covering only 80 per cent of the shares.

To summarize, evidence from the USA and Continental Europe suggests that the shareholders of VC firms are locked in for briefer periods. In addition, shareholders of US VC-backed firms are locked in with higher percentages. Given the regulation on lock-ins in France and Germany, the US result also holds for the two countries.

Espenlaub et al. (2003) look at the impact of VC presence on UK lock-in agreements among companies in the high-technology and other industrial sectors using a subsample of the IPOs examined in the present study, with less complete and detailed data on ownership and lock-in agreements. Espenlaub et al. distinguish not only between VC-backed and other offerings, but also between IPOs in high-tech and other sectors, arguing that high-tech firms are likely to face higher levels of informational asymmetries than firms outside that sector. The authors present some preliminary evidence on lock-in periods, based on the subsample of agreements with expiry dates expressed as clear-cut calendar dates ('absolute' dates). For this subsample, they find that lock-in periods are particularly long for venture-backed high-tech companies (corresponding to their higher level of information asymmetries). By contrast, for the firms outside the high-tech sector, venture capital backing appears to reduce the directors' lock-in periods. They further examine the proportion of locked-in directors' shares and find, in the non-high-tech sector, it is significantly higher in VC-backed firms than in firms without VC backing. They conclude that VC backing does not act as a strategic substitute but rather as a complement to lock-in agreements.

The present study extends this earlier analysis. It should be noted that the data and focus of this earlier study were substantially different from the analysis presented in this chapter. The scope of the earlier analysis was limited by significantly less detailed data on the lock-in agreements of VCs and other shareholders, and on post-IPO ownership. It also did not (aim to) examine the associations between the presence, ownership and lock-in agreements of VCs and the ownership and lock-in agreements of directors and other pre-IPO shareholders.

III. Data

The sample used in this study consists of 351 IPOs by UK-incorporated companies on the London Stock Exchange during January 1992 and December 1998.[7] The sample excludes IPOs of investment companies and funds, given the substantially different nature and ownership structure of such IPOs. The offerings in our sample are classified as VC-backed issues on the basis of information contained in the IPO prospectuses and further information from the British Venture Capital Association (BVCA). Specifically, we use a list of VC-backed flotations drawn up by the BVCA and the directory of BVCA members to identify (UK-based) VC funds. The BVCA list of VC-backed IPOs is not comprehensive because it only comprises details of flotations reported to the BVCA by their members. In a few cases where the details provided by the BVCA and the prospectuses are conflicting, we relied solely on prospectus information. Data on directors', venture-capitalists' and other share-holders' ownership immediately after the IPO, and about their lock-in agreements, were hand-collected from the IPO prospectuses.

IV. Descriptive Analysis and Results

Within our sample of 351 IPOs, we identified 190 offerings with VC backing (corresponding to 54 per cent of the sample). Thus, it appears that VC financing is highly prevalent among UK IPO companies. Goergen et al. (2004) find comparable proportions of VC-backed IPOs on the German Neuer Markt (47 per cent) and on the French Nouveau Marché (61 per cent).[8]

It needs to be borne in mind that a large proportion of financing termed 'venture capital' in the UK would not be considered 'venture capital' in the USA and elsewhere, where venture capital is defined primarily as seed or start-up funding. In the UK, by contrast, it also comprises later-stage financing classified elsewhere as private equity.

Frequency of locked-in venture capitalists, directors and other shareholders

An IPO and stock-market listing is generally seen to serve as an exit route for pre-IPO VC backers. It has been argued that locking in the shareholdings of existing owners serves to control the supply of shares being sold in the aftermarket to reduce any price-pressure effects. This hypothesis predicts a trade-off between the VC's desire to sell at the IPO and not to lock in any retained shares, on the one hand, and concerns with stable aftermarket share prices, on the other. The probability of being locked in under this hypothesis is likely to be linked to the magnitude of the VC's shareholdings, with larger unlocked shareholdings representing a greater danger to price stability. However, as larger shareholdings are more costly to retain and lock in, this relationship is probably not of a simple linear kind.

Other theoretical rationales of lock-in agreements focus on information and agency issues. Lock-ins may serve as a favourable signal to uninformed IPO investors. Locked-in shareholdings serve to align the objectives of existing and new shareholders, and convey the commitment of existing owners to the company and the accuracy of any information they disclose in the IPO prospectus. Asymmetric information and agency arguments predict that VCs, which are likely to have some private information and an involvement in the management of the IPO companies they back, will be locked in.

Thus it is interesting to examine the prevalence of VC lock-ins in practice, and also to assess the frequency of VC lock-ins in relation to the lock-ins of other types of shareholders. Of particular interest in this context are executive directors, who are normally the most informed players. Thus the information and agency arguments predict that directors should be most likely to be locked in irrespective of their shareholdings.

Besides directors and VCs, we also examine a third group of shareholders, so-called other shareholders (that is, all shareholders excluding executive and non-executive directors and VC backers). These include other institutional pre-IPO investors (such as pension funds), and individual investors not related to directors.[9] We hypothesize that this group is least likely to have private information and (direct) influence on company management given that they are not represented on the board. Consequently, the information and agency arguments would predict that they are least likely to be locked in. However, the price-pressure argument makes no such distinction on the basis of access to information, and predicts that any sizeable shareholdings of this group should be locked in.

Table 6.1 provides details on the prevalence of lock-in agreements of directors, VCs and other shareholders in both VC-backed and -unbacked IPOs. Consistent with our expectations and the findings of Field and Hanka (2001) for the USA, we find that directors are almost always locked in, although they are somewhat more likely to be locked in if the IPO is VC backed; specifically, 97 per cent of VC-backed IPOs lock in directors, as compared to 91 per cent of unbacked issues.

VCs and other shareholders are far less frequently locked in than directors. Still, in more than half the issues that involve VCs and/or other shareholders, they agree to be locked in. In VC-backed offerings, other shareholders are slightly less likely to be locked in than they are in issues without VC backing: 60 per cent of unbacked issuers lock in other shareholders, while only 52 per cent of VC-backed issuers do so.

VCs are somewhat more frequently locked in than other shareholders, in 63 per cent of VC-backed offerings. This may be interpreted as an indication that VCs are not as concerned with the IPO and the immediate aftermarket as an exit route, as one might have expected. Instead, they appear to take a more medium- to long-term approach, and contribute to insiders' efforts to limit the costs of information and agency problems by agreeing to lock in their shareholdings.

An interesting observation is the great similarity between VCs and other shareholders in the subsample of VC-backed IPOs in terms of their likelihood to agree to lock in their shares. Panel B of Table 6.1 shows that if other shareholders do not agree to lock-ins, VCs are likely to follow suit, and vice versa. This seems to indicate that the extent of informational asymmetries and agency problems differs widely among VC-backed companies. One group (around 17 per cent) has no need for lock-ins of shareholders other than directors, while a greater percentage (43 per cent) seeks the positive valuation effects of third-party certification, signalling and monitoring/disciplining by locking in their VC backers and other shareholders.

Types of lock-in agreements

Previous research on UK lock-in agreements (Espenlaub et al., 2001, 2003) has reported the great diversity of lock-in agreements in terms of both the type and the length of the agreements. As noted earlier, this variety observed in UK IPOs is in stark contrast to the much greater standardization of US agreements that typically specify lock-in periods of 180 days.

Table 6.1 Frequency and coincidence of lock-in agreements of directors and other shareholders of initial public offerings in the UK, 1992–98

Panel A: Initial public offerings without VC backing

| | Directors agree to lock in | | | | Directors' own no. of shares | | Total | |
| | No | | Yes | | | | | |
	No.	%	No.	%	No.	%	No.	%
Other shareholders No	1	0.62	28	17.39	0	0.00	29	18.01
Agree to lock in Yes	8	4.97	84	52.17	4	2.48	96	59.63
No other shareholders exist	1	0.62	35	21.74	0	0.00	36	22.36
Total	10	6.21	147	91.30	4	2.48	161	100.00

Panel B: Initial public offerings with VC backing

	Directors agree to lock in								Total	
	No				Yes					
	VC not locked in		VC locked in		VC not locked in		VC locked in			
	No.	%	No.	%	No.	%	No.	%	No.	%
Other shareholders No	2	1.05	0	0.00	33	17.37	10	5.26	45	23.68
Agree to lock in Yes	0	0.00	2	1.05	14	7.37	82	43.16	98	51.58
No other shareholders exist	0	0.00	1	0.53	22	11.58	24	12.63	47	24.74
Total	2	1.05	3	2.00	69	36.00	116	61.00	190	100.0

Note: While some of the firms in the unbacked IPO subsample have no ownership by directors, in the VC-backed IPO subsample, each observation has director ownership.

A further obvious difference between UK agreements and those elsewhere is the existence in the UK of a majority of lock-ins that define the expiry date relative to the announcement or publication of financial results (such as the preliminary or final, half-yearly or annual results) or, less commonly, of an event such as the Annual General Meeting. By contrast, in Continental European and US IPOs, the expiry of lock-in agreements is usually set in terms of an 'absolute', calendar date (e.g. 30 January 1997).

While most lock-in agreements allow shareholders to dispose of their entire stakes after the end of the specified period, we also observe so-called staggered lock-in periods which allow for the gradual release of locked-in shares with the first expiry date setting free only a pre-specified proportion of the locked-in shareholdings, followed by one or several additional lock-ins of ever smaller stakes. These staggered agreements are found both in the UK and on the new Continental European markets. However, their prevalence is much higher in the UK. Espenlaub et al. (2001) find that between 17 and 20 per cent of lock-in contracts are staggered. Goergen et al. (2004) find that only 8 per cent of agreements on the German Neuer Markt and 6 per cent of agreements on the French Nouveau Marché are staggered.

There is to date no clear theoretical explanation for the greater contractual diversity in the UK. Institutional inertia in the practices adopted by underwriters may be a partial explanation. We also as yet have no definitive theoretical or empirical understanding of the factors determining the adoption of different contractual features, for example the choice between absolute and relative, and between simple and staggered agreements. This study contributes to our understanding in this respect because it is the first to document empirically the nature of lock-in agreements of UK VC backers.

On the basis of theoretical insights and the limited amount of existing research, we can hypothesize about the likely factors determining the selection of absolute and relative expiry dates. First, relative expiry dates emphasize the importance of the release of the financial data relative to which they are defined. Thus it is possible that the owners of companies subject to relatively high informational asymmetries between insiders and investors, for example companies whose pre-IPO earnings and other accounting information convey little useful information to investors about the true potential and value of the company, may choose relative expiry dates to ensure the release of further pertinent information prior to their disposal of any retained shareholdings.

On the other hand, it is easier for outside investors to predict the precise timing of absolute expiry dates. By contrast, relative dates are to some extent under the control of company insiders, as the timing of the associated financial announcement or event may not be pre-determined or known to outsiders at the IPO. The predictability of the precise lock-in expiry day is of importance to investors if lock-in expiry is expected to lead to large-scale selling and price pressure, and if investors expect to trade during the subsequent period of depressed share prices.

Moreover, complex agreements, including those with staggered periods, may be difficult for outsiders to interpret *ex ante* and verify *ex post*. Also, the provision of information needed to interpret agreements may be incomplete; for example, it may be impossible to ascertain the identity of the shareholders covered by the agreement. Such an instance is reported in Espenlaub et al. (2003). It is conceivable that intentionally opaque and incomplete agreements may be adopted as part of a strategy of insiders and underwriters to obfuscate or even mislead outside investors.

Another motive for existing owners, specifically founders and directors, to lock in their shareholdings is to ensure that their valuable human capital will remain available to the firm after the IPO. Consequently the terms of the agreement should be related to their term in office and their leadership role within the company. If, for a given company, the retention motive dominates any informational considerations and is the prime driver for the decision to lock in directors' shareholdings, there would be no obvious reason to expect expiry dates of directors' lock-in periods to be set relative to financial announcements. Thus the choice of absolute dates may reflect the relative importance of the retention motive, while relative dates are associated with informational concerns.

Lock-in types and VC backing

In this study, we focus on the involvement of UK VCs in a specific aspect of financial contracting, namely the lock-in clause in the contractual agreement between issuers and underwriters. We examine in depth the extent to which these agreements are influenced by the presence of VC backing, and to what extent the VCs themselves are affected by the lock-in agreement. VCs provide strategic advice, mentoring, monitoring, certification to outside stakeholders, corporate governance and help in recruitment of senior management to the ventures they finance (Hellman and Puri, 2000). When these ventures reach the point where they decide to go public (IPO), VCs play a crucial role in the internal and external aspects of the IPO process. For the internal aspects of the IPO process, the VCs provide help with strategic and operation planning, personnel and resource allocation decisions. As for the external aspects, VCs exert influence on institutional investors, investment bankers and analysts because of their reputation and repeat interactions (Jain and Kini, 2000).

Lerner (1994) and Jain and Kini (2000) examine the extent of VC influence and involvement in the IPO process of their portfolio firms, including the selection of underwriters. However, they do not examine in depth the nature of the issuers' contracts with the IPO underwriters and the VCs' role in the IPO contracting process beyond the determination of the IPO price and share allocation. In their review of the VC literature, Kaplan and Stromberg (2001) summarize the findings of US studies, indicating the active role VCs play within their portfolio companies in terms of pre-investment screening, post-investment monitoring, financial contracting, and the implementation and modification of corporate governance mechanisms.

Based on these considerations, one can hypothesize that the presence of a VC backer has a systematic effect on the choice and nature of the lock-in agreements, including the type of expiry date. The involvement of VCs in the governance of the portfolio company is likely to reduce agency and informational problems. It may also be argued that VCs typically choose to invest in companies and industries that, *ex ante*, present greater potential for informational problems to arise. However, as noted earlier, a large part of VC investments in the UK are found in relatively mature and stable industries such as health care (that is, nursing homes rather than pharmaceutical R&D). Within the sample used in this study, 140 of the VC-backed IPO companies operated in industries outside the high-tech sector (as defined in Espenlaub et al., 2003).[10]

A priori we would expect VC backing to reduce informational asymmetries and agency problems in the portfolio companies relative to the *ex ante* levels (i.e. the levels prior to the VC investment). However, given the wide variations among VCs in terms of their experience and involvement in their portfolio companies, the residual or *ex post* levels of informational problems in VC-backed companies (i.e. the levels after allowing for the favourable effects of VC backing) are likely to differ substantially within the VC-backed sample. We would therefore expect that in some portfolio companies, VC backing is sufficient to resolve the informational issues. However, other VC-backed companies may still face relatively high residual informational problems, and will therefore have a greater need for further control mechanisms, such as the lock-in of existing shareholders, including VC backers, at the IPO stage.

VCs are repeat players in the IPO market who frequently have links with underwriters and a concern for maintaining their reputation capital with investors. We expect that as connected, repeat players in the IPO market, and as backers of companies affected (*ex ante*) by informational asymmetries, VCs are likely to push for agreements that effectively communicate information to outsiders. Thus we might expect them to shun complex and opaquely phrased agreements. They may also be associated with a greater standardization of agreements, if standardization is desirable to outside investors, for example because it reduces investors' information-processing cost of interpreting agreements.

To our knowledge, this study is the first to document the types of agreements adopted by VC backers of UK IPOs. Tables 6.2 and 6.3 give descriptive statistics on the types of agreements entered into by the directors and other shareholders of VC-backed and unbacked IPOs, while Table 6.4 presents corresponding figures for VC backers, directors and other shareholders for the VC-backed IPOs, allowing a direct comparison of the three groups of pre-IPO owners. The tables identify the numbers and percentages of agreements with simple and staggered expiry dates, and with dates defined in absolute terms or relative to the publication or announcement of a financial result. The tables provide two additional categories: 'Not clear' and 'Other'. The latter ('Other') comprises, among other things, agreements with expiry dates defined relative to an event such as the Annual General Meeting, and those using a combination of absolute and relative dates. The residual category ('Not clear') contains agreements that fail to specify a clear expiry date, or where the identity of the locked-in shareholders is impossible to determine, or both.

Comparing the agreements of directors in VC-backed and unbacked offerings in Table 6.2, there appears to be a somewhat greater frequency of simple, absolute, expiry dates among non-backed IPOs. This finding is clearly inconsistent with the joint hypothesis that absolute expiry dates are associated with low levels of informational asymmetries and agency problems, and that unbacked companies have relatively higher levels of informational problems than their VC-backed counterparts. However, as noted above, we expect the VC-backed sample to comprise companies with varying levels of (residual or *ex post*) information asymmetries and agency problems depending on whether the influence of the specific VC backers is sufficient to resolve the informational issues in the portfolio company. Another interpretation for the finding may focus on the relatively greater prevalence in the unbacked sample of the human-capital retention motive as the main driver for the decision to lock in directors' shareholdings. However, the same pattern is observed in Table 6.3 for the lock-ins of other shareholders, where the retention motive is unlikely to play much of a role.

These findings reject the hypotheses that VC backers push for expiry dates that are easy to monitor and anticipate by outsider investors, or that VC backing leads to a standardization of lock-in agreements towards the adoption of absolute dates (possibly driven by standard

Table 6.2   Lock-in agreements of the directors of VC-backed and non-VC-backed initial public offerings in the UK, 1992–98

Type of lock-in agreement	161 non-VC-backed		190 VC-backed	
	No. of agreements	%	No. of agreements	%

Panel A: Expiry relative to publication/announcement of financial results (including both simple and staggered lock-in agreements)

Simple publication of financial result	62	40.5	88	46.6
Staggered publication of financial result	18	11.8	30	15.9
Sub-total	80	52.3	118	62.4

Panel B: Absolute expiry date (including both simple and staggered lock-in agreements)

Simple absolute date	48	31.4	37	19.6
Staggered absolute dates	7	4.6	10	5.3
Sub-total	55	36.0	47	24.9

Panel C: Other types

Not clear	2	1.3	3	1.6
Other	16	10.5	21	11.1
Sub-total	18	11.8	24	12.7
Total no. of agreements	153	100.0	189	100

Notes:
This table shows the types of lock-in agreements entered into by directors. Lock-in agreements are classified in terms of the choice of absolute expiry dates or of expiry dates relative to financial announcements or publications

As one firm can have more than one type of lock-in agreement and as one firm may have no ownership by directors, the number of agreements may differ from the number of firms. In some firms, some directors are subject to lock-in agreements whereas other directors are not bound by such agreements. All percentages are expressed relative to the total number of contracts.

Staggered lock-in agreement: in addition to a first lock-in period during which sales are prohibited, these agreements include one additional period during which only a given percentage of the shares can be sold or during which sales can only happen with the consent of the sponsor

The category 'Other' (types of agreements) includes expiry dates combining absolute and relative dates, and dates relative to events such as an Annual General Meeting, among other things.

practices abroad, primarily in the USA). Instead, we observe that there are few differences between the agreements in VC-backed and unbacked offerings. The relatively small differences we do observe indicate that, in VC-backed IPOs, the directors and other shareholders are more likely to choose relative and 'other' types of expiry dates (where 'others' include combinations of one relative and one absolute date, and dates relative to events such as an AGM). However, as hypothesized above, we expect relative expiry dates to be associated

Table 6.3   *Other shareholders' lock-in agreements in VC-backed and non-VC-backed initial public offerings in the UK, 1992–98*

Type of lock-in agreement	161 non-VC-backed		190 VC-backed	
	No. of agreements	%	No. of agreements	%
Panel A: Expiry relative to publication/announcement of financial results (including both simple and staggered lock-in agreements)				
Simple publication of financial result	33	33.3	43	40.2
Staggered publication of financial result	10	10.1	8	7.5
Sub-total	43	43.4	51	47.7
Panel B: Absolute expiry date (including both simple and staggered lock-in agreements)				
Simple absolute date	38	38.4	26	24.3
Staggered absolute dates	5	5.1	6	5.6
Sub-total	43	43.4	32	29.9
Panel C: Other types				
Not clear	2	2.0	3	2.8
Other	11	11.1	21	19.6
Sub-total	13	13.1	24	22.4
Total no. of agreements	99	100.0	107	100.0

Notes:

This table shows the types of lock-in agreements by 'other shareholders', defined as those other than directors and venture capitalists. Lock-in agreements are classified in terms of the choice of absolute expiry dates or of expiry dates relative to financial announcements or publications.

As one firm can have more than one type of lock-in agreements and as one firm may have no ownership by other shareholders, the number of agreements may differ from the number of firms. In some firms, some shareholders are subject to lock-in agreements whereas other shareholders are not bound by such agreements. All percentages are expressed relative to the total number of agreements.

Staggered lock-in agreement: in addition to a first lock-in period during which sales are prohibited, these agreements include one additional period during which only a given percentage of the shares can be sold or during which sales can only happen with the consent of the sponsor

The category 'Other' (types of agreements) includes expiry dates combining absolute and relative dates, and dates relative to events such as an Annual General Meeting, among other things.

with relatively higher levels of informational problems. Thus it is likely that our result is driven by the subsample of VC-backed companies that still face high levels of residual or *ex post* information asymmetries and agency problems.

Comparing Tables 6.2 and 6.3, we find that directors are more likely to choose relative expiry dates than other shareholders irrespective of VC backing. This finding is confirmed

Table 6.4   *Lock-in agreements of the directors, venture-capitalists and other shareholders of VC-backed initial public offerings in the UK, 1992–98*

Type of lock-in agreement	Directors		Other shareholders		VC	
	No. of agreements	%	No. of agreements	%	No. of agreements	%
Panel A: Expiry relative to publication/announcement of financial results (including both simple and staggered lock-in agreements)						
Simple publication of financial result	88	46.56	43	40.19	52	42.28
Staggered publication of financial result	30	15.87	8	7.48	11	8.94
Sub-total	118	62.43	51	47.66	63	51.22
Panel B: Absolute expiry date (including both simple and staggered lock-in agreements)						
Simple absolute date	37	19.58	26	24.30	34	27.64
Staggered absolute date	10	5.29	6	5.61	4	3.25
Sub-total	47	24.87	32	29.91	38	30.89
Panel C: Other types						
Not clear	3	1.59	3	2.80	3	2.44
Other	21	11.11	21	19.63	19	15.45
Sub-total	24	12.70	24	22.43	22	17.89
Total number of agreements	189	100.00	107	100.00	123	100.00

Notes:
This table shows the types of lock-in agreements of directors, other shareholders and VC backers. 'Other shareholders' are those other than directors and venture capitalists. Lock-in agreements are classified in terms of the choice of absolute expiry dates or of expiry dates relative to financial announcements or publications.

As one firm can have more than one type of lock-in agreements and as one firm may have no ownership by other shareholders, the number of agreements may differ from the number of firms. In some firms, some shareholders are subject to lock-in agreements whereas other shareholders are not bound by such an agreement. All percentages are expressed relative to the total number of agreements. There are five firms without lock-in agreements for directors; 45 firms without lock-in agreements for the other shareholders; 71 firms without lock-in agreements for VC.

Staggered lock-in agreement: in addition to a first lock-in period during which sales are prohibited, these agreements include one additional period during which only a given percentage of the shares can be sold or during which sales can only happen with the consent of the sponsor.

The category 'Other' (types of agreements) includes expiry dates combining absolute and relative dates, and dates relative to events such as an Annual General Meeting, among other things.

further when we compare directors, venture capitalists and 'other shareholders' in Table 6.4. It is the directors who are more likely to choose relative expiry dates than either VCs or other shareholders, while VCs are somewhat more frequently associated with relative dates than other shareholders. This indicates that the choice of relative dates, especially for director lock-ins, is driven by informational considerations rather than retention motives. By contrast, the agreements of other shareholders, and their greater use of absolute expiry dates, appear to reflect concerns over price stabilization/pressure and the fact that other shareholders are less likely to have access to private information. Other shareholders may also be locked in to ensure the continued monitoring of management. Again, this would be consistent with a greater reliance on absolute expiry dates. In conclusion, we find evidence for an association between the use of relative expiry dates and the ease of access to private information of a given shareholder group.

However, the differences between VC backers and the two other groups of shareholders (directors and other shareholders) shown in Table 6.4 in terms of the proportions of different lock-in types are surprisingly small. There is clearly a much greater difference between the three groups (and certainly between directors and the two other groups) in terms of the decision whether to enter into a lock-in agreement or not (Table 6.1) than in terms of the choice of the contractual features of the agreement. This is an interesting finding suggesting that, once a shareholder agrees to lock in his/her shares, it is primarily the same set of – firm-specific – factors that drive the design of the lock-in agreements, with relatively little consideration for the characteristics of the shareholder. Specifically, the similarities in the agreements tend to ignore the fact that different types of shareholders are likely to differ significantly with respect to their relative costs of retaining shares and being locked in. For instance, the wealth of venture capitalists is much more diversified than that of directors and most individual shareholders, and therefore they bear a lower cost of retaining and locking in shares. On the other hand, venture capitalists are also under pressure from their fund investors to realize their investments within pre-determined periods.

Share ownership and the proportion of locked-in ownership

Below we examine the retained share ownership and two further characteristics of lock-ins: the proportion of shares locked in and the length of the lock-in period. The former is defined in terms of the fraction of locked-in shares as a proportion of the retained share ownership of the locked-in shareholders immediately after the IPO. The length of the lock-in period is the number of months from the first dealing date until the expiry of the lock-in agreement. The descriptive statistics are presented in Table 6.5. It should be noted that some of the statistics presented in the columns are calculated using smaller numbers of observations than those indicated at the top of the respective column. Where this is the case, the number of observations used to calculate a statistic is noted below the figure in brackets. These deviations occur because the statistics were calculated after excluding observations of zero (i.e. excluding firms without shareholdings by a given group of shareholders; and excluding firms where the proportion of the shareholdings of a given group that is locked in is zero).

Panel A of Table 6.5 presents descriptive statistics of the retained ownership of directors, venture capitalists and other shareholders immediately after the IPO, as disclosed in the prospectus. We define share ownership as beneficial ownership including any stakes held by immediate family members. Comparing the ownership structure of the 190 VC-backed and 161 unbacked firms, we find that the average stakes of other shareholders in unbacked companies are of similar magnitude to the combined holdings of venture capitalists and other shareholders of VC-backed companies. The most obvious difference between VC-backed and unbacked offerings is the substantially higher average retained shareholdings of

Table 6.5   Share ownership, proportion of locked-in shares and length of lock-in periods for directors, venture capitalists and other shareholders of VC-backed initial public offerings in the UK, 1992–98

Panel A: Average share ownership of the three shareholder groups (directors, venture capitalists and other shareholders) immediately after the IPO

Mean (Median) [Obs.]	(1) 161 non-VC-backed firms	(2) 190 VC-backed firms	(3) 119 firms VC locked in	(4) 71 firms VC not locked in	t-statistics for differences in means (medians)
Directors	34.34% (34.26%) [157; 4 firms are without ownership by directors]	19.91% (16.05%)	17.88% (13.87%)	23.29% (19.67%)	-2.198*** (-2.354)***
Venture capitalists (VCs)	/	19.53% (16.61%)	21.67% (18.83%)	15.50% (12.59%)	3.613*** (3.655)***
Other shareholders	32.66% (28.87%) [125; 36 firms have no other shareholders]	12.75% (6.97%) [143; 47 firms have no other shareholders]	16.93% (14.39%) [94; 25 firms have no other shareholders]	16.25% (10.36%) [49; 22 firms have no other shareholders]	0.270 (1.595)

Panel B: Shares locked in by directors, VCs and other shareholders as a proportion of their share ownership

	(1)	(2)	(3)	(4)	
Directors	96.54% (100.00%) [147] 10 firms have ownership but no lock-in agreements for directors	96.21% (100.00%) [185] 5 firms have ownership but no lock-in agreements for directors	96.31% (100.00%) 3 firms have ownership but no lock-in agreements for directors	96.07% (100.00%) [69] 2 firms have ownership but no lock-in agreements for directors	0.139 (0.000)
Venture capitalists (VCs)	N/A	N/A	95.82% (100.00%)	N/A	N/A

	29 firms have ownership but no lock-in agreements for other shareholders	29 firms have ownership but no lock-in agreements for other shareholders	10 firms have ownership but no lock-in agreements for other shareholders	35 firms have ownership but no lock-in agreements for other shareholders	
Other shareholders	92.00% (100.00%) [96]	88.97% (100.00%) [96]	92.91% (100.00%) [84]	70.07% (75.42%) [14]	2.576*** (2.772)***

Panel C: Length of directors', VCs' and other shareholders' lock-in periods (in calendar months). No. observations is same as in Panel B

Directors	15.0 (12.0)	12.7 (12.0)	13.2 (12.0)	12.0 (12.0)	1.629 (0.000)
Venture capitalists (VCs)	N/A	N/A	9.1 (8.5)	N/A	N/A
Other shareholders	13.1 (12.0)	10.3 (9.0)	9.9 (9.0)	13.0 (12.0)	-1.500 (-1.451)

Panel D: Length of directors', VCs' and other shareholders' lock-in periods (in calendar months) *for the subsample of agreements with absolute expiry dates*

Directors	18.5 (24.0) [57]	15.7 (12.0) [54]	16.0 (12.0) [41]	14.5 (12.0) [13]	0.894 (0.000)
Venture capitalists (VCs)	N/A	N/A	10.2 for 48 firms (10.0)	N/A	N/A
Other shareholders	14.2 (12.0) [43]	10.5 (9.5) [35]	10.0 (8.5) [30]	13.6 (12.0) [5]	-1.040 (-0.997)

Table 6.5   (continued)

Panel E: Length of directors', VCs' and other shareholders' lock-in periods (in calendar months) *for the subsample of agreements with relative expiry dates*

Directors	12.8 (12.0) [90]	11.5 (11.5) [131]	11.6 (11.75) [75]	11.4 (10.0) [56]	0.310 (2.294)***
Venture capitalists (VCs)	N/A	N/A	8.3 (8.0) [71]	N/A	N/A
Other shareholders	12.8 (12.0) [53]	10.1 (9.0) [63]	9.7 (8.5) [54]	12.6 (12.5) [9]	-1.09 (-1.475)

Notes:
The second column of the table provides descriptive statistics for the 161 non-VC-backed firms, the third column for the 190 VC-backed firms. The subsample of VC-backed firms is then further divided into two subsamples depending on whether at least one of the VC backers agrees to be locked in or not. The corresponding statistics are reported in the fourth and fifth columns. The figures in parentheses below the means are medians for the corresponding sample of observations. Where the number of observations used to calculate a specific figure differs from that noted at the top of the column, it is reported in brackets, below the median, along with a brief explanation for the deviation.

   Panel C: No. of observations as in Panel B.

   Panels D and E: No. of observations of agreements with absolute expiry dates shown in brackets. The sum of observations with absolute and relative dates equals the number of observations with lock-in agreements. Any difference between the latter and the total number of observations is due to the absence of shareholdings.

   The final, sixth, column reports the *t*-statistics for tests of equality of the subsample means (and in parentheses, for the medians) of the subsamples with and without locked-in VC (i.e. for the figures reported in the fourth and fifth columns). *** Indicates statistical significance at the 1% level.

directors of unbacked companies. This may reflect the positive signalling, certification and monitoring/disciplining effects of VC backing, and the resulting need for the insiders of companies without such backing to retain a larger stake in order to send a positive signal to investors, or to align insiders' interests with minority/outside shareholders.

An analogous argument can also explain the significant difference in the director holdings of VC-backed companies between the subsample of 119 offerings with locked-in VC backers and the 71 offerings where venture capitalists do not agree to a lock-in. Without the VC backer(s) being locked in, directors on average retain significantly higher stakes at the IPO. The decision of the VCs to agree to be locked in appears to be associated with VCs holding significantly higher average post-IPO share stakes (than those VCs who are not locked in), and it may be the positive effects of higher retained shareholdings of VCs that substitute for director shareholdings in addition to, or instead of, the VCs' lock-in agreements. In conclusion, we find indirect evidence for a positive signalling, certification and disciplining effect of VC backing of the IPO, in terms of the presence, the retained shareholdings and the willingness of the VC backer(s) to agree to lock-in clauses.

Panel B of Table 6.5 reports statistics on the shares locked in by directors, venture capital backers and other shareholders as a proportion of their retained post-IPO ownership. The first interesting observation is that directors typically lock in their entire shareholdings irrespective of the presence of venture capitalists or their agreement to lock-in clauses. This corresponds to the findings presented in Table 6.1 that, with very few exceptions (ten companies in the unbacked sample and five in the VC-backed one), executive directors are always locked in with the median locked-in proportion of shares being 100 per cent for all the subsamples in columns (1) to (4) of Table 6.5 (Panel B).

VC backers also typically lock in their entire shareholdings (with the median lock-in proportion being 100 per cent) as long as they enter into a lock-in agreement in the first place. Thus the principal decision taken by VCs (and to a lesser extent, by directors) appears to be whether or not to agree to a lock-in, rather than over the precise fraction of their holdings that is to be locked in, which is typically taken as 100 per cent.

The same appears to hold for other shareholders, at least in the absence of a VC backer (column (1)) or if the VC backer agrees to be locked in (column (3)). However, for the 71 offerings where the VC refuses to be locked in (column (4)), the other shareholders are not only reluctant to agree to a lock-in themselves, as reflected in the 35 offerings where other shareholders exist but are not locked in (see also Panel B of Table 6.1), but may also choose to lock in less than their entire share stakes, with the locked-in proportion averaging only 70 per cent. Interestingly, this reduced tendency to enter into lock-in agreements and the lower proportion of locked-in shareholdings of other shareholders if the VC backers fail to be locked in is not associated with any significant differences in the average post-IPO ownership of other shareholders as shown in Panel A of Table 6.5. The finding seems to confirm the interpretation of the results in Panel B of Table 6.1, that as expected the extent of informational asymmetries and agency problems differs widely among VC-backed companies, and that some of these companies perceive no need for locking in shareholders other than directors because the presence of VC backing and the lock-in of directors' stakes are sufficient to overcome any informational and agency problems.

The average lengths (in calendar months) of the lock-in periods of the three shareholder groups are reported in Panels C to E. For lock-in agreements specifying the expiry date as clear-cut ('absolute') calendar dates, it is simple to calculate the lock-in length as the difference between the expiry date and the first dealing date of the IPO. However, the issue is more complicated for expiry dates specified relative to a financial announcement or event. The method adopted here is to determine a lower bound by defining the length of the lock-in period as the number of calendar months from the first dealing date until the end of the financial year mentioned in the lock-in agreement (i.e. the financial year-end relating to the announcement of preliminary and final results, and the dates of Annual General Meetings). As this method ignores the delay between the financial year-end and the announcement or publication of results, it will typically result in an underestimate. This complicates the comparison of the lengths of lock-in periods with absolute and relative expiry dates. There-fore, in addition to the descriptive statistics for all lock-in periods in Panel C, we report figures separately for the two types of expiry dates in Panels D and E.

Examining the descriptive statistics in Panels C to E of Table 6.5, it appears that none of the differences in the lock-in periods between VC-backed offerings with locked-in VCs and those without are statistically significant. However, some of the differences across the four columns are likely to be of economic significance. The first interesting observation is that both directors and other shareholders agree to the longest lock-in periods in companies without VC backing. This is consistent with the view that VC backing is to some extent a substitute for lock-in agreements of directors and other shareholders. Among the sample of VC-backed offerings, the lock-in periods of directors are longer if the VC backers enter into lock-in agreements (column (4)) than if they do not (column (3)). However, for other shareholders (in VC-backed offerings) we observe exactly the opposite result: their lock-in periods are on average shorter if venture capitalists are locked in than otherwise. In fact, in VC-backed offerings where the VC backers are not locked in; other shareholders' average lock-in periods, in column (4), are of comparable length (both in terms of mean and median lengths) to those observed in unbacked offerings.

These results appear to suggest that VC lock-in agreements are complementary to the lock-ins of directors, but in relation to the lock-ins of other shareholders, they act as strategic substitutes. Viewed in conjunction with the results for other shareholders in Panel B of Table 6.1, it appears that in those VC-backed IPOs where the VC backers do not enter into lock-in agreements, other shareholders are often non-existent (in 22 offerings) or not locked in (in 35 offerings). However, in the small number of offerings (14) where other shareholders own shares and agree to be locked in while VC backers are not locked in, other shareholders lock in a smaller proportion of their holdings (on average 70 per cent; see Panel B of Table 5) but over a longer period (around three months longer, on average) than their counterparts in other VC-backed offerings.

Comparing Panels D and E, virtually all the averages in Panel D are higher than the corresponding figures in Panel E. At least to some extent, this is due to our definition of the lock-in periods with relative expiry dates, which necessarily results in underestimates of the true lengths. However, the fact that we observe similar patterns and results for both absolute and relative expiry dates (Panels D and E) suggests that this measurement error is unsystematic.

V. Conclusion

This chapter contributes to the limited body of literature on lock-in agreements in IPO companies. Using a sample of IPOs issued in the UK during 1992–98, we investigate whether VC backing of the IPO, and the existence, types and characteristics of agreements of VC backers to lock in their retained shareholdings, has any systematic association with the corresponding features of the lock-in agreements of company directors and other pre-IPO shareholders. The analysis is intended to shed light on the question whether the presence of VC backing, and the lock-in agreements of VCs, act as strategic complements or substitutes to the lock-in agreements of the directors and other shareholders. We also document the retained post-IPO share ownership of directors, VCs and other shareholders, and examine the associations between retained ownership, on one hand, and the presence of VC backing and the existence and contractual characteristics of the lock-in agreements of VCs, directors and other shareholders, on the other.

Examining the incidence and coincidence of lock-in agreements in our sample of IPOs, we find that while directors lock in their shares in almost all cases irrespective of the backing or lock-in of the VCs, the likelihood of VCs to agree to lock in their shares tends to go hand in hand with agreements of other shareholders to lock in their shares. This may indicate that some VC backed companies (around 17 per cent) perceive no need to lock in shareholders other than directors possibly because they have relatively low levels of *ex post* informational asymmetries and agency problems, while a greater percentage (43 per cent) locks in both the VCs and other shareholders. That is, the latter group uses the lock-ins of VCs and other shareholders as strategic complements to maximize the positive valuation effects of third-party certification, signalling and monitoring/disciplining.

Examining the lengths of the lock-in periods of the three shareholders groups, we find that the lock-in periods of directors and other shareholders are longest in companies without VC backing. This suggests that VC backing and the lock-in agreements of pre-IPO shareholders act as strategic substitutes. Moreover, in VC-backed offerings, the lock-in periods of directors are longer if the VC backers enter into lock-in agreements than if they do not. By contrast, for other shareholders (in VC-backed offerings) we observe exactly the opposite result: their lock-in periods are on average shorter if venture capitalists are locked in than otherwise. In fact, if the VC backers are not locked in, then other shareholders' lock-in periods are of comparable length to those observed in unbacked offerings. These results appear to suggest that VC lock-in agreements are complementary to the lock-ins of directors, but in relation to the lock-ins of other shareholders, they act as strategic substitutes. However, the latter result needs to be treated with caution because it is driven by a very small number of non-zero observations for other shareholders (14). In most VC-backed IPOs where the VC backers are not locked in, the other shareholders are either non-existent or also not locked in.

Examining the immediate post-IPO ownership of our sample companies, we find that the most obvious difference between VC-backed and unbacked offerings is the substantially higher average retained shareholdings of directors of unbacked companies. There is also a significant difference in the director holdings of VC-backed companies between offerings where the VC backers agree to lock-ins and those where they do not. If the VC backer(s) are not locked in, directors on average retain significantly higher stakes at the IPO. VCs with higher average post-IPO share stakes appear to be more likely to agree to being locked in than those with lower shareholdings. Thus there is some indirect evidence for the positive signalling, certification and monitoring/disciplining effects of VC backing and VC lock-ins. If there is either no VC backing, or the VC is not locked in, then the insiders (directors) need to compensate by retaining larger stakes after the IPO. However, we cannot disentangle the separate effect of higher post-IPO shareholdings of VC backers from the associated effect of VCs agreeing to lock in their shares because of the positive association of VC shareholdings and their likelihood to agree to lock in their shares.

Our examination of the contractual aspects of UK lock-in agreements confirms some of the findings of our earlier studies (Espenlaub et al., 2001, 2003). Specifically, we observe a much greater diversity than elsewhere in terms of the contractual features of lock-in agreements. This is apparent not only in the great degree of variation in the stipulated lengths of lock-in periods but also in the definition of the expiry dates. Our results confirm the widespread use in the UK of expiry dates specified relative to future financial announcements of the company (such as earnings announcements and publications of results).

Examining the effect of VC presence on the design of lock-in agreements, we find no evidence that VC backing leads to a significant difference in lock-in agreements in terms of the stipulation of expiry dates as either 'relative' or 'absolute' dates. Specifically, there is no evidence that VC backing results in the more frequent adoption of expiry dates that are relatively easy to monitor and anticipate by outsider investors (i.e. absolute expiry dates), or that VC backing leads to a standardization of lock-in agreements towards absolute dates for other reasons, possibly driven by the standardization of practices in the USA and elsewhere.

While we observe few differences between the agreements in VC-backed and unbacked offerings, the relatively minor differences we do observe indicate that in VC-backed IPOs the directors and other shareholders are more likely to choose relative and 'other' types of expiry dates (where 'others' include combinations of one relative and one absolute date, and dates relative to events such as an AGM). We argue that this may be due to the fact that relative expiry dates draw investors' attention to the future release of financial information, and that lock-in agreements with relative expiry dates are used to resolve the residual information asymmetries and agency problems in VC-backed companies where VC backing alone is insufficient as a control mechanism.

We find evidence for an association between the ease of access to private information of a given shareholder group and the relative tendency of the group to stipulate relative rather than absolute expiry dates in their lock-in agreements. Specifically, the group most likely to adopt relative expiry dates are directors, who typically have inside information, while those least likely (and conversely most likely to use absolute dates) are other, non-VC, shareholders. This indicates that the choice of relative dates appears to be driven by informational considerations, while the agreements of relatively less-informed shareholders appear to reflect concerns over price stabilization/pressure, or are intended to ensure the continued monitoring of management for a given period.

However, the differences between VC backers and the two other groups of shareholders (directors and other shareholders) in terms of the choice of different lock-in types are surprisingly small, and by contrast, there are much greater differences between the three groups in terms of the decision whether to enter into a lock-in agreement or not. This is an interesting finding suggesting that, once a shareholder agrees to lock in his/her shares, it is primarily the same set of *firm-specific* factors that drive the design of the lock-in agreements, with relatively little consideration for the characteristics of the shareholder.

Notes

1. We are grateful to Wissam Abdallah and Shuxing Yin for excellent research assistance.
2. However there is no restriction on the directors and major shareholders selling part or all of their pre-IPO holdings in the flotation.
3. Strictly speaking, in the USA, Rule 144 restricts sales after the IPO. However, Field and Hanka (2001, p. 475) report that only 4 per cent of IPOs out of a sample of 1948 firms are subject to this rule.
4. Before January 2000, certain UK companies such as mineral companies and scientific research based companies faced lock-in agreements. This regulation was, however, removed in 2000, and there are now no compulsory lock-in agreements for any type of firm wishing to list on the London Stock Exchange. For a detailed description of UK regulation of lock-in agreements, see Espenlaub et al. (2001).
5. This means that usually the locked-in shareholders agree not to sell for a period of 180 days after their firm goes public.
6. These new markets were part of EuroNM, an alliance of European stock markets intended to attract high-tech, high-growth firms. The German member to the alliance was the Neuer Markt and the French one the Nouveau Marché. For more details on these markets, see Goergen et al. (2003).
7. We exclude the IPOs on the Alternative Investment Market (AIM), which opened its doors in 1994. We exclude AIM firms because these firms are subject to different regulation than those on the Official List or the Unlisted Securities Market (USM). The latter market closed in 1994.
8. In comparing these figures, it needs to be borne in mind that the European 'new markets' represent growth segments designed for relatively younger and more speculative ventures. One would expect VC financing to be particularly prevalent among such companies. By contrast, the present study excludes the corresponding lower tier of the London Stock Exchange, the Alternative Investment Market (AIM).
9. Note that the shareholdings of family members of directors were added to directors' stakes.
10. Espenlaub et al. (2003) define companies as high-tech if they are included in the so-called techMARK segment of the London Stock Exchange, and comprise UK and international companies from a wide range of FTSE industrial sectors, whose success depends on technological innovation.

References

Bradley, D.J., Jordan, B.D. and Ha, Yi (2001), 'Venture capital and IPO lockup expiration: an empirical analysis', *Journal of Financial Research*, **24**: 465–92.

Brau, J.C., Lambson, V.E. and McQueen, G. (2003), 'Lockups revisited', Working paper, Brigham Young University.

Brav, A. and Gompers, P. (2003), 'The role of lockups in initial public offerings', *Review of Financial Studies*, **16**: 1–29.

Courteau, L. (1995), 'Under-diversification and retention commitments in IPOs', *Journal of Financial and Quantitative Analysis*, **30**: 487–517.

Espenlaub, S., Goergen, M. and Khurshed, A. (2001), 'IPO lock-in agreements in the UK', *Journal of Business Finance and Accounting*, **28**: 1235–78.

Espenlaub, S., Goergen, M., Khurshed, A. and Renneboog, L. (2003), 'Lock-in agreements in venture capital backed UK IPOs', in J. McCahery and L. Renneboog (eds), *Venture Capital Contracting and the Valuation of High Tech Projects*, Oxford: Oxford University Press.

Field, L. and Hanka, G. (2001), 'The expiration of IPO share lockups', *Journal of Finance*, **56**: 471–500.

Filatotchev, I. and Bishop, K. (2002), 'Board composition, share ownership and the underpricing of U.K. IPO firms', *Strategic Management Journal*, **23**: 941–55.

Goergen, M. (1998), *Corporate Governance and Financial Performance*, Cheltenham, UK and Northampton, USA: Edward Elgar.

Goergen, M., Khurshed, A., McCahery, J. and Renneboog, L. (2003), 'The rise and fall of the European new markets: on the short- and long-run performance of high-tech initial public offerings', in J. McCahery and L. Renneboog (eds), *Venture Capital Contracting and the Valuation of High Tech Projects*, Oxford: Oxford University Press.

Goergen, M., Renneboog, L. and Khurshed, A. (2004), 'Lock-in agreements in French Nouveau Marché and German Neuer Markt IPOs', mimeo, UMIST, University of Tilburg and University of Manchester.

Hellman, T. and Puri, M. (2000), 'The interaction between product market and financial strategy: the role of venture capital', *Review of Financial Studies*, **13**: 959–84.

Jain, B.A. and Kini, O. (2000), 'Does the presence of venture capitalists improve the survival profile of IPO firms?', *Journal of Business Finance and Accounting*, **27**: 1139–76.

Kaplan, S.N. and Stromberg, P. (2001), 'Venture capitalists as principals: contracting, screening and monitoring', *American Economic Review*, **91**(2): 426–30.

Leland, H.E. and Pyle, D.H. (1977), 'Informational asymmetries, financial structure and financial intermediation', *Journal of Finance*, **32**: 371–87.

Lerner, J. (1994), 'Venture capitalists and the decision to go public', *Journal of Financial Economics*, **35**: 293–316.

[7]

Insider retention and long-run performance in German and UK IPOs

Marc Goergen and Luc Renneboog

1. Introduction

Loughran et al. (1994) report that long-term underperformance, one of the three market anomalies associated with initial public offerings (IPOs), can be observed in a large number of different capital markets. We find supporting evidence of the bad long-run performance of IPOs for a sample of German and UK IPOs. Over the five years after the flotation the German and UK IPOs in our sample underperform the stock market by 14 per cent and 33 per cent respectively.

   The aim of this chapter is to explain this bad long-run performance in our sample by the agency problems caused when ownership by the original shareholders is diluted in the IPO. This study benefits from a unique set of ownership and performance data on British and German IPOs from 1981 to 1988. In a first stage, we explain differences in ownership retention by pre-IPO shareholders. Theoretical models explaining ownership retention after the IPO normally assume that the initial owners when taking their firm public face a trade-off between the benefits of keeping a concentrated holding and the benefits of selling out. Bolton and von Thadden (1998) argue that the original shareholder of a firm is subject to a trade-off between the benefits from a better portfolio diversification and the benefits from monitoring his firm. Kahn and Winton's (1996) model predicts that ownership retention by the initial shareholders will be lower in high-growth firms as these firms will need more outside financing than low-growth firms.

   In a second stage, we determine whether the often substantial changes in ownership by the pre-IPO shareholders after going public explain why IPOs underperform similar, non-issuing, companies in the long run. Two US studies have looked at the effect of different levels of ownership retention on IPO performance. Unfortunately, the studies find contradicting results. Jain and Kini (1994) argue that the bad long-term performance of IPOs can be partly explained by the decreasing ownership of managers immediately after the flotation. The decrease in managerial shareholdings following the IPO potentially leads to a worsening of managerial incentives. Jain and Kini find a positive link between operating performance and the proportion of shares retained by managers after the IPO. Mikkelson et al. (1997) record managerial ownership over the ten years following the IPO. Contrary to Jain and Kini (1994), Mikkelson et al. do not find any consistent relationship between performance and changes or levels of ownership at different points in time.

This contradicting evidence on the impact of agency costs on the performance of IPOs calls for further research on the issue. Jain and Kini (1994) use a univariate methodology whereas Mikkelson et al. (1997) use ordinary least squares (OLS). Both methodologies may be subject to biases. In addition, the OLS estimates may be inconsistent if there are omitted variables. We will use the advanced econometric techniques, developed by Blundell and Bond (1998), which do not suffer from such problems.

This paper analyses a unique set of ownership and performance data on British and German IPOs. It is interesting to study British and German IPOs for three reasons. First, the two countries are examples of the two main systems of corporate governance and corporate control, the relationship-based system and the market-based system. Second, studying German and UK IPOs, which are characterized by different levels of ownership retention by pre-IPO owners, provides an acid test for theoretical models explaining ownership retention. Third, if different degrees of ownership retention cause different levels of long-term profitability, the sample used in this study should provide significant results given a cross-sectional variation of ownership retention larger than the one in previous studies. Studying German and UK new issues should shed further light on the link between ownership and performance in IPOs.

The chapter is organized as follows. Section 2 reviews the theory relevant to the two parts of the chapter, the theory relating to ownership retention after the IPO and that relating to ownership and corporate performance. Based on these theories, we develop several hypotheses, which will be tested later in the chapter. Section 3 describes the data sample and the methodology used. Section 4 investigates whether institutional differences between Germany and the UK may cause the observed differences in the ownership retained by the initial shareholders in the two countries. Section 5 discusses the results for the econometric model explaining differences in the level of ownership retention and that explaining the bad long-run performance of IPOs by suboptimal levels of ownership retention by pre-IPO shareholders. Section 6 concludes.

2.   Theory and Hypotheses

The first part of this section reviews theories explaining the evolution of ownership in companies going to the stock market and formulates hypotheses which will be tested in Section 5. The second part of this section studies the link between long-term performance of IPOs and ownership structure.

2.1   Ownership retention

According to the pecking order theory of capital structure (Myers, 1984), firms prefer internal finance to external finance and debt finance to equity finance. Hence, if a firm grows at a steady and slow rate, it will be able to finance most of its investment decisions by retained earnings or debt. However, if the firm grows too fast, the founders may be forced to give their firm access to outside equity and consequently face a dispersion of control.

In Kahn and Winton's (1996) model the major shareholder has the choice between increasing his firm's value by monitoring the management, and trading on private information. Again, a higher demand for liquidity makes selling out more attractive than monitoring. Kahn and Winton (1996) as well as Bolton and von Thadden (1998) predict that the initial shareholders of firms with a high risk should sell off more rapidly than those of firms with a low risk. In the case of high-tech firms, once the wealth and liquidity constraints prevent shareholders from continuing to provide finance, these firms should go public and should end up with a large number of shareholders as their technologies are difficult to monitor for non-specialists.

Hypothesis 1: The faster the growth rate of the firm the lower the proportion of shares owned by the old shareholders six years after the IPO.

Hypothesis 2: The incumbent shareholders will divest rapidly out of high-risk firms as the portfolio diversification benefits from doing so are more important than the benefits from monitoring.

Furthermore, if the founder or her heirs still has a stake at the IPO, this may indicate that private benefits are still significant (e.g. the social status and power derived from controlling a listed company) and that control will only be slowly sold off. Founders may also have an important leadership role, especially in younger firms (Morck et al., 1988). Alternatively, Chung and Pruitt (1996) argue that the founder may still own a large proportion of the equity 'due strictly to historical circumstance'.

Hypothesis 3: If the founder or his heirs are still holding shares in the firm immediately before the IPO, the proportion of equity owned by the old shareholders six years after the flotation will be larger than the one in firms where the founder's family is no longer involved.

Finally, the possibility to issue non-voting shares may help pre-IPO shareholders to keep control long after the IPO by deviating from the one share-one vote rule.

Hypothesis 4: Non-voting preference shares help the initial shareholders to retain control a long time after the IPO.

Mello and Parsons (1998) argue that the IPO is only part of a lengthy process of going public and that firms go public in several stages until they achieve their optimal ownership. Our ownership data support this view. The most significant reductions in the ownership by pre-IPO shareholders occur during the first five years after the flotation. Hence we will attempt to explain ownership by the original shareholders six years after the IPO rather than explain ownership immediately after the IPO.

The regression of ownership retention, which we will be running, and the expected signs on the individual coefficients are as follows:

$$OLD6_i = \alpha - \beta_1 \cdot GROWTH_i - \beta_2 \cdot RISK_i + \beta_3 \cdot FOUNDER_i + \beta_4 \cdot PREF_i + \varepsilon_i \quad (7.1)$$

where:

$OLD6_i$ is the proportion of voting shares which are owned by the pre-IPO shareholders six years after the IPO or in the last year of listing, if the firm left the stock exchange before the six-year period.

$GROWTH_i$ is the average annual growth rate of total assets[1] calculated from the year of the IPO to year five. For some firms there may be missing data on total assets for some years. The growth rate was computed for all firms with a minimum of three years of consecutive data.

$RISK_i$ is a measure of the total risk of firm i. This is the standard-deviation of the monthly share return over the five years following the IPO (or less if the firm left the stock exchange before the end of this period).[2] Davis and Pointon (1984) and Leech and Leahy (1991) argue that given that large shareholders of firms do not hold diversified portfolios, they should be interested in total risk rather than only in undiversifiable risk (i.e. the CAPM-beta).

An alternative measure for risk, the standard deviation of the ratio of cash flow[3] to total assets over the period beginning with the year preceding the IPO and ending with the fifth year after the IPO (or less if the firm was delisted before the end of this period), was also used. However, this second measure was not significantly different from zero in the estimated regressions. As this measure is only based on a maximum of seven data points per firm, it is highly sensitive to outliers.[4]

$FOUNDER_i$ is a dummy which is 1, if the founder or his heirs own shares in firm i immediately before the IPO.

$PREF_i$ is a dummy which is 1, if firm i offers non-voting shares in the IPO.[5]

ε_i is white noise.

2.2   Long-term performance and ownership retention

In this subsection, we develop hypotheses which try to explain why IPOs perform worse than established, quoted companies during the five-year period following their flotation.

Jain and Kini (1994) as well as Mikkelson et al. (1997) argue that the reduction in ownership concentration after the flotation may increase agency problems within the firm and that this may have a negative effect on long-term performance.

Hypothesis 5: The lower the ownership retention by the pre-IPO shareholders the lower will be the long-term performance of the firm.

Mikkelson et al. (1997) argue that the higher the proportion of secondary shares (as opposed to primary shares) sold in the IPO, the worse will be the long-term performance of the firm after the flotation. They advance two reasons for this. The first is that the initial owners of the firm may time the IPO to follow a period of good performance, which should be followed by a decrease in performance. The second reason is that the secondary sale may reduce ownership concentration.

Hypothesis 6: The higher the fraction of secondary shares in the IPO the worse will be the long-run performance of the firm.

The regressions which will be estimated, as well as the expected signs on the coefficients of the explanatory variables, are as follows:

$$RETURN3_i = \alpha + \beta_1 \cdot OLD0_i + \beta_2 \cdot MAIN_i - \beta_3 \cdot SECONDARY\%_i + \varepsilon_i \qquad (7.2)$$

$$RETURN5_i = a + b_1 \cdot OLD0_i + b_2 \cdot MAIN_i - b_3 \cdot SECONDARY\%_i + e_i \qquad (7.3)$$

$$CF_{,ti} = \omega + \lambda_1 \cdot CF_{i,t-1} + \lambda_2 \cdot OLD_{i,t-1} + \gamma_i \qquad (7.4)$$

where:

$RETURN3_i$ and $RETURN5_i$ are the three-year buy-and-hold returns and the five-year buy-and-hold returns respectively, calculated from the end of month share prices and starting with the return on the second month. These returns were computed by using the market model with $\beta = 1$ and $\alpha = 0$. For Germany we used the broad-market DAFOX Index, as developed by Göppl and Schütz (1996) and as used by Ljungqvist (1997). The DAFOX Index is a value-weighted index. For the UK we used the HG 1000 Index, as used by Levis (1993).[6] Levis (1993) shows that the Hoare Govett index is a more appropriate performance benchmark for UK IPOs than the FTA Index, for example. The buy-and-hold return is the standard measure of performance used in the studies on the long-term performance of IPOs (see e.g. Ritter, 1991).

CF_i is a measure of performance based on accounting figures rather than share prices. It is the annual cash flow defined as the published profit gross of depreciation, interest, taxes and changes in provisions divided by the sum of the book values of equity and debt of the firm.[7] Both Jain and Kini (1994) and Mikkelson et al. (1997) use accounting measures of performance. We use cash flow rather than published earnings, as published earnings of German firms have been shown to be very conservative. Correia da Silva (1997) measures the published-profit per share and the cash-flow per share for a sample of 221 German firms over the period 1984–93. He finds that published profits make out only 25 per cent of the cash flow of the firm.

$OLD0_i$ is the proportion of voting shares which are owned by the pre-IPO shareholders immediately after the IPO. By definition, ownership by the old shareholders immediately before the IPO will be 100 per cent. Hence, $OLD0_i$ can also be interpreted as 100 per cent minus the change in ownership by old shareholders.

$MAIN_i$ is a dummy which is 1, if firm i was floated on the official market.

$SECONDARY\%_i$ is the proportion of secondary shares sold in the IPO.

ε_i, e_i and γ_i are error terms. The error term $\gamma_i = \eta_i + v_{i,t}$ where η_i is the fixed-effect term and $v_{i,t}$ is the intertemporal error term.

In addition, the following two dummy variables are used as alternatives to $SECONDARY\%_i$.

$PRIMARY\%_i$ is a dummy which is 1 if firm i offers only primary shares in the IPO.

$ONLY\_SEC_i$ is a dummy which is 1 if firm i offers only secondary shares in the IPO.

3.   Data Analysis

3.1   Characteristics of German and UK IPOs

Between 1981 and 1988 on average the German firms that went public were almost four times older (51 years) than the UK firms (14 years). However, the German IPOs were only twice as large as the UK IPOs (£113 million compared to £56 million of closing market capitalization of the first day of listing, adjusted for UK inflation[8]).

The industrial distribution of IPOs in Germany and the UK is also different.[9] Although the industry group with the highest proportion of IPOs is the same in both countries (the electricals, electronics and office equipment group), German IPOs seem to be concentrated in mature industries (e.g. mechanical engineering with 15.5 per cent of the total number of IPOs and motor components with 5.2 per cent), whereas about 29 per cent of the UK IPOs are in more cyclical industries (service agencies with 9.0 per cent, property with 6.0 per cent, leisure with 5.7 per cent, chain stores with 3.6 per cent and construction with 4.9 per cent).

Hence, in the UK there is a higher frequency of IPOs in the more cyclical service industries than in Germany. UK IPOs are also smaller than German IPOs in the same industry. Finally, UK IPOs seem to grow faster than German IPOs.

3.2   Data sources and methodology

Information on the identity of existing shareholders, their pre-IPO holdings and their post-IPO holdings, is obtained from the IPO prospectuses. The holdings of the old shareholders are tracked in subsequent annual reports as well as the London Stock Exchange Yearbooks for the UK and in the *Saling Aktienführer* for Germany. The period of study is 1981–88. It ends in 1988 to allow for at least six years of ownership data (not counting the year of the IPO).

Share prices were obtained from the Karlsruher Kapitalmarktdatenbank (KKMDB) and the London Share Price Database (LSPD). The characteristics of IPOs (age and industry) and the closing market capitalization for the first day of listing were obtained from Deutsche Börse AG and the London Stock Exchange. Accounting information was taken from the IPO prospectuses, company reports, the Extel Financial Company Research and Global Vantage CD-ROMs for both countries, and also from Datastream and the Extel Microfiches for the UK.

For both the UK and Germany only domestic[10] IPOs listed on the official and secondary markets are retained for this study, as data for lower market tiers are not normally available. More importantly, we also focus on German and UK IPOs whose largest shareholder of the voting equity at the IPO is an individual or a group of persons (e.g. a family or unrelated associates) to allow for a similar initial ownership.

A total of 764 British firms went public during 1981 and 1988, of which 284 were on the official market and 480 on the USM. From the 96 German IPOs, 51 were floated on the official market and 45 on the regulated market. Out of the 96 German IPOs, 80 were owned by individuals just before the IPO. Ownership could be tracked reliably for 61 of these 80 firms.[11]

We match the German IPOs by size to obtain a first UK sample. Firm size is measured by market capitalization in pounds, adjusted for UK inflation by the annual GDP deflators (base year 1985) provided by the IMF.[12] Each German company is matched with a UK company of the closest size.[13] The sample size for the size-matched sample is 54 as there was no close match for seven firms.[14]

We also perform an alternative matching by industry. For each German firm the industry description at the time of the IPO in the *Saling Aktienführer* is recorded. German firms are reclassified into the two-digit UK SE Groups. This is the industry classification used by the London Stock Exchange in its quarterly publications on new listings. Each group has a clear-cut definition of the companies that it contains.[15] The sample size for the industry-matched sample is 58 as three German IPOs could not be matched with UK IPOs.

The two German samples have 52 firms in common. However, the German sample matched by size includes two additional firms, which could be matched by size, but not by industry as there were no UK IPOs in these industries during the period. The German sample matched by industry contains six additional firms that could be matched by industry, but were so large that they could not be matched with UK IPOs of a similar size (and ownership).[16]

3.3 Data description

Table 7.1 records the number of shares held by the initial shareholders for the size sample for each of the seven years starting with the year of the IPO. Firms which are taken over before the end of the period of study are still reported in the table. They are reported as having a zero per cent ownership by the old shareholders from the year of the takeover. Similarly, firms which were taken private after the IPO are also reported over the whole period with a 100 per cent ownership by the original shareholders from the year of going private.

For a few firms which did not leave the sample, however, data on ownership were not always available for each of the individual years. In these cases, information available on the matched firm was still reported in the table. This and the bankruptcies/liquidations explain the slightly different sample sizes for some years.

Permanent reductions in sample size are due to bankruptcy and liquidation only. It is crucial to keep UK takeover targets within the sample, as in the UK investors who acquire more than 30 per cent of the equity of a firm must make an offer for the entirety of the equity,[17] and one cannot obtain majority control over a UK company without preventing it

Table 7.1   *Average proportion of voting rights held by the old shareholders in the size-matched sample*

Time after IPO	German firms		UK firms		t-statistic for difference in means
	Proportion held (%)	Sample size	Proportion held (%)	Sample size	
Immediately after the IPO	76.4	54	62.6	54	2.9***
1 year	73.6	54	51.3	54	4.6***
2 years	69.1	54	47.0	54	4.2***
3 years	63.8	54	38.7	52	4.2***
4 years	59.0	54	30.3	52	4.8***
5 years	51.2	54	25.5	52	4.1***
6 years	45.3	54	24.2	48	3.3***

Notes: If a company is taken over and leaves the stock exchange, it will be recorded as a company owned 100 per cent by its new shareholders from the year of the takeover. If a company is taken private by its original shareholders, it will be recorded as a company owned 100 per cent by its original shareholders. *** indicates that the difference in means is significantly different from zero at the 1% level.

Sources: For Germany, own calculations based on IPO prospectuses and *Saling*. For the UK, own calculations based on IPO prospectuses, company reports, London Stock Exchange and Extel.

from leaving the listing. As there is no compulsory tender offer in Germany, an investor can for example acquire a majority stake in a company and the company remains on the stock market.

For the UK size sample, 24 firms left the listing, of which 20 were taken over, two were taken private again by their initial shareholders, one was liquidated and one entered into receivership. For the UK industry sample, there was a total of 23 cancellations. Nineteen were taken over, two were liquidated and two went into receivership. Franks et al. (2001) report that on average every year 4 per cent of the listed UK companies are taken over. Hence the take-over rate among recently floated companies is higher (between 6.4 and 7.4 per cent) than that for the UK stock market. Conversely, only one German firm left the listing, the reason being a full take-over. This firm is both part of the sample matched by size and the sample matched by industry.

Table 7.1[18] shows that, first, the old shareholders of UK firms lose majority control on average after just two years whereas the old shareholders of German firms lose majority control only after five to six years. Second, although the fraction of the voting equity held by old shareholders in both German and UK firms decreases over time, ownership by the old shareholders is consistently higher in Germany than in the UK. The difference in means is consistently different from zero at the 5 per cent level.

Our UK results on ownership retention are very similar to those obtained by Brennan and Franks (1997), who find that for a sample of 69 IPOs in 1986–89 (excluding investment and closed-end mutual funds) old shareholders own 59.23 per cent immediately after the IPO.

Despite matching firms by size on one side, and matching firms by industry on the other side, there are still differences in ownership retention by the original shareholders. However, these differences may be less substantial than one may initially expect.

Three conclusions can be drawn from Table 7.1. First, even after adjusting for size and industry, the ownership of German and UK companies still evolves in a different way. Second, the pre-IPO shareholders of UK IPOs tend to retain a much smaller percentage of the equity than those of German IPOs. Third, old shareholders of British companies seem to transfer control to new shareholders much quicker than old shareholders of German firms.

Table 7.2 describes the characteristics of the size sample. UK firms seem to grow faster than German firms. The difference is economically significant but not statistically different from zero. UK firms also seem to have on average a significantly higher risk (significant at the 1 per cent level).

Although the proportion of German firms with the founder's family still being a shareholder at the time of the IPO is higher than that of UK firms, the difference in the proportions is not statistically different at any of the usual levels of confidence using a two-tailed Z-test for comparing two counts following a binomial distribution.

According to the three-year buy-and-hold returns, German firms perform better than UK firms. However, the five-year buy-and-hold returns suggest that there is no such difference in performance. The results found for the UK are similar to those found by Levis (1993): the long-term underperformance continues beyond the 36-month period after the flotation. More than a third of German IPOs comprise only primary shares. The proportion for the UK IPOs is only 11 per cent. The difference in the proportions is significant at the 10 per cent level. However, there is no significant difference between proportions of IPOs offering only secondary shares and the proportions of secondary shares offered in the IPO.

For the industry-matched sample[19] German firms are larger and less risky than their British counterparts. Again, UK firms seem to grow faster. The difference in the average growth between the two countries is, however, not statistically different from zero. At the time of the IPO, the founder or members of his family still hold shares in 93 per cent of the German companies, but hold shares in only 76 per cent of the British firms (the difference is significant at the 5 per cent level for the Z-test). A more striking observation is probably that British firms have on average a higher level of risk than German firms. There is no difference in the performance of British and German firms operating in the same industry.

The firms in the industry sample were also divided into four categories: capital goods (groups 11–35, 69), durable consumer goods (groups 36–43[20]), non-durable consumer goods (groups 45–65) and other groups (groups 66–76, excluding group 69 and group 86 (property)).[21] As previously noted, German companies are larger, except for firms producing durable consumer goods, and they are significantly smaller for firms in other groups. Although the average size of a German IPO in the former class is higher by more than 100 million pounds, the standard deviation of the size is about five times larger than for the UK. German companies in the capital goods groups, non-durable consumer goods and in other groups are on average less risky than their UK counterparts. However, there is no significant difference in means for the durable consumer goods class. Again, there is no significant difference in the share performance of British and German firms matched by industry.

The lower concentration of ownership by the initial shareholders after the IPO in UK firms, reported in Table 7.1, may be due to more stringent UK listing rules. It may be the

Table 7.2   The sample characteristics of the size-matched sample

Panel A: Mean, median, proportion = 1, minimum, maximum and sample size

Germany

Variable	GROWTH (%)	RISK (%)	FOUNDER	RETURN3 (%)	RETURN5 (%)	PRIMARY SHARES	SECONDARY SHARES	Proportion of secondary shares (%)
Mean	17.8	9.1	–	6.3	–14.2	–	–	38.3
Median	13.5	9.0	–	0.4	–13.1	–	–	29.2
Proportion =1	–	–	92.0	–	–	38.9	14.8	–
Min	–2.3	4.8	–	–85.5	–186.3	–	–	0.0
Max	75.5	15.9	–	120.9	92.7	–	–	100.0
Sample size	49	53	51	53	53	54	54	54

UK

Variable	GROWTH (%)	RISK (%)	FOUNDER	RETURN3 (%)	RETURN5 (%)	PRIMARY SHARES	SECONDARY SHARES	Proportion of secondary shares (%)
Mean	23.7	12.8	–	–32.9	–33.1	–	–	49.1
Median	18.7	12.9	–	–24.1	–25.0	–	–	50.0
Proportion =1	–	–	84.9	–	–	11.3	9.4	–
Min	–20.5	4.8	–	–261.8	–363.5	–	–	0.0
Max	111.2	22.4	–	103.5	165.7	–	–	100.0
Sample size	44	53	53	53	53	53	53	53

Panel B: t-statistics for the difference in means and Z-statistics for difference in proportions

GROWTH (%)	RISK (%)	FOUNDER	RETURN3 (%)	RETURN5 (%)	PRIMARY SHARES	SECONDARY SHARES	Proportion of secondary shares (%)
1.111	−5.645***	1.157	2.985***	1.107	3.283*	0.852	−1.630

Notes: Based on a sample of German and UK IPOs matched by market capitalization. The sample is unbalanced, i.e. if a firm leaves the listing before the sixth year after the flotation, then the shareholder for the last year of the listing is reported. Growth is the average annual growth rate of total assets. *FOUNDER* is a dummy variable which equals 1 if the founder or her family own shares in the firm at the time of the IPO. *RISK* is the standard deviation of the monthly share return over the five years following the IPO (or less if the firm was delisted before the end of this period). *PRIMARY SHARES* and *SECONDARY SHARES* are dummy variables which equal 1 if the firm offers only primary shares and secondary shares in the IPO respectively. *RETURN3* and *RETURN5* are the three-year buy-and-hold return and the five-year buy-and-hold return calculated using the market model with $\beta = 1$ and $\alpha = 0$. *** Significant at the 1% level for the two-tailed test. * Significant at the 10% level for the two-tailed test.

case that a UK firm asking to be admitted to the stock market may have to float a larger proportion of its equity than a German firm. The following section investigates whether this is really the case.

4.   UK and German Listing Conditions and Issuing Procedures

Table 7.3 summarizes the listing requirements applying to the different market tiers in the UK and Germany. The conditions relating to age, size and dispersion of equity are almost identical. The listing rules for both countries are very similar and cannot therefore be the reason for different sizes, industries and ages of IPOs in both countries.

In both Germany and the UK ordinary shares and non-voting preference shares can in principle be admitted to the listing. In both countries, ordinary shares carry one vote per share and preference shares do not normally confer the right to vote at the annual sharehold-ers' meeting. In practice, however, UK firms rarely have outstanding non-voting shares and, in contrast to German firms, if such shares exist, they are normally owned by the founders rather than by outside investors. Brennan and Franks (1997) state that 'investing institutions and the London Stock Exchange have discouraged the issuance of non-voting shares and other devices for discriminating against different shareholders'. Among all the UK firms in the two samples, only two firms had preference shares. In both cases, the preference shares were issued prior to the IPO and were not sold in the IPO. There was a total of 27 German IPOs with non-voting preference shares.[22]

5.   Results

Section 5.1 contains the results for the regression explaining ownership by the pre-IPO shareholders six years after the IPO. Section 5.2 reports the results for the regression explaining the long-run performance.

5.1   The ownership retention model

Table 7.4 displays the results from the OLS estimation of equation (7.1). The first two columns and the last two columns report the results for size and industry samples respec-tively. Each regression is run on the pooled German and UK firms. The pooled samples include all the firms, even those that were taken over or left the stock market for another reason before the end of the six-year period.

The regressions in the first and third columns were estimated using the LIMDEP software and the OLS stepwise regression technique. The four variables from equation (7.1) were forced into the regression as well as the differential intercept, *COUNTRY*.[23] Additional variables were all the variables picking up any differential effect for the German IPOs (e.g. the differential slope coefficient on *GROWTH*, measuring any additional effect of the vari-able for the German firms). The use of the stepwise procedure ensures that the OLS regressions do not include any variables whose explanatory power is low or non-existent. First, it is interesting to note that the differential intercept *COUNTRY* is not significantly

Table 7.3   Listing requirements for the London Stock Exchange and the German Stock Exchanges

Requirements	UK			Germany		
	Official market	USM	Third market	Amtlicher Handel	Geregelter Markt	(Ungeregelter) Freiverkehr
Legal form	Public limited company	Idem	Idem	AG or KGaA	Idem	Idem
Accounts/age	At least three years of published accounts	Zero, if firm has a marketable product/process; three years, otherwise		Age of at least three years	Nil	Nil
Management	No material management change during period covered by accounts					
Transferability of securities	Securities must be freely transferable	Nil		Nil	Nil	Nil
Size	At least £700 000 of market capitalization[a]		Nil	At least DM2.5 million of market capitalization	At least DM500 000 of total equity must be freely available to the market	Nil
Dispersion of shares	At least 25% of the class of shares where application for listing has been made[b]	At least 10% of the class of shares	Nil, but 10% recommended	At least 25% of the class of shares	Refer to size	Nil

Notes:

a   The market capitalization refers to the total market value of all securities to be listed. Securities of lower value may be admitted if the LSE believes that there will be an 'adequate market'.

b   The 'public' does not include directors as well as connected persons and shareholders holding at least 5 per cent of the shares.

Source: Goergen (1998).

Table 7.4   *Results from the ownership retention model for the pooled sample matched by size and the pooled sample matched by industry (p-values in parentheses)*

Model	Size		Industry	
	(1)	(2)	(3)	(4)
Constant	0.556	0.518	0.376	0.321
	(0.000)	(0.000)	(0.002)	(0.002)
COUNTRY	−0.041	−	−0.069	−
	(0.648)		(0.432)	
GROWTH	−0.298	−0.289	−0.105	−0.099
	(0.051)	(0.009)	(0.344)	(0.144)
FOUNDER	0.079	0.070	0.273	0.250
	(0.458)	(0.452)	(0.004)	(0.000)
PREF	0.272	0.253	0.233	0.203
	(0.004)	(0.010)	(0.009)	(0.033)
RISK	−2.122	−1.893	−2.094	−1.689
	(0.036)	(0.022)	(0.044)	(0.045)
R^2	0.239	0.237	0.232	0.226
$R^2_{adjusted}$	0.191	0.199	0.190	0.193
p-value of F-statistic	0.001	0.000	0.000	0.000
Sample size	85	85	98	98

Notes: The dependent variable is *OLD6*, i.e. the fraction of voting shares owned by the old shareholders six years after the IPO. *COUNTRY* is a dummy which is set to 1 if the firm is German. *GROWTH* is the average annual growth rate of total assets. *FOUNDER* is a dummy variable which equals 1 if the founder or her family own shares in the firm at the time of the IPO. *PREF* is a dummy which is equal to 1 if the firm has non-voting shares. *RISK* is the standard deviation of the monthly share return over the five years following the IPO (or less if the firm was delisted before the end of this period. The *t*-statistics are robust for heteroscedasticity. *p*-values are in parentheses.

different from zero at any of the usual levels of confidence. Second, none of the differential slope coefficients were retained by the stepwise algorithm. This suggests that differences in the levels of the explanatory variables pick up all the differences in ownership retention between Germany and the UK.

Columns 2 and 4 are standard OLS regressions run on the four variables underlying the four above conjectures.

Except for the variables *FOUNDER* in the regression run on the pooled size sample and *GROWTH* in the regression run on the pooled industry sample, the coefficients on the four explanatory variables are significantly different from zero at the 5 per cent level of confidence or better.

The results for the size sample suggest that the higher a company's growth rate, the less will be the ownership retained by the pre-IPO shareholders six years after the IPO. The results for the industry sample are less strong (at the 20 per cent level at best).[24] This is probably not surprising as firms in the same industry should have a similar growth rate and the growth rate should not be a strong explanatory variable for the different levels of ownership retention. Firms of a similar size, but operating in different industries, may have very different growth rates and growth should be better at explaining differences in insider retention.[25]

In general, we cannot reject Hypothesis 1. Alternative specifications of the growth variable were also used, such as a dummy variable set to 1 if the growth rate exceeds a given threshold (e.g. 20 per cent) and a dummy variable set to 1 if the company's growth is higher than the average growth. However, none of these alternative specifications gave any significant results.[26]

Initial owners of high-risk firms will retain less ownership of their firms than those of low-risk firms. The coefficient on *RISK* is in a consistent way significantly different from zero at the 5 per cent level of confidence. We do not reject Hypothesis 2. Our results corroborate the findings by Demsetz and Lehn (1985) and Leech and Leahy (1991) on the link between ownership and risk.

Ownership of voting shares is also higher if the founder or his family were still holding shares at the time of the IPO. This conclusion is always true for the German firms, but only true for the UK firms matched by industry. We do not reject Hypothesis 3. This result is consistent with the result found by Chung and Pruitt (1996).

There is also a higher ownership retention if the firm issued non-voting preference shares. The coefficient on *PREF* is significantly different from zero at the 1 per cent or 5 per cent level of confidence. We retain Hypothesis 4.

Our findings suggest that post-IPO ownership by the original shareholders depends on a series of corporate characteristics and other factors. These findings are consistent with those of Denis and Denis (1994). Denis and Denis compare majority-owned firms with widely held ones. They find that firms with a majority ownership have a higher family involvement, tend to have dual-class shares, and that firms with a dispersed ownership tend to have a higher variance of the residual from the market model. Denis and Denis do not include a growth rate in their model.

5.2   Long-term performance and ownership retention

In addition to the variables in Equations (7.2) and (7.3), we include the variable *MAIN* into the regressions, a dummy variable, which is set to one if the firm was floated on the official market and set to zero if it was floated on the second market tier. The estimation technique is similar to the one used for the ownership retention model. Again, a stepwise regression technique is used, forcing the ownership retention variable as well as the variables *COUNTRY*, *MAIN* and *SECONDARY%* into the regression and suggesting the differential slope coefficients as well as *PREF* and *FOUNDER* as possible additional regressors.

Table 7.5 contains the results for the buy-and-hold return and *OLD0*, i.e. ownership retention by the original shareholders immediately after the IPO. At the 10 per cent level of confidence, none of the coefficients on *OLD0* is significantly different from zero. However, there is some evidence for both models that a higher proportion of secondary shares offered in the IPO is connected with a worse long-run performance. The link exists for the UK firms, but not for the German firms: the differential slope coefficient for the German firms is of the opposite sign and of a similar magnitude in absolute terms as the general coefficient on

Table 7.5   *Long-term performance model for the pooled sample matched by size and the pooled sample matched by industry (p-values in parentheses)*

Model	Size		Industry	
	RETURN3	*RETURN5*	*RETURN3*	*RETURN5*
Constant	0.266	−0.106	0.380	0.386
	(0.064)	(0.708)	(0.045)	(0.096)
COUNTRY	0.009	0.281	0.217	−0.156
	(0.971)	(0.132)	(0.171)	(0.421)
OLD0	−0.376	−0.486	−0.547	−0.325
	(0.274)	(0.278)	(0.155)	(0.409)
MAIN	0.083	0.207	−0.169	−0.156
	(0.541)	(0.259)	(0.270)	(0.409)
SECONDARY%	−0.783	−0.099	−0.094	−0.131
	(0.014)	(0.709)	(0.665)	(0.624)
SECONDARY%_D	0.921	–	–	–
	(0.028)			
R^2	0.165	0.043	0.033	0.023
$R^2_{adjusted}$	0.122	0.003	−0.002	−0.013
p-value of *F*-statistic	0.003	0.367	0.447	0.633
Sample size	102	102	113	113

Notes: The dependent variable is the buy-and-hold return over the first three years following the IPO or the buy-and-hold return over the first five years following the IPO respectively. *COUNTRY* is a dummy which is set to one if the firm is German. *OLD0* is the percentage of the voting equity owned by the initial shareholders immediately after the IPO. *MAIN* is a dummy variable which equals one if the firm was floated on the main market tier. *SECONDARY%* is the proportion of the secondary shares sold in the IPO. *SECONDARY%_D* is *SECONDARY%* multiplied by *COUNTRY*. The *t*-statistics are robust for heteroscedasticity. *p*-values are in parentheses.

SECONDARY%. In general, the models explaining long-term performance of IPOs by ownership retention have no or only a negligible explanatory power, as the R^2, $R^2_{adjusted}$ and the *F*-test suggest. It is also interesting to note that the stepwise procedure did not retain *PREF* as an explanatory variable. This suggests that non-voting shares are not in general a means to expropriate the new shareholders in the firm. This is in line with the results found by Bergström and Rydqvist (1990). They find that for a sample of Swedish firms the existence of non-voting shares cannot normally be associated with expropriation of small shareholders.

Table 7.5 displays only one of the many specifications that were tested. Alternative specifications included variables such as the categories (e.g. firms that offer less than 25 per cent of the total equity (voting plus non-voting equity) in the IPO) and the natural logarithm of one plus the fraction of share capital offered in the IPO as used by Ljungqvist (1997), as well as quadratic specifications of the ownership variables defined at the beginning of this section. Other models regressed the buy-and-hold return for years 4–5 on ownership in year 1, 2 and 3 respectively without any significant results. None of these alternative models suggests a link between long-run performance and ownership retention.

Table 7.6   *Performance model with cash-flow ratio (CF) and the total stake held by all pre-IPO shareholders for the size sample*

Constant	0.053
	(0.331)
COUNTRY	0.034
	(0.562)
$CF1_{i,t-1}$	0.638
	(0.000)
$CF1\_D_{i,t-1}$	−0.221
	(0.313)
$Told_{i,t-1}$	0.024
	(0.762)
$Told\_D_{i,t-1}$	0.024
	(0.791)
p-value of m_1	0.000
p-value of m_2	0.207
p-value of Sargan test (d.f.)	0.664
	(46)
Observations	265

Notes: $CF_{i,t}$ is the dependent variable in each model. It is the cash flow adjusted for depreciation, interest, taxes and changes in provisions divided by the book values of equity and debt. *COUNTRY* is the differential intercept, COUNTRY is set to 1 if firm i is German. $Told_{i,t}$ is the total percentage of the voting equity held by the pre-IPO shareholders. Variable names marked with a D are the differential slope coefficients for German firms. The model contains time dummies and industry dummies. m_1 and m_2 are tests for the absence of first-order and second-order correlation in the residuals respectively. These test statistics are asymptotically distributed as $N(0,1)$ under the null of no serial correlation. The Sargan test statistic is a test of the over-identifying restrictions, asymptotically distributed as $\chi^2(k)$ under the null of valid instruments, with k degrees of freedom reported in parentheses. The model is a linear system of first-differenced and levels equations. The instruments are levels of *CF1*, *CF1_D*, *Told*, and *Told_D* dated t–2 to t–99 for the differenced equations and first differences dated t–1 for the levels equations. p-values, based on standard errors asymptotically robust to heteroscedasticity, are reported in parentheses.

Table 7.6 reports the results for model (4), the model based on the accounting measure of performance. The model is a dynamic panel data model, estimated using the generalized method of moments (GMM) in first differences and in levels as developed by Blundell and Bond (1998). Contrary to OLS, this estimation method provides consistent estimates if there are unobserved effects. The method uses a system of equations. The system consists of the equations in levels as well as the equations in first differences. The estimation method uses the lagged differences of the dependent variable and the independent variables as instruments for the equations in levels. In addition, it uses the lagged levels of the dependent variable and the independent variables as instruments for the equations in first differences. For model (4) we use a similar methodology to one of models (2) and (3), i.e. we use a differential intercept, *COUNTRY*, and differential slope coefficients.

Table 7.6 shows that for the size sample there is no evidence that past ownership by the initial shareholders influences current performance. The results for the industry sample are similar. This is consistent with the results found by Mikkelson et al. (1997) on US IPO data.

Ljungqvist (1997) finds a negative link between ownership retention and long-run performance for a sample of German IPOs. However, his sample includes several privatizations and spin-offs, and firms are not of a homogeneous initial ownership. Similarly to Jain and Kini (1994), we split the sample into firms whose ownership retention exceeds the sample median and those whose ownership retention is below the median. Again, there is no evidence of a link between performance and ownership retention.[27]

The likely absence of a link between long-run performance in IPOs and ownership characteristics is a very interesting result, especially in the context of the results obtained from the estimation of the ownership retention model. All in all, the results suggest that ownership retention depends on corporate characteristics such as risk and growth rate, and that firms choose an ownership structure, which maximizes their firm value. These results are consistent with an increasing amount of studies using different samples and estimation techniques and that also do not find a link between financial performance and ownership characteristics (see e.g. Agrawal and Knoeber, 1996; Kole, 1996 and Loderer and Martin, 1997).

6. Conclusion

This study has found that German IPOs are in more mature industries than UK IPOs. They are also older and larger than their UK counterparts. Analysing ownership retention after the IPO as well as its evolution during subsequent years shows that the initial shareholders of UK IPOs lose control much quicker than those of German IPOs and that the fraction of shares owned by new shareholders is significantly higher in UK IPOs at all times.

Differences in ownership retention can be explained by corporate characteristics such as the firm's growth rate, its total risk, the involvement of the founder as well as the issue of non-voting shares. This suggests that results obtained from studies on corporate performance and ownership that have assumed ownership to be exogenous may suffer from serious econometric biases.

This study sheds further light on the link between ownership by the initial shareholders and financial performance. Contrary to existing studies, the study uses advanced econometric techniques, which provide consistent estimates even if there are omitted variables. We find that the bad long-term performance of IPOs cannot be explained by the observed dilution of ownership by the original shareholders after the IPO and possible agency conflicts caused by this dilution. Our findings are consistent with Mikkelson et al. (1997), but are in direct contradiction with Jain and Kini (1994).

Notes

1. Accounting figures are taken from the consolidated company accounts, if available.
2. Share price returns are adjusted for dividends, scrip issues and rights issues, and are log-returns.
3. Cash flow was defined as the published profits gross of tax and interest (before any dividend payments on both ordinary and preference shares) + depreciation of tangibles + amortization of intangibles + change in pension provisions (for German firms only) + deferred and future tax (for UK firms only) + change in other provisions (for German firms only) + change in temporar-

ily tax-exempt reserves (for German firms only). Data sources for the accounting data were the company reports for Germany and Datastream, the company reports, Extel and the LSE microfiches for the UK.

4.   The measure of risk retained is an *ex post* measure of risk (relative to the IPO) rather than an *ex ante* measure. However, Pagano et al. (1998) argue that if the relevant decision makers have rational expectations, *ex ante* data as well as *ex post* data should give consistent answers.

5.   Instead of this dummy variable, an alternative model was estimated using the proportion of non-voting shares in the equity. The results are not substantially different from those obtained using PREF. Among our sample firms only German firms offer non-voting preference shares in their IPO.

6.   Note that *OLD6*, *RISK*, *RETURN3* and *RETURN5* are expressed as percentages.

7.   We also used an alternative version of this cash flow ratio, using the same cash flow figures, but using the market value of equity and the book value of debt in the denominator. This measure is similar to the one used by Healy et al. (1992). The results from estimating the model were not substantially different.

8.   These amounts are in constant 1985 pounds sterling.

9.   Section 3.3 provides further detail on the industrial classification.

10.   For the UK, given the different legislation, we do not retain companies registered in the Channel Islands.

11.   For most of the other IPOs, the identity of the shareholders was available, but not the exact size of their holdings.

12.   As several German firms in our sample have dual class shares of which one class is not listed, the market capitalization for these firms was obtained by multiplying the total number of shares by the market price of the listed class.

13.   The average difference in size is 2.7 per cent. The median is 0.5 per cent and the standard deviation is 4.7 per cent.

14.   A close match is defined as a match within a ±25 per cent difference in size.

15.   Groups 27 (Misc. Mechanical Engineering) and 28 (Machine and Other Tools) were merged. Groups 19 (Electricals), 35 (Electronics) and 69 (Office Equipment) were also merged as groups 35 and 69 did not exist at the beginning of the 1980s and computer and software manufacturers were first assigned to group 19, then to group 69 and later only to group 35.

16.   It may be argued that another matching based on the age of firms should have been performed. However, a reasonable match (± two years of difference) could only be found for about 19 German firms. Similarly, we tried to match firms simultaneously by size and industry. However, again for more than three quarters of the firms no match could be found.

17.   This obligation does not apply to the incumbent shareholders whose holding after the IPO still exceeds 30 per cent. See Weinberg and Rabinowitz (1989), paragraphs 3-939, 3-946, 3-952.

18.   A table similar to Table 7.1, but based on the industry sample, is available from the author on request.

19.   A table similar to Table 7.2 is available from the author for the industry sample.

20.   Group 44 does not exist in the classification.

21.   Other groups comprises plastic and rubber fabricators (66), pharmaceutical products (67) and agencies (75) as well as groups 68–74, which were however not represented by firms in our sample.

22.   Hay and Morris (1984) argue that in the UK inheritance taxes often force families owning large unlisted firms to sell off a substantial part of the equity on the stock market at the death of the founder to meet the tax liability. Inheritance taxes may be significantly higher in the UK than in Germany. If this is true, then when the founder of a UK company dies, his heirs may be forced to sell a much more important part of the equity to meet the tax bill than is the case for a German company. Goergen (1998) analyses inheritance tax rates applying to an average-sized German IPO and an average-sized UK IPO over the period 1980–95. His findings suggest that the German IPO would have faced a tax charge of 35 per cent of its value whereas the UK IPO would have faced a tax charge ranging from 20 to 37.5 per cent of its value. Thus inheritance

taxes incurred by families owning large companies in the UK have been on average lower than those incurred by families in Germany.

23. Dropping the differential intercept *COUNTRY* from the list of forced variables does not influence the results in columns (1) and (3) in Table 7.4.

24. Due to the nature of accounting figures (past and present price data), time dummies were also included in the model. This did not change the significance of the coefficient on *GROWTH*.

25. The significance of the coefficient on *GROWTH* does not change in both models, if a size variable and industry dummies are included.

26. A variable measuring company size (market capitalization at the end of the first day of trading) was also added to the models run on the industry. However, this did not improve the significance of the coefficient on *GROWTH*.

27. Industry dummies were also added to the model run on the pooled size sample and a size variable was added to the industry sample. This did not, however, affect the results in any substantial way.

References

Agrawal, A. and Knoeber, C. (1996), 'Firm performance and mechanisms to control agency problems between managers and shareholders', North Carolina State University, mimeo.

Bergström, C. and Rydqvist, K. (1990), 'Ownership of equity in dual-class firms', *Journal of Banking & Finance*, **14**, 255–69.

Blundell, R. and Bond, S. (1998), 'Initial conditions and moment restrictions in dynamic panel data models', *Journal of Econometrics*, **87**, 115-43.

Bolton, P. and von Thadden, E.-L. (1998), 'Liquidity and control: a dynamic theory of corporate ownership structure', *Journal of Institutional and Theoretical Economics*, **154**(1), 177–211.

Brennan, M. and Franks, J. (1997), 'Underpricing, ownership and control in initial public offerings of equity securities in the UK', *Journal of Financial Economics*, **45**, 391–413.

Chung, K. and Pruitt, S. (1996), 'Executive ownership, corporate value, and executive compensation: A unifying framework', *Journal of Banking & Finance*, **20**, 1135–59.

Correia da Silva, L. (1997), 'Corporate control and financial policy. An empirical investigation of dividend policy in Germany', unpublished DPhil thesis, University of Oxford.

Cutik, U. (1988), 'Aus der Sicht der Banken. Auch bei verändertem Umfeld an die Börse', in H. Herdt, E. Padberg and D. Walther (eds), *Der Gang an die Börse*, Frankfurt am Main: Verlag Börsen-Zeitung, 16–27.

Davis, E. and Pointon, J. (1984), *Finance and the Firm*, Oxford: Oxford University Press.

Demsetz, H. and Lehn, K. (1985), 'The structure of corporate ownership: causes and consequences', *Journal of Political Economy*, **93**, 1155–77.

Denis, D.J. and Denis, D.K. (1994), 'Majority owner-managers and organizational efficiency', *Journal of Corporate Finance*, **1**, 91-118.

Franks, J., Mayer, C. and Renneboog, L. (2001), 'Who disciplines the management of poorly performing companies?', *Journal of Financial Intermediation*, **10**, 209–48.

Goergen, M. (1998), *Corporate Governance and Financial Performance. A Study of German and UK Initial Public Offerings*, Cheltenham: Edward Elgar Publishing.

Göppl, H. and Schütz, H. (1996), 'Die Konzeption eines Deutschen Aktienindex für Forschungszwecke (DAFOX)', Discussion Paper No. 162, University of Karlsruhe.

Hay, D. and Morris, D. (1984), *Unquoted Companies: Their Contribution to the United Kingdom Economy*, London: Macmillan.

Healy, P., Palepu, K. and Ruback, R. (1992), 'Does corporate performance improve after mergers?', *Journal of Financial Economics*, **31**, 135–75.

Jain, B. and Kini, O. (1994), 'The post-issue operating performance of IPO firms', *Journal of Finance*, **49**, 1699–726.

Kahn, C. and Winton, A. (1996), 'Ownership structure, liquidity demand, and shareholder monitoring', University of Illinois and Northwestern University, mimeo.

Kole, S. (1996), 'Managerial ownership and firm performance: incentives or rewards?', *Advances in Financial Economics*, **2**, 119–49.

Leech, D. and Leahy, J. (1991), 'Ownership structure, control type classifications and the performance of large British companies', *Economic Journal*, **101**, 1418–37.

Levis, M. (1993), 'The long-run performance of initial public offerings: the UK experience 1980–1988', *Financial Management*, **22**, 28–41.

Ljungqvist, A. (1996), 'Can firms outwit the market? Timing ability and the long-run performance of IPOs', in Levis, M. (ed.), *Empirical Issues in Raising Equity Capital*, Amsterdam: Elsevier.

Ljungqvist, A. (1997), 'Pricing initial public offerings: further evidence from Germany', *European Economic Review*, **41**, 1309–20.

Loderer, C. and Martin, K. (1997), 'Executive stock ownership and performance: tracking faint traces', *Journal of Financial Economics*, **45**, 223–55.

Loughran, T., Ritter J. and Rydqvist, K. (1994), 'Initial public offerings: international insights', *Pacific-Basin Finance Journal*, **2**, 165–99.

Mello, A. and Parsons, J. (1998), 'Going public and the ownership structure of the firm', *Journal of Financial Economics*, **49**, 79–109.

Mikkelson, W., Partch, M. and Shah, K. (1997), 'Ownership and operating performance of companies that go public', *Journal of Financial Economics*, **44**, 281–307.

Morck, R., Shleifer, A. and Vishny, R. (1988), 'Management ownership and market valuation. An empirical analysis', *Journal of Financial Economics*, **20**, 293–315.

Myers, S. (1984), 'The capital structure puzzle', *Journal of Finance*, **39**, 581–2.

Pagano, M., Panetta, F. and Zingales, L. (1998), 'Why do companies go public? An empirical analysis', *Journal of Finance*, **53**, 27–64.

Ritter, J. (1991), 'The long-run performance of initial public offerings', *Journal of Finance*, **46**, 3–27.

Weinberg, M. and Rabinowitz, L. (1989 and updates), *Weinberg and Blank on Take-overs and Mergers*, London: Sweet & Maxwell.

[8]
Divestment, remuneration and corporate governance in mature firms[1]

Michelle Haynes, Steve Thompson and Mike Wright

1. Introduction

Jensen (1993) has argued that technological and market changes have left many corporations needing to exit from some activities and re-deploy their resources elsewhere. Existing research on downsizing that typically explores the determinants of voluntary divestments has identified the role of corporate governance characteristics (Hoskisson et al., 1994; Haynes et al., 2000).

One of the shortcomings of this research has been its treatment of executive incentives. Typically divestment has been examined as a function of insider equity ownership. However, this assumption is problematic in an agency theoretic context since insider ownership will also restrain managerial preferences for diversifying expansions (Jensen, 1986) and so result in a lower stock of value-generating divestment opportunities. Murphy (1997) has observed that traditional pay practices, in which executive remuneration is tied to company size and/ or the span of control, would tend to reinforce managerial preferences for size/growth objectives and do nothing to encourage the divestment of those activities that might be more profitably undertaken elsewhere. Therefore he conjectured that to motivate executives to downsize their companies and divest activities would require stock-based inducements, generally stock options. In an agency context, more intensive use of executive stock options would be expected to occur in precisely those cases where incentives provided by existing equity ownership are weak.

This chapter therefore presents a novel extension to research on the determinants of divestment. Using a unique dataset on voluntary divestment by UK firms, we explicitly incorporate executive incentive effects, as suggested by Murphy. We construct a series of alternative measures of relative compensation sensitivity, adapting an approach suggested by Conyon and Sadler (2001). This involves considering the marginal impact of a share price change on executive wealth, comprised of fully owned shares and options weighted by their Black–Scholes (1973) options delta, relative to the same executives' cash compensation.

The chapter reveals qualified support for the importance of incentives. While there is no significant uniform incentive effect, there is a statistically significant and robust effect for those firms below the median level of insider equity ownership, that is, those firms for which the agency problem might be anticipated to be most acute: executive compensation arrangements do appear to influence the downsizing decision.

Section 2 develops hypotheses relating to the determinants of divestment. Section 3 outlines the sources of data and defines variables. The results are presented as Section 4 and a brief conclusion follows.

2. Development of Hypotheses

Remuneration incentives

If corporate refocusing is a reversal of prior managerial empire-building stimulated by a slack market for corporate control (Jensen, 1986), we would expect refocusing firms to be characterized by low levels of prior management equity ownership. Hoskisson et al. (1994) do not directly employ insider ownership as a determinant of divestment, but they do find it to be negatively related to diversification and therefore anticipate a similar effect with respect to high levels of insider ownership. Denis et al. (1997) find higher levels of insider ownership in more focused firms and argue that reductions in agency costs associated with concentrated managerial ownership are associated with lower levels of diversification. Anderson et al. (2000) find that diversified firms have lower equity ownership by CEOs.

Since executive share ownership will change relatively slowly under normal conditions, the opportunities for profitable downsizing might also be expected to correlate *negatively* with the *current* extent of executive shareholding. Of course, divestment opportunities may be additionally generated through exogenous changes in the firm's circumstances, perhaps including a reduction in interfirm transactions costs or the comparative advantage of the M-form, as Bhide (1990) and Hoskisson and Turk (1990) suggest. If so, it would be expected that these opportunities would be more fully exploited by managers incentivized by higher levels of insider ownership.

Hypothesis 1a: Divestment is positively related to the board's equity holding.

A very substantial literature on the determinants of executive compensation – see Murphy (1999) and Bruce and Buck (1997) for recent surveys – has established the importance of corporate size, whether measured by sales, assets or employment, as a driver of senior managers' pay. Indeed, Rosen (1992) and others have commented on the unusually robust nature of this finding, with the compensation-size elasticity typically in the 0.25–0.35 range. This relationship alone might be expected to make managers reluctant to downsize their firms. However, Murphy (1997) notes that other factors will tend to reinforce it: first, non-monetary compensations, such as perquisites, power and prestige, also tend to correlate with size and growth. Second, personal disutility may accompany unpopular downsizing decisions. And finally, he notes that performance bonuses, designed to align manager and shareholder interests, may have a perverse effect in this case if these are tied to accounting profitability, since disposals, for example, are frequently accompanied by restructuring charges that reduce accounting profits in the short run.

It is clearly possible for a remuneration committee to encourage downsizing in particular circumstances by setting up suitable specific compensation arrangements. However, large corporations typically face simultaneous opportunities for growth in some activities alongside the need for contraction in others. In such circumstances detailed intervention by the remuneration committee is difficult and inappropriate if it involves the committee in the design of strategic objectives. Hence Murphy concludes that an optimal solution involves the provision of generic incentives to downsize by linking executive compensation more strongly to share performance, generally by the use of stock options.

Murphy's conjecture suggests an important testable hypothesis: namely that downsizing activity is positively related to the sensitivity of executive compensation to the share price. If downsizing does enhance shareholder value, as evidence from the stock market's response to divestments, de-mergers and so on suggests,[2] those corporations whose executives' well-being is most strongly tied to the stock price should *ceteris paribus* be those that experience the greatest downsizing activity. Furthermore, the observed growth in the extent of both executive options – see Abowd and Bognanno (1995) – and voluntary divestment – see Markides (1995) – in the 1980s and 1990s need not be coincidental. However, there is a complete lack of formal evidence on this relationship.

Hypothesis 1b: Divestment is positively related to the sensitivity of executive compensation to the share price

The anticipated incentive effect of option holding on downsizing is unambiguous but has been ignored in the literature, at least unless and until such options have been exercised. This has two potentially unfortunate consequences: First, depending on the current parameter values for the relevant option pricing model, the option value may be highly sensitive to changes in the share price, implying that the omission of option holdings will seriously understate the executive incentive effect. And second, agency theory suggests that stock options should be effective in precisely those situations where the executive stock holdings are low.

Corporate governance hypotheses

Firms with a weak governance regime may have a greater propensity to postpone taking unwelcome restructuring decisions, with the result that high levels of diversification persist (Bethel and Liebeskind, 1993; Hoskisson et al., 1994). Under a strong corporate governance regime, timely action to address underperformance is likely. Outsider blockholders of equity provide the basis for active shareholder influence over management and the reduction of entrenchment behavior by management with large equity holdings. Similarly, the presence of outside, non-executive directors on the board is likely to lead to greater influence on management to pursue shareholders' interests. Hence:

Hypothesis 2a: Divestment will be positively related to the presence of a non-managerial blockholder.

Hypothesis 2b: Divestment will be positively related to a greater presence of non-executive outside directors on the board.

Corporate reorganization may be associated with the introduction of a new management team. A radical change in the strategy of the firm is usually undertaken when a new management team arrives – either because they have a weaker emotional commitment to the old activities or because the changes indicate deeper shareholder dissatisfaction (Ravenscraft and Scherer, 1987; Markides, 1995).

Hypothesis 2c: Divestment is positively related to a change in top management.

A firm's debt burden may influence its decision to change the scope of its activities. Jensen (1986, 1993) and others have argued that debt constrains managers' capacities to allocate free cash flow to unprofitable diversification as it precommits cash flows to meet debt service obligations. The incentive effects associated with highly leveraged firms foster better asset utilization, not least because it forces the company to divest divisions to repay its debt (Ravenscraft and Scherer, 1987) and reduce this constraint on managerial discretion. John and Ofek (1995) argue that the coinsurance effect of bringing imperfectly correlated activities together in a diversified firm *increases* the debt capacity of that firm, leading to a *negative* association between refocusing and leverage. However, we suggest that those incentives for refocusing associated with leverage will tend to dominate any coinsurance effect. It is therefore expected that divesting firms will be characterized by high leverage.

Hypothesis 2d: Divestment will be positively associated with high leverage.

Finance hypothesis

The ability of a firm to generate and maintain a suboptimal configuration of activities appears likely to depend upon its performance. US studies find diversified firms are associated with a discount in their stock market value compared to focused firms (Berger and Ofek, 1996). Deterioration in performance is expected to raise the pressure on managers of diversified firms to divest. US evidence by Markides (1995) appears to support this conjecture. Similarly, John and Ofek (1995) find that divestments improve operating performance where these are associated with increased focus. Accordingly, we offer:

Hypothesis 3: Divestment will be negatively related to firm performance.

Strategy hypotheses

Anderson et al. (2000), Hoskisson et al. (1994) and Matsusaka (2001) among others have suggested that factors relating to firms' strategies may influence divestment. If, as is widely argued (Penrose, 1959), there exists an optimal limit to which a firm can diversify without adversely affecting its performance, then profit-maximizing firms that find themselves in breach of this optimum will attempt to reduce the scope of their activities by trying to improve performance. This line of reasoning implies that refocusing firms will be characterized by high levels of diversification relative to their industry counterparts. Reasoning from the strategic literature also suggests that larger firms are more likely to have breached some Penrose (1959) type constraint on expansion and are more likely to refocus. Hence:

Hypothesis 4a: Divestment will be positively associated with relatively high levels of diversification.

Hypothesis 4b: Divestment will be positively associated with firm size.

Markides (1995) argues that core market conditions such as concentration, market share and a large core business determine the attraction of a refocusing strategy. A firm would not be expected to refocus on its core business if that business were stagnating or unprofitable. Rather, the higher the attractiveness of the core industry, the higher the likelihood that a firm will refocus. Chatterjee and Wernerfelt (1991) provide some evidence to support this view. If vertical *disintegration* is accompanied by the divestment of business units supplying intermediate products, as might be expected, divestment may be particularly prominent in firms with high initial levels of vertical integration. Therefore, we offer:

Hypothesis 4c: Divestment will be positively related to core concentration.

Hypothesis 4d: Divestment will be positively related to core market share.

Hypothesis 4e: Divestment will be positively related to the degree of vertical integration.

Finally, a firm's acquisition activity may be associated with divestment. Existing evidence indicates that divestment and acquisition activity is often conducted simultaneously as part of an unbundling or corporate restructuring process (Ravenscraft and Scherer, 1987; Kaplan and Weisbach, 1992). Acquisition by a firm provides a means of reconfiguring the structure of resources with divestment being a consequence of this process (Capron et al., 2001). Acquisition raises a firm's stock of potentially divestable businesses and is predicted to be related positively to refocusing. Where firms experience problems in controlling unrelated activities, as a result say of an absence of managerial resources and capabilities, reductions in scope through the divestment of those activities may be a means of restoring control (Barney et al., 2001). Refocusing may also be associated with the sale of activities in declining sectors in order to focus on profitable growth sectors (Hoskisson et al., 1994). However, resource deployment following horizontal acquisitions may lead to significant divestment of related activities that may therefore not have a downward impact on diversification (Capron et al., 2001). Thus:

Hypothesis 4f: Divestment will be positively related to acquisition activity.

3.   Data and Methodology

The data on which this chapter based involved an unbalanced panel of 158 UK publicly quoted companies over the period 1985 to 1993. The period was chosen partly because the available evidence (see Haynes et al., 2002, 2003) indicated that it was one in which divestment had become commonplace. Furthermore, as indicated above, it was a period characterized by a high level of hostile merger activity that has been conjectured to make for an uncomfortable environment for highly diversified firms. The sample period also runs between two recovery years in adjacent macroeconomic cycles. The criterion for inclusion in the sample was an appearance in the leading 300 companies in the 1988–89 *Times 1000* list. Financials, foreign-owned and trading companies were excluded since their accounts are not comparable to those of other firms.

Data on *financial variables* and *firm size* were taken from the Datastream database, which holds information on quoted companies. Corporate governance variables and diversification indices were constructed from company annual reports and the *Financial Times*. Market share and concentration figures were constructed using information on firm and industry sales from Datastream.

Divestment was defined to include sales to third parties and disposals via management buy-outs. Information regarding sales to third parties was obtained from *Acquisitions Monthly* and the *Financial Times* from 1985 through to 1993. Information on divestment to management buy-outs was obtained from The Centre for Management Buy-out Research database, which is compiled from a number of published and non-published sources, including twice-yearly surveys of practitioners and effectively covers the population of management buy-outs in the UK. The CMBOR source includes deals that are never reported in the press at all as well as deal price information that may not be reported even though the deal itself is public knowledge.

Executive compensation. Conyon and Sadler (2001) – see also Sadler (1999) – have suggested as a measure of the sensitivity of executive compensation to share price performance the sum of shares and option grants held, with the latter weighted by the relevant option delta. Thus:

$$\Delta W_i = \sum_j \partial_j O_{ij} + S_i \tag{8.1}$$

where

ΔW_i is the impact on the wealth on executive i of a marginal increase in the share price,
O_{ij} represents the jth tranche of options held by executive i,
S_i represents executive i's holding of ordinary shares, and
∂_j is the Black–Scholes (1973) European call option delta for the jth tranche of options held by executive i.

The logic of this formulation is that the option delta[3] represents the marginal sensitivity of the valuation of each share held in that tranche to a change in the value of the underlying asset, in this case the price of the ordinary share. Hence, weighting the amount of each option tranche by its delta allows the incentive effect of options ownership to vary with the firm's underlying circumstances. In particular, the value of the Black–Scholes delta increases with the difference between the current share price and the option strike price (i.e. the extent to which the option is 'in the money'), with the underlying volatility of the share and with the time before the option expires.[4] Weighting option holdings in this way is

Table 8.1 The determinants of divestment activity: Poisson and negative binomial estimates

Independent variable	1a	1b	2a	2b	1c	1d	2c	1e	2d
CEOINCENT1	1.36 (6.55)	–	1.04 (1.82)	–	–	–	–	–	–
ALLEXINCENT1	–	7.17 (3.88)	–	6.17 (1.30)	–	–	–	–	–
CEOINCENT2	–	–	–	–	3.10 (6.57)	–	2.36 (1.83)	–	–
ALLEXINCENT2	–	–	–	–	–	24.2 (5.25)	–	–	–
CEOINCENT1* MANUF	–	–	–	–	–	–	–	2.92 (6.18)	2.37 (1.85)
CEOINCENT1* SERVICE	–	–	–	–	–	–	–	-0.200 (-4.22)	-1.06 (1.25)
Accounting performance	-0.001 (0.18)	-0.002 (0.45)	0.001 (0.08)	0.000 (0.05)	-0.001 (0.18)	-0.002 (0.41)	-0.001 (0.82)	-0.001 (0.29)	0.002 (0.17)
Firm leverage	0.018 (7.27)	0.019 (7.85)	0.018 (3.31)	0.019 (3.39)	0.018 (7.28)	0.019 (7.62)	0.018 (3.31)	0.018 (7.07)	0.017 (3.05)
Board composition	0.218 (1.62)	0.253 (1.88)	0.338 (1.00)	0.356 (1.04)	0.217 (1.61)	0.246 (1.82)	0.172 (1.00)	0.241 (1.80)	0.344 (1.02)
Blockholder	0.225 (3.13)	0.169 (2.43)	0.171 (0.99)	0.134 (0.77)	0.225 (3.13)	0.198 (2.79)	0.150 (0.80)	0.225 (3.14)	0.169 (0.99)

	(1)	(2)	(3)	(4)	(5)	(6)	(7)	(8)	(9)
Board equity	-0.860	-0.817	-0.837	0.819	-0.861	-0.810	-0.838	-0.888	-0.940
	(2.35)	(2.23)	(1.22)	(1.18)	(2.35)	(2.21)	(1.22)	(2.41)	(1.37)
Diversification level	0.497	0.447	0.451	0.426	0.498	0.476	0.450	0.483	0.444
	(7.85)	(7.20)	(3.33)	(3.12)	(7.86)	(7.56)	(3.33)	(7.63)	(3.32)
Firm size	0.336	0.336	0.264	0.259	0.337	0.338	0.264	0.319	0.270
	(11.85)	(11.77)	(3.90)	(3.79)	(11.88)	(11.86)	(3.90)	(11.23)	(4.00)
Market share	0.375	0.382	0.570	0.569	0.374	0.384	0.570	0.430	0.527
	(2.61)	(2.66)	(1.57)	(1.55)	(2.60)	(2.67)	(1.57)	(2.97)	(1.47)
Concentration	-0.302	-0.314	-0.454	0.461	-0.302	-0.295	-0.455	-0.249	-0.376
	(1.69)	(1.76)	(1.15)	(1.15)	(1.69)	(1.65)	(1.15)	(1.36)	(0.95)
Change in management	0.068	0.062	0.098	0.099	0.068	0.060	0.099	0.091	0.117
	(1.02)	(0.92)	(0.62)	(0.62)	(1.01)	(0.89)	(0.62)	(1.36)	(0.74)
Acquisition	0.007	0.006	0.015	0.015	0.007	0.006	0.015	0.110	0.016
	(4.62)	(3.95)	(2.90)	(2.75)	(4.63)	(4.11)	(2.89)	(6.14)	(3.14)
Vertical integration	0.302	0.500	0.731	0.834	0.302	0.383	0.732	0.281	0.576
	(1.01)	(1.71)	(1.16)	(1.30)	(1.30)	(1.29)	(1.16)	(0.94)	(0.91)
Constant	-3.515	-3.475	-2.789	2.699	-3.525	-3.522	-2.781	-3.379	-2.817
	(7.90)	(7.80)	(2.71)	2(2.59)	(7.92)	(7.90)	(2.70)	(7.63)	(2.75)
Ln L	-496.8	-506.7	-390.9	391.9	-496.6	-502.1	-390.9	-486.8	-390.9
Variance parameter α	–	–	0.294	0.303	–	–	0.293	0.293	0.285
Pseudo R^2	0.46	0.45	0.11	0.11	0.46	0.46	0.11	0.47	0.11
N	118	118	118	118	118	118	118	118	118

necessary since firm circumstances will alter the incentive effects of holding any option to buy stock. For example, a marginal improvement in the stock price will have little impact on the Black–Scholes valuation of a deep 'out-of-money' option with a proximate expiry date. By contrast, the holder of a deep 'in-the-money' option experiencing the same share price improvement will enjoy a wealth gain approaching that of an actual shareholder.

We construct a series of measures of ΔW_i/cash compensation for the CEO and the entire set of executive directors of a sample of UK firms: the wealth impact of a 1 percent rise in the share price relative to the cash compensation of the CEO (*CEOINCENT1*) or the entire set of executives (*ALLEXINCENT1*); the same variables recalculated under the assumption of a uniform options delta of unity (*CEOINCENT2* and *ALLEXINCENT2*); and finally the first set of variables recalculated (as *CEOINCENT3* and *ALLEXINCENT3*) under the assumption of a one penny rise in the share price. In every case the variable was interacted with a dummy variable equal to one for firms at or below the median insider ownership level: i.e. the incentive effect was evaluated in those cases where lower insider executive might be considered to have generated a more acute agency problem.

The ratios were intended to proxy the relative importance of share-based remuneration to the executive. It is recognized, of course, that the denominator may include cash bonuses, if any, which may be performance-related. However, an extensive literature on UK executive remuneration – see Bruce and Buck (1997) for a survey – reports that the impact of performance, including share price performance, on executive pay is generally insignificant. Moreover, as Murphy (1997) points out, bonuses are more usually tied to accounting profits that may even fall following downsizing decisions of the type considered here.

There are a number of problems in incorporating an options-based incentive measure into a regression framework. First, it is necessary to assume, with the executive compensation literature (e.g. Main et al., 1996), that executive options are realistically valued as European call options. Murphy (1999) has pointed out that the non-tradable executive option, to which exercise restrictions may apply, technically violates several of the Black–Scholes (1973) assumptions.[5] Second, institutional factors are likely to produce patterns of time series development that violate the usual regression requirements. For example, a substantial general decline in share prices will leave many corporate executives with deep 'out-of-the-money' options, thus eliminating any incentive effect and necessitating a new general round of option grants. An additional problem with UK data in our period concerns a stock exchange restriction that limits the par value issue of new options to a multiple of four times an executive's base salary. Therefore, if firms operate at this constraint, time series variation may be limited. Third, option delta evaluation with multiple tranches of options and multiple executives is extremely demanding in its data requirements; see Conyon and Sadler (2001). Until recently, some of these data were either unavailable to the outsider, or only available at a prohibitive cost.[6]

To accommodate these difficulties it was necessary to use a cross-sectional framework. Divestment data had been collected for the years 1985–91 and since research elsewhere (e.g. Conyon and Schwalbach, 2000) suggested that option use was increasing over this period, an incentive measure evaluated at the mid-point of the period would have been desirable. However, the earliest publicly available complete count of options held by individual executives in our sample firms was for late 1989.[7] The data source employed, the Hemmington–Scott Corporate Register, did not distinguish separate tranches of options, so all outstanding options were considered as a single tranche. Neither did the Corporate Register indicate the option exercise dates. Therefore option deltas were calculated using the following assumptions.

First, since executive options typically appeared to be granted for a period of about four years, it was assumed that the extant holding of options had an average of two years to maturity. Second, the current market price was taken to be the 1989 year-end price and the strike price was assumed to be an average of the year-end prices for 1987–89. Third, the risk-free rate was assumed to be 10 percent. Fourth, in conformity with the literature, volatility was proxied by the standard deviation of the share price returns and this and the yield were taken from the London Business School's Risk Measurement Service.

The calculated option deltas did not appear to be particularly sensitive to small changes in these assumptions, but as a check on the robustness of our results the incentive measures were recalculated under a delta = 1 assumption for the empirical estimation.

Board composition is defined as the ratio of non-executive to executive board members.

Board equity is defined as the proportion of voting equity controlled by the board.

Blockholder ownership is represented (here defined as the ownership of 5 percent or more of the firm's ordinary shares by a single shareholder) by a dichotomous variable equal to 1 if there was a blockholder immediately prior or during the period and 0 otherwise.

Change in top management is measured as a dichotomous variable equal to 1 if there was a change in CEO/managing director and 0 otherwise.

Firm leverage is measured as the ratio of debt to total assets and the ratio of debt to equity, both measured as book values.

Performance. Alternative accounting-based performance measures were employed. The reported results are for return on capital employed (ROCE), defined as the ratio of pre-tax profit to capital employed. Alternatively, market performance is measured as the ratio of market value to book value of assets (an approximation to Tobin's q).

Diversification level. Start-of-period level of diversification was included to capture mean-reversal behaviour. Two measures of diversification are employed: first, a count of the number of 3-digit SIC industries in which a firm operates; and second, the entropy index of diversification. The entropy index = $\Sigma P_i \ln (1/P_i)$, where P_i is the share of the ith segment in the total sales of the firm and $\ln(1/P_i)$ is the weight for each segment i. The index was calculated using sales data and SIC codes for each of the principal segments of the company at the 3-digit level. Given the nature of the data it is not possible to disaggregate a firm's sales to the 4-digit level. In the cases where it was not possible to assign a unique SIC code to an activity, an upper-bound estimate of two industry segments was assumed. For these reasons, the extent of firm diversification will tend to be underestimated. The index was calculated using data from Datastream and company accounts (analysis of turnover by activity). Some previous research has used a discrete classification scheme (see the discussion in Whittington et al., 1999) to measure diversification. However, the use of a continuous measure, as adopted here, appears preferable in a quantitative study primarily concerned with analysing changes in diversification.

Firm size is calculated by taking the book value of total assets, total sales, and the number of employees.

Concentration was measured using the Herfindahl index of concentration which is calculated as the sum of the squared market shares, S_i, of the firms in an industry:

$$H = \sum_{i=1}^{n} S_i^2$$

where S_i is the market share of the ith firm measured as the sales of the ith firm divided by total sales. H takes values between zero and one. The closer H is to one, the more concentrated is the industry. This is a standard measure in many studies on industry concentration (for example, Liebeskind et al., 1996). A Datastream program was utilized to identify all firms within an industry and their reported sales (approximately equivalent to the 3-digit SIC level).

Market share is calculated in the standard manner as total firm sales divided by industry sales. Again, a Datastream program was used to identify all firms assigned to a Datastream industry. To calculate industry sales, the sales for all firms within an industry were summed.

Vertical integration, or start-of-period value added/sales ratio. This measure is widely used as a proxy for the degree of vertical integration.

Acquisitions were defined to include the purchase of independent companies and of sales of subsidiaries from other groups. Acquisitions data were obtained from *Acquisitions Monthly* and *The Financial Times* from 1985 through to 1993.

Start-of-period values of the explanatory variables (except management change and recent acquisition indicator variables) are used to avoid problems of reverse causality.

4.   Results

The hypotheses were initially estimated as a Poisson model, which is widely adopted in the analysis of count data, that is where the dependent variable is discrete and defined for non-negative integers corresponding to the number of events in a given time interval. However, the Poisson model strictly requires equality between the conditional mean and variance, an assumption violated in many applications (see Cameron and Trivedi, 1986). For example, if there is unobserved heterogeneity or interdependence between the occurrence of separate events, each condition likely when working with firm-level data, the variance of y_i may exceed its mean, implying 'overdispersion'. This may lead to a downward bias in the covariance matrix, implying spuriously small standard errors and correspondingly inflated t-statistics.

To counter possible concerns with overdispersion, we re-ran the analysis using a negative binomial model. The latter (see Haynes et al., 2000, Cameron and Trivedi, 1986) introduces an additional stochastic component to capture unobserved heterogeneity. An examination of the coefficient (α) from this exercise leads, using a straightforward procedure proposed by

Cameron and Trivedi (1990), to a test for overdispersion. When this is undertaken, say by comparing columns 1a and 2a in Table 8.1, we find that α is significantly greater than zero or, equivalently, that a likelihood ratio statistic of 211.8 [$= 2*(496.8 - 390.9)$] supports its inclusion. That is we cannot reject the possibility of overdispersion.

Board equity, the proportion of voting equity controlled by the board, which Haynes et al. (2000) found to exert a significant *positive* effect on divestment, after the inclusion of the incentive variable, now attracts a *negative* sign. Hypothesis 1a is therefore not supported.

The variables capturing the executive incentive to take value-enhancing, but personally less preferred, downsizing decisions show a reasonably consistent picture. The CEO incentive variable is positive and significant, at or above the 10 percent level, in all estimations. By contrast, the all executive incentive variable is invariably positive but significant only in the Poisson model. The results do not appear to be sensitive to the assumptions used in the calculation of the Black–Scholes delta weights. Indeed, making a uniform delta equals one assumption, as in *CEOINCENT2* and *ALLEXINCENT2*, makes no material difference.[8] It was suspected that some within-sample differences existed between manufacturing and service sector firms, with the decoupling of activities being in some sense less costly in the former.[9] In the event, while there was little evidence of lower absolute levels of divestment among service sector firms, there was some indication that executive incentive effects were more important for manufacturers. For example, when the sample was split into manufacturing and service firms on the basis of each firm's principal activity and the resulting dummies were interacted with *CEOINCENT1*, it was clear that the incentive effects appeared to be concentrated in the former sector. Hypothesis 1b is therefore supported.

The presence of a blockholder is positively and significantly associated with divestment in some specifications (Hypothesis 2a is partly supported). Divestment is a positive function of leverage (Hypothesis 2d is supported). Divestment is also unambiguously a positive function of the start-of-period levels of diversification (entropy index) (Hypothesis 4a supported) and firm size (log of sales) (Hypothesis 4b supported). Less robust is the positive effect of market share in the firm's core product, although it is suggestive of at least limited refocusing by dominant product firms (Hypothesis 4d is therefore partly supported). Intra-period acquisition exerts the expected strong positive effect, reflecting the usual result that much divestment activity represents the unbundling of activities acquired in the recent takeover of multi-product firms. Hypothesis 4f is therefore supported.

Some check on the robustness of our findings is possible by analyzing the determinants of the proportion of assets disposed of over the interval of investigation. However, measuring divestment by the extent of asset disposals is problematic here for two reasons. First, about 20 percent of disposals, usually the smaller ones, have no recorded price, even in the annual reports of the buyers and sellers. And second, any measure will be sensitive to the intrinsic lumpiness or indivisibility of many disposals. However, following a procedure suggested in Haynes et al. (2000), the unpriced deals were valued and an alternative measure of divestment intensity constructed as the ratio of the value of assets divested to start-of-period assets.[10] The latter variable was then regressed on the same set of explanatory variables as before. The incentive coefficients, together with *t*-statistics generated by estimating heteroskedasticity-robust standard errors, are summarized in Table 8.2. While the overall explanatory power of these regressions is quite low, probably reflecting the lumpiness problem referred to above, the results do provide general confirmation of those of the count data analysis. In particular, it can

Table 8.2   Incentive variable coefficients from a regression of the determinants of the proportion of assets divested

Incentive variable	Coefficient* (standard error)	Model R^2
CEOINCENT1	4.85 (2.55)	0.14
CEOINCENT2	2.09 (2.48)	0.14
ALLEXINCENT1	2.34 (0.73)	0.14
ALLEXINCENT2	0.64 (0.10)	0.13

Note: * $\times 10^{-7}$.

be seen that the CEO incentive variables continue to exert a significant positive effect, while the effect of the all-executive incentive is positive but non-significant.

It is not clear whether the apparently greater importance of CEO incentives than those for the executive body as a whole is a real phenomenon or merely the result of some noise in the executive share- and option-holding data. It is clear after scrutinizing ownership data that some firms, even within the top 300, have large residual shareholders from the founding families. Their presence may impact on the measured ownership to cash compensation ratios in unpredictable ways. By contrast, it is suspected that most of the firms in our sample were hiring CEOs from outside the founding family nexus.

5.   Conclusion

This chapter has extended previous work on the determinants of divestment. Although a number of studies have identified the role of corporate governance factors, attention to the role of incentives for managers has been problematical. This chapter presents the first attempt to test for the importance of share-based incentives in motivating managers to take non-preferred downsizing decisions. Following Murphy (1997), conventional size-based remuneration and non-pecuniary benefits of executive employment would tend to generate an incentive to build and maintain corporate empires. If the modern economy requires large firms to divest non-core activities, as Jensen (1993) and others have argued, the shareholder–principals need to provide alternative incentives. These are most obviously supplied in the form of share-based compensation.

The chapter has constructed a series of share-based measures aimed at combining the incentive effects of actual share ownership with the wealth-augmenting effect of share price appreciation on the stock of options held by executives. In particular, we have used the option delta from the Black–Scholes pricing model, being the marginal wealth effect of a change in the share price under current firm circumstances, as a weight to allow option holdings to be added to fully owned shares. It is recognized that such an exercise can, at best, only offer an approximation to the incentives faced by executives across a period of years. The full information required to produce a Black–Scholes valuation of executive options is highly demanding and is necessarily incomplete for the period of our investigation. The valuation of executive share options, with all their limitations, as European call options is itself a problematic – even if widely adopted – exercise. Furthermore, we have had to construct an incentive measure that is assumed to hold across an entire period, even though elements of that measure will be subject to continuous fluctuation in response to firm and financial market circumstances.

However, whilst acknowledging the difficulties of including options in any measure of executive incentives, we would argue that to exclude them is potentially even more unsatisfactory. Agency theory suggests that options are a cost-effective form of providing high-powered incentives (Sadler, 1999). We might expect them to be employed in precisely those situations where existing incentives are weakest. Furthermore, given the strong role attributed to managerial share ownership in the existing literature on firm performance, the near-complete omission of options from that literature appears to us surprising.

The chapter used the incentive measures constructed to augment the divestment model of Haynes et al. (2000) for a somewhat longer interval of investigation. The results provided support for the contention, advanced by Murphy (1997), that share-based incentives might be necessary to persuade managers to take downsizing decisions that might otherwise harm their pecuniary and non-pecuniary well-being. This research is highly provisional and a number of questions need to be addressed. In particular, we intend to explore why the incentive effect appears to be significant at the CEO level but less obviously so at the level of the entire set of executives and whether firms that employ more intensive use of executive option grants over time are more likely to adopt product refocusing strategies.

Notes

1. Acknowledgement: the authors are grateful to Martin Conyon for many useful suggestions on the design of this research. The data was collected with financial support from the ESRC (grant R000236343), which is acknowledged with gratitude.
2. See Jain (1985) etc.
3. The Black–Scholes model calculates the value (V) of a European call option as:

$$V = Se^{-qT}N(d_1) - Xe^{-rT}N(d_2)$$

where

$$d_1 = \lfloor l_n(S/X) + (r - q + \sigma^2/2)T \rfloor / \lfloor \sigma T^{1/2} \rfloor$$

and

$$d_2 = \lfloor l_n(S/X) + (r - q + \sigma^2/2)T \rfloor / \lfloor \sigma T^{1/2} \rfloor$$

and S is the share price, X is the strike price, T is the time to expiry, q is the dividend yield, r is the risk-free rate of interest and σ is the standard deviation of share price returns. $N(\cdot)$ represents the cumulative probability distribution for a standard normal variable.

The options delta (δ) for a European call option on a dividend paying share is given by

$$\delta = e^{-qT} N(d_1) \text{ where } 0 \leq \delta \leq 1$$

4. These issues are discussed in Sadler (1999).
5. In particular, the impossibility of short-selling her own stock and the requirement to hold an undiversifiable position in an asset whose return typically correlates with that on her actual stock holdings and her human capital leaves the executive with risks that would not exist in a Black–Scholes world – see Murphy (1999).
6. Main et al. (1996) point out that for the period of our investigation option disclosure was incomplete and then required the payment of a fee to inspect the privately held Register of Directors' Interests for each company.
7. The Hemmington–Scott Corporate Register held in Warwick University Library.
8. The results using *CEOINCENT3* and *ALLEXINCENT3* – i.e. assuming a one penny rise in the share price – are very similar again. These are not reported for space reasons, but are available from the authors.
9. Retailers, for example, may find it hard to divest subsidiaries as going concerns if these subsidiaries trade under the parent's name.
10. The deals whose value went unreported were generally small; typically they fell beneath the threshold of £1m operated by *Acquisitions Monthly* for inclusion in their divestment listings. Therefore, following the argument of Haynes et al. (2000), a value of 0.1 percent of market value of the vendor is assigned to the deal. The results do not appear to be sensitive to even quite large changes in this assumption, perhaps because of the lumpiness of divestment. We style our measure the 'proportion' of assets divested, but note that it is not a true proportion since intra-period acquisitions allow it to rise beyond 100 percent.

References

Abowd, J. and Bognanno, M. (1995), 'International differences in executive and managerial compensation', in R. Freeman and L. Katz, eds, *Differences and Changes in Wage Structures*, Chicago: University of Chicago Press.

Anderson, R., Bates, T., Bizjak, J. and Lemmon, M. (2000), 'Corporate governance and firm diversification', *Financial Management*, Spring: 5–22.

Barney, J., Wright, M. and Ketchen, D. (2001), 'The resource based view of the firm: ten years after 1991', *Journal of Management*, **27**: 625–42.

Berger, P.G. and Ofek, E. (1996), 'Bust-up takeovers of value destroying diversified firms', *Journal of Finance*, **51**: 1175–200.

Bethel, J.E. and Liebeskind, J. (1993), 'The effects of ownership structure on corporate restructuring', *Strategic Management Journal*, **14**: 15–31.

Bhide, A. (1990), 'Reversing corporate diversification', *Journal of Applied Corporate Finance*, **3**(2): 70–81.

Black, F. and Scholes, M. (1973), 'The pricing of options and corporate liabilities', *Journal of Political Economy*, **81**: 637–54.

Bruce A. and Buck, T. (1997), 'Executive reward and corporate governance', in K. Keasey et al. (1997).

Cameron, A.C. and Trivedi, P.K. (1986), 'Econometric models based on count data: comparisons and applications of some estimators and tests', *Journal of Applied Econometrics*, **1**: 29–53.

Cameron, A.C. and Trivedi, P.K. (1990), 'Regression-based tests for overdispersion in the Poisson model', *Journal of Econometrics*, **46**: 347–64.

Capron, L., Mitchell, W. and Swaminathan, A. (2001), 'Asset divestiture following horizontal acquisitions: a dynamic view', *Strategic Management Journal*, **22**: 817–44.

Chatterjee, S. and Wernerfelt, B. (1991), 'The link between resources and the type of divestment: theory and evidence', *Strategic Management Journal*, **12**: 33–48.

Conyon, M. and Sadler, G. (2001), 'CEO compensation, option incentives and information disclosure', mimeo, The Wharton School, University of Pennsylvania, August.

Conyon, M. and Schwalbach, J. (2000), 'Executive compensation: evidence from the UK and Germany', *Long Range Planning*, **33**(4): 504–26.

Denis, D.J., Denis, D.K. and Sarin, A. (1997), 'Agency problems, equity ownership and corporate diversification', *Journal of Finance*, **52**: 135–60.

Haynes, M., Thompson, S. and Wright, M. (2000), 'The determinants of corporate divestment in the UK', *International Journal of Industrial Organization*, **18**: 1201–22.

Haynes, M., Thompson, S. and Wright, M. (2002), 'The impact of divestment on firm performance: empirical evidence from a panel of UK companies', *Journal of Industrial Economics*, **50**(2): 173–96.

Haynes, M., Thompson, S. and Wright, M. (2003), 'Divestment in the UK: a panel data study', *Journal of Economic Behavior and Organization*, **52**: 147–66.

Hoskisson, R.E., Johnson, R.A. and Moesel, D.D. (1994), 'Corporate divestment intensity in restructuring firms: effects of governance, strategy and performance', *Academy of Management Journal*, **37**(5): 1207–51.

Hoskisson, R.E. and Turk, T.A. (1990), 'Corporate restructuring: governance and control limits of the internal capital market', *Academy of Management Review*, **15**(3): 459–77.

Jain, P.C. (1985), 'The effect of voluntary sell-off announcements on shareholder wealth', *Journal of Finance*, **40**(1): 209–34.

Jensen, M.C. (1986), 'Agency costs of free cash flow, corporate finance and takeovers', *American Economic Review*, **76**: 323–9.

Jensen, M.C. (1993), 'The modern industrial corporation: exit and the failure of internal control systems', *Journal of Finance*, **48**(3): 841–80.

John, K. and Ofek, E. (1995), 'Asset sales and the increase in focus', *Journal of Financial Economics*, **37**: 105–26.

Kaplan, S. and Weisbach, M. (1992), 'The success of acquisitions: evidence from divestitures', *Journal of Finance*, **47**: 107–38.

Liebeskind, J., Opler, T. and Hatfield, D. (1996), 'Corporate restructuring and the consolidation of US industry', *Journal of Industrial Economics*, **44**: 53–68.

Main, B., Bruce A. and Buck, T. (1996), 'Total board remuneration and company performance', *Economic Journal*, **106** (November): 1627–44.

Markides, C. (1995), *Diversification, Refocusing and Economics Performance*, Boston, MA: MIT Press.

Matsusaka, J. (2001), 'Corporate diversification, value maximization and organizational capabilities', *Journal of Business*, **74**: 409–31.

Murphy, K.J. (1997), 'Executive compensation and the modern industrial revolution', *International Journal of Industrial Organization*, **15**(4): 413–532.

Murphy, K.J. (1999), 'Executive compensation', in O.C. Ashenfelter and D. Card (eds), *Handbook of Labor Economics* (volume 3b), Amsterdam: North-Holland, 2485–563.

Penrose, E. (1959), *The Theory of the Growth of the Firm*, Oxford: Basil Blackwell.

Ravenscraft, D.J. and Scherer, F.M. (1987), *Mergers, Sell-offs and Economic Efficiency*, Washington, DC: The Brookings Institution.

Rosen, S. (1992), 'Contracts and the market for executives', in L. Wein and H. Wijkander (eds), *Contract Economics*, Oxford: Blackwell.

Sadler, G. (1999), 'Executive compensation and share options in UK quoted companies', unpublished PhD thesis, University of Warwick.

Whittington, R., Pettigrew, A., Peck, S., Fenton, E. and Conyon, M. (1999), 'Change and complementarities in the new competitive landscape: a European panel study, 1992–1996', *Organization Science*, **10**(5): 583–600.

Appendix: Explanatory Variables

All these variables are start-of-period (i.e. pre-1985) values and are derived from firm data in Datastream or from the firms' annual reports and accounts:

Accounting performance: measured as return on capital employed.

Leverage: measured as the debt-to-equity ratio.

Board equity: the percentage of voting held by the entire board of directors, including non-executives.

Blockholder: represented by a dichotomous variable equal to 1 for firms with an identifiable shareholder holding 5 percent or more of the voting equity.

Diversification: measured using the entropy index $= \Sigma P_i \ln(1/P_i)$, where P_i is the share of the ith segment in the total sales of the firm and $\ln(1/P_i)$ is the weight for each segment. The derivation of the segment data is outlined in Haynes et al. (2000).

Firm size: measured as the log of total sales.

Market share: calculated as the total sales of the principal segment of the firm over the relevant total industry sales.

Concentration: measured as the Herfindahl index for the industry containing the firm's principal segment.

Vertical integration: the ratio of the firm's value added to total sales.

The following binary variables relate to the entire period:

Change in management: a dichotomous variable equal to 1 if there was a change in the identity of the CEO/managing director over the period.

Acquisition: a dichotomous variable equal to 1 for any sample firm making an identifiable acquisition over the period.

[9]

Corporate governance and financial constraints on strategic turnarounds

Steve Toms and Igor Filatotchev

Introduction

There has been considerable recent debate about the role of retrenchment as part of the turnaround process. Robbins and Pearce (1992: 287) suggest that retrenchment might comprise 'restructuring', 'downsizing' and 'downscoping', with a particularly strong emphasis on cost and asset reduction required for mitigation of the conditions responsible for financial downturn. This view has been challenged, both in terms of its precise attribute as a cause or effect (Barker and Mone, 1994), and in terms of whether such retrenchment strategies are necessary conditions at all as precursors for subsequent strategic turnaround actions (Castrogiovanni and Bruton, 2000). According to the latter view, strategic actions may be sufficient for successful turnarounds in some contexts and recourse to retrenchment strategies may be unnecessary or even counterproductive (Schreuder et al., 1991). This view is consistent with a wider literature, which, as Robbins and Pearce (1992: 287–8) point out, concentrates on strategic aspects of turnarounds and ignores the financial aspects. Although it is certainly true that the research literature has given due weight to the strategic aspects of turnarounds, the omission of financial considerations is in general surprising. Indeed, financial distress, which occurs where firms fail to maintain their capital and hence the value of the claims of financial stakeholders, might be expected to be an important feature of most (if not all) strategic crises faced by business organizations. The contention of this chapter is that turnarounds cannot be sensibly analysed without taking into account the context of the financial obligations imposed by governance arrangements.

By placing these arrangements at the centre of a theoretical model, the chapter supports and extends the Robbins and Pearce (1992) view of the role of retrenchment in the turnaround process. Earlier research did not provide a suitable theory of turnaround or useful framework for its analysis (Cameron et al., 1987). The Robbins and Pearce (1992) framework is an exception, although its underpinnings are disputed by subsequent empirical findings. However, the disparate nature of these large-sample cross-sectional and case-study-based research studies has hindered progress towards further theoretical developments (Chowdhury, 2002). Although the Robbins and Pearce (1992) framework is a useful starting point, it is therefore underdeveloped in certain respects. According to this framework, depending on the severity of the crisis, strategic repositioning must be preceded by cost reduction or asset sales (Robbins and Pearce, 1992). The assumption is that these financial strategies exist freely as options in all cases. Hence although this and other studies recognize the importance of retrenchment, they assume it to be non-problematic (Hambrick and Schecter, 1983; Slatter, 1984; Grinyer et al., 1988; Grinyer and McKiernan, 1990). There are many cases where retrenchment is possible and indeed made easier for management when the onset of a crisis provides justification for unpopular decisions (Grinyer et al., 1988: 95), but as this chapter illustrates, this is not always the case. Where it is not, there will be a failure of an important necessary condition for turnaround success. Specifically, the contention of this chapter is that if the turnaround model is extended to include governance and ownership factors, there are circumstances in which ownership and liability structures may have the effect of preventing entirely the pursuit of all subsequent strategic options. These options therefore include those that have otherwise rightly attracted the most attention in the literature. The reasons why financial arrangements may impose serious constraints on such strategic options are twofold. These are explained in detail below. In summary, they arise first because financial structure imposes fixed costs that are accordingly difficult to reduce without altering ownership rights; and second because in a crisis there might be a greater economic benefit to owners from the continued employment of all deployed assets relative to their opportunity cost.

The principal motivations of this chapter therefore are twofold; first to emphasize the importance of financial constraints in explaining the success or otherwise of corporate turnarounds; second to show that there are circumstances where financial constraints arising from crisis situations may impose a hard constraint on other strategic options, thereby preventing endogenous turnaround regardless of the attitudes, competencies and strategies of incumbent management. In other words, although prior studies have emphasized managerial inaction as an important cause of turnaround failure (e.g. Barker and Mone, 1994; Hambrick and Schecter, 1983; Hofer, 1980; Schendel et al., 1976; Weitzel and Jonsson, 1989), such inaction may not in itself be the product of poor-quality management, particularly where financial constraints operate.

Finance research, but not the strategy research, has identified financial restructuring as an integral component of corporate turnaround strategy (e.g. Brown et al., 1993; DeAngelo and DeAngelo, 1990; Franks and Tourous, 1994; Gilson, 1989; John et al., 1992). The contention of this chapter is that the strategic and financial aspects of turnarounds are inseparable. To examine these propositions the remainder of the chapter is divided into three further sections. The first develops a theoretical model explaining the circumstances in which it might be expected that financial constraints impact directly on strategic decisions. The second examines an empirical case providing an exemplification of failure to restructure under hard financial constraints. The final section draws conclusions.

A Governance-based Model of Turnarounds

The turnaround process commonly focuses around pre-identified stages. For example, these might be the efficiency/operating turnaround strategy stage and the entrepreneurial/strategic

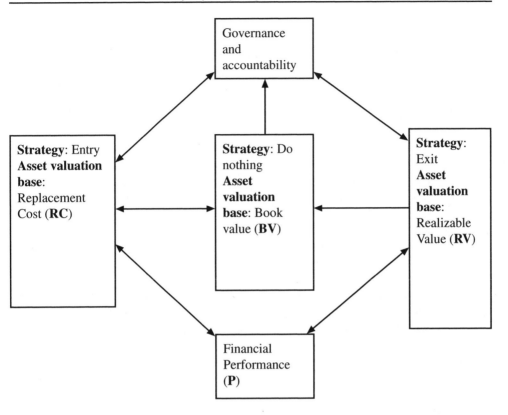

Figure 9.1   A governance-based model of turnarounds

stage (e.g. Bibeault, 1982; Robbins and Pearce, 1992; Slatter, 1984). Process research links the inner mosaic of the firm with the outer context of the political, social and economic, and competitive environments (Pettigrew, 1992: 9). The outer context may be constraining, enabling or neutral (Chowdhury, 2002). For the environmental context to operate in this fashion, a mediating mechanism is required and the obvious linkage is the governance devices responsible for the channelling of strategic resources in and out of the business. To consider strategic resources and their allocation through governance mechanisms in tandem, a strategic model is developed in this section, in which several strands of theory are synthesized. These are the resource-based view of the firm, corporate governance and financial returns determined by accounting rules of asset valuation. The result is a model, summarized in Figure 9.1, that can be used to analyse strategic repositioning where the principal features are financial restructuring, exit from existing lines of activity, and reinvestment in new ones. Each theoretical element of the analytical model is now discussed in turn.

The resource-based view (RBV) of the firm offers a theoretical basis for rationalizing decisions, common to turnaround situations, to enter or exit specific activities and markets or market segments. In the economist's standard model of perfect competition, barriers to any such repositioning do not exist. According to the RBV, however, competitive advantage, and by corollary, super-normal profits arise from firm-specific assets and managerial scope economies as identified by Penrose (1959) and Teece (1980). According to this perspective, diversification enhances performance if it allows the firm to access skills, resources and competencies that cannot be acquired by non-diversifying firms in a competitive market, and this may explain why related diversification can enhance performance (Markides and Williamson, 1994). The horizontal axis in Figure 9.1 presents a continuum of strategic decisions ranging from entry into new markets on the left, continuation in present markets in the centre and exit from present activities on the right. Empirical studies support resource-based theory by showing a systematic relationship between the nature of market chosen to enter and firms' resource profile. In other words, a firm tends to diversify into industries where similar resources are employed for production (Lecraw, 1984; Montgomery and Hariharan, 1991). For Teece (1980), managerial scope economies reflect tacit, human capital assets and these together with asset specificity and underutilized capacity explain why diversified firms exist. For multi-product businesses, where interdivisional cross-subsidization and divestments are options, there is a further dimension, related to constraints in the supply of capital. Strategic cures such as diversification, divestment and vertical integration have little applicability at independent business unit or business level unit of a multi-unit organization (Chowdhury, 2002: 254). Capital infusion may be an option, but single business firms may lack the necessary access to outside capital (Castrogiovanni and Bruton, 2000).

Governance arrangements are implicitly important in Teece's (1980) analysis and in subsequent developments of the RBV. Although Teece (1980) demonstrates that managers can never be fully monitored through the medium of fully efficient capital markets, market efficiency is but one aspect of corporate accountability. Indeed, a full integration of the resource-based view of the firm with corporate governance has yet to be developed. None the less, recent research has increasingly acknowledged the importance of governance factors as a constraint on managerial activity and as part of the turnaround process (Daily and Dalton, 1998). For example, where management fails to respond to an actual or anticipated deterioration of organizational resources due to a changing economic environment, effective corporate governance may be an important determinant of managerial ability and willingness to undertake restructuring actions (Hoskisson et al., 1994; Johnson, 1996; Zahra and Pearce, 1989). Effective implementation of strategy may depend on managerial 'capacity to change', where considered as a function of such firm characteristics as size, diversity and debt levels (Dunphy and Stace, 1988; Barker and Duhaime, 1997; Singh, 1986). These research results have contributed to the debate on the relationship between governance and corporate performance. Figure 9.1 reflects these relationships by suggesting that decisions about entry, exit or continuation are mediated by governance arrangements.

An important reason for such decisions is the change in asset value associated with the strategies of new markets entry, continuation and exit. Providers of capital, be they banks or equity market participants, assess the future cash flows of proposed new investments in the case of entry decisions or may force exit from existing activities where these are perceived as inadequate. Asset values, as collateral and as points of reference for ultimate realizations from investments, are important inputs into decisions by governance agents about whether strategic redirection is supported. Figure 9.1 shows three different bases of asset valuation consistent with these three strategies: replacement cost, capitalization of current profit streams and realizable value. Theoretical models show that economic profit reconciles to the cash flows generated by an asset or group of assets in any given time period and the difference in their opening and closing valuations (Edwards and Bell, 1961; Edey, 1962). Strategic entry and exit decisions can be related to level of profit and the valuation of assets (Edwards et al., 1987; Shleifer and Vishny, 1992). Consistent with the RBV, strategic resources generate economic quasi-rents that sustain superior performance and restrict entry (Peteraf, 1993). Conversely, if there are changes in the level of technology the replacement cost of assets may change, resulting in a loss of capital for the firm. This may depend on whether the firm or its competitors have made *ex ante* investments in proprietary R&D activities. Where incumbent firms lose capital, there are stronger entry incentives for new firms to enter the market. Another way in which firms lose capital is if existing assets are underutilized, either through temporary changes in demand or through longer-run overcapacity problems. In such cases, losses are incurred as a result of spreading fewer units of output over a higher cost base. In certain conditions of asset specificity, managers have an incentive to diversify the uses of such assets (Teece, 1980). In conditions of changing technology capital losses arising from obsolescence may also be expressed as asymmetries between realizable values and the book value of assets on the assumption of continuing use. Further, declining realizable values of specific assets may create exit barriers where their use can be continued at low marginal but high average cost, for example in conditions of excess capacity.

The final point of reference influencing the relationship between entry, exit and governance is the level of profitability. As already noted, profit levels will affect the value of deployed assets perceived by external stakeholders. The rate of return depends on the profits generated by assets and their valuation, which depends on intended managerial decisions about market entry and asset deployment. In Figure 9.1 these decisions depend on a comparison between the rates of return from alternative strategies. Financial performance generates profit stream P. In Figure 9.1, where RC refers to replacement cost, BV refers to book value and RV refers to realizable value, opportunity rates of return are derived as P/RC, P/BV or P/RV, reflecting altered asset valuations in the context of the strategic decision. In conditions of moral hazard and information asymmetry, managers and owners may evaluate these opportunities differently. Intervention by capital suppliers utilizing governance mechanisms is more likely and may be more effective when the base of asset valuation alters, because owners and managers will simultaneously seek new information about asset valuations in the new circumstances.

A further aspect of financial performance that must be taken into account is the cost base of the firm. Where industries are affected by downturns and crisis conditions the cost base of the firm, and the extent to which the firm bears costs which are not easily variable in the short run, will be a crucial determinant of realized profit and the ability of managers to stabilize cash flows. Fixed costs typically arise from sunk and specialized assets, which are the sources of entry barriers and competitive advantage under the assumptions of the RBV. However, the greater the investment in these assets, the more problematic it becomes for non-specialist outside investors to evaluate their actual profit potential. The information asymmetries that arise will mediate the effectiveness of governance arrangements. Continuous technical change in some industries means there will be divergences between the values of assets in use and the values of new assets required by incumbent firms and new entrants. Demand for new finance is high and there will be pressures to alter governance, accountability and reporting structures in favour of outside financial stakeholders.

Taking these factors together, the conditional availability or non-availability of finance may under certain conditions act as an entry barrier. Similarly, in conditions of industry decline, exit decisions will be mediated by governance and accountability arrangements. Whether or not firms exit will depend in part on whether the realizable value of assets allows financial stakeholders to liquidate their position without loss of capital. If such values are low compared to the value profit streams from continued use, then active monitoring by financial stakeholders may prevent exit (Jensen, 1993). The governance and financial performance relationship is a further important factor. For example, firms in mature but profitable industries generating free cash flows will systematically overdiversify (Jensen, 1986). In contrast, possession of knowledge-based resources and financial resources from external sources are associated with more related diversification (Chatterjee and Wernerfelt, 1991).

The model in Figure 9.1 summarizes the principal relationships. Its vertical axis encapsulates a governance, strategy and performance dimension. Horizontally the axis offers a continuum of options consistent with the resource-based view. On the horizontal axis, the rates of entry and exit through time are a function of financial performance and hence asset value and stakeholders' monitoring of financial performance, or the accumulation and maintenance of capital. On the vertical access the transparency of these processes influences the extent of monitoring by financial stakeholders and their attitude to strategic entry and exit decisions.

Although several potentially important aspects are missing from Figure 9.1, the relationships suggested offer several advantages in the analysis of strategic decision making. To begin with, it presents a logical framework for the analysis of financial performance using accounting data. Although the structure conduct performance paradigm remains important in the field of industrial organization, many economists are reluctant to use accounting data due to their perceived lack of reliability (Mueller, 1990; Schmalensee and Willig, 1989). However, the Edwards et al. (1987) analysis, whose assumptions are integrated into the model, provides an analytical solution to these problems provided appropriate valuation rules are followed. Those rules are consistent with the replacement cost, economic value in use and realizable values that govern entry, do-nothing and exit decisions, and which are also consistent with Figure 9.1. Whilst financial performance may be a worthwhile measure for evaluating strategic outcomes, it is also useful for analysing the effectiveness of governance systems. For example, the market for corporate control can be analysed with reference to wealth effects, where the distribution of gains from merger transactions is a function of differences in replacement costs of assets, values in use and realizable values. Financial theory has begun to depart from the traditional propositions of the value irrelevance of capital structure and dividend decisions, and is beginning to examine the relationships between active or passive investor monitoring arrangements and the value of the firm (Jensen, 1993). These relationships are increasingly recognized elsewhere, particularly in comparative and historical analysis of governance systems (Whittington and Mayer, 2000: 13–14). However, the model does not merely examine the governance and exit relationship implied by Jensen's hypothesis. Of equal importance are the process of value and the establishment of entry barriers. The model recognizes that investments in organizational learning, the development of firm-specific intangible and physical assets and the concomitant exploitation of scale and scope economies is also mediated by the processes of governance and accountability. In Figure 9.1, scale and scope economies are manifested in the horizontal relationship between entry barriers, strategy (decisions to diversify or refocus) and exit barriers and mediated by the effectiveness of the system of governance and accountability.

It is expected that the five variables in the model are measurable empirically and are historically and economy specific. For example, the rates of entry and exit from an industry allow the modelling of the industry life cycle, mediated by levels of profit and accountability to financial stakeholders. Similarly there is also a governance life cycle modelled in terms of the venture capital function. At an early stage in the life cycle the venture capital function is entrepreneurial but is usually surrendered to outside stakeholders as size, and lines of credit, increase. Later, financial stakeholders may again take on an active role to enforce exit decisions. Governance-based interventions on strategic position are mediated through time by the relative importance of entry and exit barriers. Cross-sectional multiple industry content studies are inadequate for capturing these sequential patterns and for the assessment of underresearched turnaround processes (Chowdhury, 2002). These are better examined by longitudinal single industry case studies. The next section of the chapter examines a set of circumstances derived from the model in the general case showing the relationship between a profit crisis, asset valuation and strategic paralysis followed by an exemplification from the British textile industry.

Hard Financial Constraints on Turnaround

An empirical illustration

In 1920 the British cotton textile industry enjoyed a postwar boom. Many firms recapitalized, selling equity to financial syndicates and investment groups (Thomas, 1973: 156). Within a year the boom, along with export orders, collapsed (Burnett-Hurst, 1932; Dupree, 1996: 270–71; 283–90). According to the Robbins and Pearce (1992) model, the first response should have been at least cost reduction, and given the severity of the crisis, asset reduction. Neither of these responses materialized, although as the crisis lengthened they became increasingly important.

As suggested in the discussion above, to explain the paralysis, the Robbins and Pearce model requires extending to include the cost base of the firm. In the case of the textile firms their cost bases were relatively fixed. Recapitalized assets created high depreciation charges and extensive use of loan finance led to high interest charges (Thornley, 1923: 187–9). The leverage effects of these fixed charges accentuated the downturn in reported profits (Higgins and Toms, 2003). To stabilize profits and cash flow required managers to reduce the book values of assets and in some cases to make asset disposals in order to repay loans. Governance arrangements prevented these strategies. In terms of Figure 9.1 investors needed to compare the expected profits from existing operations with the profitability of the exit strategy. Putting aside some expectations that the downturn was cyclical and temporary (by 1922 the industry had formed an emergency committee), even low profit expectations from continuation were preferable to the alternative. Asset write-downs would entail a reordering of financial claims to the detriment of the new investors who had bought at the height of the boom, capital losses and immediate recognition of losses in future dividend streams. Asset disposals at other than scrap value were prevented by the collapse of the second-hand machinery market (Bowker, 1928). The collapse of the export market created spare capacity, whilst new technical advances in spinning and weaving processes rendered deployed assets increasingly obsolete (Ryan, 1930). Overcapacity was made progressively worse during the 1920s by the failure of firms to exit the industry in significant numbers (Keynes, 1981: 583–4, 591). At the level of the individual firm, investors chose rationally, according to Figure 9.1, to accept marginal profitability on their sunk investments to the almost total loss of capital that would arise from exit. Some profits could still be made by accepting contracts that covered marginal costs and by undercutting competitors (*Economist*, 9 December 1922: 1076).

The result was paralysis, and the second-stage strategic options that ought to have opened up in the Robbins and Pearce model failed to materialize. A crucial question that remains is why, since the exit option was closed, did firms not consider other strategic alternatives? Figure 9.1 suggests a comparison of the expected profits from deployed assets with those from the purchase of new assets. Newer and more efficient machinery was available (Board of Trade, 1932: 135) that would have assisted firms seeking marginal contracts and the option to undercut their competitors. However, there were several objections to this strategy. The most obvious from the investors' point of view was that having lost capital already, this would be throwing good money after bad. A further consideration was that the machinery was under patent protection, more efficient and therefore more expensive (Joshi, 1935; Sandberg, 1974). To deploy these machines efficiently required the integration of spinning, intermediate processes and weaving (Mass and Lazonick, 1990): in other words, the complete reorganization of existing vertically specialized factory buildings or the construction of new ones. Taken together this strategy amounted to heavy commitment to high fixed-cost assets in conditions of uncertain demand. Small expected cash flow streams would amount to a high-risk, low rate of return on such a large capital.

Ultimately the crisis conditions and the failure of individual firm responses to the crisis prompted outside intervention. To save the banks from bad loans and financial collapse, the Bank of England set up a new company whose function was to buy up existing companies in order to close them down (Bamberg, 1988). This was not the first or last occasion of government intervention in lieu of strategic action by industry participants and where such interventions are necessary there may be further examples of strategic paralysis and turnaround failure.

Implications

The empirical example shows that the linkages in process between the main stages of the Robbins and Pearce (1992: 291) model are far from automatic. In the light of the example it is worth reconsidering this model and extending its scope with reference to Figure 9.1. In the Robbins and Pearce model, financial problems are addressed at the first *retrenchment* stage, which aims to stabilize operations and restore profitability by pursuing cost and/or asset reductions. Recall that the realized level of profit in Figure 9.1 factors in the cost base of the firm. Where cost reduction strategies are pursued, the process is facilitated where the cost base of the organization is variable. Where the cost base is fixed, it is more difficult for the firm to stabilize cash flow without also altering the strategic basis of its activities. To the extent that financial distress is severe and/or strategic health is weak, asset reduction becomes increasingly imperative for turnaround (Hofer, 1980; Pearce and Robbins, 1993). However, as the illustration suggests, the causes of financial distress may also impact on the disposal value of the assets. This is very important because the effectiveness of asset reduction strategies as a precursor to subsequent recovery depends substantially on the ability of the firm to generate cash flow from these disposals. Although the literature uniformly presupposes this to be possible, there are clearly associated practical difficulties. In the empirical illustration and in the general case these difficulties reflect the degree of asset specificity, liquidity in the second-hand market and similar exit barriers.

Special cases may be derived from the model in Figure 9.1 which illustrate the impact of combined factors on turnaround strategies. The first case to consider is where asset values impose a hard constraint on exit strategies and prevent constrained firms developing second-stage recovery strategies through reinvestment in product/process innovation. The typical economic model assumes no capital rationing (Weingartner, 1977), but the allocation of capital to an industry depends on governance structures and lending conditions. With very high levels of capitalization, high asset specificity and low resale values in the external market, the supply of financial and physical capital becomes highly inelastic, or subject to hard rationing. In other words, positive net present value (NPV) projects will be rejected even when the outcome is positive with a high degree of certainty. Where these conditions apply, it is difficult or perhaps even impossible for incumbent management to apply the standard turnaround prescription. In the case of British textiles sunk investment in old machinery and the attitudes of capital suppliers prevented investment in new machinery. It is interesting to speculate how high the NPV from investment in the new machines might have been and still be at a level consistent with investors' refusal to commit fresh capital.

Low resale values for highly specific assets prevent stabilization of cash flow in the retrenchment phase. Even leaving that problem aside, nothing can be done in the recovery phase even if it can be entered, as the positive NPV projects that must now be rejected are the necessary investments in new product and process. In terms of Figure 9.1 parameters this means that however much crisis conditions drive down financial performance, the economic rate of return from the 'do-nothing' strategy is superior to the loss of capital associated with exit at low resale value. Meanwhile the lack of cash flow from such realizations and the hard rationing constraint prevent reinvestment in new products and processes, however profitable they may be. Financial claim holders will therefore, through the governance structure, rationally impose the 'do-nothing' strategy on management. In doing so they will extract any remaining value from assets in use by undercutting competitors to obtain marginal contracts. Such limited strategies may further intensify competition. Where the crisis is generated by a sudden and sustained fall in demand, failure to exit due to the relationships suggested above will accentuate the crisis further by creating overcapacity. These were the features that characterized many staple industries in the UK and other industrialized economies in the 1920s and 1930s.

Discussion and Conclusions

Some turnaround researchers suggest that retrenchment strategies involving the sale of critical assets might be detrimental as a result of trading short-run survival for longer-run strategic advantage (Barker and Mone, 1994). The model presented in this chapter, in contrast, suggests a more complex story. First, retrenchment is argued to be an integral part of the turnaround process according to a rational decision-making model with financial and governance constraints. The supporting empirical case confirms retrenchment to be a necessary condition for subsequent turnaround. Second, and closely linked, the chapter has illustrated that asset sales are not always discretionary and the governance arrangements may prevent such disposals. This problem is less likely to occur in multi-product firms where managers are more likely to be able to re-deploy resources from one sector to another. However, even these advantages of such strategic flexibility are only apparent where managers avoid investment in highly specific assets with associated high levels of fixed cost. Investments in such assets, which have entry barrier characteristics associated with difficulty of replication by competitors, are the *sine qua non* of superior performance according to the RBV. In short, firms cannot have their cake and eat it. They either commit themselves to high fixed-cost sunk investments and pay the price in the event of a crisis, or they avoid them and thereby avoid crisis, but instead fail to achieve competitive advantage and only receive the normal profit levels at the given stage of the business cycle.

References

Bamberg, J.H. (1988), 'The rationalisation of the British cotton industry in the inter-war years', *Textile History*, **19**: 83–102.

Barker, V.L. and Duhaime, I.M. (1997), 'Strategic change in the turnaround process: theory and empirical evidence', *Strategic Management Journal*, **18**: 13–38.

Barker III, V.L. and Mone, M.A. (1994), 'Retrenchment: cause of turnaround or consequence of decline?', *Strategic Management Journal*, **15**: 395–405.

Bibeault, D.B. (1982), *Corporate Turnaround: How Managers Turn Losers into Winners*, New York: McGraw-Hill.

Board of Trade (1932), *An Industrial Survey of the Lancashire Area (Excluding Merseyside)*, London: HMSO.

Bowker, B. (1928), *Lancashire under the Hammer*, London: Hogarth.

Brown, D.T., James, C.M. and Mooradian, R.M. (1993), 'The information content of distressed restructuring involving public and private debt claims', *Journal of Financial Economics*, **33**: 93–118.

Burnett-Hurst, A. (1932), 'Lancashire and the Indian market', *Journal of the Royal Statistical Society*, **95**: 395–440.

Cameron, K.S., Kim, M.U. and Whetten, D.A. (1987), 'Organizational effects of decline and turbulence', *Administrative Science Quarterly*, **32**: 222–40.

Castrogiovanni, G. and Bruton, G. (2000), 'Business turnaround process following acquisitions: reconsidering the role of retrenchment', *Journal of Business Research*, **48**: 25–34.

Chatterjee, S. and Wernerfelt, B. (1991), 'The link between resources and type of diversification: theory and evidence', *Strategic Management Journal*, **12**: 33–48.

Chowdhury, S.D. (2002), 'Turnarounds: A stage theory perspective', *Canadian Journal of Administrative Sciences*, **19**(3): 249–66.

Daily, C.M. and Dalton, D.R. (1998), 'The role of governance in corporate decline: a review and research agenda', in L. Foster and D. Ketchen (eds), *Advances in Business Strategy Vol.5. Turnaround Research: Past Accomplishments and Future Challenges*, Stamford, CT: JAI Press.

DeAngelo, H. and DeAngelo, L. (1990), 'Dividend policy and financial distress: an empirical investigation of troubled NYSE firms', *Journal of Finance*, **45**: 1425–31.

Dunphy, D.C. and Stace, D.A. (1988), 'Transformational and coercive strategies for planned organizational change: beyond the OD model', *Organization Studies*, **9**: 317–34.

Dupree, M. (1996), 'Foreign competition and the inter-war period', in M.B. Rose (ed.), *The Lancashire Cotton Industry*, Preston: Lancashire County Books, pp. 265–95.

Edey, H. (1962), 'Business valuation, goodwill and the super-profit method', in W. Baxter and S. Davidson (eds), *Studies in Accounting Theory*, London: Sweet and Maxwell.

Edwards, E. and Bell, P. (1961), *The Theory and Measurement of Business Income*, Berkeley, CA: University of California Press.

Edwards, J., Kay, J. and Mayer, C. (1987), *The Economic Analysis of Accounting Profitability*, Oxford: Oxford University Press.

Franks, J.R. and Tourous, W.N. (1994), 'A comparison of financial recontracting in distressed exchanges and Chapter 11 reorganisations', *Journal of Financial Economics*, **35**: 349–70.

Gilson, S.C. (1989), 'Management turnover and financial distress', *Journal of Financial Economics*, **25**: pp. 241–62.

Grinyer, P.H., Mayes, D.G. and McKiernan, P. (1988), *Sharpbenders: The Secrets of Unleashing Corporate Potential*, Oxford: Basil Blackwell.

Grinyer, P.H and McKiernan, P. (1990), 'Generating major change in stagnating companies', *Strategic Management Journal*, **11** (special issue): 131–46.

Hambrick, D.C. and Schecter, S.M. (1983), 'Turnaround strategies for mature industrial-product business units', *Academy of Management Journal*, **23**(2): 231–48.

Higgins, D.M. and Toms, J.S. (2003), 'Financial distress, corporate borrowing and industrial decline: the Lancashire cotton textile industry, 1918–1938', *Accounting Business and Financial History*, **13**(2): 207–32.

Hofer, C.W. (1980), 'Turnaround strategies', *Journal of Business Strategy*, **1**(1), 19–31.

Hoskisson, R.E., Johnson, R.A. and Moesel, D.D. (1994), 'Corporate divestiture intensity in restructuring firms: effects of governance, strategy and performance', *Academy of Management Journal*, **37**: 1207–51.

Jensen, M. (1986), 'The agency costs of free cash flow: corporate finance and takeovers', *American Economic Review*, **76**: 323–9.

Jensen, M. (1993), 'The modern industrial revolution, exit and the failure of internal control systems', *Journal of Finance*, **48**(3): 831–80.

John, K., Lang, L.H.P. and Netter, J. (1992), 'The voluntary restructuring of large firms in response to performance decline', *Journal of Finance*, July: 891–917.

Johnson, R.A. (1996), 'Antecedents and outcomes of corporate restructuring', *Journal of Management*, **22**: 439–83.

Joshi, B. (1935), *Articles on Preparatory Machines, Cotton Weaving, Yarn Testing etc.*, Bombay: Times of India Press.

Keynes, J.M. (1981), *The Return to Gold and Industrial Policy II, Collected Works*, Cambridge: Cambridge University Press, pp. 578–637.

Lecraw, D.J. (1984), 'Diversification strategy and performance', *Journal of Industrial Economics*, **33**: 179–98.

Markides, C. and Williamson, P.J. (1994), 'Related diversification, core competences and corporate performance', *Strategic Management Journal*, **15** (Special Issue): 149–65.

Mass, W. and Lazonick, W. (1990), 'The British cotton industry and international competitive advantage: the state of the debates', *Business History*, **32**: 9–65

Montgomery, C.A. and Hariharan, S. (1991), 'Diversified expansion by large established firms', *Journal of Economic Behavior and Organization*, **15**(1): 71–89.

Mueller, D. (1990), *The Dynamics of Company Profits: An International Comparison*, Cambridge: Cambridge University Press.

Pearce, J.A. and Robbins, K.D. (1993), 'Towards improved theory and research on business turnaround', *Journal of Management*, **19**: 613–36.

Peteraf, M. (1993), 'The cornerstones of competitive advantage: a resource-based view', *Strategic Management Journal*, **14**(3): 179–91

Penrose, E. (1959), *The Theory of the Growth of the Firm*, Oxford: Oxford University Press.

Pettigrew, A. (1992), 'The character and significance of strategic process research', *Strategic Management Journal*, **13**: 5–16.

Robbins, K.D. and Pearce, J.A. (1992), 'Turnaround: retrenchment and recovery', *Strategic Management Journal*, **13**(4): 287–309.

Ryan, J. (1930), 'Machinery replacement in the cotton trade', *Economic Journal*, **40**: 568–80.

Sandberg, L. (1974), *Lancashire in Decline*, Columbus: Ohio State University Press.

Schendel, D., Patton, G.R. and Riggs, J. (1976), 'Corporate turnaround strategies: a study of profit decline and recovery', *Journal of General Management*, Spring: 3–11.

Schleifer, A. and Vishny, R.W. (1992), 'Liquidation values and debt capacity: a market equilibrium approach', *Journal of Finance*, **47**: 1343–66.

Schmalensee, R. and Willig, R.D. (eds) (1989), *Handbook of Industrial Organisation*, Vol. 2, Amsterdam: North-Holland, ch. 16.

Schreuder, H. Van Cayseele, Jaspers, P. and DeGraff, B. (1991), 'Successful bear-fighting strategies', *Strategic Management Journal*, **12**: 523–34.

Slatter, S. (1984), *Corporate Recovery: Successful Turnaround Strategies and Their Implementation*, Harmondsworth, UK: Penguin.

Singh, J.V. (1986), 'Performance, slack and risk taking in organizational decision-making', *Academy of Management Journal*, **29**: 562–85.

Teece, D. (1980), 'Economies of scope and the scope of the enterprise', *Journal of Economic Behaviour and Organisation*, **3**: 223–47.

Thomas, W. (1973), *The Provincial Stock Exchanges*, London: Frank Cass & Co.

Thornley, T. (1923), *Modern Cotton Economics*, London: Scott Greenwood and Co.

Weingartner, H.M. (1977), 'Capital rationing: "n" authors in search of a plot', *Journal of Finance*, **32**: 1403–31.

Weitzel, W. and Jonsson, E. (1989), 'Decline in organisations: a literature integration and extension', *Administrative Science Quarterly*, **34**, 91–109.

Whittington, R. and Mayer, M. (2000), *The European Corporation*, Oxford: Oxford University Press, pp. 13–14.

Zahra, S.A. and Pearce, J.A. (1989), 'Boards of directors and corporate financial performance: a review and integrative model', *Journal of Management*, **15**: 291–334.

[10]

Corporate governance and the public-to-private threshold

Charlie Weir, David Laing and Mike Wright

1. Introduction

Considerable research on the firm life cycle, as reflected in other chapters in this volume, has focused on the thresholds between founder management and the entry of venture capital firms and between private ownership and IPO (initial public offering). A further threshold of growing importance concerns the taking private of listed companies. For several reasons, these transactions involve significant corporate governance and ownership issues. First, the decline in hostile take-over activity as a governance device and the recognition that it was, in any case, always a minor part of the market for corporate control has called for a reassessment of approaches based on the implicit assumption that the most appropriate way to differentiate between take-over targets is to treat them as either hostile or friendly.[1,2]

Second, recent years have seen an increased focus on the development of new 'best-practice' codes for enhancing internal corporate governance through, for example, the strengthening of corporate boards (e.g. Cadbury, 1992). Enhanced corporate governance has also been associated with an increase in emphasis on the role of performance-related remuneration for management, notably in the form of equity incentives (Murphy, 1999).

Third, the decline in the importance of hostile acquisitions coincided with the increase in public-to-private transactions (PTPs) in the UK. Over the period 1991–97, 4.8 per cent of acquisitions involving publicly quoted companies were PTPs. During 1998–2000, the figure rose to 23.7 per cent, with the figure increasing in each of the years. In a PTP, the publicly owned equity of a company is acquired and the new company is taken private so that its shares are no longer quoted on the stock market. Thus a PTP creates a new independent, privately owned entity typically with close monitoring by private equity firms as opposed to being subsumed within a group.

These developments give rise to several important questions concerning the implications of corporate governance and ownership for the sale of businesses. In particular, this chapter examines the notion that PTP targets are distinct from other acquisition targets. Central to this analysis, we extend previous work that has examined the undervaluation, free cash flow and market for corporate control hypotheses relating to the acquisition of firms (Jensen, 1986). We incorporate the impact of internal governance mechanisms and the role of ownership structure on firms that are acquired by an existing corporation or are subject to a PTP.

Our findings show that for the whole sample, PTPs have higher board shareholdings and higher institutional shareholdings than other acquisitions. In addition, the stock market regards them as having poorer growth prospects. PTPs appear to experience greater pressure from the market for corporate control, but this is sensitive to variable definition. However, there is no evidence that they have different internal governance structures, have more free cash flow or spend different amounts on capital projects. If the sample is split by PTP board shareholdings, the results are more consistent with financial incentives than the incentive realignment model. Overall the results show that firms going private and other acquired firms have significantly different characteristics. The homogeneity hypothesis can therefore be rejected. It was also found that the premiums received by shareholders in firms going private were lower than those received by shareholders of other acquired firms, which suggests that PTPs represent poor value for external shareholders.

The chapter is structured as follows. In the next section the literature relating to acquisitions and PTPs is discussed. Then the data and research design are outlined. The results are then discussed and finally some conclusions drawn.

2.   Previous Literature and Hypothesis Development

PTP transactions are a type of take-over; however, there are a number of important differences between them and other acquisitions. First, a PTP means that the company will have been taken out of public control and will no longer be quoted on the stock market. This means that the company will no longer be subject to public monitoring and hence will not incur the bonding and monitoring costs associated with being publicly quoted. Second, PTP transactions tend to be funded by private equity firms. For example, over the period 1998–2000, 68.7 per cent of all PTPs were funded by private equity firms. The figure increases as the value of the PTP increases, with private equity firms funding 90.75 per cent for PTPs that were in excess of £50 million (CMBOR, 2003).

Third, the funding of PTPs usually involves a higher proportion of debt whereas other acquisitions tend to be funded by cash or shares. For example, Sudarsanam and Mahate (2003) found that over the period 1983–95 in the UK, 18.7 per cent of acquisitions were financed only by cash, 19.8 per cent only by equity and 61.5 per cent by a mixture of the two. In contrast, over the period 1991–2000, debt provided an average of 42.4 per cent of the funding of UK PTP transactions (CMBOR, 2003). Fourth, the motives of acquisitions in general are characterized as synergistic if the acquisition is friendly and disciplinary if hostile (Martin and McConnell, 1991). However, it is clear that neither of these alternatives applies easily to firms going private. They are neither hostile, because the objective is not to replace poorly performing management, nor are they synergistic, because the outcome does not involve the association of two complementary companies. These differences suggest that PTPs form a distinct subgroup of acquired firms and this chapter assesses how far we can differentiate between the two groups.

We are not aware of any study that has attempted to differentiate between PTPs and other acquisitions in a period when non-hostile acquisitions are the rule.[3] One US study, Halpern et al. (1999), compared leveraged buy-outs (LBOs) with a random sample of other acquired firms. Their discussion stresses the importance of the threat of hostile take-over but does not indicate what the composition of their acquired firms sample is in terms of the proportions of hostile or non-hostile acquisitions. The period they studied was 1981–86, a time when hostile acquisitions were much more common in the USA than now. They find that the probability of engaging in an LBO increases as managerial share ownership increases and is higher if take-over interest had been reported in the *Wall Street Journal*. They find no evidence of any difference in either growth prospects or free cash flows.

In terms of our initial analysis, the effective elimination of hostile acquisitions means that we construct our null hypothesis in terms of non-hostile acquisitions. Franks and Mayer (1996) and Powell (1997) find that friendly targets are not poor performers and Morck et al. (1988) conclude that friendly targets are 'just regular firms' which possess some specific synergistic characteristic that the acquirer wants. In addition, North (2001) finds that, in a period in which acquisitions are becoming 'friendlier', acquired firms do not perform worse than non-acquired firms. Thus the null hypothesis is that there is no difference between the characteristics of PTPs and other acquired firms. This means that the population of acquired firms is homogeneous and that it is not possible to differentiate between the two subgroups in terms of growth prospects, governance structures or ownership. In contrast, the maintained hypothesis is that acquired firms are heterogeneous and that there are differences between PTPs and other acquired firms. Two specific hypotheses are tested to assess heterogeneity: the incentive realignment hypothesis and the financial incentive hypothesis.

2.1   Incentive realignment hypothesis

The incentive realignment hypothesis argues that PTP transactions will realign shareholder interests by reducing the ability of management to pursue their own non-shareholder value objectives. Thus firms involved in PTP transactions will have characteristics associated with interest misalignment before the decision to go private and so will have incurred higher agency costs than other acquired firms.

The extent of any misalignment of interests may be assessed by investigating the following characteristics. Traditionally, three main approaches have been adopted: the free cash flow hypothesis; low growth prospects and the role of the market for corporate control. First, the incentive realignment hypothesis proposes that PTPs will have higher free cash flows than other acquired firms. Free cash flow measures the cash flow that is greater than that required to fund all projects that have a positive net present value. Jensen (1986) argues that firms going private will have substantial free cash flow and that the PTP transaction will return some of it to the shareholders. This is unlikely to be present in the other take-overs because there is no evidence that they are being driven by this issue (e.g. Morck et al., 1988; Powell, 1997). Going-private transactions, which are usually highly leveraged, will mean that management is committed to paying out these funds to cover the debt repayments rather than spend them on unprofitable projects. Therefore a PTP transaction will reduce agency costs.

Second, consistent with Jensen (1986) and Lehn and Poulsen (1989), the incentive realignment hypothesis argues that firms going private will have lower growth prospects, as measured by the Q ratio, than other acquired firms. High growth prospects will generate a high Q whereas a relatively low Q will indicate that the market is not optimistic about the firm's future. Not only will low growth prospects make it difficult for firms to identify profitable projects; it will also make firms vulnerable to the threat of hostile acquisition. Faced with this possibility, going private presents an opportunity to return some of the lost residual claims to shareholders by offering them a premium on the current share price.

The third element associated with the incentive realignment hypothesis involves the market for corporate control and the threat of take-over. The impact of an acquisition on the employment of the senior management of the acquired team is well documented. For example, in the UK, Kennedy and Limmack (1996) report that in the first year after acquisition, 40.14 per cent of companies changed their CEO and 25.7 per cent changed them in the second. Franks and Mayer (1996) found that 50 per cent of directors of target firms resigned after the bid had been accepted. Dahya and Powell (1999) show that 35.24 per cent of top management teams leave in the first year post take-over and 25.80 per cent in year 2. In the USA, Martin and McConnell (1991) found that 41.9 per cent of CEOs left within one year. Thus there are significant changes in the top management teams of acquired firms in the post-acquisition period. Given this, the threat of acquisition would provide the impetus to return some of the residual claims to other shareholders. The incentive realignment hypothesis therefore predicts that firms going private are more likely to encounter a take-over threat than other acquired firms.

More recent developments stress the potential importance of internal governance mechanisms and ownership. Hence a fourth aspect of the incentive realignment hypothesis implies the presence of board structures that are not consistent with the perception of good governance. In the UK, guidance on this is provided in the Code of Best Practice (Cadbury, 1992), later amended by the Hampel Report (1998) in the Combined Code of Best Practice. The reports were the outcomes of concerns that were being expressed about the quality of financial reporting and the issues of integrity and accountability in UK quoted companies. The reports identified internal governance characteristics that were regarded as best practice and which would, therefore, ensure the effective and transparent governance of quoted companies.

Both the Code and the Combined Code identified two key internal mechanisms for controlling the executive directors. The first is a significant non-executive director representation. Fama (1980) and Cadbury (1992) argue that non-executive, or outside, directors bring the necessary objectivity, skills and experience that enable them to perform an effective monitoring role. This ensures that policies consistent with shareholder objectives are followed. Thus we expect PTPs to have fewer independent directors than other acquired firms.

The second important governance mechanism identified in the Codes relates to duality, the situation where one person takes on the posts of chairman and CEO. Both reports concluded that duality was undesirable given the degree of control that it invests in one person. However, Hampel (1998) did recognize that it may be appropriate in certain circumstances, for example if a company is small. However, given the negative perceptions about duality (Cadbury, 1992), the incentive realignment hypothesis predicts that PTPs will have a higher incidence of duality than other acquired firms.

There is evidence that UK quoted companies have been adopting the internal governance structures recommended in the reports (Weir and Laing, 2000; Dahya et al., 2002), particularly with the appointment of additional non-executive directors and in reducing the incidence of duality. It should be noted that there is no legal requirement to adopt these structures, but companies must include a governance statement in their accounts detailing how far they have implemented the Code of Best Practice. The incentive realignment hypothesis suggests that PTP targets have ineffective internal governance mechanisms and this sends signals to the market that the company is incurring high agency costs.

Fifth, the incentive realignment hypothesis implies that PTPs will have lower internal, and lower external, shareholdings than other acquired firms. As a result they will have higher agency costs. Jensen and Meckling (1976) argue that low shareholdings reduce the incentives for management to pursue wealth maximization policies because the financial returns are so small. It also reduces the incentives for external shareholders to monitor management's actions because the costs do not justify the potential rewards.

Finally, it is also proposed that the extent of capital expenditure is consistent with the incentive realignment hypothesis. However, the direction of the relationship is open to question. High capital expenditure is indicative of the use of funds on projects that will produce negative net present values (Halpern et al., 1999). However, as Long and Ravenscraft (1993) and Lichtenberg and Siegel (1990) argue, lower capital expenditure will increase the ability of going-private firms to service the increased post-PTP debt. Thus, consistent with this hypothesis, firms going private may have higher or lower capital expenditure than other acquired firms.

2.2 Financial incentives hypothesis

The second general explanation of PTPs relates to the financial incentives hypothesis (North, 2001). Within the context of a take-over offer being made, managers are more willing to accept a bid the higher their shareholding in the company. This is because a bid for a company must place a higher value on it than its current market value. The greater the internal shareholdings, the greater the financial incentive to take a company private and so increase personal wealth. DeAngelo et al. (1984) report significant increases in returns when the market finds out that a PTP is proposed. Lehn and Poulsen (1989) found that the premiums paid in PTP transactions were statistically significant. Maupin et al. (1984) and Walkling and Long (1984) found higher shareholdings in non-hostile bids, a finding also reported by Morck et al. (1988). Halpern et al. (1999) found firms involved in LBOs had significantly higher managerial share ownership than in other acquired firms. Thus PTPs are expected to have higher internal shareholdings than other acquired firms.

There are also incentive effects present with external shareholdings. For example, Morck et al. (1988) and North (2001) find a positive relationship between external shareholdings and the probability of acquisition. If the market undervalues the company, the institutions will have a financial incentive to accept the premium offered by the buyer. Therefore the financial incentive hypothesis predicts a positive relationship between going private and institutional shareholdings.

The financial incentive hypothesis, like the incentive realignment hypothesis, argues that PTPs will have lower Q ratios than other acquired firms. This would be consistent with information asymmetry, or private information, which causes the management to expect higher future returns than those being signalled by the market. This expectation will force the management and private equity firms to offer a bid in excess of the current market valuation because both believe that management has private information. In addition, the private equity firms believe that their specialist skills enable them to identify growth opportunities that the market does not know about.

The hypotheses are summarized in Table 10.1.

Table 10.1   Summary of hypotheses

	Incentive realignment hypothesis	Financial incentive hypothesis
Board shareholdings	Negative	Positive
Institutional shareholdings	Positive	Positive
Duality	Positive	Not significant
Non-executive director representation	Negative	Not significant
Q ratio	Negative	Negative
Free cash flow	Positive	Not significant
Take-over		
• bid rumours	Positive	Not significant
• multiple bidders	Positive	Not significant
Capital expenditure	Positive/negative	Not significant
Boardpower	Positive	Positive
Free cash flow*Q	Positive	Not significant

Notes:
Positive – a high value increases the probability of being involved in a PTP.
Negative – a low value decreases the probability of being involved in a PTP.
Not significant – no difference between the firms going private and other acquired firms.

3.   Data and Research Design

3.1   Sample

The sample consists of a total of 362 UK quoted acquisitions. Of these, 99 were PTP transactions and 263 were other publicly quoted companies that were acquired during the period 1998 to 2000. To be included, acquired companies had to have complete financial and governance data available and they had to exclude the acquisition of companies in the financial services sector. Firms in the financial services sector have non-standard accounts and cannot be compared to firms in the other sectors. They are also subject to external scrutiny by the Financial Services Authority, which means that the usual governance–agency issues may not apply. Over the period there were 500 acquisitions of UK public companies. Of these, 100 were in the financial services sector and 38 had missing or incomplete data. This gives the final sample of 362.

The PTP and acquisitions data were collected from a number of sources. First, *Acquisitions Monthly*, which publishes information on acquisition activity in the UK. Second, data on the PTP transactions were supplied by the Centre for Management Buyout Research *Quarterly Review*, which is based at the University of Nottingham, the *Financial Times* Intelligence Service and Vickers (2000). Financial information was taken from Extel Primark Company Analysis, which provides accounting and financial data on UK quoted companies. The corporate governance and shareholding data were taken from the PriceWaterhouseCoopers Corporate Register. This provides information on internally held shareholdings and also details external shareholdings in excess of 3 per cent. It also gives details of board structure. Information on take-over rumours came from FT Intelligence, which provides newspaper text reports. The data are measured at the date of the last accounts before the acquisition.

The following model was estimated by logistic regression and the logit results reported. Logistic regression estimates the probability of a company being involved in a PTP, rather than being acquired, given a matrix of explanatory variables.

$$y = X\beta$$

where

$$y_i = \beta_0 + \beta_1 PIND + \beta_2 DUALITY + \beta_3 FCF + \beta_4 Q + \beta_5 BOARDSHARE$$
$$+ \beta_6 INSTITSHARE + \beta_7 TAKEOVER + \beta_8 LNMC + \beta_9 CAPEX$$

and

$$P_i = \frac{1}{1 + e_i^{-y}}$$

P_i is the probability that the *i*th firm will be a PTP transaction and $1 - P_i$ is the probability that the *i*th firm will be a different type of acquisition and *e* is the natural log.

The variables are defined as follows:

Y – a binary dependent variable. It takes the value 1 if the acquisition was a PTP and zero if a company was acquired by other means.

PIND – the percentage of independent non-executive directors on the board. To be defined as independent, a non-executive director must not have previously been an executive director of the company or an adviser to the company. Also excluded are directors who are related to executive directors or who work for firms with large shareholdings.

DUALITY – a binary variable. It is equal to 1 if the posts of CEO and chairman are held by the same person and zero if they are not.

FCF – measures a company's free cash flow. It is defined as the operating cash flow minus interest, taxes and dividends divided by sales.

Q – measures the company's growth prospects. It is defined as the market value of the company plus debt minus cash divided by the book value of assets.

TAKEOVER – represents the market for corporate control and is defined in two ways:

(i)   *RUMOUR* – a binary variable that takes the value 1 if there had been, within the period 1 month to 18 months before the bid being made, a report in the financial press that the company may be taken over and zero if not (Lehn and Poulsen, 1989).

(ii)   *THREAT* – a dummy variable that takes a value of 1 if there were hostile or multiple bidders for a company and zero if not. This shows the actual presence of alternative bidders and is hence a stronger measure of interest than the reporting of rumours.

BOARDSHARE – the percentage of issued capital owned by the whole board.

INSTITSHARE – the percentage of the issued capital held by all institutions that have a shareholding in excess of 3 per cent. In the UK, shareholdings below this do not need to be declared.

LNMC – the natural log of market capitalization, included to control for size.

CAPEX – net capital expenditure divided by the book value of total assets expressed as a percentage. It controls for investment in new and existing businesses.

BOARDPOWER – a dummy variable that takes the value 1 if the board has a larger shareholding than *INSTITSHARE*. It provides another measure of the extent to which PTP transactions are insider-driven. Both the financial incentive and incentive realignment hypotheses predict a positive relationship between the probability of the board owning more shares than the largest institutions and the decision to go private.

FCF*Q – a dummy variable that has the value of 1 if a firm has above median free cash flow and below median *Q* and zero if not. Opler and Titman (1993) argue that the appropriate test of Jensen's free cash flow, or incentive realignment, hypothesis is to look at the interactive relationship between free cash flow and *Q* rather than treat them separately. This leads us to expect a positive relationship between *FCF*Q* and being involved in a PTP.

4.   Empirical Results

4.1   Sample characteristics

Table 10.2 reports the characteristics of the sample. In terms of ownership, the mean *BOARDSHARE* is 11.92 per cent but only 10 per cent of the sample had shareholdings in excess of 20 per cent. This shows that in relatively few cases did the board have a large absolute shareholding. Institutions held an average of almost one third of the shares, 31.62 per cent, of acquired firms. The board structure statistics show that 20 per cent of the sample had one person undertaking the dual roles of CEO and chairman. Boards had an average of 38 per cent independent non-executive directors. Over half of the firms, 52 per cent, experienced take-over rumours in the press. In terms of specific take-over pressures, 18 per cent of firms were subjected to publicly reported competition from another buyer. On average, the sample had a *Q* ratio of 1.12, which suggests that the market had a marginally positive overall view of the growth prospects of acquired firms before take-over. However, 66.4 per cent had a *Q* ratio of less than 1, which indicates that, in general, the market regarded

Table 10.2 Sample descriptive statistics

	Minimum	Maximum	Mean	Standard deviation
BOARDSHARE (%)	0.01	85.00	11.92	17.39
INSTITSHARE (%)	0.00	83.49	31.59	20.59
DUALITY	0.00	1.00	0.20	0.40
RUMOUR	0.00	1.00	0.52	0.50
THREAT	0	1.00	0.18	0.38
Q ratio	-0.25^1	10.81	1.12	1.11
PIND (%)	0.00	80.00	38.71	15.98
FCF	−163.78	51.33	3.59	13.79
BOARDPOWER	0	1.00	0.23	0.42
FCF*Q	0	1.00	0.21	0.41
BIDPREM	0.12	25.93	1.74	2.19
CAPEX (%)	−137.19	79.65	5.14	16.35
Market capitalization (£m)	1.08	43 049.00	361.62	2406.58

Notes:
BOARDSHARE is the percentage of issued capital owned by the board. *INSTITSHARE* is the sum of all institutional shareholdings in excess of 3 per cent. *DUALITY* is a dummy variable that has a value of 1 if the posts of CEO and chairman are undertaken by a single person and zero if they are separated. *RUMOUR* is a dummy variable that has a value of 1 if take-over rumours had been reported in the financial press and zero if there had been no rumours. *THREAT* is a dummy variable that has a value of 1 if a firm experienced multiple bidders and zero if not. *Q* is market capitalization plus debt minus cash over the book value of assets. *PIND* is the percentage of independent non-executive directors on the board. *FCF* is operating cash flow minus interest, taxes and dividend divided by sales. *BIDPREM* is defined as the value of the accepted bid divided by the market capitalization at the date of the last accounts. *PRIVATE EQUITY* is a dummy variable that takes a value of 1 if a private equity provider led the transaction and zero if not. *REPUTATION* is a dummy variable that takes a value of 1 if a private equity firm had been involved in more than two of the deals in the sample. *BOARDPOWER* is a dummy variable that takes a value of 1 if the board has a larger shareholding than the combined shareholdings of those institutions with more than 3 per cent and zero if not. *FCF*Q* is a dummy variable that has the value of 1 if a firm has above median free cash flow and lower than median *Q* and zero if not. CAPEX is the percentage net capital expenditure over total assets. Market capitalization is the market value of equity.

1. One company had cash reserves greater than the combined value of its market value and debt. This gives a negative value for *Q*.

acquired firms as having poor growth prospects, regardless of the type of acquisition. The mean free cash flow for the sample is 3.59, with 83 per cent of firms having positive free cash flows.

In 23 per cent of acquired firms, the board held more shares than the largest institutions. Twenty-one per cent of firms combined above average free cash flow with a poor *Q* ratio. The average bid premium was 74 per cent, showing that shareholders did well when their shares were bought. In terms of capital expenditure, the mean figure is 5.14 per cent, with 28 per cent of firms spending in excess of 10 per cent of the value of their assets on capital projects. The mean size of acquired firms is £361.62 million.

4.2   Univariate results

Table 10.3 presents the initial univariate comparison of PTPs and acquired firms. Because of the non-normal distribution of the variables, the non-parametric Mann–Whitney and chi square tests were used. We find that PTPs had significantly higher board shareholdings, more duality and were more likely to experience press take-over speculation than other acquired firms. They also had lower *Q* ratios and were smaller. In addition, PTPs had significantly more cases where board shareholdings exceeded institutional shareholdings, with *BOARDPOWER* significant at 1 per cent. However, there is no difference in the extent to which the two groups faced public take-over competition from other firms. Neither are there any differences in institutional shareholdings, the percentage of non-executive directors, free cash flow or capital expenditure. Although higher, the interactive free cash flow–*Q* ratio term was insignificant. The initial results therefore appear to offer support for the heterogeneity hypothesis.

4.3   Multivariate results

Table 10.4 presents the logistic regression results. A number of models are tested. Models 1 and 2 show the basic analysis, including different measures of the market for corporate control. Models 3 and 4 further investigate the financial incentive hypothesis by including a dummy variable that measures the relative shareholdings of the board and institutions. Opler and Titman (1993) argue that free cash flow and *Q* should be treated interdependently rather than separately. To take account of this, Models 5 and 6 include an interactive term for free cash flow and *Q*.

The results show that PTPs are more likely to experience rumours of take-over speculation in the press than other targets. They also have significantly lower *Q* ratios, are more likely to have higher board shareholdings and are more likely to have higher institutional shareholdings. Models 3 and 4 show that PTPs are more likely to have a more closely held internal share structure with *BOARDPOWER* being both significant and positive. However, none of the models suggests that PTPs have fewer non-executive directors or are more likely to combine the posts of CEO and chairman.[4] Neither is there any difference in the extent of free cash flows generated, the intensity of capital expenditure or size. Further, in Models 5 and 6, the interaction free cash flow–*Q* ratio variable is insignificant, casting doubt on the part played by free cash flow measures in UK PTPs.[5]

However, the Halpern et al. (1999) argument that the expression of take-over interest is a proxy for hostile intent, and hence shows pressure from the market for corporate control, is not borne out by the statistics in the UK. As Table 10.3 shows, 62 per cent of PTPs had press reports highlighting take-over interest; however, only 15 per cent were specifically reported as experiencing opposing bids. In terms of other acquired firms, 49 per cent experienced press speculation but only 18 per cent were actually reported as involving multiple bidders. This is consistent with Maupin et al. (1984), who found that PTPs were predominately friendly. The existence of hostile intentions does not, therefore, appear to be the reason for the greater press speculation associated with PTPs.

In addition, there are a number of problems associated with using press speculation as a proxy for the market for corporate control. For example, press coverage may simply be

Table 10.3   Univariate analysis of PTP transactions and other acquired companies

	Mean		Median		Z statistic
	PTP	Acquired	PTP	Acquired	
BOARDSHARE (%)	17.80	9.69	7.84	3.02	3.94 (0.00)
INSTITSHARE (%)	33.47	30.92	34.14	29.17	1.18 (0.23)
DUALITY	0.28	0.17	0.00	0.00	4.74** (0.02)
THREAT	0.15	0.18	0	0	0.59 (0.43)
RUMOUR	0.62	0.49	1.00	0	4.55** (0.03)
Q	0.87	1.22	0.76	0.86	2.36** (0.18)
PIND (%)	36.63	39.49	40.00	40.00	1.12 (0.26)
FCF	4.23	3.35	3.39	4.21	0.75 (0.44)
BOARDPOWER	0.32	0.20	0	0	5.93** (0.01)
FCF*Q	0.22	0.20	0	0	0.12 (0.72)
CAPEX (%)	2.83	6.01	4.78	6.25	1.02 (0.30)
Market capitalization (£m)	91.49	463.30	30.43	46.15	2.35** (0.01)

Notes:
** significant at the 5% level.
p-values in parentheses.
Mann–Whitney test used for all variables except chi square test applied to the dummy variables *DUALITY, RUMOUR, THREAT, BOARDPOWER* and *FCF*Q*.
See also notes to Table 10.2.

reporting the intention to take a firm private rather than reporting an alternative bid. Alternatively, the press may not comment on the bids for small quoted companies. In addition, Pound and Zeckhauser (1990) found that only 43 per cent of firms that were the subject of take-over rumours had actually received a bid within a year. Therefore care should be taken when drawing inferences that the reporting of take-over rumours shows that the market for corporate control is operating as if the rumour were hostile.

To overcome this problem, an alternative measure of the market for corporate control was used, *THREAT*. It measures the reporting of an alternative bid to the one initially

Table 10.4   Logistic regression explaining the differences between PTPs and other acquired firms

	Model 1	Model 2	Model 3	Model 4	Model 5	Model 6
RUMOUR	0.7221		0.7545		0.7185	
	(0.000)***		(0.005)***		(0.007)***	
THREAT		−0.2486		−0.1484		−0.1615
		(0.472)		(0.660)		(0.639)
PIND	−0.0021	0.0001	−0.0063	−0.0040	−0.0038	−0.0016
	(0.807)	(0.995)	(0.437)	(0.616)	(0.651)	(0.849)
DUALITY	0.4868	0.5015	0.4489	0.4470	0.4608	0.4634
	(0.122)	(0.106)	(0.158)	(0.134)	(0.132)	(0.123)
FCF	0.0191	0.0131	0.0181	0.0121		
	(0.147)	(0.288)	(0.167)	(0.330)		
Q ratio	−0.5809	−0.6342	−0.3743	−0.4286		
	(0.013)**	(0.007)***	(0.060)*	(0.031)**		
BOARDSHARE	0.0436	0.0423			0.0345	0.0328
	(0.000)***	(0.000)***			(0.000)***	(0.000)***
INSTITSHARE	0.0198	0.0224			0.0188	0.0212
	(0.007)**	(0.002)***			(0.010)***	(0.003)***
LNMC	−0.0026	0.0565	−0.1453	−0.0969	−0.0636	−0.0347
	(0.981)	(0.588)	(0.131)	(0.297)	(0.500)	(0.708)
CAPEX	−0.0066	−0.0061	−0.0087	−0.0079	−0.0084	−0.0089
	(0.415)	(0.456)	(0.252)	(0.296)	(0.290)	(0.226)
BOARDPOWER			0.6697	0.5303		
			(0.026)**	(0.073)*		
*FCF*Q*					0.1057	0.0828
					(0.729)	(0.785)
Constant	−2.0959	−1.9431	−0.5362	−0.2453	−2.1529	−1.9656
	(0.002)***	(0.000)***	(0.290)	(0.614)	(0.001)***	(0.003)***
Chi square	49.99***	43.38***	32.06***	23.88***	37.31***	29.91***
	(0.000)	(0.000)	(0.000)	(0.000)	(0.000)	(0.000)

Notes:
p-values in parentheses; *** significant at the 1% level; ** significant at the 5% level; * significant at the 10% level.
See also notes to Table 10.2. LNMC is the natural log of the market value of equity.

received and provides an indication of the extent to which there was publicly known competition to acquire a company. This is consistent with Schwert (2000), who stresses the importance of public auctions as a means of identifying hostility. As Table 10.4 shows, *THREAT* is insignificant in all models, which shows that there is no difference in the extent of public auctions across types of acquisition. The analysis was then developed to address the issues of the extent of bid premiums offered to shareholders and managerial entrenchment.

The first development to be analysed is the size of the bid premium, *P*, which was measured by the value of the accepted bid, V^*, divided by the market value of the company, V_c, the latter being the figure at the end of the last financial year-end. Assuming an efficient market and no information asymmetry, we would expect

$$P_{PTP} = P_{AD},$$

where PTP = PTP transactions and AD = other acquired firms.

In terms of the wealth windfall returned to shareholders on the change of ownership, the incentive realignment hypothesis predicts that the premiums gained by other shareholders will be less than those received by the shareholders of other acquired firms. This is because the other shareholders will be more willing to accept a relatively lower bid given that they know that the presence of a large internal shareholding will make an alternative bid less likely. The relatively lower premium therefore adds to the other shareholders' agency costs. Thus:

$$P_{PTP} < P_{AD}$$

Second, if the main objective were to maximize their own shareholder wealth and to potentially liquidate a significant proportion of their own wealth, we would expect higher premiums to be offered to the other shareholders. This would mean that internal and external shareholders would benefit and is consistent with the financial incentive hypothesis. Thus:

$$P_{PTP} > P_{AD}$$

In contrast, low board ownership is not likely to offer financial incentives and so the bid premium is not expected to be significantly different for low ownership. Equally, the incentive realignment hypothesis does not specify the extent of the premium where board ownership is low.

As Table 10.5 shows, the Mann–Whitney test means that we can reject the null hypothesis of no difference between the bid premiums paid to shareholders of PTPs and those paid to the shareholders of other acquired firms.[6] The results show that the shareholders of PTPs received significantly lower premiums than those paid to the shareholders of the other acquired firms. On average, the shareholders of other acquired firms received a premium of 58 per cent. In contrast, shareholders of PTPs with low board shareholdings received a premium of 37 per cent and high board shareholdings PTPs generated a premium of only 18 per cent.

Table 10.5   Incentive effects and bid premiums

	PTP mean	Acquired mean	t test	Z statistic
Whole sample	1.32	1.58	(0.006)***	(0.003)***
High board shareholdings	1.18	1.58	(0.018)**	(0.040)***
Low board shareholdings	1.37	1.58	(0.063)*	(0.046)**

Notes:
p-values in parentheses; *** significant at the 1% level; ** significant at 5% level, * significant at 10% level.
Bid premium is defined as the value of the accepted bid divided by the market capitalization at the date of the last accounts.

Although the premium paid to shareholders of PTPs was higher with low board shareholdings than with high board shareholdings, the difference was not significant. It should also be noted that the premiums paid to both sets of shareholders were significantly greater than zero, which offers some support for the financial incentive hypothesis. However, as shown, the effect is less strong for PTP shareholders.

The second development addresses the argument that, unlike the Jensen and Meckling (1976) model, internal ownership and agency costs do not have a linear relationship but rather exhibit a non-linear one. At low levels of inside ownership, inside owners pursue non-value-maximizing objectives by consuming large amounts of perks and/or engaging in suboptimal investment behaviour. At high levels of internal ownership, the board becomes entrenched and the directors can continue their non-optimal behaviour. Their ability to do this derives from the protection they receive from their relatively large voting rights. Therefore there is a misalignment of interests at both low and high levels of internal ownership. A number of studies, including Halpern et al. (1999), Morck et al. (1998) and McConnell and Servaes (1990), have found evidence consistent with the non-linear entrenchment hypothesis.

There are a number of ways to investigate the entrenchment hypothesis. Morck et al. (1988) use piecewise regression but recognize that there is an element of trial and error in finding the appropriate turning point(s). We follow Halpern et al. (1999) and use cluster analysis to split PTP board shareholdings into high and low board ownership. The low board shareholding cluster has a mean of 6.37 per cent and the high ownership cluster a mean of 45.61 per cent. The low ownership cluster included 70 PTPs and the high ownership cluster had 29 PTPs. As in Halpern et al. (1999), each cluster was then regressed against all other acquired firms.

If entrenchment is present, PTPs with high board shareholdings are more likely to exhibit higher agency costs than other acquired firms. They would have lower Q ratios, higher free cash flows, fewer non-executive directors and more duality. However, they should experience less alternative take-over interest because of the potential difficulties faced by outside bidders when trying to buy a company that already has a significant internal blockholding, particularly one that may not wish to sell. For example, potential bidders may believe that a firm that has a closely held ownership structure may try to extract too high a premium from a bidder such that any anticipated gains will not accrue to the bidder. Therefore the presence of large internal shareholdings may persuade a potential buyer to look elsewhere, which will reduce the liquidity of the wealth of both the internal and external shareholders.

We also expect low board ownership to be consistent with high agency costs because of the associated excessive consumption of perks. The key difference between high and low board shareholdings is that the latter will experience a greater take-over threat than other acquired firms. This is because the low internal ownership firms going private would lack a significant block of shareholdings that may be used to oppose a bid.

Table 10.6 presents the logistic regression results for both of the board shareholdings subsamples. Splitting the sample into high and low ownership PTPs reveals significant differences between the subgroups and other acquired firms. Shareholders of PTPs that had high board ownership received lower premiums than those paid to the shareholders in other acquisitions.[7] These companies also had significantly lower growth prospects. There is some evidence that duality is more common and free cash flows higher in the high ownership group. How-

Table 10.6 *Impact of shareholdings and bid premiums on the probability of differentiating between PTPs and other acquired firms.*

	High board shareholdings			Low board shareholdings		
	Model 8	Model 9	Model 10	Model 11	Model 12	Model 13
BIDPREM	−1.0371	−0.8885	−0.6165	−0.4501	−0.4022	−0.4274
	(0.059)*	(0.068)*	(0.152)	(0.044)**	(0.057)*	(0.046)**
THREAT	0.0347	0.5880	−0.2594	−0.2141	−0.1034	−0.1322
	(0.973)	(0.548)	(0.800)	(0.565)	(0.776)	(0.721)
PIND	0.0042	−0.0168	−0.0079	−0.0003	0.0005	−0.0008
	(0.823)	(0.280)	(0.632)	(0.973)	(0.960)	(0.936)
DUALITY	1.1261	0.8722	0.9582	0.2432	0.2526	0.2341
	(0.077)*	(0.113)	(0.087)*	(0.514)	(0.496)	(0.523)
FCF	0.0606	0.0509		0.0052	0.0065	
	(0.091)*	(0.126)		(0.687)	(0.697)	
Q ratio	−2.3165	−0.8421		−0.3931	−0.3600	
	(0.002)***	(0.044)**		(0.117)	(0.134)	
BOARDSHARE	0.1106		0.0679	−0.0018		−0.0111
	(0.000)***		(0.000)***	(0.905)		(0.454)
INSTITSHARE	−0.0170		0.0132	0.0258		0.0252
	(0.406)		(0.458)	(0.001)***		(0.002)***
LNMC	0.2886	−0.0465	0.0394	−0.0222	−0.1218	−0.1011
	(0.270)	(0.824)	(0.848)	(0.851)	(0.248)	(0.342)
BOARDPOWER		4.8634			−1.4296	
		(0.000)***			(0.010)**	
FCF*Q			0.6446			−0.1477
			(0.324)			(0.681)
CAPEX	0.0114	−0.0126	0.0015	−0.0043	−0.0057	−0.0060
	(0.0551)	(0.442)	(0.943)	(0.642)	(0.521)	(0.510)
Constant	−2.8380	−3.2251	−3.1042	−1.1009	0.2305	−1.0616
	(0.065)*	(0.042)**	(0.036)**	(0.183)	(0.723)	(0.197)
Chi square	99.95***	90.36***	77.61***	27.42***	22.73***	23.99***
	(0.000)	(0.000)	(0.000)	(0.000)	(0.000)	(0.000)

Notes:
p-values in parentheses; *** significant at the 1% level; ** significant at the 5% level; * significant at the 10% level.
See also notes to Table 10.2. LNMC is the log of the market value of equity.

ever, the insignificant free cash flow–*Q* ratio interaction term suggests that the free cash flow model does not explain PTPs in the UK. Board shareholdings of PTPs are higher in the high board shareholdings group relative to the board ownership of other acquired firms. Institutional shareholdings are not significant in the high shareholdings sample.

These results are supported by the significant board power variable, which shows that overall, internal ownership dominates the decision to go private. However, the lack of competition from other potential buyers suggests that the decision to go private is not being driven by the fear of acquisition and possible job loss. This is borne out by the fact that over half of the firms going private in the high board ownership group were not subjected to takeover rumour and speculation.

Thus PTPs that have high board ownership may be characterized as having lower growth prospects, higher free cash flows, more duality and lower bid premiums, all of which suggest the presence of managerial entrenchment. The results imply that the decision to go private, when coupled with high internal ownership, is driven by the incentive realignment hypothesis.

The results for the low board shareholdings sample also show that lower premiums are paid for firms going private. The only other difference relates to institutional shareholdings, which are significantly higher and suggests that institutional ownership and board ownership are substitute mechanisms. However, in spite of the fact that their growth prospects were no worse than those of other acquired firms, these shareholders received significantly lower premiums than those received by shareholders of other acquired firms.

Thus, overall, PTPs do not represent good value for external shareholders because they receive a smaller proportion of the residual claims than shareholders of other acquired firms. Control is likely to be retained post-PTP but only a proportion of the forgone wealth is returned to other shareholders. Contrary to expectations, the extent of the premium paid does not appear to reflect a trade-off between returning cash to shareholders and the desire to retain control.

5.   Conclusions

This chapter has addressed governance issues relating to the PTP threshold. We have shown that PTP transactions can be distinguished from other acquisitions in terms of a number of governance and other characteristics. Firms going private were more likely to have higher internal and external ownership, and were more likely to experience take-over speculation in the press. They were also more likely to have lower growth prospects and their shareholders were more likely to receive lower premiums. We found no evidence of differences in governance mechanisms between types of acquired firm or that free cash flow explained the difference.

Our results raise a number of additional research questions. In particular, analysis of the extent of CEO and other executive director turnover post-PTP may provide additional insights into the desire to avoid public monitoring by going private. The bid premium and the relationship with the type of acquisition is also something that requires further investigation, particularly as external shareholders appear to get a particularly poor deal when board ownership is high.

Notes

1.   The analysis of publicly quoted firms that have been acquired tends to be undertaken from one of the following methodologies. First, the comparison of all characteristics of acquired firms with those of non-acquired firms (e.g. Palepu, 1986). Second, the comparison of firms acquired in hostile and non-hostile take-overs (e.g. Martin and McConnell, 1991; Franks and Mayer, 1996; Kennedy and Limmack, 1996). Third, a comparison of the characteristics of firms acquired by friendly take-over with those of non-acquired firms (e.g. Song and Walkling, 1993; Nuttall,

1999). Fourth, a comparison of firms involved in hostile acquisitions with those of non-acquired firms (e.g. Shivdasani, 1993).

2. Even this split, however, may not accurately reflect the true situation. For example, Schwert (2000) argues that any initial rejection of an approach may simply indicate an attempt to get the bidder to enter into an auction process the purpose of which is to increase the value of the bid. In addition, Boone and Mulherin (2002) argue that the traditional definition ignores potential private auctions.

3. In the USA, the literature on PTP transactions tends to compare PTPs with firms that remain public (e.g. Halpern et al., 1999; Kaplan, 1989; Lehn and Poulsen, 1989; Maupin et al., 1984; Kieschnick, 1998). Alternatively it looks at the impact of PTPs on the share price (e.g. DeAngelo et al., 1984; Frankfurter and Gunay, 1992; Torabzadeh and Bertin, 1987).

4. The results are therefore consistent with studies such as Kini et al. (1995) and Weir et al. (2002) that show substitutability between agency mechanisms. One possibility for the insignificance of the governance variables is multicollinearity. However, the correlations are not high enough to suggest problems. The correlation between *BOARDPOWER* and duality and non-executive directors is 0.16 and –0.21 respectively. The correlation between board shareholdings and duality and non-executive directors is 0.17 and –0.29 respectively. In addition, the variation inflation factors showed no evidence of multicollinearity.

5. We also attempted to take account of industry effects through industry dummies. Using the *Financial Times* Classification System, 27 sectors were identified. However, the small number of PTPs and acquisitions in some of the sectors meant that the matrix was singular. To overcome this, sectors had to be omitted from the regressions. For example, to include industry effects in Table 10.4, 30 per cent of the classification groups would have had to be omitted. To include them in Table 10.6, the high CEO shareholdings models, 35 per cent of the sector classifications would have had to be omitted; the figure for the low CEO shareholdings sample was 40 per cent. It was concluded that the omission of so many sectors would have cast doubt on the meaningfulness of the results. We defined industry effects as the extent of actual take-over activity in the industry of each target firm. This would capture industry effects such as the sensitivity to general market conditions, product life cycle effects and technological effects. The variable was insignificant, suggesting that industry effects do not differentiate between types of acquisition.

6. The bid premium variable had five observations that were in excess of three standard deviations from the mean. Two were PTPs and the other three were other acquired firms. The results presented in Tables 10.5 and 10.6 are obtained by excluding these outliers. The sample mean was 1.79 and the omitted companies had premiums ranging from 11.30 to 25.93.

7. The raw bid premium was also calculated for the percentage change in the share price one day before the announcement date and the share price the day after. The results were similar to those given in Table 10.6. The low CEO shareholdings sample had significantly lower premiums, at the 10 per cent level, and the high CEO shareholdings sample had insignificant share price changes.

References

Boone, A.L. and Mulherin, J.H. (2002), 'Corporate restructuring and corporate auctions', working paper, College of William and Mary.

Cadbury Committee (1992), *Report of the Committee on the Financial Aspects of Corporate Governance*, London: Gee.

CMBOR (2003), *Quarterly Review* from the Centre for Management Buy-out Research, Nottingham University Business School, Spring.

Dahya, J. and Powell, R. (1999), *Top Management Changes Following Hostile and Friendly Takeovers*, ACCA Research Report, 61, London.

Dahya, J., McConnell, J.J. and Travlos, N.G. (2002), 'The Cadbury Committee, corporate performance and top management turnover', *Journal of Finance*, **57**: 461–83.

DeAngelo, H., DeAngelo, L. and Rice, E. (1984), 'Going private: minority freeze outs and stockholders' wealth', *Journal of Law and Economics*, **27**: 367–402.

Fama, E. (1980), 'Agency problems and the theory of the firm', *Journal of Political Economy*, **88**: 134–45.

Frankfurter, G. and Gunay, E. (1992), 'Management buyouts: the sources and sharing of wealth between insiders and outside shareholders', *Quarterly Review of Economics and Finance*, **32**: 163–81.

Franks, J. and Mayer, C. (1996), 'Hostile takeovers and the correction of managerial failure', *Journal of Financial Economics*, **40**: 163–81.

Freshfields, Bruckhaus, Deringer (2002), *Public Takeovers in the UK*, London: Freshfields, Bruckhaus, Deringer.

Halpern, P., Kieschnick, R. and Rotenberg, W. (1999), 'On the heterogeneity of leveraged going private transactions', *Review of Financial Studies*, **12**: 281–309.

Hampel, R. (1998), *Committee on Corporate Governance: Final Report*, London: Gee.

Jensen, M. (1986), 'Agency costs and free cash flow, corporate finance and take-overs', *American Economics Review*, **76**, 323–9.

Jensen, M. and Meckling, W. (1976), 'Theory of the firm: managerial behaviour, agency costs and ownership structure', *Journal of Financial Economics*, **13**: 305–60.

Kaplan, S. (1989), 'Management buyouts: evidence on taxes as a source of value', *Journal of Finance*, **64**: 611–32.

Kennedy, V. and Limmack, R. (1996), 'Takeover activity CEO turnover and the market for corporate control', *Journal of Business Finance and Accounting*, **23**: 267–93.

Kieschnick, R. (1998), 'Free cash flow and stockholder gains in going private transaction revisited', *Journal of Business Finance and Accounting*, **25**: 187–202.

Kini, O., Kracaw, W. and Mian, S. (1995), 'Corporate takeovers, firm performance and board composition', *Journal of Corporate Finance*, **1**: 383–412.

Lehn, K. and Poulsen, A. (1989), 'Free cash flow and stockholder gains in going private transactions', *Journal of Finance*, **44**: 771–87.

Lichtenberg, F.R. and Siegel, D. (1990), 'The effects of leveraged buyouts on productivity and related aspects of firm behaviour', *Journal of Financial Economics*, **26**: 165–94.

Long, W.F. and Ravenscraft, D.J. (1993), 'LBOs, debt and R and D intensity', *Strategic Management Journal*, **14** (special issue): 119–35.

Martin, K.J. and McConnell, J.J. (1991), 'Corporate performance, corporate takeovers and management turnover', *Journal of Finance*, **46**: 671–87.

Maupin, R., Bidwell, C. and Ortegren, C. (1984), 'An empirical investigation of the characteristics of publicly quoted corporations which change to closely held ownership through management buyouts', *Journal of Business Finance and Accounting*, **11**: 345–59.

McConnell, J.J. and Servaes, H. (1990), 'Additional evidence on equity ownership and corporate value', *Journal of Financial Economics*, **27**: 595–612.

Morck, R., Shleifer, A. and Vishny, R. (1988), 'Characteristics of targets and friendly take-overs', in A.J. Auerbach (ed.), *Corporate Take-overs: Causes and Consequences*, Chicago: University of Chicago Press.

Murphy, K.J. (1999), 'Executive compensation', in O. Ashenfelter and D. Card (eds), *Handbook of Labour Economics*, Volume 3, Amsterdam: North-Holland.

North, D. (2001), 'The role of managerial incentives in corporate acquisitions: evidence from the 1990s', *Journal of Corporate Finance*, **7**: 125–49.

Nuttall, R. (1999), 'Takeover likelihood models for UK quoted companies', Nuffield College Working Paper, University of Oxford.

Opler, T. and Titman, S. (1993), 'The determinants of leveraged buyout activity: free cash flow vs. financial distress costs', *Journal of Finance*, **48**: 1985–99.

Palepu, K.G. (1986), 'Predicting take-over targets: a methodological and empirical analysis', *Journal of Accounting and Economics*, **8**: 3–35.

Pound, J. and Zeckhauser, R. (1990), 'Clearly heard on the street: the effect of takeover rumours on stock prices', *Journal of Business*, **63**: 291–308.

Powell, R.G. (1997), 'Modelling take-over likelihood', *Journal of Business Finance and Accounting*, **24**: 1009–30.

Schwert, G.W. (2000), 'Hostility in take-overs: in the eyes of the beholders', *Journal of Finance*, **55**: 2599–640.

Shivdasani, A. (1993), 'Board composition, ownership structure and hostile take-overs', *Journal of Accounting and Finance*, **16**: 167–98.

Song, M. and Walkling, R. (1993), 'The impact of managerial ownership on acquisition attempts', *Journal of Financial and Quantitative Analysis*, **28**: 439–57.

Sudarsanam, P.S. and Mahate, A.A. (2003), 'Glamorous acquirers, method of payment and post-acquisition performance: the UK evidence', *Journal of Business Finance and Accounting*, **30**: 329–41.

Torabzadeh, D. and Bertin, W. (1987), 'Leveraged buyouts and shareholder returns', *The Journal of Financial Research*, **20**: 313–19.

Vickers, M. (2000), *Public to Private Takeovers: The New Paradigms*, London: Ashurst, Morris Crisp.

Walkling, R. and Long, M. (1984), 'Agency theory, managerial welfare and take-over bid resistance', *Rand Journal of Economics*, **15**: 55–68.

Weir, C.M. and Laing, D.L. (2000), 'The performance–governance relationship: the effects of Cadbury compliance on UK quoted companies', *Journal of Management and Governance*, **4**: 265–81.

Weir, C., Laing, D. and McKnight, P.J. (2002), 'Internal and external governance mechanisms: their impact on the performance of large UK public companies', *Journal of Business Finance and Accounting*, **29**: 579–611.

[11]

Corporate governance, strategy and structure: US and British comparatives, 1950–2000

Steve Toms and Mike Wright

Introduction

The literature on international comparative governance research has a tendency to combine the salient features of American and British capitalism into a single 'Anglo-American' model. Such a combination serves the purpose of more easier comparison with the sharper contrasts offered by the governance models of Germany and Japan. As a result, US/UK comparative work has been neglected. This is a pity, since although there are important similarities, the differences have not been fully investigated. Such an investigation is particularly worthwhile in so far as there may be opportunities to refine the positive aspects of the 'Anglo-American' model by combining the best aspects of each. This might be particularly worthy in view of the criticisms that the model has faced in the past and which seem likely to dominate the agenda of governance and economic regulators in the future.

The main area that this chapter is concerned to contrast is the relationship between changes in corporate governance and changes in firms' exploitation of scale and scope economies, to explain the exploitation of the firm's strategic resource base by entrepreneurial and managerial groups. In the period 1950–80, US corporations successfully exploited scale and scope economies, adoption of scientific management, the multi-divisional structure and the associated benefits of large-scale high-throughput production.[1] Meanwhile British business has been criticized for failure to emulate these practices.[2] Even so, the perceived value of flexibility in smaller-scale production has received greater attention in the research literature.[3] The essence of this debate is the contrast between Chandler's model of how organizations successfully capture scale and scope economies and the alternative model of flexible specialization.[4] Since 1980, there has been a pronounced trend towards divestment of subsidiaries in multi-divisional organizations in both countries.[5] Although these tendencies have been well documented in both countries, there has been little systematic comparison of causes, although they are generally assumed to be similar. None the less, if it is the case that firms had overdiversified, then it is necessary also to investigate the causes of diversification, and these were clearly different. It is important therefore to document differences in the earlier period in order to identify and investigate the causes of differences in the later period.

A related issue is the impact of governance and firm structure on economic performance. Evidence suggests British companies performed poorly relative to international competition in the postwar period, including the USA,[6] which was also its period of greatest M-form (multi-divisional form) adoption. Other studies show that performance for both countries improved during the 1980s.[7] The trends are empirically uncertain and also paradoxical, since the literature suggests that performance improvements are linked to changes in governance and accountability structures in both countries since the 1980s, whilst the USA enjoyed a different, but apparently equally successful, basis of comparative advantage relative to Britain in the earlier period.

To address these questions this chapter proceeds as follows. The first section reviews relevant theory incorporating the resource-based view of the firm and theories of corporate governance as a synthesized model to explain the dynamic aspects of entrepreneurial and managerial behaviour. This synthesized view is then tested with reference to two contrasting historical episodes: diversification, conglomeration and the multi-divisional, 1950–80 and divestment and restructuring, 1980–2000. A final section evaluates the strengths and weaknesses of the proposed framework, indicating a possible research agenda that could provide useful insights into the nature of business evolution.

Theoretical Framework

The research questions listed above require corporate governance mechanisms to be considered in conjunction with the resource-based view (RBV) of the firm. This section outlines a dynamic framework for such a synthesis, set out in Figure 11.1. In summary the framework deals with determinants of the firm's resource base, then considers the mechanics of corporate governance and shows how their combination might be used to explain entrepreneurial and managerial behaviour.

Figure 11.1 shows the resource base of the firm to be diversified or specialized. Internalized, firm-specific factors are considered as the major drivers of strategic change according to the resource-based view.[8] Firm-specific assets include managerial scope economies as identified by Penrose and later Barney and Teece.[9] Hence diversification enhances performance if it allows the firm to access skills, resources and competencies that cannot be acquired by non-diversifying firms in a competitive market and this may explain why related diversification can enhance performance.[10] However, specialization may promote flexibility, replacing standardization and scale economies.[11] Firms in industrial districts, trade associations and other networks may share resources and draw on local pools of experience and skilled labour, exploiting knowledge pools or agglomeration-based external economies of scale.[12] In this case, specialization narrows the resource base and pushes other strategic resources outside the firm. Access to internalized resources within firms and external shared resources provide opportunities for managers to earn rents via the exploitation of these unique inimitable assets.

Hence the importance of also considering the governance arrangements.[13] As suggested by Figure 11.1, ownership determines the effectiveness of these arrangements depending upon

		Ownership structure	
		Dispersed	**Concentrated**
Resource location	**Diversified**	*Quadrant 1* **Managerial resource utilization**: routine **Managerial objective/incentive**: growth through planning and diversification	Quadrant 3 **Managerial resource utilization**: routine **Managerial objective/incentive**: efficiency through accountability
	Specialized	*Quadrant 2* **Managerial resource utilization**: entrepreneurial **Managerial objective/incentive**: growth through alliance	*Quadrant 4* **Managerial resource utilization**: entrepreneurial **Managerial objective/incentive**: efficiency through innovation

Figure 11.1   Framework for corporate governance mechanisms in conjunction with the resource-based view of the firm

whether it is dispersed or concentrated. Where ownership is concentrated, monitoring arrangements are less problematic. Diffuse shareholders may weaken the effectiveness of the market for corporate control through well-known free-riding problems.[14] Alternatively, institutional blockholders may provide the concentration of ownership to put pressure on management through using their voting powers to elect their own nominees to boards of directors and through the threat to fight proxy votes more aggressively.[15] In a corporate governance system based on strong voice, managers may give greatest credence to stakeholders with the deepest commitment and the weakest threat of exit. Family or entrepreneurial ownership may affect managerial strategies via voice-based policy direction but at the same time inhibit growth and the development of professional managerial hierarchies.[16] Also, in adverse economic conditions, effective corporate governance in the form of voice, exit or both may be an important determinant of managerial ability and willingness to undertake restructuring actions.[17] Such political institutional arrangements become more aligned during periods of prosperity, but break down in periods of declining profitability.[18] These scenarios and responses are clearly related to the process of resource acquisition or threats of reductions in the resource base.

Entrepreneurial opportunity is promoted by a unique, idiosyncractic understanding of a situation and is therefore likely to be associated with specialization. Conversely an absence of idiosyncratic human capital is likely to be linked to routine learning based on structured decisions and quantifiable outputs and therefore associated with a diversified resource base.[19] The ownership of the business and the ability of owners to monitor and govern managerial incentives will moderate the opportunities created by these differences in managerial style. The possession of superior or idiosyncratic skills/resources does not necessarily lead to superior performance or innovation. There is a need for effective governance and incentives to ensure that management both generate the rents as well as capture some of the gains from those rents for themselves.[20] Where ownership is dispersed, monitoring is more costly; therefore the traditional managerial objective of growth in the size of the resource base will tend to predominate. If ownership is concentrated, monitoring is easier and more likely to be aligned with ownership objectives. Hence in quadrant 1, routine managerial style combined with limited opportunities for monitoring leads to growth through diversification. In quadrant 2, specialization promotes an entrepreneurial style, with growth as the principal managerial incentive, due to the specialized resource base through alliance. In quadrant 3, closer monitoring attenuates managerial opportunism and promotes profit orientation. When combined with a routine managerial style, this promotes efficiency. Finally, in quadrant 4, close monitoring promotes profit-seeking objectives, but this time because it is combined with an entrepreneurial management style it leads to innovative activity.

Whilst this model may be useful for analysing businesses at a given point in time, it is also of benefit to consider the dynamic implications. The first is the impact of growth. Quadrants 1, 2 and 4 all involve business growth as an outcome. In quadrant 3 the implication is that divestment will be highest since outside monitors are in the best position to demand the return of inefficiently deployed resources. Even in quadrant 3, however, growth may be a corollary of efficiency orientation. The model is therefore broadly congruent with the growth paths that might be taken in an industrial economy. However, once such growth is undertaken, the consequence is that businesses will be repositioned in the model. This will be the case especially if the consequence of growth is investment in managerial hierarchy. However, managerial entrenchment may in turn have its limits, for example through the exhaustion of managerial economies of scale and scope and/or changes in ownership. In the latter case, although managers may benefit personally through ownership dispersal, they are usually relatively powerless to prevent the reconcentration of capital. Regulation is therefore the second dynamic dimension of the model. Concentration of economic resources, for example in quadrants 1 and 3, while potentially empowering corporate lobbyists, will also promote regulatory intervention, either through restrictions on market power (i.e. a vertical movement in the model), or through empowerment of outside monitors (i.e. a horizontal movement in the model).

To explore these dynamics further, the model also outlines the dominant paradigm, using examples from the US and British corporate economies, reflecting their significant reorganizations in the last half century. The remainder of the chapter provides detailed empirical evidence as a test of the model and explores the main dynamic changes in the two economies.

Diversification, Conglomeration and the Multi-divisional, 1950–80

An important corollary of the relationships suggested in Figure 11.1 is that there are no timeless or universally superior models of business organization. Rather, change will reflect historically and nationally contingent conditions of business organization and ownership. This section considers a period in which many European countries appeared to adopt the American model. However, in the British case, such adoption was partial and where adoption occurred inappropriate to British conditions.

Differences in scale and scope economies

The USA emerged from the Second World War with its productive capacity intact and enlarged and in a stronger position than the war-damaged European economies. Cold war pressures prompted a need to rebuild European economies urgently. Successive British governments, desperate to restore export earnings, were receptive to calls for productivity improvements and to a greater or lesser extent willing to consider adopting the American model of business organization.

The principal features of this model are well known.[21] In 1950 vertically integrated firms that had promoted industrial growth through investment in capital goods, research and development and product innovation dominated the US economy.[22] By the 1960s, US corporations were already large enough to dominate their sectors of the global economy. The apparent success of this model, relative to British 'personal' capitalism, was driven by investment in scale and scope economies.[23] It is true that in comparison, the British economy reflected poorly in terms of productivity. In cotton textiles British productivity was around half that of the USA, and rayon, considered by many to be the most efficient branch of the UK textile industry, was also considered to be well behind.[24] According to one view, this inefficiency was caused by the tendency of British firms to engage in price-fixing cartels and perpetuate a system of restrictive practices.[25] The response of successive governments was to modify industrial policy to increase industrial concentration. In the electrical engineering industry, the government used the Industrial Reorganisation Corporation to underwrite the GEC/AEI merger in the 1960s.[26]

Other aspects of the American model, such as its aggressive competition framework and supporting legal structure, were not adopted in Britain.[27] Unlike the USA, British governments took a permissive approach to competition policy. The Americans regarded the Monopolies and Restrictive Practices Act 1948 as ineffective, particularly because it had the discretion to treat each case on its merits. In contrast the Celler–Kefauver Act (1950) placed strict limits on horizontal and vertical acquisition under threat of litigation.[28] This had the effect of promoting conglomerate diversification by large US corporations.[29] In the period 1963–72, 75 per cent of assets acquired were in unrelated products and 50 per cent in the period 1973–77.[30] In Britain, the consequence was that governments were able to promote concentration in industries, strategic or otherwise, without resorting to nationalization.

In theory, these structural changes made British firms more adaptable to the American '3S' model of standardization, simplification and specialization.[31] However, the structure of the British economy imposed constraints on the extent to which the American model could be adopted. In the 1960s, there was only a small number of industries, for example, aircraft, mainframe computers, cars and electric motors, that required more than half the British market to be able to operate at efficient scale. In other industries, for example, brewing at 3 per cent, cotton spinning and weaving at 2 per cent and machine tools at 0.75 per cent, the required share was much smaller.[32] By the 1950s, in electrical engineering most scale-based economies were exhausted, with the top five firms (AEI, GEC, English Electric, Plessey and Parsons-Peebles) already controlling 42 per cent of domestic production.[33] Hence, in the period 1957–68 diversification became increasingly horizontal and in many cases conglomerate, with acquisitions of firms in unrelated industries.[34] British business also developed into internationally diversified firms, primarily to exploit the opportunities associated with size and market attractiveness.[35]

These restrictions on scale prevented any startling improvements in productivity. As a result, the gap in productivity between the two countries has remained roughly constant through time, with little difference in productivity between the large and small firm sectors in either Britain or the USA.[36] Even in British industries where the 3S, Fordist-productivity-oriented approach was most likely to succeed, there were some clear difficulties. For example, the cost-leadership-based marketing strategies of the British motor vehicle industry failed to recoup investment in design, the underpricing of the mini being the leading example.[37] All British manufacturers tended to rely on quality and variety rather than cost and price.[38] Their strategies were marketing led, rather than product led as in the USA, so that the dominance of design became a barrier to production efficiency.[39] US methods were, however, particularly unsuited to Britain's sizeable small-firm sector. Instead of copying inappropriate methods developed by large US firms, these companies adopted innovative management and accounting techniques that were more flexible and responsive to changing circumstance.[40] In terms of Figure 11.1, these contrasts suggest that US industry was positioned on the top row and Britain on the bottom. In Britain, those firms and industries that moved upwards did so because diversification was driven by restrictions on scale in the domestic market, whilst in the USA such diversification was driven by legislation. Even so, the changes in the US corporate economy provided a useful model in the multi-divisional form for those British firms that did diversify. Chandler and Lazonick, while supportive of the large firm, condemn the separation of decision making from organizational learning in this model.[41] However, the model presented in this chapter (Figure 11.1) suggests that there are two levels of learning, routine and entrepreneurial, and this may be the product of the differences noted above in scale and scope economies. The evidence suggests that the British model was more entrepreneurial, but it is difficult to reconcile this view with the apparent poor performance of the 1950s and 1960s. It is possible, as suggested above, that adoption of the American model was not the best prescription for Britain. However, another important condition, discussed below, is the dynamic and atavistic relationship between entrepreneurial opportunity and accountability.

Differences in governance and accountability

Another important dimension of the American model adopted by British firms after 1950 was the M-form. The earliest pioneers of this structure, such as DuPont, had adopted it in the 1920s and it was rapidly emulated.[42] By 1959, 49.6 per cent of the largest 120 firms were M-form and 84.2 per cent by 1979.[43] They were most closely adopted by British businesses in the 1950–80 period.[44] British companies evolved the holding company form, which offered certain advantages in the adverse economic conditions of the 1930s, facilitating rationalization in some industries, such as textiles and diversification in others, such as shipbuilding.[45] Consultants such as McKinsey and their recommendation that the multi-divisional form be adopted had an important influence.[46] A related influence was the adoption of the 'firm as portfolio' model of strategic planning, particularly the Boston Consulting Group's growth share matrix.[47]

There is evidence that although multi-divisional structures were nominally adopted in the 1950s and 1960s as British businesses diversified, they retained many features of the holding company. To begin with, they were reluctant to adopt professional managerial hierarchies. British managers resisted specialist management education, preferring instead to rely on the artistry and intuition of generalist education and this became especially true at higher levels of the hierarchy.[48] The notable exception was the rise of accountancy and finance specialists.[49] As they rose to dominate the British boardroom, their solution to the monitoring problems associated with diversification was the use of financial controls. However, in this respect, British big business suffered a serious lag compared to the USA in that the techniques of standard costing and discounted cash flow which helped US companies manage internal capital markets more effectively were slow to develop.[50] So although British companies were prone to the risks and inefficiencies associated with the US model of conglomerate diversification, they were less able to implement the control techniques considered by theorists such as Williamson as essential to make them effective.[51]

Growth was a dominant political object in Britain and a dominant managerial objective in the USA. In the USA this meant the conglomerate diversification exemplified by Gulf & Western Industries (G&W), whose managerial objective was to diversify operations thereby countering business cycles and stabilizing earnings growth. By the 1980s, G&W had 155 lines of business.[52] In Britain this meant that government-backed promotion of internal economies of scale became dependent on industrialists such as Weinstock, who were simultaneously able to deliver value to the stock market.[53] This reflected financial control so characteristic of the UK economy in this period and an absence of integrated managerial systems. So, whilst GEC became a very profitable firm in a rapidly declining sector, it failed to invest in high-tech ventures in semiconductors or consumer electronics. Although GEC's cash surplus was envied by many, its investment in bank accounts represented poor value for shareholders, demonstrating failures in capital market accountability.[54] At the same time, both the late 1960s Labour government's reluctance to impose new corporate governance regulations on business and the growing influence of new share trading operators contributed to the persistence of opaque accountability.[55] This allowed business leaders like Weinstock to continue to run their firms without extensive ownership interference, provided investment returns were acceptable.[56] Reliance on financial controls, as in the GEC case, illustrates how British companies remained wedded to important tenets of the holding company model.

Theory suggests and evidence confirms that diversification strategies were a mistake from a financial point of view.[57] *The Economist* refers to them as a 'colossal mistake'.[58] It is therefore likely that diversification in both economies during this period arose from ineffective governance arrangements, in particular lack of effective monitoring from shareholders.

The market for corporate control and the rise of the institutional investor were important elements of transformation in both economies, but occurred at different times and for different reasons in the USA compared to the UK. In the USA, weak shareholder control dated back to the Securities and Banking Acts of 1933 to 1935.[59] Increased liquidity was associated with the rise of the pension funds and other institutional investors in the 1960s.[60] Later the impact of the Employment Retirement Income Security Act (ERISA) of 1974 led to more rapid growth in private trust stock ownership, ultimately helping to promote the asset bubble of the 1990s,[61] although this is still constrained by Securities and Exchange Commission (SEC) regulations.[62] None the less by the mid-1980s block trading by institutional investors dominated the stock market.[63]

British stock ownership followed a similar pattern. In 1963, individual persons controlled 54 per cent of shares, whereas pension funds and insurance companies held 16 per cent.[64] Dispersed share ownership prevented the formation of voting coalitions hostile to directors, whilst sales of shares by individuals was unlikely to have a major impact on share price. The collapse of Rolls-Royce in the early 1970s starkly illustrates the lack of involvement of institutional shareholders in corporate governance, although in this case the banks belatedly exerted pressure on management when crisis conditions developed.[65] In certain sectors such as textiles, capital market illiquidity made exit difficult.[66] Meanwhile the regulatory framework did little to facilitate active monitoring. The Companies Act, passed in 1948, reflected several compromises, one of which was a directors' and industry lobby for reduced disclosure on the grounds of commercial secrecy.[67] Although the Jenkins Report of 1962 aimed to promote greater accountability, disclosures such as directors' remuneration were not introduced until the Companies Act of 1967, whilst sales turnover, nominee shareholdings, directors' private interests and other important disclosures required a further White Paper in 1973 and only became law in 1976.[68]

Unlike in the USA, developments in the market for corporate control facilitated diversification but without corresponding threats to inefficient managers in the form of hostile takeovers. The earliest, Clore's bid for Sears in 1953, the battle for British Aluminium in 1958 and the ICI bid for Courtaulds in 1961, were exceptional and provoked regulatory responses from the government.[69] In the last case, although an attempt was made to purchase the shares of a firm in the open market that was perceived as underperforming and undervalued, neither group of managers perceived the market to be an efficient valuation mechanism. The transaction contrasted with the gentlemanly, agreed mergers that remained prevalent in business combinations. It was not until the boom in merger activity between 1968 and 1973 (Tables 11.1 and 11.2) that such corporate control transactions became widespread, with 22 per cent of the top 200 listed firms in 1969 having been acquired by 1972. In terms of Figure 11.1, the dispersion of ownership and the underdeveloped market for corporate control meant that both the USA and Britain occupied the left-hand column of the matrix, with powerful managers subject to relatively weak accountability. If this positioning is combined with the more significant differences discussed earlier in terms of scale economies and business strategy, it can be seen that US businesses predominantly occupied quadrant 1 and British businesses quadrant 2. The changes occurring in the 1960s and 1970s tended to push larger British firms up towards quadrant 1 as they adopted elements of the American model. Developments in capital market scrutiny exerted a weak push for both economies in a rightward direction towards quadrants 3 and 4.

Table 11.1   UK and US markets for corporate control compared (numbers)

	UK (% of deal numbers)			US (% of deal numbers)		
	Independent acquisitions	Parent-to-parent divestments	LBOs	Independent acquisitions	Parent-to-parent divestments	LBOs
1980	63.9	17.5	18.6	89.5	6.7	3.8
1981	56.8	21.7	21.5	75.3	20.4	4.3
1982	42.2	23.1	34.7	68.4	24.5	7.1
1983	43.8	20.4	35.8	53.9	35.1	11.0
1984	48.6	20.8	30.6	53.0	35.7	11.3
1985	44.3	17.5	38.2	41.0	44.3	14.7
1986	51.3	18.2	30.5	43.9	42.8	13.3
1987	60.6	17.3	22.1	49.3	39.7	11.1
1988	56.3	18.8	24.9	45.7	41.8	12.5
1989	48.1	23.7	28.2	47.6	43.5	8.9
1990	31.6	24.8	43.6	50.1	45.3	4.6
1991	26.9	19.8	53.3	42.6	51.2	6.2
1992	22.6	19.5	57.9	46.5	46.2	7.3
1993	33.1	18.6	48.3	47.8	46.1	6.1
1994	37.8	17.0	45.2	54.6	40.9	4.5
1995	27.2	18.7	54.1	57.3	38.4	4.3
1996	27.4	20.2	52.3	59.7	36.5	3.8
1997	32.0	10.2	57.8	64.5	32.1	3.4
1998	37.1	11.5	51.4	68.4	28.3	3.3
1999	35.5	8.2	56.3		29.5	
2000	39.4	10.2	50.4	68.6	28.1	3.3

Restructuring the 'Anglo-American' Model: Some Contrasts, 1980–2000

The previous section analysed the historical antecedents to the restructuring of the Anglo-American model that began in the 1980s. Changes in share ownership meant greater scrutiny of the diversification strategies adopted by corporate management teams. From 1980 onwards in both the USA and the UK, there was growing scepticism about the role of diversified multi-divisional firms. The 1987 stock market crash in the USA was followed by greater 'relational investing' by institutional investors to get companies to follow strategies that would increase the value of their investments.[70] In the USA, a number of recent studies on the efficacy of internal capital markets suggest that funds may actually flow in the wrong direction (i.e. from divisions with excellent investment opportunities to divisions with poor opportunities).[71] In the UK, institutional ownership also increased significantly after 1980 and the rate at which institutional investors voted increased to 50 per cent in 1999 from 20

Table 11.2   UK and US markets for corporate control compared (value)

	UK (% of deal numbers)			US (% of deal numbers)		
	Independent acquisitions	Parent-to-parent divestments	LBOs	Independent acquisitions	Parent-to-parent divestments	LBOs
1980	83.0	13.8	3.2	81.6	14.7	3.7
1981	70.1	20.8	9.1	80.9	14.7	4.4
1982	48.9	28.0	23.1	80.4	13.8	5.8
1983	69.7	15.9	14.4	63.4	30.5	6.1
1984	73.9	19.0	7.1	58.6	29.3	12.1
1985	75.7	9.5	14.8	53.0	33.7	13.3
1986	72.9	18.4	8.7	42.7	36.9	20.4
1987	59.4	23.4	17.2	43.3	38.3	18.4
1988	62.1	19.9	18.0	44.0	38.9	17.1
1989	62.1	16.3	21.6	47.6	28.5	23.9
1990	47.2	25.8	27.0	50.1	42.5	7.4
1991	56.1	22.1	21.8	56.5	39.2	5.3
1992	44.4	19.8	35.7	49.5	42.9	7.6
1993	30.1	41.1	28.8	50.1	43.8	6.1
1994	48.2	21.2	30.6	58.3	37.0	4.7
1995	67.5	18.3	14.2	58.4	36.2	5.4
1996	60.5	19.2	20.3	61.5	33.3	5.2
1997	60.1	11.7	28.2	69.2	27.1	3.7
1998	54.6	12.3	33.1	75.7	21.3	3.0
1999	51.8	9.2	39.0		19.7	
2000	76.9	4.9	18.2	77.3	20.5	2.2

per cent in 1990.[72] A possible reason for the transfer of US style relational investing was the take-over of British stock market firms by US-dominated integrated investment banks following the 1987 crash.[73]

Both economies began the 1980s with moves at the macro level towards monetary stringency, corporate and financial deregulation and attacks on organized labour. An important difference was the depth of recession in the UK in 1980 and the degree of exit from declining manufacturing industries during that period. Another was that whereas strategic concentrated industries such as steel and coal remained powerful as private-sector lobbyists in the USA, these industries were now privatized in the UK. In Britain, this presented incumbent managers with entrepreneurial opportunities.[74] When combined with differing sources of finance and greater level of specialization in the UK economy, this presented contrasting opportunities and restrictions on entrepreneurial action in the restructuring process.

An important vehicle of restructuring in both economies was the buy-out, with specialist buy-out financiers in the US like Kohlberg, Kravis Roberts & Co. emerging as new financial controllers of enterprises.[75] As distinct from a conglomerate firm, these LBO associations own and control stand-alone enterprises which do not cross-subsidize each other. Tables 11.1 and 11.2 provide details and contrasts in levels of activity in relation to aggregate merger and acquisition transactions. These contrasts are provided through time in terms of number and value for the two economies. As the tables suggest and the evidence illustrates, there were some notable differences in the extent and nature of parent to parent divestment and of leveraged and management buy-out activity between the USA and the UK.

A very important difference was that the taking private of whole listed companies was more in evidence in the USA than in the UK throughout this period but especially in the 1980s, while divestment buy-outs were more important in the UK. In the USA, the number of buy-outs of listed firms in 1979–88 was 48 per cent of the number of divestment buy-outs, but their average value was over eight times that for divestment buy-outs.[76] In the UK, during the same period, the number of divestment buy-outs was 11.4 times that of buy-outs listed firms and their value was 3.5 times that of listed buy-outs.[77]

A second important difference was that the extent and nature of leverage finance was also greater in the USA than in the UK. In America, junk bonds arose as surplus capital in the wake of the conglomeration movement of the 1950s and 1960s.[78] Equity finance remained more important in the UK and the deregulation of financial services in the 1980s created new flows of equity investment into the corporate sector.[79] Also, the tax advantage of financing firms through debt rather than equity applied more to the USA than to the UK.[80] Accordingly, financial innovations such as junk bonds became an important part of the US buy-out market from the early 1980s but failed to materialize in the UK until the late 1990s, and then only for a very limited number of transactions. UK banks following overcommitment to risky overseas lending in the early 1980s[81] generally took a more prudent view of leverage in buy-outs. However, there was significant upward movement as a result of the increase in privately placed mezzanine debt and competition in the senior debt market from new entrants from the USA and Japan.[82] In 1989, the mean senior plus mezzanine debt in UK buy-outs with a value above £10 million accounted for over three quarters of the financing structure, although this subsequently fell in the recession of the early 1990s. Even in the boom period of the late 1990s, the levels of debt that featured in the earlier decade were not regained.[83] Financing structure is important in interpreting the Figure 11.1 model, since debt finance is more likely to be used where the desired outcome is efficiency and the return of free cash flow to shareholders per quadrant 3. Where quadrant 4 outcomes are desired, equity finance may be more appropriate. This also follows because higher business risk associated with specialized assets is not then compounded by the financial risk associated with debt finance.

A third difference was that although hostile LBOs and subsequent break-up always accounted for a minority of transactions in the USA, they were much less in evidence in the UK. An important reason was that there were concerns on the part of banks to extend leverage on the basis of asset sales at predicated prices that may not be realized.[84] In the recession of 1980 many exiting firms had obsolete equipment reflecting decades of underinvestment and the fast rate of new capital goods development by overseas suppliers. These gained easy access to the UK market following the removal of exchange controls. At the same time newer sectors emerged. Post-1980 witnessed the re-emergence of flexible specialization and the resurgence of the smaller firm in Britain.[85] In 1949 small firms accounted for 20.5 per cent of output and 22.5 per cent of employment. Following the period of concentration, these percentages declined to 18.2 per cent and 21.7 per cent respectively by the early 1970s. By 1990, however, they had risen to 21.7 per cent and 29.1 per cent.[86] Although this does not suggest that these changes were related to improvements in productivity, they did reflect changes in opportunity brought about by changes in scale economies.[87] In contrast, new external economies in the USA, such as transport, telecom and the Internet, promoted further industrial concentration. In 1990, four airlines accounted for 66 per cent of US revenue and four software companies controlled 55 per cent of the market.[88] Since then further technical advance and concentration have promoted further anti-trust cases but without breaking up the Microsoft monopoly.

A fourth difference was that in the USA the buy-out and venture capital markets have traditionally been viewed as quite separate, with the former focusing on the financing of businesses in mature sectors using high degrees of leverage and the latter on early-stage fast-growing innovative firms. In the UK there has traditionally been a much closer link between the buy-out and venture capital markets. While the UK venture capital market has been criticized for being less positive towards early-stage investments, it has been more involved in buy-outs. This difference has partly contributed to the generally lower degrees of leverage in UK buy-outs and may also have contributed to a greater emphasis on growth opportunities than in the USA. This also accounts for the delay in divestment activity in the UK, since the venture capital industry was slow to develop in earlier decades.[89] In part this reflected the role of quasi-government organizations in promoting private-sector investment associated with perceptions of market failure.[90]

A fifth difference concerns the public perception of buy-outs. Much more so than in the UK, in the USA a serious national debate about the detrimental effects of leveraged buy-outs took place with close scrutiny by committees of Congress. Corporate managers claimed that the threat of such transactions detracted from their efforts to enhance competitiveness, while financiers and academics argued the opposite. In the UK, buy-outs were generally viewed much more positively. While there had been some concern from trade unions in particular about buy-outs' role in privatizations, employees often took a different view as they saw opportunities for share ownership and capital gain.[91] Hostile buy-outs did not appear until 1988, and then only fleetingly.[92]

In part, differences in economic structure may account for another important contrast, which is that the level of parent-firm-to-parent-firm disposal in the USA was much higher than in Britain (Table 11.1). The simplest explanation for the high relative proportion of parent-to-parent transfers is the impact of the Tax Reform Act of 1986, which introduced tax relief on such tranfers provided subsidiary status was retained.[93] However, as is clear from Table 11.1, this trend was important before the passage of that legislation. A possible explanation is that powerful corporations lobbied for tax relief in order to reduce the transaction costs of existing strategies, whose effectiveness was reinforced once the tax relief provisions were available.[94] However, this would not account for the adoption of what some authors have described as the multi-subsidiary form (MSF). Unlike Britain, where as discussed earlier aspects of the H-form remained embedded in the period of M-form transition, MSF adoptions represent concerted attempts to re-entrench managerial power and respond to the debt overhang that had prompted the LBO wave in the early 1980s. The rate of increase in MSF was rapid in 1981–85, but five times higher in 1986–93.[95] The specific mechanisms in addition to tax relief were internalization of capital, including the transfer of parent debt and parent risk reduction through legal firewalls between holding company and subsidiary. Public offerings of subsidiary stock became a common source of finance, allowing the proportion of assets held by the largest corporations to increase in this period. This shift from debt to internalized equity allowed managers to regain control after 1993, using stock swaps.[96] Unlike the LBOs of the 1980s, these firms consolidated vertically, combining sector-similar small firms to realize efficiencies in business services provided by central HQ.[97] The net effect was reduction of liability and risk in the parent company balance sheet,[98] and these apparent advantages help explain the prevalence of parent-to-parent transfers in the USA.

In contrast, L/MBOs accounted for a greater proportion of take-overs in the UK, with a significant majority of such transactions being divestments. A key factor affecting the growth of management buy-outs in the UK from 1981 was the relaxation of the law regarding financial assistance in the purchase of a company's own shares that made it easier for buy-out financiers to take security.[99] This coincided with the initial development of the venture capital market, notably the important role of the development capital subsidiaries of the clearing banks for whom buy-outs represented a less risky alternative than early-stage investments. Divisional management in the UK may have been in a stronger position to effect a buy-out than in the USA, especially as the initial development of the UK market in the early 1980s was focused on the acquisition of smaller underperforming divisions that may have been less attractive to corporate acquirers and which could be acquired without an auction process. There is evidence that in the 1980s at least corporate management gave preference to managers attempting to buy out, although this position appeared to change later in the period. In the USA, divestments have tended to be larger and less likely to involve underperforming activities (see below). Moreover, while the fiduciary duties of directors are important in both countries, the development of legislation in the USA to emphasize the maximization of shareholder value in the disposal of subsidiaries[100] seems to have occurred earlier and to be much stronger than in the UK.[101] This would seem to make auctions of divisions more likely, in which management buy-outs may find it more difficult to compete with corporate buyers who are not constrained to meet the cost of the purchase out of current cash flow. In the USA, this process of divestment was given impetus by the development of hostile LBOs and other corporate raiders,[102] which only appeared in the UK towards the very end of the 1980s.

The deconglomeration that provided the junk finance associated with much US restructuring in the 1980s began around a decade earlier. By 1975 divestitures were around 33 per cent of all mergers and acquisitions activity greater than announced mergers and acquisitions,[103] and these sales often accompanied financial duress.[104] In the UK this percentage was not reached until 1982.[105] This evidence suggests detectable underperformance by US capital markets around ten years earlier than the UK. Conglomerate discounts were identified in the USA as early as 1970.[106] More recent studies consistently report a diversification discount in the market value of unrelated diversifiers.[107] This suggests that, for example, a US corporation operating in, say, two unrelated business segments may experience a market value discount of 12–15 per cent compared to the notional value were its segments to operate as freestanding concerns.[108] In addition, event studies of merger activity report that diversifying mergers have been viewed more pessimistically than merger activity in general, certainly since the 1970s.[109] More recent evidence also suggests that diversified listed firms in the UK were subject to a 'conglomerate discount'.[110] This reflects evidence based on accounting data that firms undertaking unrelated acquisitions from the 1980s onwards performed less well than those undertaking related acquisitions.[111]

Although underperformance by conglomerates coupled with increased capital market scrutiny may have prompted some reduction in diversification in both countries, the precise impact on corporate diversity is difficult to quantify. In the USA, median diversification among the US Fortune 500 firms in 1980, 1985 and 1990 based on an entropy measure fell from 1.0 in 1980 to 0.9 in 1985 and 0.67 in 1990.[112] In the UK, aggregate diversification, as measured by the *categorization* of firms as diversified or not among the largest 100 firms in each year, does not appear to have fallen since 1970,[113] suggesting a qualitative rather than a quantitative change in diversification. Analysis of the behaviour of a cohort of large firms from 1985 to 1993 shows that, using an entropy measure, there has been some degree of decline in diversification among larger UK firms after 1970.[114] Within the net figures, many firms refocused but others increased diversification.

US evidence suggests that in the period 1977 to 1987, 30 per cent of all publicly traded manufacturing firms were involved in corporate restructuring through acquisitions or being taken private through a leveraged buy-out, with the importance of the latter increasing during the latter part of the period.[115] Divestments as a share of all acquisitions rose sharply from the early 1980s compared with the 1970s. In the UK, the period 1980–2000 also saw a remarkable increase in the number and value of divestments and restructuring transactions, especially management buy-outs and buy-ins. This activity was extensive in relation to the assets of larger firms, accounting for an average of 4 per cent of assets per year (median 1 per cent, std dev. 12.7) over the period 1985–91.[116] A significant proportion of divestments were conglomerate in nature.[117]

In addition to the differences noted above, there are also some clear similarities. These follow from survey evidence, much of which concentrates on the performance effects of restructuring. Both US and UK evidence is consistent in showing that divestment decisions are systematically related to leverage, corporate governance, management changes, the size and diversification of the firm and to some extent market structural characteristics.[118] Greater financial leverage is positively associated with divestment, as is greater managerial equity and a larger proportion of outside to insider directors. This is consistent with the view that gains from divestment are likely to be greatest for those firms with control problems associated with experiencing a proportionately greater fall in their optimal levels of size and diversity.

Similarly, divestment appears to raise the performance of the vendor firm. A substantial number of US event studies show that the announcement of sell-offs, spin-offs or divestment MBOs is associated with significant average wealth gains for the vendor's shareholders.[119] Divestments associated with reductions in diversification or greater refocusing have been associated with greater wealth gains to shareholders as well as improved accounting performance.[120] UK studies of the announcement effects of corporate sell-offs are less extensive but report positive value gains, especially for those sell-offs that increased the corporate focus upon a core business.[121] In contrast, divestments as management buy-outs have been found to generate negative abnormal returns to divestors and tend to follow a period of abnormally positive returns.[122] Accounting data from an unbalanced panel of large UK quoted companies suggests that divestment has a significant effect in raising the profitability of the vendor company and is greater for larger and/or more diversified firms and firms operating with weak governance arrangements.[123]

US evidence shows that leverage buy-outs have taken place in sectors with low R&D expenditure and stable cash flows. They have also led to higher total factor productivity after buy-out and higher total factor productivity (TFP) than other firms in their sector and maintained R&D employment growth while non-production employment fell.[124] In contrast to LBOs, financial restructurings with no changes in control experienced substantial falls in R&D where there was a move to higher leverage, with there being some decline in investment for those firms making acquisitions. Evidence from hostile take-overs in the USA, which have mainly taken place in only a few stable sectors, finds considerable unbundling and allocation of assets to owners who can make higher value use of them and a reduction in R&D.[125] In contrast, friendly mergers which were the dominant form, mainly involved closely related businesses and were seldom followed by cuts in R&D. Besides tax incentives and agency costs associated with free cash flow, Hall also argues that the fall in the net return to capital in US manufacturing fell below the real cost after 1980, leading to greater pressure for financial restructuring to force managers to face the real external cost of capital rather than the artificially low internal cost. This has been viewed as positive since it forces mature corporations to disgorge free cash flow.[126] In contrast to the US evidence on TFP, which found that plant productivity was greater than the industry mean before buy-out, preliminary UK evidence using plant-level data indicates that plants were less productive than their industry mean pre-buy-out.[127] However, after buy-out UK plants also display significant increases in TFP.

What is notable in both the USA and the UK is that the most significant positive influence on post-buy-out returns is the incentive effect due to the size of the managerial equity stake, suggesting reduced opportunism as managerial objectives are aligned with those of shareholders.[128] The influence of the pressure from high leverage has been found to be at best mixed. Despite the evidence of buy-out gains arising from cost efficiencies, in both the USA and the UK there is evidence that buy-outs are followed by entrepreneurial actions such as new product development in a significant proportion of cases. These findings emphasize the importance of governance mechanisms that enable wealth to be generated rather than just focusing on reducing inefficiencies. They also emphasize the importance of providing scope for managers who have identified entrepreneurial opportunities to realize those opportunities.

The focus on agency cost control from the 1980s onwards in the USA and the UK, epitomized in attempts to enhance shareholder value through better corporate governance, divestment and refocusing, and in leveraged buy-outs, has been criticized for viewing managerial discretion as negative and for ignoring the new investments in organizational learning that can potentially generate greater returns in the future.[129] Discretion may be a necessary condition for management to undertake strategic learning and innovation. On the other hand, there are some concerns that corporate governance innovations have served to inflate executive salaries with a weak link to performance improvements and have failed to enhance managerial accountability.

These developments suggest a need to combine enhanced corporate governance with a greater recognition of the human capital resources of managers and other organizational capabilities, and that the nature of corporate governance may need to vary with particular circumstances. Corporate governance *per se* may not be a source of competitive advantage, especially where necessary idiosyncratic human resources are missing. However, some firms may be better than others at implementing otherwise common corporate governance devices in order to realize fully the benefits of the resources they control.[130] Similarly, boards need to reconcile minimizing agency costs with maximizing rent generation potential.

Developments in the leverage buy-out market, for example, provide some evidence that these changes may be happening. The skills of private equity firms involved in classic leveraged buy-outs may be more attuned to financial monitoring than in providing involvement that will enable management to become more innovative. However, more recent developments have seen attempts by private equity financiers to fund transactions where there is scope for entrepreneurial activity. Indeed, managers in subsidiaries are frequently the main initiators of buy-outs as they perceived opportunities to undertake radical entrepreneurial actions that they were prevented from carrying out under the previous ownership and control structure and/or are unable to obtain a share of the gains that reflect their tacit knowledge.[131] In some cases, the financing of these transactions has involved alliances between traditional buy-out and venture capital firms in order to bring together the necessary financial and technical resources.[132] In the case of the buy-out of Seagate Technology in the USA, the traditional buy-out firm Texas Pacific aligned with the newly created Silver Lake Partners which comprised several general partners with venture capital experience. Texas Pacific also combined with the venture capital firm Mayfield to effect the buy-out of the troubled listed computer-chip manufacturer Zilog. These transactions have also involved the use of lower degrees of leverage because of the perceived need for greater flexibility if opportunities for upside gains are to be realized.

In both countries there has been a regulatory response to corporate restructuring and to deal with continued concerns over managerial accountability. In the USA, concerns about managerial behaviour spawned several reports,[133] and in view of similar concerns in the UK,[134] their recommendations were subsequently emulated in the Cadbury Report. In 1987, the Treadway Report offered 11 recommendations to enhance the effectiveness of audit committees, which were to be the keystone of corporate financial governance. However, management in the USA seem to have been more intransigent to reform. In 1990 the Business Roundtable turned back from commitments undertaken in the 1970s to introduce greater accountability to shareholders, claiming instead that the large firm's internal hierarchy was the best means for selecting board members and for reviewing corporate performance.[135] In a 1992 response to a recommendation by the Treadway Commission, a study and exposure draft was commissioned by the COSO, representing CPAs, internal auditors, management accountants, financial executives and accounting educators. Subsequent developments in US corporate governance have been encompassed in statements by the California State Pension funds (Calpers), the US Council of Institutional Investors Policies on Corporate Governance and the TIAA–CREFF Policy Statement on Corporate Governance.

In the UK a number of pronouncements were made, starting with the Cadbury Committee's Code in 1992, developing through various iterations to the Combined Code in 1999 and continuing with the UK government's proposals to reform company law.[136] The evolution of these Codes has been from a stress on accountability to shareholders to enabling managers to create value within a framework that promotes accountability. To achieve accountability, the Cadbury Report placed emphasis on the need to strengthen the link between managerial incentives and performance through remuneration committees. Cadbury also placed emphasis on enhancing shareholder monitoring through the influence of institutions and outside directors. The UK government's more recent review suggests a shift in emphasis back towards accountability.[137] A notable difference between the USA and the UK is the proportion of outside directors on boards. While US boards typically have a majority of outside directors, this is not the case in the UK. Perhaps the most important difference has been the greater reluctance on the part of American executives to concede to demands for accountability from outside the corporate hierarchy.

To summarize these trends in terms of Figure 11.1, both countries witnessed increases in monitoring by shareholders over managers during the 1980–2000 period. The strength of the rightward shift across quadrants was more pronounced in the UK than in the USA. In the USA, the adoption of the MSF has provided a vehicle for historically rooted managerial entrenchment and resistance to demands for greater accountability. In Britain, the role of the buy-out has been more pronounced and reflected greater transparency in capital markets. The British adoption of diversification and the M-form was always partial, and resistance to the professionalization of management more effective, thereby simplifying the retreat from conglomerate diversification. The prevalence of subsidiary buy-outs in Britain was also a function of resource specialization and the re-emergence of the small firm, reflecting the continued relative importance of external economies. In terms of Figure 11.1, British firms were operating in quadrant 4, whilst US firms were in quadrant 3.

Conclusions

The main source of the differences between the two countries lies in the differing roles played by economic institutions in the process of industrialization, particularly in terms of exploitation of economies of scale and scope in the period following maturity of the original industries of the Industrial Revolution. Large-scale businesses in the USA have concentrated economic power, posing serious conflicts between accountability and efficiency. Regulatory restrictions pushed growth in the conglomerate direction. In contrast, the lack of opportunity to develop large-scale industries forced British capital abroad and left domestic entrepreneurs dependent upon network and alliance style capitalism. Hence the British tended to perform badly when importing, albeit partially and half-heartedly, US models of concentrated industry, productivity and managerial capitalism during the 1950s and 1960s. Ironically, this half-heartedness meant British firms were relatively well placed to exploit the return to shareholder capitalism in the 1980s. In turn this abreaction was prompted by the demise of managerial and particularly conglomerate capitalism in the USA. As in Britain, changes in ownership in the USA provided important momentum to corporate restructuring, but with less apparent impact on the concentration of power.

Notes

1. The multi-divisional as defined by A. Chandler, *Strategy and Structure* (Cambridge, MA: MIT Press, 1962) or as the M-form (O. Williamson, 'Managerial discretion, organisational form and the multi-divisional hypothesis', in R. Marris and A. Wood (eds), *The Corporate Economy*, London: Macmillan, 1971, p. 382) possesses certain key features: (1) centralized control over strategic decision-making investment in new products and markets and (2) delegation of operational decision making to divisions monitored as profit centres. In this article where these features are present, the term 'multi-divisional' is used. Scientific management is concerned with divisionalization as an extension of Taylorism from the shopfloor to the corporate level (R. Whittington and M. Mayer, *The European Corporation*, Oxford: Oxford University Press, 2000, p. 67) and refers to the application of systematic principles for managing the large firm as described by Chandler, *Strategy and Structure*. High throughput production refers to the transformation of high fixed cost into low unit costs via coordination of work flow through production processes as defined by A. Chandler, *The Visible Hand* (Cambridge, MA: MIT Press, 1977) and W. Lazonick, *Business Organisation and the Myth of the Market Economy* (Cambridge: Cambridge University Press, 1991, p. 134). For the critique of British firms' failure to invest in managerial hierarchies see A. Chandler, *Scale and Scope* (Cambridge, MA: Harvard University Press, 1990, p. 235), slow adoption of multidivisional (D. Channon, *The Strategy and Structure of British Enterprise*, London: Macmillan, 1973, p. 69), and high throughput (Lazonick, *Business Organisation*, pp. 110–11), B. Elbaum and W. Lazonick (eds), *The Decline of the British Economy* (Oxford: Oxford University Press, 1986) and Chandler, *Scale and Scope*.
2. Channon, *Strategy and Structure of British Enterprise*.
3. C. Sabel and J. Zeitlin, *World of Possibilities: Flexibility and Mass Production in Western Industrialisation* (Cambridge: Cambridge University Press, 1997), p. 33.
4. J. Zeitlin, 'Flexibility in the "Age of Fordism": Technology and production in the international automobile industry', *Enterprise and Society*, Vol. 1, No. 1 (2000), pp. 4–8.
5. M. Wright, K. Robbie, B. Chiplin and M. Albrighton, 'The development of an organisational innovation: management buy-outs in the UK 1980–97', *Business History*, Vol. 42, No. 4 (2000), pp. 137–84.
6. S.N. Broadberry and N.F.R. Crafts, 'British economic policy and industrial performance in the early post-war period', *Business History*, Vol. 38, No. 4 (1996), pp. 65–91. S. Broadberry, *The Productivity Race: British Manufacturing in International Perspective, 1850–1990* (Cambridge: Cambridge University Press, 1997).
7. N.F.R. Crafts, 'Reversing relative economic decline? The 1980s in historical perspective', *Oxford Review of Economic Policy*, Vol. 7, No. 3 (1991), pp. 81–98.
8. J.B. Barney, *Gaining and Sustaining Competitive Advantage* (New York and Amsterdam: Addison-Wesley, 1997).
9. E. Penrose, *The Theory of the Growth of the Firm* (Oxford: Blackwell, 1959); D. Teece, 'Economies of scope and the scope of the enterprise', *Journal of Economic Behaviour and Organisation*, Vol. 1, No. 3 (1980), pp. 223–47. J.B. Barney, 'Firm resources and sustained competitive advantage', *Journal of Management*, Vol. 17, No. 1 (1991), pp. 99–120.
10. C. Markides and P.J. Williamson 'Related diversification, core competences and corporate performance', *Strategic Management Journal*, Vol. 15, Special Issue (1994), pp. 149–65.
11. M. Piore and C. Sabel, *The Second Industrial Divide* (New York: Basic Books, 1984).
12. Originally described by Alfred Marshall. See A. Marshall, *Principles of Economics* (London: Macmillan, 1890). M. Kamien, E. Mueller and I. Zang, 'Research, joint ventures and R&D cartels', *American Economic Review*, Vol. 82, No. 5 (1992), pp. 1293–306. C. Oughton and G. Whittam, 'Competition and co-operation in the small firm sector', *Scottish Journal of Political Economy*, Vol. 44, No. 1 (1997), p. 6.
13. As suggested elsewhere as part of a developing research agenda. J. Barney, M. Wright and D. Ketchen, 'The resource-based view of the firm: Ten years after 1991', *Journal of Management*, Vol. 27, No. 6 (2001), pp. 625–41.

14. S. Grossman and O. Hart, 'Takeover bids, the free rider problem and the theory of the corporation', *Bell Journal of Economics*, Vol. 11, No. 1 (1979), pp. 42–64.
15. C.W.L. Hill and T.M. Jones, 'Stakeholder-agency theory', *Journal of Management Studies*, Vol. 29, No. 2 (1992), pp. 131–54.
16. Chandler, *Scale and Scope*. D. Palmer, P. Jennings and M. Powers, 'The economics and politics of structure: The multi-divisional form and the large US corporation', *Administrative Science Quarterly*, Vol. 32, No. 1 (1987), pp. 25–87. J. Mahoney, 'The adoption of the multi-divisional form of organisation: a contingency model', *Journal of Management Studies*, Vol. 29, No. 1 (1992), pp. 42–72.
17. R.E. Hoskisson, R.A. Johnson and D. Moesel, 'Corporate divestiture intensity in restructuring firms: effects of governance, strategy and performance', *Academy of Management Journal*, Vol. 37, No. 5 (1994), pp. 1207–51. R.A. Johnson, 'Antecedents and outcomes of corporate refocusing', *Journal of Management*, Vol. 22, No. 3 (1996), pp. 439–83. S. Zahra and J. Pearce, 'Boards of Directors and corporate financial performance: A review and integrative model', *Journal of Management*, Vol. 15, No. 2 (1989), pp. 291–334.
18. D. Gordon, R. Edwards and M. Reich, *Segmented Work, Divided Workers* (Cambridge: Cambridge University Press, 1982); D. Gordon, *Fat and Mean: The Corporate Squeeze of Working Americans and the Myth of Managerial Downsizing* (New York: Free Press, 1996).
19. M. Wright, R. Hosskisson, L. Busenitz and J. Dial, 'Entrepreneurial growth through privatization: The upside of management buyouts', *Academy of Management Review*, Vol. 25, No. 3 (2000), pp. 591–601.
20. R. Castanias, and C. Helfat, 'The managerial rents model: theory and empirical analysis,' *Journal of Management*, Vol. 27, No. 6 (2001), pp. 661–78.
21. This discussion used the received notion of the American model. It is not intended that the US economy is treated in a homogeneous fashion. For example the Silicon Valley 'west-coast' model utilizing external economies-of-scale-based networking using flexible specialization was successfully developed in the 1930–70 period. C. Lecuyer, 'Making Silicon Valley: Engineering culture, innovation and industrial growth, 1930–1970', *Enterprise and Society*, Vol. 2, No. 4 (2001), pp. 666–72.
22. R.T. Averitt, *The Dual Economy* (New York: W.W. Norton, 1968).
23. Chandler, *Scale and Scope*.
24. N. Tiratsoo and J. Tomlinson, 'Exporting the gospel of productivity: United States technical assistance and British industry, 1945–1960', *Business History Review*, Vol. 71 (Spring 1977), pp. 44 and 45.
25. Broadberry and Crafts, 'British economic policy and industrial performance', Broadberry, *The Productivity Race*.
26. P. Armstrong, 'The rise of accounting controls in British capitalist enterprises', *Accounting, Organisations and Society*, Vol. 12, No. 5 (1987), pp. 415–36. S. Young and A.V. Lowe, *Intervention in the Mixed Economy* (London: Croom Helm, 1974), p. 74.
27. B. Kogut and D. Parkinson, 'The diffusion of American organising principles in Europe' in B. Kogut (ed.), *Country Competitiveness* (New York: Oxford University Press, 1993).
28. N. Fligstein, *The Transformation of Corporate Control* (Cambridge, MA: Harvard University Press, 1990).
29. G. Davis, K. Diekmann and C. Tinsley, 'The decline and fall of the conglomerate firm in the 1980s: The deinstitutionalisation of an organisational form', *American Sociological Review*, Vol. 59, No. 4 (1994), pp. 547–70.
30. D. Ravenscraft and F. Scherer, *Mergers, Sell Offs and Economic Efficiency* (Washington, DC: Brookings Institute, 1987) ch. 6; Chandler, *Scale and Scope*, pp. 622–3.
31. Tiratsoo and Tomlinson, 'Exporting the gospel of productivity', p. 67.
32. P. Hart and R. Clarke, *Concentration in British Industry* (Cambridge: Cambridge University Press, 1980), M. Utton, *The Political Economy of Big Business* (Oxford: Martin Robinson, 1982).
33. Hannah, *Rise of the Corporate Economy*, p. 126.

34. Channon, *Strategy and Structure of British Enterprise*, p. 67. Hannah, *Rise of the Corporate Economy*, p. 174.
35. G. Jones, *The Evolution of International Business* (London: Routledge, 1998).
36. A. Booth, 'British manufacturing did not fail in the Golden Age' (University of Exeter, mimeo).
37. J. Zeitlin, 'Reconciling automation and flexibility? Technology and production in the post-war British motor vehicle industry', *Enterprise and Society*, Vol. 1, No. 1 (2000), pp. 9–62.
38. Board of Trade, *Working Party Reports: Cotton* (London: Board of Trade, 1946), pp. 242–9. J. Jewkes, *Ordeal by Planning* (London: Macmillan, 1948).
39. *Engineering*, 8 June 1956.
40. J.R. Edwards, T. Boyns and M. Matthews, 'Standard costing and budgetary control in the British iron and steel industry: A study of accounting change', *Accounting, Auditing & Accountability Journal*, Vol. 15, No. 1 (2002), pp. 12–45(34).
41. Chandler, *Scale and Scope*. W. Lazonick and M. O'Sullivan, 'Finance and industrial development. Part 1: The United States and the United Kingdom', *Financial History Review*, Vol. 4, No. 1 (1997), p. 16.
42. Chandler, *Scale and Scope*.
43. N. Fligstein, 'The spread of the multidivisional form among large firms, 1919–1979', *American Sociological Review*, Vol. 50 (1985), pp. 377–91.
44. Channon, *Strategy and Structure of British Enterprise*.
45. R. Fitzgerald, 'The competitive and institutional advantages of holding companies: British businesses in the inter-war period', *Journal of Industrial History*, Vol. 3, No. 2 (2000), pp. 1–30.
46. Channon, *Strategy and Structure*, p. 239.
47. M. Goold, A. Campbell and M. Alexander, *Corporate-Level Strategy: Creating Value in the Multibusiness Company* (New York: John Wiley & Sons, 1994), p. 54.
48. Tiratsoo and Tomlinson, 'Exporting the gospel of productivity', p. 73.
49. Armstrong, 'The rise of accounting controls', p. 415.
50. Ibid. Investment appraisal techniques such as discounted cash flow were not used anywhere in the UK economy until the mid-1960s, when they became rapidly established. This was partly due to the advocacy of A.M. Alfred of Courtaulds, who did much to pioneer the technique. A.M. Alfred, 'Investment in the development districts of the United Kingdom and discounted cash flow', *Journal of Accounting Research*, Vol. 2, No. 2 (1964), pp. 174–82.
51. O.E. Williamson, *Markets and Hierarchies* (New York: Free Press, 1975).
52. Ravenscraft and Scherer, *Mergers, Sell Offs and Economic Efficiency*.
53. Armstrong, 'The rise of accounting controls', p. 74.
54. K. Williams, T. Williams and D. Thomas, *Why are the British Bad at Manufacturing?* (London: Routledge and Kegan Paul, 1983).
55. S. Bowden and A. Gamble, 'Corporate governance and public policy: "new" initiatives by "old" Labour to reform stakeholder behaviour in the UK, 1965–69', *Journal of Industrial History*, forthcoming.
56. S. Aris, *Arnold Weinstock and the Making of GEC* (London: Aurum, 1998).
57. H. Levy and M. Sarnat, 'Diversification, portfolio analysis and the uneasy case for conglomerate mergers', *Journal of Finance*, Vol. 25 (1970), pp. 795–802. R. Rumelt, *Strategy, Structure and Economic Performance* (Boston, MA: Harvard University, 1974).
58. *The Economist*, 1991, p. 44.
59. A.W. Sametz, 'An expanded role for private pensions in US corporate governance', *Journal of Applied Corporate Finance*, Vol. 8, No. 2 (1995), pp. 97–110.
60. Chandler, *Scale and Scope*, p. 625.
61. J. Cassidy, *Dot Con.* (London: HarperCollins, 2002). Tax relief on Individual Retirement Accounts was introduced 1978 and extended to all income under 401(k) plans.
62. Sametz, 'An expanded role for private pensions'.
63. Chandler, *Scale and Scope*, p. 625.

64. J. Scott, *Corporate Businesses and Capitalist Classes* (Oxford: Oxford University Press 1997), p. 86.
65. S. Bowden, 'Ownership responsibilities and corporate governance: the crisis at Rolls-Royce 1968–71', *Business History*, Vol. 42, No. 3 (2002), pp. 31–62.
66. D. Higgins and J.S. Toms, 'Public subsidy and private divestment: the Lancashire cotton textile industry, *c*.1950–*c*.1965', *Business History*, Vol. 42, No. 1 (2000), pp. 59–84.
67. J. Maltby, 'Was the 1947 Companies Act a response to a national crisis?', *Accounting History*, Vol. 5, No. 2 (2000), pp. 31–60.
68. Companies Acts 1967 and 1976. *Jenkins Report* (1962), Cmnd 1749, *White Paper on Company Law Reform* (1973), Cmnd 5391.
69. R. Roberts, 'Regulatory response to the rise of the market for corporate control in Britain in the 1950s', *Business History*, Vol. 34, No. 1 (1992), pp. 183–200. J. Littlewood, *The Stock Market* (London: Financial Times, 1998), p. 103.
70. M. Blair, *Ownership and Control: Rethinking the Corporation for the Twenty-First Century* (Washington, DC: Brookings Institute, 1995).
71. H. Servaes, 'The value of diversification during the conglomerate merger wave', *Journal of Finance*, Vol. 51 (1996), pp. 1201–55. H.H. Shin and R.M. Stultz, 'Are internal capital markets efficient?' *Quarterly Journal of Economics*, Vol. 113 (1998), pp. 531–53. R. Rajan, H. Servaes and L. Zingales, 'The cost of diversity: The diversification discount and inefficient investment', *Journal of Finance*, Vol. 55 (2000), pp. 35–80. D.J. Denis, D.K. Denis and A. Sarin, 'Agency problems, equity ownership, and corporate diversification', *Journal of Finance*, Vol. 52 (1997), pp. 135–60. D.J. Denis, D.K. Denis and K. Yost, 'Global diversification, industrial diversification, and firm value', *Journal of Finance*, Vol. 57 (2002), pp. 1951–79.
72. *Report of the Committee of Inquiry into UK Vote Execution*, National Association of Pension Funds, 2000.
73. P. Augar, *The Death of Gentlemanly Capitalism* (Harmondsworth, UK: Penguin, 2000).
74. Wright, Hoskisson, Busenitz and Dial, 'Entrepreneurial growth through privatization', p. 598.
75. A. Kaufman and E. Englander, 'Kohlberg, Kravis Roberts & Co and the restructuring of American capitalism', *Business History Review*, Vol. 67 (Spring 1993), pp. 52–97. These deals generally began as friendly deals but later transactions involved hostile LBOs.
76. *Mergerstat Review*.
77. Centre for Management Buy-out Research.
78. R.A. Taggart, 'The growth of the junk bond market in its role in financing takeovers', in A. Auerbach (ed.), *Mergers and Acquisitions* (London: University of Chicago Press, 1988).
79. P. Coggan, *The Money Machine* (Harmondsworth, UK: Penguin, 1996).
80. A. Dicker, 'Tax issues', in B. De Caires (ed.), *Corporate Restructuring* (London: Euromoney, 1990).
81. Coggan, *The Money Machine*.
82. M. Wright, S. Thompson, B. Chiplin and K. Robbie, *Buy-ins and Buy-outs: New Strategies in Corporate Management* (London: Graham and Trotman, 1991).
83. Centre for Management Buy-out Research. Management Buy-outs: *Quarterly Review* (Autumn 2001), p. 78.
84. The main exceptions in the UK were the hostile LBO bid for BAT Industries in 1989 which was predicated on divesting underperforming assets. Incumbent management reacted to the bid by divesting assets as a defence. Although the bid thus subsequently lapsed, it had an important effect in pressurizing management to exit certain businesses that would not otherwise have happened so speedily, if at all. The successful hostile LBO of Gateway superstores in 1989 was accompanied by significant divestment of unwanted stores and divisions. These cases very much represented a brief emergence of US behaviour in the UK. M. Wright, N. Wilson, K. Robbie and C. Ennew, 'Restructuring and failure in buy-outs and buy-ins', *Business Strategy Review*, Vol. 5, No. 2 (1994), pp. 21–40.
85. Oughton and Whittam, 'Competition and co-operation'.
86. *Censuses of Production*, Summary Tables.
87. Oughton and Whittam, 'Competition and co-operation', p. 27.

88. *Business Week*, 'The age of consolidation', 14 October 1991, 'Making the perfect connection', *Wordperfect Report*, Summer/Fall 1994, p. 2.

89. R. Coopey, *3i: Fifty Years of Investing in Industry* (Oxford: Oxford University Press, 1995). R. Coopey, 'The first venture capitalist: Financing development after 1945, the case of ICFC/3I', *Business and Economic History*, Vol. 23, No. 1 (1994) pp. 262–72. Wright, Robbie, Chiplin and Albrighton, 'The development of an organisational innovation'.

90. Wright, Robbie, Chiplin and Albrighton, 'The development of an organisational innovation'.

91. M. Wright, B. Chiplin, S. Thompson and K. Robbie, 'Management buy-outs, trade unions and employee ownership', *Industrial Relations Journal*, Vol. 21, No. 2 (1990), pp. 137–46.

92. M. Wright, S. Thompson, B. Chiplin and K. Robbie, *Buy-ins and Buy-outs*, ch. 3.

93. H. Prechel, *Big Business and the State* (Albany, NY: SUNY, 2000), p. 129.

94. M. Zey, *Banking on Drexel, Junk Bonds and Buyouts* (New York: De Gruyter, 1993), M. Zey, 'The transformation of corporate control to owners and form to the multi-subsidiary, 1981–1993', *Research in Organizational Change and Development*, Vol. 11 (1998), pp. 271–312. M. Zey, 'The subsidiarization of the securities industry and the organisation of securities fraud networks to return profits in the 1980s', *Work and Occupations*, Vol. 26 (1999), pp. 50–76.

95. Zey, 'The transformation of corporate control'. M. Zey and B. Camp, 'The transformation from multi divisional to corporate groups of subsidiaries: Capital crisis theory', *The Sociological Quarterly*, Vol. 37 (1996), pp. 327–51.

96. M. Zey and T. Swenson, 'The transformation and survival of Fortune 500 industrial corporations through mergers and acquisitions, 1981–1995', *The Sociological Quarterly*, Vol. 42, No. 3 (2001), pp. 461–86.

97. D. Wise and M. Zey, 'The convergence of production and financial organisations: KKRs integration of corporate control for continued profits in the 1990s', *Social Science Quarterly*, Vol. 80 (1999), pp. 487–503.

98. Zey, *Banking on Drexel*; Zey and Camp, 'The transformation'; Zey and Swenson, 'Corporate tax laws, corporate restructuring and subsidiarization of corporate form, 1981–1995', *The Sociological Quarterly*, Vol. 39 (1998), pp. 555–81. Zey and Swenson, 'The transformation of the dominant corporate form from multi-divisional to multi subsidiary: the role of the Tax Reform Act', *The Sociological Quarterly*, Vol. 40 (1999), pp. 241-267.

99. M. Sterling and M. Wright, *Management Buyouts and the Law* (Oxford: Blackwell, 1990).

100. US buy-outs in the early 1980s were accused of involving cosy deals with management (L. Lowenstein, 'Management buy-outs', *Columbia Law Review* (1985), pp. 730–84.

101. The Delaware Supreme Court ruled in the case of Revlon Inc. vs MacAndrews & Forbes Holdings Inc. that once sale becomes inevitable, directors should no longer see their role as 'defenders of the corporate bastion' but as 'auctioneers charged with getting the best price for the stockholders' (D. Ridl, 'Buy-outs in the United States', ch. 12 in G. Sharp (ed.), *The Management Buy-out Manual* (London: Euromoney, 1993)). Sterling and Wright (p. 137) suggest that the position is less clear in the UK but that directors have a duty not to mislead shareholders, to provide sufficient information and advice to enable shareholders to reach a properly informed decision and not to exercise fiduciary power in a way which would prevent or inhibit shareholders from accepting the best competing offer.

102. Kaufman and Englander, 'Kohlberg, Kravis Roberts & Co', p. 82.

103. Chandler, *Scale and Scope*, p. 624. *Mergerstat Review* (Chicago: W.T. Grimm & Co., 1987), pp. 103–4. Lazonick and O'Sullivan, 'Finance and industrial development. Part 1', p. 17. Merrill Lynch Advisory Services, *Mergerstat Review* (New York: Merrill Lynch, 1994), p. 120.

104. Ravenscraft and Scherer, *Mergers, Sell Offs and Economic Efficiency*, p. 190.

105. S. Toms and M. Wright, 'Corporate governance, strategy and structure in British business history, 1950–2000', *Business History*, Vol. 44, No. 3 (2002), pp. 91–124.

106. L. Rosenthal and T. Sullivan, 'Some estimates of the impact of corporate diversification on the valuation and leverage of USA firms: Estimates from 1972 data', *Journal of Business Finance & Accounting*, Vol. 12, No. 2 (1985), pp. 275–312.

107. See Rajan, Servaes and Zingales, 'The cost of diversity'. L. Lang and R. Stulz, 'Tobin's q, corporate diversification and firm performance', *Journal of Political Economy*, Vol. 102 (1994),

pp. 1248–80; P.G. Berger and E.Ofek, 'Bust-up takeovers of value destroying diversified firms', *Journal of Finance*, Vol. 51 (1996), pp. 1175–200. K. Lins and H. Servaes, 'International evidence on the value of corporate diversification', *Journal of Finance*, Vol. 54 (1999), pp. 2215–39.
108. Lins and Servaes, 'International evidence'.
109. H. Servaes, 'The value of diversification'. Although it should be pointed out that recent evidence suggests that many studies have identified conglomerate discounts by misspecification of subsidiary benchmarks. J. Graham, M. Lemmon and J. Wolf, 'Does corporate diversification destroy value?', *Journal of Finance*, Vol. 57, No. 2 (2002), p. 695.
110. Lins and Servaes, 'International evidence'.
111. S. Thompson, M. Conyon, P. Wright and S. Girma, 'Merger activity and firm employment', *European Economic Review*, Vol. 46 (2002), pp. 31–49. This change in performance evidence relating to diversifying acquirers compared to evidence from the pre-1980 period suggests that such firms moved beyond a situation where diversifying acquisitions could be accommodated efficiently within a divisionalized structure, effectively becoming overdiversified.
112. Davis, Diekmann and Tinsley, 'The decline and fall of the conglomerate firm in the 1980s'.
113. R. Whittington, M. Mayer and F. Curto, 'Chandlerism in post-war Europe: Strategic and structural change in France, Germany and the UK, 1950–1993', *Industrial and Corporate Change*, Vol. 8, No. 3 (1999), pp. 519–55.
114. M. Haynes, S. Thompson and M. Wright, 'The determinants of corporate divestment in the UK', *International Journal of Industrial Organisation*, Vol. 18, No. 8 (2000), pp. 1201–22.
115. B. Hall, 'Corporate restructuring and investment horizons in the United States, 1976–1987', *Business History Review*, Vol. 68 (Spring 1994), pp. 110–43.
116. Based on 143 of the top 500 manufacturing companies in the UK for which data were available (Haynes, Thompson and Wright, 'Determinants of corporate divestment'.
117. M. Wright and S. Thompson, 'Vertical disintegration and the life-cycle of firms and industries', *Managerial and Decision Economics*, Vol. 7, No. 2 (1986), pp. 141–4.
118. Haynes, Thompson and Wright, 'Determinants of corporate divestment'.
119. See M. Wright, B. Chiplin and S. Thompson, 'The market for corporate control: Divestments and buy-outs', in M. Bishop and J. Kay (eds), *European Mergers and Merger Policy* (Oxford: Oxford University Press, 1993) for a review.
120. C. Markides, 'Consequences of corporate refocusing: Ex ante evidence', *Academy of Management Journal*, Vol. 35 (1992), pp. 398–412; K. John and E. Ofek, 'Asset sales and increase in focus', *Journal of Financial Economics*, Vol. 37 (1995), pp. 105–26.
121. K.A. Afshar, R.J. Taffler and P.S. Sudarsanam, 'The effects of corporate divestment on shareholder wealth: The UK experience', *Journal of Banking and Finance*, Vol. 16, No. 1 (1992), pp. 115–35.
122. B. Saadouni, R. Briston, C. Mallin and K. Robbie, 'Security price reaction to divestments by healthy and financially distressed firms: The case of MBOs', *Applied Financial Economics*, Vol. 6, No. 1 (1996), pp. 85–90. These findings are in contrast to US evidence.
123. M. Haynes, S. Thompson and M. Wright, 'The impact of divestment on firm performance: empirical evidence from a panel of UK companies', *Journal of Industrial Economics*, Vol. 50, No. 2 (2002), pp. 173–96. These findings are consistent with US studies using cross-section data (C. Markides, *Diversification, Refocusing and Economic Performance* (London: MIT Press, 1995) but have the advantage of taking into account the effects of corporate restructuring programmes spread over a period of time.
124. F. Lichtenberg and D. Siegel, 'The effects of leveraged buyouts on productivity and related aspects of firm behavior', *Journal of Financial Economics*, Vol. 27 (1990), pp. 165–94.
125. S. Bhagat, A. Shleifer and R. Vishny, 'Hostile takeovers in the 1980s: The return to corporate specialization', *Brookings Papers on Economic Activity: Microeconomics* (1990), pp. 1–72.
126. M. Jensen, 'The agency cost of free cash flow, corporate finance and takeovers', *American Economic Review*, Vol. 76 (1986), pp. 323–9.
127. R. Harris, D. Siegel and M. Wright, 'Assessing the impact of management buyouts on economic efficiency: Plant-level evidence from the United Kingdom', paper presented at the North

American Productivity Workshop at Union College, Schenectady, New York, 20–22 June 2002.

128. For the USA see for example P. Phan and C. Hill, 'Organizational restructuring and economic performance in leveraged buyouts: An ex post study', *Academy of Management Journal*, Vol. 38, No. 3 (1995), pp. 704–40.

129. Lazonick and O'Sullivan, 'Finance and industrial development', p. 29.

130. J. Barney, M. Wright and D. Ketchen, 'The resource-based view of the firm: Ten years after 1991', *Journal of Management*, Vol. 27, No. 6 (2001), pp. 625–42.

131. Wright, Chiplin, Thompson and Robbie, *Management Buy-ins and Buy-outs*; R. Coff, 'When competitive advantage doesn't lead to performance: The resource-based view and stakeholder bargaining power', *Organization Science*, Vol. 10, No. 2 (1999), pp. 119–33. Castanias and C. Helfat, 'The managerial rents model'.

132. M. Wright, R. Hoskisson and L. Busenitz, 'Firm rebirth: Management buy-outs and wealth creation', *Academy of Management Executive*, Vol. 15, No. 1 (2001), pp. 111–25.

133. Principally the Treadway (known as the Report of the National Commission of Fraudulent Financial Reporting) and Committee of Sponsoring Organizations (COSO) Reports.

134. H. Short, K. Keasey, M. Wright and A. Hull, 'Corporate governance: From accountability to enterprise', *Accounting and Business Research*, Vol. 29, No. 4 (1999), pp. 337–52; I. Demirag, S. Sudarsanam and M. Wright, 'Corporate governance: Overview and research agenda', *British Accounting Review*, Vol. 32, No. 4 (2000), pp. 341–54. M. Maclean, 'Corporate governance in France and the UK: Long-term perspectives on contemporary institutional arrangements', *Business History*, Vol. 41, No. 1 (1999), pp. 88–116.

135. Kaufman and Englander, 'Kohlberg, Kravis Roberts & Co'.

136. For a discussion see the special issue of *Hume Papers on Public Policy*, on corporate governance and the reform of company law, Vol. 8, No. 1 (2000).

137. Short, Keasey, Wright and Hull, 'Corporate governance: From accountability to enterprise'.

[12]

Corporate directing in large plcs: reflections on (the concept of) corporate governance

Annie Pye and Ian Colville

Introduction

This chapter addresses change at board level in a sample of large UK organizations, classi-cally described as at a mature stage in their life cycle, in the context of changing environ-mental conditions. In so doing, it raises the question of the concept of organization life cycle as our research reveals patterns of metamorphosis which are not quite as cyclical as the life-cycle metaphor implies. This finding also draws attention to the fascinating dynamic be-tween micro- and macro-level life-cycle issues, represented at and through board-level behaviour, where it appears that perhaps the role of boards and executive management is to 'interrupt' organization life cycles. The chapter also contributes to the development and theorizing about corporate governance, prompted in part by changing practice as well as changing the theoretical lens, and by putting forward a model of corporate directing.

There are two ESRC-funded projects which lie at the heart of this chapter, conducted some ten years apart in large UK plcs.[1] In 1987, chairmen, chief executives (CEs) and selected board members were interviewed in 12 large UK plcs, for example Hanson, Pru-dential, BTR, Marks & Spencer (Mangham and Pye, 1991). In 2001, a second ESRC-funded project returned to these contributors and to their 'current equivalents' in these organizations (as far as it was possible to identify them), effectively with the same question: 'how do you "run" a large organization?' (Pye, 2002b). The 1987–89 project was neither conceived as a corporate governance study nor did it draw specifically on corporate governance literature: it was broadly based in organization studies and drew on 'upper echelons' literature in the process of developing our understanding of 'the doing' of managing at executive and board level: the continual, purposive, relentless action which underpinned their organizing (Mangham and Pye, 1991). Above all, context was viewed as important to the data and to theorizing, which meant that time and timing were also relevant to directors' explanations and accounts.

Against this conceptual backdrop, context and time continue to have great relevance, from both academic and practitioner points of view (Pye, 2005). The current corporate climate is, in some ways, very different to that of 1987–89. A series of corporate scandals at the start of the 1990s (e.g. Maxwell, BICC, Polly Peck and Barings Bank) prompted a decade of governance committees in the UK. The early 2000s have been characterized by a global array of corporate collapses and scandals, including Enron, Tyco, WorldCom, Marconi, Equitable Life, Ahold and Parmalat, which has seriously damaged public and investor confidence in large mature organizations and their boards. Hence their governance is of great public interest. So the chapter begins with a reflection on recent corporate history, changing times in the corporate context, which sketches the environment in which these people and their firms now operate.

We then briefly set out the changing times in the academic context, which influences how we address (and research) this area. For all the wealth and variety of literature which contributes to our understanding of this subject, Daily, Dalton et al. (2003) propose that governance research is at a "crossroads" and in need of a more 'multitheoretic approach' (p. 372). Our aim is to contribute to new theorizing about governance in terms of how people run organizations, by drawing on deliberately selected contributions from organization studies rather than specifically corporate governance literature, which help to set the scene for this chapter. In particular, we will broaden the scope beyond agency theory to explore and develop an integrated analysis of processes of interaction in making sense of boards and their sense making. In so doing, we shall emphasize the 'doing'/enacting of governance and strategy in our endeavour to contribute to the call for new perspectives which take a holistic approach, not just considering what boards do but also how and why they do it.

The third section will then introduce changing times in the fieldwork, where we will sketch the background to the fieldwork and analysis underpinning the two projects which span the 13 years. In the UK, the decade of committees on corporate governance, from Cadbury (1992) onwards, has resulted in the London Stock Exchange adopting the Combined Code of Practice (1998) for all listed companies, revised again in 2003. So not only has the sample changed, but so also have the behaviours and expectations of the participants, held both by themselves and by others. Indeed, for these reasons, a selection of investors was also added to the interview sample in 1998–2000.

The discussion section, entitled life cycles and corporate directing, goes on to draw on these data to explore governance in these mature firms and to articulate a model of corporate directing. First, changes in relationships between boards and shareholders are seen to impact on what happens inside the boardroom, with consequences at the macro level, for example the demise of conglomerates which impacts on organization life cycle, and the more micro level, for example location and frequency of investor meetings. This leads to some interesting implications for the concept of organization life cycle, where the role of directors appears to become one of interrupting the cycle.

The second part of the discussion section goes on to outline our model of corporate directing, which reframes what boards do by retaining emphasis on the integrative, continuous process themes which underpin their organizing at this micro–macro-level interface. This brings together the governance (conformance) and the strategizing (performance) side of director roles, brought alive/enacted through board leadership. This creates a framework which most importantly reflects the broad cultural differences through which their leading, governing and strategizing are expressed. This process-oriented description of board practice seeks to capture the link between micro and macro level, represented in board action in a way that reflects the importance of context, time and trust which are considered crucial to our appreciation of transparent and effective governance.

The conclusion draws attention to the implications of our research. Our findings illustrate how organization life cycle is not just about age, maturity and structure, but also reflects something of the organizational mindset and cultural heritage. Likewise, the reframing of what boards do does not necessarily require 'dismantling fortresses' (Daily, Dalton et al., 2003) so much as, again, challenging the mindset and cultural heritage, that is, a new way of thinking rather than taking apart the old. The model of corporate directing maintains an emphasis on the enacting of board leadership, which ensures recognition of the importance of board culture for determining much about how governance, strategy and leadership are 'done'.

At the macro–micro interface, this leads to a curious paradox of corporate governance codes, where they may appear to have an 'equal and opposite' effect: that is, greater reliance on codes of conduct encourages more to happen 'off-stage', which works against the drive for greater openness and transparency. In turn this raises the question of accountability, which is of course a key driver of the continual refining of governance codes. Our conclusion is that more process-oriented descriptions of board practice, such as corporate directing and so on, which capture this link between micro- and macro-level issues represented in board action and which reflect context, timing and trust, are essential to our development of the concept of corporate governance in a way that has relevance to both practitioners and academics.

Changing Times in Context

Although authors tell us that change now happens faster than ever before (Beer and Nohria, 2000), it is simply a fact of life (i.e. basic biology/physiology) that change is continuous even though – and for whatever reasons – our perceptions of the scale and scope of change are likely to vary. There have been significant changes across the last decade in the economic, political and social environment of the UK and globally as well, as huge technological developments which impact on ways of living and working. Just compare the information that you carry in your pocket now with that of ten years ago: mobile phones with Internet and cameras, palm tops, wireless Internet access and so on are commonplace!

As the focus of this chapter is on corporate governance and its practice in large, mature UK-listed plcs, we will concentrate more specifically on those changes that have had a significant impact on board-level thinking and practice in these enterprises. These include the fact that the Berlin Wall came down in 1989 and the cold war effectively drew to a close, reflecting a major shift in the global superpower balance; the Far East experienced severe economic downturn following the collapse of the Thai currency in 1987 and Japan, in particular, has suffered recession ever since; more recent events such as the attack on the World Trade Center in 2001 signal the rise of religious 'war' which has had multiple effects on business; and the UN finds that 21 of the world's largest 100 multinationals have programmes for dealing with HIV/Aids.[2]

The 1990s have been described as the era of the growing 'equity culture' (Bogler, 2000), starting in the UK from the stock market crash in 1992 which was then followed by a bull period until a second cycle of recession in 2001 wiped billions off the market value of companies.[3] During the latter half of this decade, the 'dot.com bubble' was an important driver of interest in equity investment, mirrored on both sides of the Atlantic, with fantastic valuations of technology stocks which then fell dramatically in the early 2000s. There have been inevitable peaks and troughs in the climate for mergers and acquisitions (M&A) throughout this time, with 2003 showing a decline from previously increased levels of M&A activity. In the mid-1990s, the UK economy also suffered what was known as 'pensions mis-selling', which led to tightened regulatory oversight and laid the foundations for what, in 2004, was predicted to be a 'looming pensions crisis' ahead, as insurers predict significant shortfalls in future provision at a time of growth in an ageing population.

Other significant economic changes in the UK during this time include continuing consolidation amongst institutional investors, which has had the effect of concentrating share ownership and investor influence. By 1997, Gaved had established that over 60 per cent of UK equity was owned by 20 fund managers (Gaved, 1997). Important structural change in the financial and business services field includes the demise of Andersen's following the collapse of US energy company Enron and the growing trend to separate the audit and consulting arms of others of the 'Big Five'. In addition, a host of corporate collapses has also raised concern about the integrity and reliability of board decision making and of corporate reporting, for example Marconi, WorldCom, Tyco, Parmalat, Equitable Life.

The regulatory context has changed too. The 1990s saw a series of committees in the UK which sought to improve the governance of companies, starting with the Cadbury Committee in 1992. This was followed by the Greenbury Committee (1995) which specifically addressed executive remuneration, and the Hampel Committee (1997) which was set up to review the implementation of Greenbury's and Cadbury's findings, which then led to the Combined Code of Practice (1998), and was seen to encourage practices which were by now already common to many large organizations. However, the Turnbull Committee Report (1999) of the Institute of Chartered Accountants for England and Wales, which contained guidance for directors on internal control issues in implementing the combined code, was felt to require much closer attention and thought likely to have greater impact on changing risk management practices. These committees were, in effect, formalizing what the best were already doing and also legislating against what the worst were already doing: ironically, as one subsequently finds in a case such as Enron, the catch is that it may be possible for a firm to illustrate both positions simultaneously.

The Higgs Report (2003) on the role and effectiveness of non-executive directors (NEDs) and the Smith Report (2003) on the role of audit committees have been more recently focused on tightening up perceived weaknesses in governance, following recent corporate collapses in the USA and the UK. The outcome has been a revised Combined Code of Practice (2003), affirming the UK governance culture of 'comply or explain'. Interestingly, while the Higgs Review was widely debated in the press and brought out an array of views, relatively little significant change is felt likely to occur on the boards of large organizations as many already largely comply. However, the audit committee guidance requires much closer attention and is likely to have much greater impact on changing practice. The Myners Review of Institutional Investment (2001) has also encouraged changes to bring greater transparency and accountability to investment practices, proposing, among other things, a code of practice for pension fund trustees.[4]

In 1997, the Chancellor of the Exchequer brought banking supervision and investment services regulation together under the span of a new regulatory body, the FSA (Financial Services Authority, formerly the Securities and Investment Board). Its powers and responsibilities extend to regulating 'pretty much the whole of the financial services industry', as its former chairman, Sir Howard Davies (2000), put it. For many large companies, managing the FSA is now a full-time job for members of their finance staff, responding to regular consultation papers and updating accounting practices to comply with ever-changing regulation. The FSA also takes a close view of practices at board level and of City briefings, in particular, which can lead to very time-consuming and gruelling investigations by FSA officials, should any impropriety be suspected. This degree of scrutiny was not the case in the late 1980s and has serious consequences for what is said by and to board members.

On a global scale, the OECD (2000) has also proposed a code of corporate governance which sets a broad governance agenda for what companies should do, and other countries, for example the USA and Germany, have further developed their own codes. Change in the USA has been concentrated through bodies such as the Securities and Exchange Commission (SEC). Following the collapse of Enron, for example, it implemented the Sarbanes–Oxley code in 2002, requiring CEOs and finance directors to sign off their accounts as being accurate. The effect of this has been widespread and deeply felt, particularly among board audit committees, where paperwork and time commitment have increased dramatically.

Technological change has also played a part in this process, given changes to computing power and database software, access to information, performance measurement and ease of data manipulation. In addition, it has been a key driver for changing operations, often well beyond the shopfloor effects, through to partnerships, people and processes. Not only has purchasing become a much more significant operational role than was the case in 1989, but the whole field of logistics and operations, based on software and equipment almost inconceivable before, means considerable change in terms of factory operations and robotics as well as global satellite positioning systems for mapping the supply chain, delivery and logistics. Such very different technologies of stock control, for example, make the whole organizational context very different in terms of what performance may be expected, how it is achieved and, importantly, how and against what criteria it is measured and evaluated.

This brief overview of the history of the last 15 years is inevitably only partial but it gives a broad flavour of some of the more important changes in context which have significant effect on boards, what they do and how they do it. Interestingly, as a final comparator, 1988–89 was a significant year for Marks and Spencer as their CE explained at the time, becoming the first UK retailer to achieve over £500 million pre-tax profit on a turnover of £4577 million. Marks and Spencer has been a more volatile performer in the late 1990s, with pre-tax profit falling from over £1 billion in 1997 to £700m in 2003.[5] Against this backdrop, the academic literature of management and corporate governance has also seen change during this time, although in different ways and for different reasons, some of which are now considered in the next section.

Changing Times in the Academic Context

The origins of the concept of corporate governance are usually traced back to the work of Berle and Means (1932), which drew attention to problems inherent to the separation of ownership and control of the public corporation. Jensen and Meckling's (1976) classic paper further developed an agency-theory-framed explanation, based on the assumption that managers are self-interested and are financially relatively immune from the impacts of their decisions. And from here, agency theory has since dominated much of the corporate governance literature, and can be found regularly summarized in review articles that claim to set the agenda (e.g. Johnson et al., 1996; Shleifer and Vishny, 1997; Huse, 2000; Daily et al., 2003).

Although earlier voices offered a notably different perspective (e.g. Mace, 1971 and Lorsch and McIver, 1989), agency theory continues to provide the starting point for many authors and sometimes seems to be the only element shared by some of this literature. However, the scope of corporate governance literature is potentially much wider, as authors such as Keasey et al. (1997) or Turnbull (1997) suggest. While acknowledging its roots in economics and finance literature, these authors identify other perspectives, for example stewardship, stakeholder and political, based on different sets of assumptions, which provide a contrast to an agency approach. Each has potential relevance here as we seek to widen the canvas, although each also has its limitations, not least because these approaches are developed in 'other' fields and are applied to boards and their governance practices rather than offering a holistic, integrative perspective on 'doing' governance.

The 1987–89 project had developed on the assumption that top management is somehow different to 'other' management, a deep-rooted assumption going back Barnard's (1932) definition of executive process: 'the synthesis in concrete action of contradictory forces, reconciling conflicting forces, instincts, conditions, positions and ideals' (p. 231). The project had drawn on the work of Hambrick and Mason (1984), who had identified and distinguished the 'upper echelons' perspective. This promulgated the view that not only are board directors different to other managers, in terms of values and characteristics, but also they make a difference to their organizations (see also Nadler and Tushman, 1990; Tichy and Charan, 1995; Finkelstein and Hambrick, 1996).

Like all small groups, there are two dimensions against which their actions and interactions can be viewed: task and group maintenance functions (Benne and Sheats, 1948). Most board research has concentrated on the task aspects of what boards do. From this point of view, the board director's task comprises two primary elements: one is around the governance/conformance-to-regulation type agenda and the other is around the strategic direction/performance side of their agenda (Stiles, 2001). These form the core of much of the work on board behaviour although each takes a slightly different direction. For instance, Garratt (1996) elaborates these two themes into his notion of the learning board, which helps to draw attention to both external and internal elements of the director role and both long- and short-term horizons in their decision making. He conceptualizes this as a framework for the learning board, from which he develops notions of review cycles (of policy, strategy, operations and governance), which underpin a fully effective learning board and offers implications for board development.

Some US authors take a different perspective and describe director roles in terms of control and service which, in turn, puts a different emphasis on what it is that directors do. For example, working from 'upper echelons' literature, Forbes and Milliken (1999) propose a model of strategic decision-making effectiveness which considers three elements of board/group dynamics (effort norms, cognitive complexity and use of skills and knowledge) in performing its control and service functions. In contrast, Rindova (1999) compares a traditional governance perspective and a cognitive perspective through analysis of the role of boards in strategy formation and offers several important implications for policy, practice and research. However, there remains a need for empirical research to underpin the development of these lines of theoretical analysis.

This is perhaps where the real difficulty lies since our own research in this field suggests that operationalizing some of these concepts can be practically impossible. For example, whether one prefers to frame board roles in terms of conformance and performance or control and service, fundamentally these are not discrete segments or distinctive aspects or pieces of action – they are closely interwoven into everything directors do. As a result, distinguishing between (and measuring) actions and their effects on performance becomes conceptually very challenging. On the one hand, this makes it a very interesting field, yet on the other such a difficult area to research, and may also contribute to the sense of unease which seems prevalent in current literature about progress in governance research and conceptualization.

For example, Daily, Dalton et al. (2003) provide a comprehensive summary of governance literature in their description of the 'crossroads' faced by governance researchers, proposing that 'alternative theories and models are needed to effectively uncover the promise and potential of corporate governance' (p. 371). This is particularly notable because, although they themselves have been influential authors in this field for some time, they observe that for governance researchers to fulfil these needs, they will have to engage with the challenge of 'dismantling fortresses', and will doubtlessly face a barrier of 'empirical dogmatism' (Daily et al., 2003, p. 379). This perhaps says something about why corporate governance theory is in this situation in the first place, as well as indicating something of the scale of the intellectual climb which lies ahead in order to stimulate new thinking and perspectives.

In facing these crossroads and endeavouring to develop a holistic, integrative approach to thinking and theorizing about how small groups of people run large organizations, our research in this field shows that rarely, if at all, do directors talk in terms of conformance/ performance, or control/service roles, nor do they ever talk of agency theory or resource dependency. Instead they talk of shareholder value, strategic focus and corporate governance and, in essence, they talk of the things that they do. They talk of actions that they have taken; issues with which they are concerned; of people they have met and conversations they have had; plans which they are shaping; and so on. Their emphasis throughout is on *process* – integrative, relentless and purposive, about shaping strategic direction and governing rather than about adherence to a strategy or describing governance practice, for example.

For this reason, our preference is to reframe the subject more broadly around what happens in organizations: that is, the doing of managing/organizing/leading and, ultimately, the doing of corporate directing. Hence we draw on the work of authors such as Weick (1979, 1995) to help express this social psychological analysis of organizing. Weick (1987) offers four sentences taken from academic papers in which one word is missing. The author is invited to consider whether the word 'culture' or 'strategy' has been taken out: it is of course an intellectual challenge as either word could be inserted and each sentence would still make sense. His point is that whether it is labelled strategy or culture matters much less than the sense which it generates. Our research agrees with this point. As Pye (1995, p. 457) notes: 'it is not so much whether or not you have something called strategy which is important ... what really matters is that if by communicating that your organization has a strategy, this helps to focus people's minds and actions and to define meaning, then strategy may be a helpful construct. Ultimately however, managing at senior executive level is about dialogue and doing: that is, the process and outcome of sensemaking.'

Likewise, the same conclusion could be drawn of governance, to the extent that it is not so much having a code of conduct which is important but if it helps to focus people's minds and actions and to define meaning, then it may be helpful as a communicative device. Ultimately, it is boards in general, and chief executives in particular, who are seen to embody these principles; that is, they are seen to be where the buck stops as far as strategic decision making and corporate governance are concerned, from both an internal and an external point of view. Hence, in terms of what they do, these remain the two key board themes which are brought alive through particular leadership actions in particular board situations: that is, they are enacted in ways which are particular to each board case, time and context. This leads to the conclusion that the director's role is, in essence, that of directing: where corporate directing is taken to comprise governing and strategizing, enacted through leading which reflects the outcome of individual and collective dynamics, located in time and context.

Changing Times in Fieldwork

In 1987–89, we studied chairmen, CEs and board members in 12 large UK plcs to explore who they were and what they did, by asking them how they ran their organizations. The sample was drawn up based on a variety of criteria. We aimed to go to firms which were listed in the FTSE 100 and had a reputation among critical opinion formers, in particular, for doing something 'interesting' or noteworthy in terms of their management, for example by asking analysts and business journalists/commentators. This led to letters, phone calls and visits to offices in London of an array of key people, and we also obtained articles on relevant firms from a press-cutting service illustrating fieldwork before the Internet era.

As a consequence, we finally gained access to the chairman and chief executive, and selected board members at Beazer, BTR, Coats Viyella, Glynwed, Hanson, Lucas, Marks and Spencer, Metal Box, Prudential, Reckitt and Colman, and TSB. The twelfth firm in our list was an exception to our selection criteria: this was Avon Rubber plc, which was chosen as a local firm where we had access to the chief executive who was prepared to allow us to test our method with his senior management. We were not entirely sure that interviewing would be the best way to answer our core question and, indeed, as a consequence of this pilot study, made some changes to how we framed our approach. However, the practice of interviewing different directors and then preparing a case on the company, which was then read and discussed between us, became our grounded theory method in action. Initial case drafts were raw and the analysis unrefined but as each case and each discussion meeting went on, so the process became more complex, with cross-comparisons of organizations and people, and the analysis became more refined. Gradually, we began to agree the pattern and shape of our analysis among our 46 transcripts, appreciating the importance of process in what we called 'the doing of managing' at this level.

Among the group dynamics we saw described in our data, then, was the classic tension between individual and collective: where individual and collective responsibility come together, sometimes finely balanced and on occasions, violently opposed. Our pilot study confirmed that no matter how carefully one may describe the competencies or qualities of individuals or the rationale for actions they take in carrying out their responsibilities, it is actually their effect in a collective dynamic (i.e. a small group of people engaged in purposive action) which leads to actions that provide the basis for attributions made about the quality of their performance, both dramatic and financial as well as individual and collective. The meaning of these actions, we noted, lay in the responses of key others.

Looking more closely at how small groups of directors ran large organizations in 1989, the variety was considerable: for example at Hanson Trust, two central directors supported by a select group of key people created a very tightly driven financial management system in what was almost essentially an investment company; at Glynwed International, the shared ambition of board members was that of becoming the lowest-cost producer; while at Lucas, they were aiming to be one of the top three in their key markets; and so on. What was common to all, however, was that they had strategic ambition and engaged in continuous and (usually) consistent communication (largely within but also outside their organizations) about how it was they were collectively going to achieve that ambition and beyond (Mangham and Pye, 1991): we described this as *organizing as explaining* (Pye, 1993).

Some ten years later, in 1998–2000, former contributors were asked again, how do you run a large organization?[6] Three of the original 12 companies were under different ownership (BTR, Lucas and Metal Box) and composition, although the remaining nine were still largely UK owned and based. Of the remaining nine, several had undergone radical change in strategic scale and focus, even though their name may have remained the same. For example, Hanson had demerged into five organizations and Hanson plc focused on aggregates; Avon Rubber no longer made rubber, even though this had been its core business for the preceding hundred plus years; likewise, Glynwed had sold its original founding metals business; and TSB was now part of the much bigger clearing bank, LloydsTSB group.

In 1998–2000, interviews were conducted with 25 people who had contributed to the first study;[7] and with 35 current board members in Avon, Beazer, Coats Viyella, Glynwed, Hanson, LloydsTSB, Marks and Spencer, Prudential, Reckitt and Colman and Scottish Power. A tenth firm, Scottish Power, was added to the sample as they were/are a utility firm, representing a type of organization which had not been available as a listed company ten years previously and which offered an interesting case of changing organizational composition and culture. Soon into the fieldwork, it became apparent that major investors were now felt by contributors to be significantly more powerful 'observers' of their explanations of corporate performance. Given substantial concentration among the UK financial services sector across the last ten years, it was felt important to appreciate investors' perspectives. Hence interviews were also conducted with five chief executives at selected institutional investors: Hermes, Gartmore, LionTrust, Merrill Lynch, and Philips and Drew. The grounds for selection were that they were all, with the exception of LionTrust, 'active' investors, hence were committed to 'shaking up sleepy management'. LionTrust, introduced to the research via another contributor, added an alternative viewpoint as a 'passive' investor to sharpen the perspective. Although a non-random sample, they were none the less a highly influential group of investors to the extent that between these five firms, they controlled over 10 per cent of UK equity in 2000 (Golding, 2001).

In addition to archive searching on the companies and people interviewed, data were drawn from a variety of other sources including annual reports, press releases, fieldnotes and observations, corporate websites and databases such as FT.com and LexisNexis. All interviews (between one and three hours long) were taped, fully transcribed and a copy returned to the contributor for their information. It was agreed that no quotations would be used and attributed without prior permission. Four people sought to amend their transcripts at this stage, in effect translating spoken into written English, although none sought to change the substantive content or to change the interpretation of what had been said.

In essence, this approach is best described as interpretative (Morgan, 1980) in its methodological position, has been rooted in social constructionist assumptions (Sandberg, 2001) and data analysis has followed the grounded theory method (Strauss and Corbin, 1994; Locke, 2000). Based on observations of change made by the primary researcher in both studies, a conceptual model is developed here which we encourage others to test for robustness and validity and which we hope will lead to further conceptual debate.

Life Cycles and Corporate Directing

This section will first identify three particular changes observed across the two studies and then consider their impact, first, on the organization life cycle and the role of boards, and then on the life cycle of the concept of corporate governance and the need to develop alternative theories and models. In so doing, we will also explore the notion of corporate directing. Throughout, this analysis will highlight the fascinating position of boards on the cusp between micro- and macro-level issues in organization, its practice and its theorizing.

There are similarities between the two projects in terms of findings, although there are also important differences in terms of *how* directors conduct their roles. For example, in 1987–89, not one person in our interviews used the phrase 'corporate governance', whereas now, almost all contributors raised this subject of their own volition, implying greater awareness of and sensitivity to such issues. Relationships with major shareholders have changed significantly across the decade and directors now see accounting for their strategic direction as crucial in this context. The role of director, both executive and non-executive, is also felt to be more critically under the spotlight.

Organization life cycle and the role of boards

These three observations all have important bearing on corporate life-cycle issues at both the macro and micro level. An example of macro-level consequence relates to conglomerates which have effectively disappeared as a major corporate form during the 1990s. The scale and composition of their agglomerations seemed to have reached saturation point, where there were few sufficiently undervalued companies of sufficiently large enough scale to represent good investment. At the same time, index tracker fund managers were developing positions which made conglomerates no longer attractive as investments, in part because their comparative base had become more difficult to track. This also made it difficult to ascertain what value a board can add to this breadth. Hence the two largest UK conglomerates of the time, Hanson and BTR, metamorphosed dramatically.

This leads to a curious situation where, on the one hand, organizations appear to have changed because of demerger (e.g. Hanson), merger (Reckitt and Colman with Benkiser) or take-over (Siebe took over BTR), yet on the other hand, organizations which bear the same name (e.g. Avon, Glynwed) may often have changed substantially from their original core founding businesses, each of which has over 150 years' heritage. So from a life-cycle point of view, Hanson plc is likely to be considered mature in that it was first founded in 1967 and has grown up from the Yorkshire transport company from which it began and expanded and developed, in effect, into an investment company, both in the UK and the USA, where Lord Hanson and Sir Gordon White kept a close eye out for underperforming, undervalued assets.

In 1995, the Hanson board decided to demerge and, steadily, over the next two years, five organizations were constructed out of Hanson operations, each with deeply engrained and tightly controlled Hanson criteria for financial management and evaluating investments, measuring in close financial terms the value added by each element of any process. So although there remains an organization called Hanson plc, its focus is on the aggregates business and it bears little resemblance to its predecessor in Hanson Trust plc. Indeed, the current Hanson plc organization shows evidence of being at an earlier stage in the life cycle,[8] parts of which are overlaid on more deeply engrained, mature cultural patterns.

Prudential plc is another mature organization which offers an interestingly, micro-level illustration. Although their core business remains largely unchanged to outside observers – the insurance industry – closer inspection reveals considerable and continuing change. This is not brought about just by changing insurance products but by more fundamental change in financial services and the regulatory environment too. Prudential had bought estate agencies in 1989 which transpired to be a poor investment from which they withdrew in the early 1990s. Following acknowledgement of their role in pensions mis-selling in 1995, Prudential went through a period of significant change, starting at board level. Among other things, they also ceased employing the 'man from the Pru' approach to direct selling, launched Egg, their Internet banking business in 1998, and went into partnership with Accenture IT to run part of this business. Given government interventions on ISAs and stakeholder pensions as well, they anticipated that a significant portion of business that the sales force was currently doing would not be viable in two years' time. This problem created an urgency for change, through a very changed context for Prudential, leading to changing networks of significant relationships, all of which require time and effort to sustain.

The role of investors is considered very important in these networks and so, for example, the new CE, Sir Peter Davis, chose to visit major shareholders rather than expect them to come to him, as his predecessor had done. He described his approach as being one of 'no surprises', such that he would take time to call major shareholders if felt necessary, to ensure they were kept informed. This style of relationship was illustrated by the majority of interviewees and was welcomed by active investors, too. Although time-consuming and, on occasions, particularly for the smaller, less significant firms in the sample, frustratingly wasteful from the corporate point of view (especially where the investor was ill informed or ill prepared), most agreed that this was simply a key part of their role, taking around 30 per cent of their time.

The interplay between macro- and micro-level issues of this kind is brought vividly to light by the recent example of Sir Philip Watts, who resigned in early 2004 as Chairman of Royal Dutch Shell, under pressure from shareholders. He had caused great disquiet among investors for choosing not to front a briefing which told investors that Shell had mistakenly overvalued its oil reserves by 20 per cent: the share price dropped instantly and dramatically. Sir Philip had earlier been the (executive) director responsible for valuations of mining reserves so this major revision was of even greater significance. His reputation among the City was already one of being distant and aloof, hence his inaction further compounded matters, and the pressure on him to resign increased. Shareholders have also seen this as an opportunity to push for change in the board structure of Shell and now the acting chairman, Joeren Van de Vijver, has agreed that all options will be considered in order to improve governance practice at Royal Dutch Shell and, above all, to regain investor confidence in them. Interestingly, behind the stories of resignation and people also lies the macro-level influence of the SEC: it was a change to SEC requirements for reserve-level reporting that apparently prompted Shell to make the revaluation in the first place.

As these cases illustrate, the ability to forge and sustain good relationships with key people both inside and outside their organizations has become a much more critical part of the director role than was previously the case. However, it is not an element of director competence which is routinely or easily evaluated because, in many ways, it runs against the grain of much of the emphasis of corporate governance reform. For example, much governance attention (e.g. Hermes website) is given to ensuring that NEDs are 'independent' and the Higgs Review (2003), in particular, sought to break up the 'old boys' network' image of directors and their appointments. In contrast, our research reveals director independence to be a *non sequitur*, in some respects. That is, effective directors are well known if not also well interconnected: that is, one does not even get to be considered for selection by a head-hunter unless one already has network credibility. Part of the evaluation of director ability includes one's relationships – their strength, quality and efficacy – as well as one's ability to relate. This is something of a catch-22 for board directors as well as for governance reviews.

Corporate directing

With such wide and deep changes in practice, it is not surprising that we need some change in our thinking to make sense of change in practice. Although Dalton et al. (2003) describe this as being at a crossroads, our evidence suggests it may be more appropriate simply to reframe our focus. That is, the crossroads metaphor implies choice between this route or that, whereas reframing suggests, literally, changing the framework; so it is not the navigator's choice of left or right but instead, a move into a different plane (*sic*). For example, Dalton et al. (2003) suggest that to develop more holistic thinking requires bringing together things that have claimed separate areas of intellectual interest for some time. Board directors conform to regulation and seek to perform, and they generate wealth for themselves and for their owners. They also do perfectly normal and natural human activities, such as talk and develop relationships, listen and learn, and ultimately given their power and influence, shape direction and lead.

Hence, we argue, they are corporate directors doing corporate directing: in so doing, they are 'doing' governing and strategizing, while being seen as the figureheads and as the centre of attention and accountability, so they can also be described as leading their firms or enacting leadership. Pye (2002a) has elaborated more fully this conception and model of corporate directing, reflecting the integrative process of governing/conforming and strategizing/performing which is brought to life through leading: that is, what directors do in enacting their roles (individually and collectively), as a board/decision-making body. It is argued that it is important to attend the ongoing 'active process' emphasis of direct*ing* rather than direct*ion* (i.e. govern*ing*, strategiz*ing* and lead*ing* rather than governance, strategy and leadership). That is, as companies such as Enron, Marconi and now, recently, Parmalat have shown, it may be possible to have ticks in all the right governance boxes (i.e. meet all the criteria) and strategy boxes (i.e. have one and know what it is); and leadership boxes too (i.e. have leaders who 'make things happen'). However, as these companies illustrate, it is not whether or not you have them but how you actually *do* or *enact* governing, strategizing and leading which makes the key difference. For this reason, the process emphasis represented through the use of the present participle is crucial.

The notion of corporate directing also helps to acknowledge the importance of the relationship between chief executive and chairman in determining the culture of the board and senior management group. To what extent they feel able to ask questions, to challenge, to interrogate and so on is largely circumscribed by the climate created through this powerful relationship and, most particularly, acts as the axis around which this evolves and revolves and on which trust may or may not be placed. Board members have to feel confident of the information that they receive, to believe that they are kept appropriately informed of issues, that they are well briefed and helped to make good decisions. Several participants noted that, without this confidence, there was little they could do unless there was a strong enough grouping of counter-views to challenge the 'dominant logic'. And as one NED pointed out, if one was already thinking in this way, then this would not be a board to which one would wish to continue to belong.

Several noted that they had had experience of boards where they had seen 'bad behaviour', or tension between directors which was not appropriately handled and so resigned. The consequence of this, however, is to further concentrate this behaviour rather than to encourage it to change. Although active major shareholders are supposed to step forward in this kind of situation and influence change, only one example was identified where this had happened to remove a chairman. The only other examples were of shareholders challenging remuneration policy and, in one case, rejecting the strategy document of a FTSE 100 firm. Although the sample is relatively small, in corporate governance terms these are big issues and suggest a tension between micro–macro-level issues here, where greater reliance on codes of conduct appears to encourage more discussion to take place 'off stage', which works against the drive for greater openness and transparency. It also ensures that NEDs, in particular, need to have absolute faith and confidence not only in the information they are receiving but also in the way in which such information is shaped and influenced before it even gets to being in a board paper.

Conclusion and Reflections on Corporate Governance

This chapter has covered an array of issues in addressing the organizational life cycle and corporate governance through data that have been generated across 17 years of researching in this field. The two projects that lie at the heart of this work provide a unique database in tracking change at board level, in practice and in theory, as well as providing a foundation for continuing theorizing about practice. This particular chapter has paid attention to the fascinating confluence of micro- and macro-level governance issues which are represented in board-level practice, in the process of addressing organization life cycle and corporate governance.

The notion of firm life cycle raises an interesting question about whether it is age and structure alone that defines maturity or whether mindset and cultural heritage also play a part. Some firms in the sample have changed significantly, selling off their founding business, for example, and in some cases, spawning a 'new' level of maturity, rather than more classic assumptions of a mature organization. The second is that the board role is about 'interrupting' the corporate life cycle – changing direction in some way rather than progressing on to the next stage of development or metamorphosis.

The notion of interrupting life cycles is perhaps also relevant to governance academics. Rather than progressing along the traditional governance conceptions borne of its agency theory heritage and 'dismantling fortresses' as suggested by Daily et al. (2003), it is perhaps time to interrupt this thinking by engaging in some radical reframing. In this chapter, we have tried to do this by working from a social constructionist/process-oriented perspective to generate a more holistic and integrative notion such as corporate directing, interweaving govern*ing*, together with strategiz*ing* which is brought to life through lead*ing*, as a means by which to develop a framework which offers useful implications for both academics and practitioners. More simply, corporate directing can be used to describe a twenty-first-century update of Barnard's executive process, acknowledging the influence of upper echelons which is now more diluted with more outside directors on boards. It offers a process-oriented description rather than prescription of what boards should do, in which some organizations create constructive and trusted cultures and others do not.

This brings together the two themes of 'how do small groups of people "run" large organizations?' and the role played by the concept of corporate governance in developing our understanding of their behaviour, and looks ahead to areas for future development. Like all small groups, boards develop patterns to their interactions, a board culture, which has an essential impact both on board process and practice as well as on the ability of individual directors to be effective. The relationship between chief executive and chairman, around which board culture (r)evolves, is crucial in shaping the ability of directors to be effective although it lies beyond the prescriptive powers of governance codes. Key to effective board working is a sense of trust, both inside, among directors and outside, amongst a much wider interest group, from shareholders, and analysts onwards.

It is here that corporate governance codes appear to have a polar – that is, equal and opposite – effect. On the one hand, they are designed to underpin trust – that is, everyone follows the codes, so we must be able to trust them. Yet on the other hand, they may actually undermine trust – by codifying governance principles which may encourage 'more' discussion and action to happen away from the spotlight, back- or off-stage rather than front-stage.[9]

For this reason, the future research agenda must encourage more wide-ranging consideration of process-oriented analyses of board practice, such as corporate directing, which seek to capture this link between micro- and macro-level issues represented in board action. Together, which would help draw close attention to context, timing and trust which are essential to developing our understanding of (the concept of) corporate governance with relevance both to practitioners and academics.

Notes

1. We are grateful to the ESRC for their support in funding this work under grant numbers: WF 2925 0020 (1987–89) and R 000236868 (1998–2000).
2. With around 40 million people infected worldwide, the business case for such programmes is becoming clearer – for example, according to AngloGold, one of South Africa's top mining groups, 'HIV/Aids programmes for its employees cost \$5 for every ounce of gold produced – but inaction would cost \$9 an ounce' (*FT*, 2003).
3. By 31 December 2003, the UK FTSE Share Index returned to the 4200 levels for the first time since some four years previously, and having reached almost 7000 in early 2001 and around 2500 in early 2003.
4. There is also now a host of advisory and pressure groups, some of which are relatively new to the scene. For example, in the UK, the Pensions and Investment Research Company (PIRC) acts as a lobbyist on governance issues, compiling reports and analyses of companies and their governance, a role fulfilled by others, including the Corporate Library and TIAA-CREF in the USA. Organizations such as Manifest, the proxy voting agency, also claim to offer 'independent, impartial and informative support services to all those working in the corporate governance field' and are frequently now found among those who take an active role in challenging organizational governance practice. Likewise, Hermes (an institutional fund, independent of any broader financial services group whose largest client is the BT Pension Scheme) also takes a lead in being an active investor and has, for some time, published its own code of corporate governance on its website. Other organizations such as Incomes Data Services also provide annual surveys of remuneration and its relationship (or lack of it) with performance. Longer-standing associations such as the Association of British Insurers, the National Association of Pension Funds, the Confederation of British Industry, the Chartered Institute of Company Secretaries, the Institute of Directors and Chartered Institute of Managers all have codes and guidance to their members and others offering standards for practice, widely adopted in the UK.
5. These figures are in turn dwarfed by the recent corporate profit record reported by HSBC of £7.7 billion in 2004.
6. The authors are grateful to ESRC for their continued funding of this work, under grant number R 000236868.
7. Of the original 46 contributors, 26 had remained active in corporate life and of these, all except one agreed to contribute.
8. Perhaps what Greiner (1972) would classically describe as between the delegation and coordination phases.
9. The notion of 'more' must be qualified as it is impossible to measure. It also raises significant questions about how one can conduct good research which gains unobtrusive or uncontaminating access to both front- and back-stage arenas. However, there is not sufficient space to answer these here as this subject warrants extensive consideration in another paper.

References

Barnard, C.I. (1932), *The Functions of the Executive*, Boston, MA: Harvard Business School Press.

Beer, M. and Nohria, N. (eds) (2000), *Breaking the Code of Change*, Boston, MA: Harvard Business School Press.

Benne, K.D. and Sheats, P. (1948), 'Functional roles of group members', *Journal of Social Issues*, **4**: 41–9.

Berle, A. and Means, G.C. (1932), *The Modern Corporation and Private Property*, New York: Macmillan.

Bogler, D. (2000), 'Equity culture becomes the new Pied Piper', *Financial Times*, 21 February.

Cadbury, S.A. (1992), *Report of the Committee on the Financial Aspects of Corporate Governance*, London: Gee & Co Ltd.

Combined Code of Practice (1998), London: Gee & Co Ltd.

Combined Code of Practice (2003), London: Financial Reporting Council.

Daily, C.M. et al. (2003), 'Corporate governance: decades of dialogue and data', *Academy of Management Review*, **28**(3): 371–82.

Davies, Sir Howard (2000), 'The regulatory environment for a changing world', Swiss Bankers' Association, St Gallen, Switzerland, 1 September.

Financial Times leader column, 28 Nov 2003: 'Global companies have a vital role in fighting the epidemic'.

Finkelstein, S. and D.C. Hambrick (1996), *Strategic Leadership: Top Executives and their effects on organizations*, Minneapolis, MN: West Publishing Co.

Forbes, D.P. and Milliken, F.J. (1999), 'Cognition and corporate governance: understanding boards of directors as strategic decision making groups', *Academy of Management Review*, **24**: 489–505.

Garratt, B. (1996), *The Fish Rots from the Head*, London: HarperCollins.

Gaved, M. (1997), *Closing the Communications Gap: Disclosure and Institutional Shareholding*, London: Institute of Chartered Accountants of England and Wales.

Golding, T. (2001), *The City: Inside the Great Expectation Machine*, London, FT/Prentice-Hall.

Greenbury, Sir Richard (1995), *Directors' Remuneration*, London: Gee & Co. Ltd.

Greiner, L. (1972), 'Evolution and revolution as organizations grow', *Harvard Business Review*, **50**(4): 37–46.

Hambrick, D.C. and Mason, P.A. (1984), 'Upper echelons: the organization as a reflection of its top managers', *Academy of Management Review*, **9**: 193–206.

Hampel, Sir Ronnie (1998), *Committee on Corporate Governance, Final Report*, London: Gee & Co. Ltd.

Higgs, D. (2003), *Review of the Role of Non-Executive Directors*, DTI, UK Govt.

Huse, M. (2000), 'Boards of directors in SMEs: a review and research agenda', *Entrepreneurship and Regional Development*, **12**: 271–90.

Jensen, M., Thompson, S. and Meckling, W. (1976), 'Theory of the firm: managerial behaviour, agency costs and ownership structure', *Journal of Financial Economics*, **3**: 305–60.

Johnson, J.L., Daily, C.M. and Ellstrand, A.E. (1996), 'Boards of directors: a review and research agenda', *Journal of Management*, **22**: 409–38.

Keasey, K. and Wright, M. (1997), *Corporate Governance*, Oxford: Blackwell.

Locke, K.D. (2000), *Grounded Theory in Management Research*, London: Sage.

Lorsch, J.W. and MacIver, E. (1989), *Pawns or Potentates: The Reality of America's Corporate Boards*, Boston, MA: Harvard Business School Press.

Mace, M.L. (1971), *Directors: Myth and Reality*, Boston, MA: Harvard Business School Press.

Mangham, I. and Pye, A. (1991), *The Doing of Managing*, Oxford: Blackwell.

Morgan, G. (1980), 'Paradigms, metaphors, and puzzle solving in organization theory', *Administration Science Quarterly*, **25**: 605–22.

Myners, P. (2001), *Institutional Investment in the UK: A Review*, London: HM Treasury.

Nadler, D.A. and Tushman, M.L. (1990), 'Beyond the charismatic leader: leadership and organizational change', *California Management Review*, **32**(2): 77–96.

OECD (2000), *OECD Principles of Corporate Governance*, Paris: Organization for Economic Cooperation and Development.

Pye, A. (1993), '"Organizing as explaining" and the doing of managing: an integrative appreciation of processes of organizing', *Journal of Management Inquiry*, **2**(2): 157–68.

Pye, A.J. (1995), 'Strategy through dialogue and doing: a game of Mornington Crescent?', *Management Learning*, **26**(4): 445–62.

Pye, A. (2002a), 'Corporate directing: governing, strategizing and leading in action', *Corporate Governance: An International Review*, **10**(3): 153–62.

Pye, Annie (2002b), 'The changing power of explanations: directors, academics and their sensemaking from 1989–2000', *Journal of Management Studies*, **39**(7): 907–26.

Pye, A. (2005), 'The importance of context and time for understanding board behavior: some lessons from social capital research', *International Studies in Management and Organization*, **34**(2): 64–90.

Rindova, V.P. (1999), 'What corporate boards have to do with strategy: a cognitive perspective', *Journal of Management Studies*, **36**(7): 953–75.

Sandberg, Jörgen (2001), 'The constructions of social constructionism', in Sven-Erik Sjöstrand, Jörgen Sandberg and Mats Tyrstrup (eds), *Invisible Management: The Social Construction of Leadership*, London: Thomson Learning.

Shleifer, A. and Vishny, R.W. (1997), 'A survey of corporate governance', *Journal of Finance*, **52**(2): 737–83.

Smith, Sir Robert (2003), 'Audit Committees' Combined Code Guidance', Report to the Financial Reporting Council, London: FRC.

Stiles, P. (2001), 'The impact of the board on strategy: an empirical examination', *Journal of Management Studies*, **38**(5): 627–50.

Strauss, A. and Corbin, J. (1994), 'Grounded theory methodology: an overview', in N.K. Denzin and Y.S. Lincoln (eds), *Handbook of Qualitative Research*, London: Sage.

Tichy, N.M. and Charan, R. (1995), 'The CEO as coach: an interview with Allied Signal's Lawrence A. Bossidy', *Harvard Business Review* (March–April): 69–78.

Turnbull, N. (1999), *Corporate Guidance for Internal Control*, London: Gee & Co. Ltd.

Turnbull, S. (1997), 'Corporate governance: its scope, concerns and theories', *Corporate Governance*, **5**(4): 180–205.

Weick, K.E. (1979), *The Social Psychology of Organizing*, 2nd edn, Reading, MA: Addison Wesley.

Weick, K. (1987), *Substitutes for Strategy*, New York: Ballinger.

Weick, K.E. (1995), *Sensemaking*, London: Sage.

[13]
The impact of corporate governance on firm performance and growth potential: an analysis of three different European governance regimes[1]

Carles Gispert, Abe de Jong, Rezaul Kabir and Luc Renneboog

I. Introduction

Countries around the world are characterized by alternative corporate governance systems (Shleifer and Vishny, 1997). Considerable debate is going on illustrating how good, superior or effective these systems are. Prowse (1995) suggests that such judgments are inherently subjective because of the sparse evidence on the relative performance of different corporate governance systems. A question of major interest is therefore: do differences in these systems lead to differences in firm performance? While existing studies usually examine corporate governance characteristics of firms in one country, there is, to our knowledge, no study yet which thoroughly analyzes the influence of cross-country governance characteristics on company performance. In this study, we take a step towards filling this gap. We empirically analyze the effect of different corporate governance systems on firm performance by examining a sample of matched industrial companies listed on stock exchanges of three countries, namely Belgium, the Netherlands and the United Kingdom. In particular, we investigate whether differences in the two key aspects of a corporate governance mechanism, namely control concentration and the board structure of firms of these countries, affect their performance. This chapter focuses on the governance of listed mature companies which are at the top (or over the top) of their systemic life cycle. We pay particular attention to the role of corporate governance in poorly performing companies (in terms of both share and accounting performance) as poor corporate performance may not only be the result of bad managerial decisions but also of a lack of efficient corporate governance. In addition, we also focus on the contribution of corporate governance to the growth potential of firms as measured by their Tobin's Q.

The three countries represent three different corporate governance systems. The United Kingdom – an example of the market-based model – falls under the Common Law family with the strongest protection of shareholders and creditors (La Porta et al., 1998). The stock market is a well-established feature of the UK economy and shareholders occupy the central position as their interests are the ones British companies tend to promote. Share ownership is widely dispersed and the 'Berle–Means' type of corporations (the separation of ownership and control) is broadly prevalent. An active market for corporate control functions as an important disciplinary mechanism (Franks and Mayer, 1996). On the other hand, Belgium is an example of French Civil Law family, which is characterized by relatively weak investor protection and corporate law enforcement. Belgian companies have features like high ownership concentration, cross-shareholdings and pyramid structure (Renneboog, 2000). These features make Belgium typical of some Continental European countries. In between the UK and Belgium is the Netherlands, which falls under the German Civil Law system, having somewhat stronger protection of creditors. Share ownership is not as dispersed (concentrated) as in the UK (Belgium). Shareholders of Dutch listed companies have divergent cash-flow and control rights that do not arise from pyramiding and cross-holdings, but from various mechanisms leading to the issue of depository (non-voting) shares and priority shares, and the reduction of certain rights of common shareholders (Kabir et al., 1997). The two-tier corporate board structure is the norm in the Netherlands while one-tier boards are typical in Belgium and the UK.

Do these and other cross-country differences in corporate governance features lead to significant differences in performances of firms in these countries? In order to study this question, we assemble a panel data set consisting of 150 listed non-financial firms from these three countries covering a time period of five years. The firm-level panel regressions that we perform in our analysis are based on approximately 720 observations.

We have several principal findings. First, there is a significant cross-country variation of commonly described corporate governance characteristics such as board size, board composition and ownership structure of listed firms. We thus confirm earlier findings reported in the literature. Second, these common features do not have similar cross-country relationships with corporate performance. While one characteristic has a positive relationship with performance in one country, it has negative or no relationship in another country. For example, an analysis of stock returns shows that financial institutional investors only have a significant impact in the UK, which is positive. Apparently, the role of these institutions differs in this setting, which induces this positive effect. Third, specific corporate governance features of a country play an important role in determining corporate performance, relative to the common characteristics. For example, for each of the three performance measures we use, a significantly negative impact of so-called holding companies is found in Belgium. This characteristic is unique to the Belgian setting. These findings are relevant for the literature on governance for at least two reasons. First, findings in a specific country cannot be generalized to other countries. Second, a set of variables that is used to study a specific country is most likely not the complete set of variables in another country.

The rest of the chapter is organized as follows. In the next section, we discuss the relevant literature analyzing the relationship between corporate governance mechanisms and firm performance. In Section III, we describe the data used in our analysis; we also discuss firm and corporate governance characteristics of three countries. Section IV outlines the research methodology. The empirical results are presented in Section V. The summary and conclusions of this study are presented in Section VI.

II. Literature Review

Jensen and Meckling (1976) and Fama and Jensen (1983) argue that the diffusion of ownership has an important impact on the validity of the profit-maximizing goal of corporations because the separation of control may enable corporate managers to pursue their own interests. Without a managerial remuneration system geared towards value maximization, managers of firms face an asymmetrical reward structure: poor performance will negatively affect them whereas they will not be excessively rewarded for good corporate performance. Consequently, managers of widely held firms may be more risk-averse than those of blockholder-controlled firms. The alternative view is that there exist several managerial disciplining mechanisms, such as blockholder monitoring, the (threat from the) market for corporate control, pay-for-share price performance remuneration schemes, managerial labour markets and so on, which curb managerial opportunistic behaviour.

A large number of studies spanning a few decades have investigated the relationship between ownership structure and corporate performance, but have not yielded clear-cut results. It has been argued that as ownership concentration increases, the incentives and the abilities of shareholders to properly monitor managers increase too. This creates beneficial effects for firms in the sense that performance or profitability improves (Morck et al., 1989). On the other hand, there are studies which find that higher ownership concentration leads to detrimental effects for corporations as large blockholders and managers can collude to extract rents from small shareholders (Lehman and Weigand, 2000).

Demsetz and Lehn (1985) state that a relation between ownership and performance is not to be expected because ownership-induced inefficiencies cannot be maintained. Ownership concentration will be adjusted to maintain the highest possible profitability. In a rational world, equity can act as a commitment device to delegate a certain degree of authority from shareholders to management (Burkart et al., 1997 and Bolton and von Thadden, 1998). Equity control should be state-contingent: in some states of the world (e.g. with low corporate profitability), close monitoring resulting from strong ownership concentration is desirable. In other states, close monitoring may reduce managerial discretion and hence management's effort. The study by Demsetz and Villalonga (2001) provides recent evidence that there is no significant relation between ownership structure and firm performance.

However, if (insufficient) monitoring by shareholders or other control mechanisms cannot avoid a decrease of profitability, low-quality monitors may sell their stakes and new (controlling) shareholders could improve future corporate performance by substituting incumbent management. Bethel et al. (1998) find empirical support for US companies: activist shareholders hold large blocks in diversified companies with poor profitability. Likewise, poor corporate performance triggers changes in control to remove top management (Franks et al., 2001).

Another dimension of ownership structure is concerned with the identity of shareholders, which also has implications for corporate governance. Demsetz and Lehn (1985) point out that individuals and families, financial institutions and corporations may have different objectives, monitoring skills and different monitoring incentives. Individual blockholders are usually strongly involved with the events of a firm, and their monitoring can significantly enhance firm performance. Financial institutions have the skills and resources to monitor managers, but they can also align with managers in order to foster their other interests in the firm.

A deficiency of most of the US empirical research is that it usually only focuses on insider ownership concentration and thus ignores the presence of blockholders. Insider ownership concentration *per se* is not a good proxy for agency costs, but rather *relative* insider control. Morck et al. (1988) and McConnell and Servaes (1990) show that the impact of equity ownership may change over different levels of ownership. Morck et al. (1988) discover a non-monotonic relation between Tobin's Q and insider ownership. Increasing insider ownership between 0 and 5 percent has a positive impact on Tobin's Q. This effect reverses for insider control over 5 to 25 percent of the voting rights, and is again positively related to Q if management holds more than 25 percent of the equity. It seems that at low levels of insider ownership, the agency costs decrease with rising insider ownership, that at higher levels of insider control, performance suffers from managerial entrenchment and that at high levels of insider control, management maximizes shareholder value. The McConnell and Servaes (1990) study does not confirm these results. They find a curvilinear relation between Q and insider ownership. The relation increases up to ownership levels of 40–50 percent and subsequently decreases. Still, these findings are not confirmed by Loderer and Martin (1997), Cho (1998) and Himmelberg et al. (1999), who consider equity ownership as endogenous.

In addition to the ownership structure, the board of directors is expected to play an important role in corporate governance. But its role has been controversial too. On the one hand, the board of directors is expected to perform effective monitoring of the actions of top corporate managers. The board replaces poorly performing managers and determines their compensation. It is also believed that boards dominated by non-executive/independent directors are better monitors. On the other hand, directors may have their own interests which are not aligned with those of shareholders. Hence it is possible that directors are not effective monitors as they are not selected independently and are more dependent on management for obtaining firm-specific information. Several outside directors are in fact former employees or advisers of a firm. Numerous studies (predominantly in the USA) have investigated the role of boards, specifically their tasks and composition, and found no clear-cut evidence regarding their effects on firm performance (Denis and Denis, 1995; Borokhovich et al., 1996; Agrawal and Knoeber, 1996).

Both ownership and board characteristics of firms are found to be interrelated. Agrawal and Knoeber (1996) examine the role of different corporate governance mechanisms and find evidence of interdependence among these mechanisms. They conclude that a greater use of one mechanism need not be positively related to firm performance.

In sum, both theoretical and empirical studies suggest that the relation between corporate governance characteristics and corporate performance can be positive, negative or absent. Therefore, we do not put forward specific hypotheses describing the relationships in one or another direction. Rather, our stance is that the precise manner in which corporate governance characteristics affect corporate performance has to be determined empirically.

III. Sample

A. Data sources

We identify a time period of five years and construct a sample of 150 non-financial firms. These firms are listed on Amsterdam, Brussels and London Stock Exchanges, and are selected after first matching on the basis of industry and then on firm size.[2] Companies in our sample range from very small (22 percent of the sample firms have sales of less than £25 million) to very large (24 percent have sales of at least £1000 million).

We use a wide variety of sources in the three countries to collect firm-level panel data. All financial data for the Belgian companies are collected from 'Balanscentrale' (a CD-ROM database maintained by the National Bank of Belgium) and annual publications of *Memento der Effecten*. Corporate governance data are hand-collected from the Brussels Stock Exchange and annual publications of *Memento der Effecten*. For the Netherlands, financial data are collected from yearbooks of Dutch companies, 'REACH' (a CD-ROM database) and annual reports. Corporate governance data are again hand-collected from different publications (yearbooks of Dutch companies and a daily financial newspaper *Het Financieele Dagblad*) and annual reports of companies. The financial data from the UK companies are collected from 'Worldscope' and, wherever needed, from company annual reports. All corporate governance data of British companies are also hand-collected from annual reports.

These data are collected for the five-year period from 1993 through 1997. The sample period is 1992–96 for Belgian firms because complete 1997 data were not available. This minor difference in time-period is not likely to lead to different results. Nevertheless, as a robustness check we have performed the analysis covering the single common period of four years' data (1993–96) and the empirical results of this study remain qualitatively similar.

B. Variable definitions

The variables used in our analysis are classified into three categories: firm characteristics, corporate governance characteristics and performance measures. The definitions are presented in Table 13.1. Although firm characteristics are not of primary interest, we include these in our analysis as control variables because differences on these dimensions can affect the relative performance of firms. Prior studies show that both firm size and leverage are two important determinants of company performance. The book value of total assets (*BVTA*) of a firm is used as a proxy for firm size. We use the natural logarithm of the book value of total assets in the regression analyses to account for inherent skewness of this variable. The leverage variable (*LEV*) used in our analysis is the percentage of total assets financed by total debt (in book value terms). We also separate firms with leverage ratios reporting a profit from those reporting a net loss (*LEVPROF* and *LEVLOSS*) as these firms tend to have differentiated patterns of corporate governance.

Table 13.1   Definition of variables

Firm characteristics

BVTA	Firm size	Book value of total assets (£ million)
LEV	Leverage	Book value of total debt/book value of total assets (%)
LEVPROF	Leverage (profit)	Leverage of firms reporting a profit (%)
LEVLOSS	Leverage (loss)	Leverage of firms reporting a loss (%)

Common corporate governance characteristics

BRDSIZE	Board size	Total number of board members
BRDEXT	Board fraction external	Percentage of external board members
BLOCK	Total blockholdings	Percentage of common shares owned by all blockholders
FINAN	Financial blockholdings	Percentage of blocks of common shares owned by financial institutions
INDIV	Individual and family blockholdings	Percentage of blocks of common shares owned by individuals and family members
INSIDE	Insider blockholdings	Percentage of blocks of common shares owned by insiders
INDUS	Industrial blockholdings	Percentage of blocks of common shares owned by industrial firms

Country-specific corporate governance characteristics

CEO	CEO dummy	Equals 1 if CEO is also the chairperson of the board (Belgium, UK)
SR	Structured regime	Equals 1 if firm adopted structured regime (Netherlands)
HOLDING	Holding company blockholdings	Percentage of blocks of common shares owned by holding companies (Belgium)

Performance measures

ROA	Return on assets	(Earnings before interest, taxes and depreciation)/book value of total assets (%)
Q	Tobin's Q	(Market value of equity + book value of debt)/book value of total assets
RET	Stock return	Annual stock return (%)

We identify widely used corporate governance characteristics of firms. These are grouped under board structure and ownership structure categories. The total number of directors sitting on the board is used to calculate the board size variable (*BRDSIZE*). Both Belgium and the UK have a unitary board structure. The Netherlands has a two-tier board system and our measure includes the size of both boards. We also classify all directors as either internal or external. In Belgium and the UK internal members are normally called executives, while in the Netherlands they are referred to as managerial board members. External directors are non-executives in Belgium and the UK and supervisory board members in the Netherlands. The variable board fraction external (*BRDEXT*) is the percentage of external board members. The size of total block ownership (*BLOCK*) is computed as the percentage of firm's total outstanding shares owned by all blockholders, which is defined as those owning at least 5 percent of a firm's total outstanding shares. We also construct additional variables related to the identity of share ownership. The percentages of shareholdings by financial institutions including banks and insurance companies (*FINAN*), individuals and family members (*INDIV*), insiders (*INSIDE*), and industrial corporations (*INDUS*) are computed separately.

In addition to the above-mentioned common governance characteristics, we define three variables that are specific to one or two of the three countries. The variable CEO dummy (*CEO*) has a value of 1 in case the chairperson of the internal and external boards is the same. Such a situation is not possible in the Netherlands. The dummy variable structured regime (*SR*) has a value of 1 in case a firm has adopted the structured regime. Under this regime many of the powers of shareholders are delegated to the external (supervisory) board (see de Jong et al., 2002). A governance characteristic that is specific in Belgium firms is the blockholdings of holding companies. We measure the percentage of shares held by holding companies (*HOLDING*) (see Renneboog, 2000).

We examine three different measures of firm performance. The return on assets (ROA) is a purely accounting-based measure and is computed from company financial statement data. Each firm's annual earnings before interest, taxes and depreciation are divided by the average of the book value of total assets at the beginning and ending of the year and are denoted as ROA. Accounting performance measures (like ROA) have an advantage because they are backward looking. Still, they are prone to manipulation by management and usually do not reflect investment in intangible assets. This distorts performance comparisons across firms with differing proportions of intangible assets.

The second performance measure, Tobin's *Q*-ratio (*Q*), is a hybrid one. It is measured by dividing the sum of the market value of equity and the book value of debt by the book value of total assets. The last performance metric we use is stock return (*RET*), which is a capital-market-based performance measure. It is computed from annual changes in share price plus dividends divided by the previous year's share price. Stock return is considered to be a purely forward-looking benchmark. It should be pointed out that almost all published empirical studies on the control–performance relation are set within the Anglo-American context and usually take one performance measure: Tobin's *Q*, or an accounting measure like ROA. Since no consensus exists in the literature on the use of a reliable performance measure, we believe that these three variables will reflect company performance in a robust way.

Table 13.2   *Descriptive statistics for firm characteristics, corporate governance characteristics and performance measures*

Panel A. Firm characteristics

	Mean	Median	25th	75th	St. dev.	Obs.
Belgium						
BVTA	665.07[u, n]	124.35	46.06	712.84	1321.65	250
LEV	53.20[u, n]	54.53[u, n]	38.55	70.59	22.23	250
LEVPROF	52.29[u, n]	53.54[n]	38.49	68.87	21.68	234
LEVLOSS	–	–	–	–	–	–
Netherlands						
BVTA	1203.03[b]	161.94	27.23	904.67	2950.87	247
LEV	61.26[b]	62.71[b, u]	52.73	70.59	13.49	247
LEVPROF	61.16[b]	62.55[b, u]	52.74	70.59	13.76	224
LEVLOSS	61.71	58.51	51.15	73.97	11.44	20
UK						
BVTA	1876.94[b]	121.11	25.44	1204.00	6463.12	249
LEV	59.18[b]	55.84[b, n]	44.60	70.87	21.49	248
LEVPROF	58.77[b]	55.21[n]	44.45	70.87	19.98	210
LEVLOSS	60.95	60.28	43.96	70.04	28.85	37

Panel B. Corporate governance characteristics

	Mean	Median	25th	75th	St. dev.	Obs.
Belgium						
BRDSIZE	10.29[u, n]	9[u, n]	6	11	6.05	248
BRDEXT	75.27[u, n]	80.00[u, n]	62.94	91.66	21.68	248
BLOCK	58.86[u, n]	57.40[u, n]	46.22	70.50	18.85	250
FINAN	10.85[u]	0	0	8.18	20.68	249
INDIV	12.78[u]	0	0	19.5	21.02	249
INDUS	35.24[u, n]	36.40[u, n]	5.62	56.30	28.17	249
Netherlands						
BRDSIZE	8.48[b]	7[b]	5	11	3.98	247
BRDEXT	64.47[b, u]	66.66[b, u]	60	73.33	11.28	247
BLOCK	46.35[b, u]	47.23[b, u]	25.11	68.51	28.51	247
FINAN	11.00[u]	6.01[b, u]	0	14.78	14.36	247
INDIV	13.35[u]	0	0	20.37	23.21	247
INDUS	10.08[b, u]	0	0	6.01	20.32	247

Table 13.2   *(continued)*

Panel B. Corporate governance characteristics

	Mean	Median	25th	75th	St. dev.	Obs.
UK						
BRDSIZE	8.17^b	8^b	6	10	3.12	249
BRDEXT	$43.30^{b,\,n}$	$44.44^{b,\,n}$	33.3	55.55	15.99	249
BLOCK	$25.55^{b,\,n}$	$24.96^{b,\,n}$	8.69	37.96	19.14	249
FINAN	$15.20^{b,\,n}$	$11.1^{b,\,n}$	0	25.81	15.13	249
INDIV	$5.77^{b,\,n}$	0	0	0	13.88	249
INDUS	$4.98^{b,\,n}$	0	0	0	12.08	249

Panel C. Performance measures

	Mean	Median	25th	75th	St. dev.	Obs.
Belgium						
ROA	$10.44^{u,\,n}$	$8.94^{u,\,n}$	5.48	15.04	7.84	249
Q	$1.34^{u,\,n}$	$1.23^{u,\,n}$	0.99	1.58	0.50	244
RET	11.22^n	7.04^n	−7.81	27.22	31.41	240
Netherlands						
ROA	15.61^b	15.28^b	10.40	20.32	6.79	247
Q	$1.59^{b,\,u}$	$1.37^{b,\,u}$	1.06	1.85	0.76	247
RET	$30.29^{b,\,u}$	$22.72^{b,\,u}$	4.03	51.33	40.99	245
UK						
ROA	12.86^b	13.88^b	6.96	20.53	14.31	246
Q	$1.74^{b,\,n}$	$1.51^{b,\,n}$	1.16	2.12	0.82	249
RET	15.18^n	13.11^n	−6.66	30.53	41.84	247

Notes: The sample consists of 150 matched Belgian, Dutch and UK listed firms. Annual data for a five-year period are analyzed. All variables are defined in Table 13.1. ^{b}, ^{n} and ^{u} denote if there are statistically significant differences (at the 5% level) in mean and median values between the country and Belgium, the Netherlands and the UK, respectively. We use a two-tailed *t*-test for means and Wilcoxon signed rank test for medians.

C. Descriptive statistics

Table 13.2 reports descriptive statistics for firm characteristics (Panel A), corporate governance characteristics (Panel B) and firm performance measures (Panel C) for each country separately. Note that the number of observations for each country is approximately 250. Conforming to prior research analyzing financial statement data, we truncate the most extreme observations (larger/smaller than the mean plus/minus three standard deviations) in order to mitigate the influence of outliers. According to Panel A, the mean (median) total assets of Belgian firms in our sample amount to £665 (£124) million, compared to £1203 (£162) million for Dutch firms and £1877 (£121) million for UK firms. The values from five different years have been converted into 1997 pounds in order to adjust for inflation. Although the mean total assets of Dutch and UK firms are significantly different from those of Belgian firms, none of the median differences is statistically significant. It should be noted that the average Belgian listed firm is smaller as the Belgian economy is characterized by small and medium-sized firms and multinational firms are less prevalent. The median firm in our sample of all three countries is roughly of equal size.

Looking at the leverage ratio of the Belgian, Dutch and UK firms, we observe that these are significantly different from each other. The average leverage ratios of Belgian, Dutch and UK firms in the sample are 53 percent, 61 percent and 59 percent, respectively. The median value of each country does not differ much from the mean. We also find that the leverage ratio of Belgian firms reporting positive earnings is significantly different from that of Dutch and UK firms.

Analyzing the corporate governance characteristics in Panel B, we observe that country means or medians of almost all variables are significantly different from each other. Companies in Belgium have the largest boards. The average board size of Belgian firms is ten compared to eight for Dutch and UK firms. These differences are statistically significant. A significantly larger percentage of board seats (75 percent) of Belgian companies are held by non-executives. The corresponding figure for the Netherlands is 64 percent and 43 percent for the UK. Prior studies report similar findings (Dahya et al., 2002).

The functioning of the board systems prevailing in these three countries can be described as follows: directors of the UK firms are, in general, expected to take into account the 'interests of shareholders' in company decision making; those of the Dutch firms are expected to take into account the 'interests of the company'; and those of the Belgian firms are expected to take into account the 'interests of the company' in which non-shareholders interests are limited to long-term goals.

With regard to ownership, we observe that Belgian firms have, on average, significantly higher ownership concentration (59 percent), compared to Dutch firms (46 percent) and UK firms (26 percent). Shareholdings by financial institutions are the largest for the UK firms. The average blockholdings by financial institutions in the UK is 15 percent which is significantly different from those of Belgium and the Netherlands (11 percent). The average ownership by individuals and families in both Belgium and the Netherlands is equal to 13 percent. It is significantly larger compared to the average share ownership of individuals in the UK (5.7 percent).[3] Block ownership by industrial corporations is the largest in Belgium (the average is 35 percent), which is significantly different from that of the Netherlands (11 percent) and the UK (5 percent).

In Belgium, 31.2 percent of the firms unify the position of chairperson of the executive and non-executive board in one person. On average 22.8 percent of the shares is held by holding companies. In the UK 20.9 percent of the firms have the dual position of the chairperson. In the sample for the Netherlands, 54.8 percent of the firms have the structured regime.[4]

Panel C of Table 13.2 reports summary statistics of our three performance measures. Most of these variables are significantly different from each other. The mean (median) ROA of the Belgian sample of firms is 10.44 (8.94). Both Dutch and UK samples have a significantly higher average (median) ROA: 15.61 (15.28) for the Netherlands and 12.86 (13.88) for the UK. The mean (median) Q-ratio of Belgian firms in our sample is 1.34 (1.23), compared to 1.59 (1.37) for Dutch firms and 1.74 (1.51) for UK firms. These values are also significantly different from each other. Our last performance measure is stock return. We find that during the sample period both mean and median annual stock returns of Dutch companies (30.29 and 22.72) are significantly higher relative to Belgian and UK companies. Over the period 1993–97, Dutch companies have substantially outperformed those of other continental European countries as well as those of the UK (see Dimson et al., 2001).

IV. Research Design

The descriptive analysis above shows that there are significant differences among corporate governance characteristics as well as performance in the samples of companies from the three countries. In order to study whether the observed differences in performance are related to the differences in corporate governance characteristics associated with each country, we estimate the following basic regression model:

$$\text{Performance} = f \text{(corporate governance variables, control variables)} \qquad (13.1)$$

The model uses firm performance as the dependent variable. As mentioned earlier, three different proxies (*ROA*, *Q* and *RET*) are used to measure firm performance. We use two types of proxies to represent a country's corporate governance system: board characteristics and ownership characteristics. The variables *BRDSIZE* (board size) and *BRDEXT* (board fraction external) represent the number of directors and the percentage of non-executive directors, while the variables *FINAN*, *INDIV* and *INDUS* represent percentages of block ownership by institutions, individuals and families and industrial corporations, respectively. It is possible that corporate performance is driven purely by non-governance factors. Therefore, we specifically control for differences in two most important firm characteristics by using *BVTA* (firm size) and *LEV* (leverage) variables. The first set of regression equations that we estimate can be specified as follows:

$$\begin{aligned}
\text{Performance}_{i,t} = {} & \beta_0 + \beta_1 \, BRDSIZE_{i,t} + \beta_2 \, BRDEXT_{i,t} + \beta_3 \, FINAN_{i,t} + \qquad (13.2)\\
& \beta_4 \, INDIV_{i,t} + \beta_5 \, INDUS_{i,t} + \beta_6 \, LOG(BVTA)_{i,t} + \\
& \beta_7 \, LEVPROF_{i,t} + \beta_8 \, LEVLOSS_{i,t} + \\
& \Sigma\gamma_j \, \text{Country dummies} + \Sigma\lambda_l \, \text{Time dummies} + \varepsilon_{i,t},
\end{aligned}$$

where i and t represent all 150 firms in our sample and the five time periods, respectively, and $\varepsilon_{i,t}$ is an error term. The country dummies capture the performance differentials related to country characteristics. The time dummies capture the potential effect of general market conditions and other systematic factors that may vary across years.

To control for all other unobservable firm-level features that can influence performance, we estimate a fixed-effects regression model in which each firm is assigned a unique intercept. The important advantages of a panel regression are that it will yield more accurate estimators and reduce the effect of omitted variables in comparison to pure cross-section or time-series regressions. The firm dummies capture the potential effect of all firm-specific omitted variables. The second set of regression equations that we estimate can thus be specified as follows:

$$\text{Performance}_{i,t} = \beta_0 + \beta_1 \, BRDSIZE_{i,t} + \beta_2 \, BRDEXT_{i,t} + \beta_3 \, FINAN_{i,t} + \qquad (13.3)$$
$$\beta_4 \, INDIV_{i,t} + \beta_5 \, INDUS_{i,t} + \beta_6 \, LOG(BVTA)_{i,t} +$$
$$\beta_7 \, LEVPROF_{i,t} + \beta_8 \, LEVLOSS_{i,t} +$$
$$\Sigma\lambda_l \, \text{Time dummies} + \Sigma\eta_m \, \text{Firm dummies} + \varepsilon_{i,t}.$$

One can ask whether our empirical tests are robust to the generic relation between corporate performance and corporate systems of these three countries. In order to find out whether the change in performance is specifically related to each country's corporate governance charac-teristics, we model several interaction variables which measure the relationship of firm performance with country-specific corporate governance characteristics. Therefore, our third set of regression equations is specified as follows:

$$\text{Performance}_{i,t} = \beta_0 + \beta_1 \, BRDSIZE_{i,t} + \beta_2 \, BRDEXT_{i,t} + \beta_3 \, FINAN_{i,t} + \qquad (13.4)$$
$$\beta_4 \, INDIV_{i,t} + \beta_5 \, INDUS_{i,t} + \beta_6 \, LOG(BVTA)_{i,t} +$$
$$\beta_7 \, LEVPROF_{i,t} + \beta_8 \, LEVLOSS_{i,t} +$$
$$\Sigma\varphi_k \, \text{Interaction variables}_{i,t} + \Sigma\lambda_l \, \text{Time dummies} + \varepsilon_{i,t}.$$

Finally, we estimate three separate set of regressions per country, in which we include an intercept, time dummies, control variables and the common governance variables, as in equations (13.2) to (13.4). In addition, in these regressions we include the country-specific governance variables.

V. Empirical Results

Table 13.3 presents the results of the different regression models using the full data set. There are about 720 observations pooled across the three countries. The regressions of various corporate performance measures using firm-specific explanatory variables include time dummies, and are performed both with and without country dummies and company fixed effects.

In Panel A, we start with pooled data from the three countries for all firm-years with firm characteristics, country dummies and time dummies used as control variables (equation (13.2) in Section IV). We include the basic set of explanatory variables. The results in the column *ROA* show that the accounting return is significantly negatively influenced by the fraction of external board members, industrial shareholdings and leverage of firms with a loss. The dummy for Dutch firms has a significantly positive coefficient. The regression includes an intercept and five period dummies (results not reported).

We can compare the results in Panel A for the three performance measures. Board size has a significantly positive impact for *Q*, while the other measures yield insignificant results. The evidence for external board members is stronger, because both *ROA* and *Q* have a significantly negative sign. The blockholdings of financial and industrial firms are

Table 13.3   *Estimation of relationship between corporate governance characteristics and corporate performance: international evidence*

Panel A. Regressions with country effects

	ROA	*Q*	*RET*
BRDSIZE	−0.075	0.017**	0.344
BRDEXT	−0.047**	−0.004**	0.031
FINAN	0.018	−0.004**	0.106
INDIV	0.005	−0.002	0.070
INDUS	−0.066***	−0.001	0.083
NL	3.662***	0.233***	21.952***
UK	0.504	0.351***	9.351*
LOG(*BVTA*)	0.697	−0.162***	−1.503
LEVPROF	0.006	0.001	0.134*
LEVLOSS	−0.224**	−0.004***	−0.131
Adj. R^2	0.232	0.102	0.055
Obs.	720	719	713

Panel B. Regressions with firm-fixed effects

	ROA	*Q*	*RET*
BRDSIZE	0.117	0.011	0.034
BRDEXT	0.032	−0.006**	−0.251
FINAN	0.002	0.0001	−0.103
INDIV	0.104***	0.003	−0.113
INDUS	0.050	−0.001	−0.064
LOG(*BVTA*)	0.384	−0.391***	−2.254
LEVPROF	0.009	0.007***	0.320*
LEVLOSS	−0.168***	0.005**	0.129
Adj. R^2	0.531	0.690	0.099
Obs.	720	719	713

Panel C. Regressions with country-governance interactions

	ROA	*Q*	*RET*
BRDSIZE	−0.119	0.015*	0.315
BRDEXT	−0.006	−0.006***	0.075
FINAN	−0.006	−0.002	−0.043
INDIV	−0.048	−0.004	−0.318*
INDUS	−0.076**	−0.004*	−0.239*
NL*BRDSIZE	0.321*	0.006	−0.191

Table 13.3   (continued)

Panel C. Regressions with country-governance interactions

	ROA	Q	RET
NL*BRDEXT	−0.027	−0.002	0.097
NL*FINAN	0.075	0.001	−0.123
NL*INDIV	0.094**	0.006*	0.487**
NL*INDUS	0.062	0.005	0.435**
UK*BRDSIZE	0.448**	0.024*	−1.167
UK*BRDEXT	−0.028	0.003	−0.073
UK*FINAN	−0.033	−0.013***	0.374*
UK*INDIV	0.060	−0.014***	0.501**
UK*INDUS	−0.204***	0.015***	0.564**
LOG(BVTA)	−0.141	−0.211***	1.100
LEVPROF	−0.005	0.003**	0.155*
LEVLOSS	−0.232***	−0.001	−0.122
Adj. R^2	0.250	0.177	0.061
Obs.	720	719	713

Notes: Results of regressions of corporate performance on corporate governance and firm-specific variables. The sample consists of matched firms from Belgium, the Netherlands and the UK. Annual data for a five-year period are analyzed. NL (UK) is a dummy with value of 1 for Dutch (UK) firms, and zero otherwise. All other variables are defined in Table 13.1. The regressions include a constant and time-specific dummies (results not reported). The regressions in Panel B are estimated for the firm-fixed effects model (firm-specific estimators not reported). ***, ** and * denote statistical significance at 1%, 5% and 10% levels, respectively.

both significantly negative for one of our measures, while the blockholdings of individuals and families have no significant effect on performance. The two country dummies in Panel A clearly show that the Dutch firms and the UK firms have outperformed the Belgian firms. The influence of firm size and leverage of profitable firms is only significant for a single measure. Leverage in firms with a loss has the expected negative sign for two measures.

In Panel B we introduce controls for firm-specific fixed effects (equation (13.3) in section IV). Here, we observe that five coefficients remain significant, with the same sign. Four coefficients that were significant in Panel A become insignificant. We find two new significant coefficients; that is, individuals have a positive impact on *ROA* and leverage of profitable firms influences *Q* positively. The fact that statistical significance of corporate governance variables changes with the inclusion of fixed firm effect suggests that omitted firm characteristics are correlated with the included explanatory variables. We observe that the adjusted R^2 increases dramatically: for example, for *ROA* from 23 percent in Panel A to 53 percent in Panel B. This indicates that a substantial amount of cross-sectional variation in firm performance is explained by firm characteristics. It is reassuring to notice that, although our findings are never significant in all of the six regressions, the results that are significant are never contradictory across regressions.

The analysis in Panel A and B assumes that the impact of our governance variables is the same across countries. This assumption can be tested by introducing country-specific interactive corporate governance variables. This allows us to see to what extent corporate governance variables produce a differential effect across the three countries. Our results are reported in Panel C (equation (13.4) in Section IV). For example, for Tobin's Q the coefficient for board size is significantly positive in the base case, Belgium. The interaction term for board size and the Netherlands is insignificant, which implies that for Dutch firms the influence is not significantly different from the base case. UK firms have a significantly higher positive influence of board size, in comparison with the base case.

The overall results in Panel C point to some similarities, but also distinct differences between the three countries. As mentioned above, a larger board size has a positive effect in each of the countries. The similarity is stronger for the fraction of external board members. In Belgium a significantly negative effect is found for Q. None of the coefficients in the Netherlands and the UK is significant, which means that the result is similar across countries. Differences seem to appear in the ownership structures. Financials are only significant in the UK, but the result is negative for Q and positive for stock returns. Individuals and families are significantly negatively related to stock returns in Belgium. However, the coefficients in the Netherlands and the UK are larger, which leads to positive effects in these countries. For the Netherlands, this positive effect is confirmed by significant results for Q and *ROA*, while in the UK the results are mixed. Industrial firms clearly have a negative impact in Belgium, because all three regressions show significantly negative coefficients in the base case. For Dutch firms, this negative effect becomes positive for stock returns. Also in the UK a positive effect results for the market-based measures, that is, Q and stock returns. A puzzling result is the more negative effect in the UK for *ROA*.

Two conclusions can drawn from Panel C. First, board size and the fraction of outsiders have similar influence across the countries. Second, the variables for ownership structure show pronounced differences across the countries in their relations to performance. So far, our analysis has included variables that represent part of the institutional setting that is present in each of the three countries. However, some variables are unique to one or two countries. We therefore analyze the three countries separately and provide more attention to specific institutional features of each country. Table 13.4 presents the results of country-level regressions of corporate performance on firm-specific corporate governance variables.

The results for the separate analyses of the countries are presented in three panels. For Belgian firms (Panel A), we find that the board characteristics (size and external members) are similar in comparison with the previous table. As mentioned earlier, Belgian firms have a one-tier board. It can be argued that if the CEO of a firm is also the chairperson of the board, no effective monitoring can be expected. We therefore use the CEO dummy as an explanatory variable, but we do not find a systematic relationship with performance. The variables representing ownership by financial institutions and individuals and families also do not show any significant relationship with any of the performance measures.

An analysis of the ownership of Belgian companies reveals that by far the largest category of shareholders is that of the holding companies. We therefore split corporate shareholders into two sub-categories: holding companies and other companies, and use these variables in regression analysis. Our results show that ownership by holding companies is significantly negatively related to performance. The sign on the holding companies variable is negative

Table 13.4   *Estimation of relationship between corporate governance characteristics and corporate performance: national evidence*

Panel A: Belgium

	ROA	Q	RET
BRDSIZE	−0.043	0.013**	0.068
BRDEXT	−0.005	−0.005***	0.020
CEO	0.970	−0.027	−5.896
FINAN	−0.023	−0.001	−0.035
INDIV	−0.045	−0.003	−0.164
HOLDING	−0.103***	−0.006***	−0.242*
INDUS-HOLDING	−0.048*	0.001	−0.082
LOG(BVTA)	0.281	−0.120**	4.071
Adj. R^2	0.078	0.103	0.185
Obs.	247	243	240

Panel B: The Netherlands

	ROA	Q	RET
BRDSIZE	−0.043	−0.028	0.072
BRDEXT	−0.185***	−0.013***	0.109
SR	−0.981	−0.122	−10.377***
INSIDE	−0.073*	−0.001	−0.035
FINAN	0.029	−0.003	−0.151
INDIV	0.053*	0.001	0.091
INDUS	−0.070***	−0.001	0.115
LOG(BVTA)	−0.881	−0.002	0.148
Adj. R^2	0.121	0.097	0.039
Obs.	244	244	242

Panel C: The United Kingdom

	ROA	Q	RET
BRDSIZE	0.245	0.075***	−1.261
BRDEXT	−0.102*	−0.002	−0.087
CEO	−7.170***	0.039	−12.644*
INSIDE	0.104	−0.019***	0.354
FINAN	−0.156**	−0.020***	0.244
INDIV	0.065	−0.025***	0.286
INDUS	−0.270***	0.005	0.277
LOG(BVTA)	0.661	−0.409***	2.717
Adj. R^2	0.118	0.200	0.098
Obs.	246	249	246

Notes: Results of regressions of corporate performance on corporate governance and firm-specific variables. The sample consists of matched firms from Belgium, the Netherlands and the UK. Annual data for a five-year period are analyzed. All variables are defined in Table 13.1. The regressions include a constant and time-specific dummies (results not reported). ***, ** and * denote statistical significance at 1%, 5% and 10% levels, respectively.

and statistically significant in all three regressions. Renneboog (2000) and Banerjee et al. (1997) also document evidence that holding companies destroy value for Belgium and France, respectively.

The regression results for the Dutch sample (Panel B of Table 13.4) show that board size has no relationship with any of the performance measures used in the analysis. On the other hand, the percentage of external directors is significantly negatively related with performance (*ROA* and *Q*). As mentioned earlier, Dutch firms have a two-tier board structure where supervisory board members are expected to look after the interests of all stakeholders. It is argued that the composition of the supervisory board is controlled by the management board and, therefore, these 'external' directors (supervisory board members) are not that effective in disciplining corporate managers. One specific institutional feature of many Dutch companies is the 'structured regime' which reduces certain rights of the shareholders and grants them to the supervisory board (see Kabir et al., 1997 and de Jong et al., 2002). In particular, it is not the common shareholders but the supervisory directors who appoint and dismiss directors, approve the annual accounts of the corporation, and approve certain major decisions such as issue of new securities, file for bankruptcy and so on. Nearly half of the Dutch firms in the sample fall under this regime and we use a dummy variable in the regression analysis to proxy for this feature. The structured regime appears to have a negative effect on stock returns, while it is insignificant for the other measures. We observed in Table 13.3 that blockholdings by individuals and families in the Netherlands had a positive impact on corporate performance. Splitting the ownership of individuals and family members into ownership of insiders (management and supervisory board members) and others, we find that for *ROA* insiders block ownership has a significantly negative effect on firm performance while ownership by outside large shareholders has a significant positive effect.

Unlike Belgium and the Netherlands, the UK is a typical Anglo-Saxon country. We use the common corporate governance features as explanatory variables in the regression analysis. The results presented in Panel C of Table 13.4 indicate that board size has a positive effect (*Q*) and the fraction of outsiders has a negative effect (*ROA*). The *CEO* dummy (CEO acting as a chairperson of the board) has a negative effect on firm performance (*ROA* and stock return). We find that when the management owns a high proportion of equity, *Q* is lower. We also observe that large shareholdings by financial institutions and corporations in the UK seem to reduce corporate performance.

As a robustness check, we try a variety of alternative regression specifications. First, we control for industry fixed effects instead of company fixed effects. It is possible that firm performance is affected by industry factors which are not captured by the explanatory variables we use. Second, we perform regressions using five-year average values of all variables. One can argue that yearly performances of firms are usually quite erratic and therefore can cause insignificant relationships. None of these specification checks significantly changes the above mentioned results.

Overall, our results show that country-specific corporate governance features are important in multi-country studies for two reasons. First, variables have different impacts on performance across countries. Second, countries have unique institutional features that influence performance.

VI. Conclusions

The purpose of this chapter is to examine whether differences in corporate governance features across countries can explain the differences in corporate performance. Whereas most studies on the relation between performance and control focus on the USA, this study takes a comparative approach and researches the relation in different countries. We assemble a small but unique data set comprising matched industrial firms listed on stock exchanges of three countries: Belgium, the Netherlands and the UK. We focus on the governance of listed mature companies which are at the top (or over the top) of their systemic life cycle. These countries are chosen because their corporate governance characteristics differ significantly on many dimensions. Moreover, these countries can be considered as examples of three different corporate governance systems having close similarities with many countries of the world. The UK represents countries with a market-based system, Belgium is prototypical for most Continental Europe whereas the Netherlands has unique corporate governance features but is close to the German governance system. We pay particular attention to the role of corporate governance in poorly performing companies (in terms of both share and accounting performance) as poor corporate performance may not only be the result of bad managerial decisions but also of a lack of efficient corporate governance. In addition, we also focus on the contribution of corporate governance to the growth potential of firms as measured by their Tobin's Q.

We can draw the following major conclusions from this study. First, a significant cross-country variation in stylized corporate governance characteristics is present among Belgian, Dutch and UK firms. The average board size and the proportion of non-executives in Belgian firms is larger than that of the Netherlands and the UK. Ownership concentration is the highest in Belgium and the lowest in the UK. Second, these common corporate governance features do not have a similar relationship with firm performance across countries. Our results indicate that in cases where a statistically significant relationship with performance is observed, there is no consistency across countries concerning the direction of such a relationship. Third, country-specific corporate governance characteristics are found to be more important in determining performance of firms. The significantly negative relationship between corporate shareholdings and performance observed in Belgium is driven by the ownership and lack of monitoring by holding companies. The legal obligation for many Dutch firms to create a separate supervisory board with outsiders and to reduce rights of shareholders also negatively influences the governance–performance relationship.

The empirical evidence provided in this study therefore suggests that it would not be sufficient to consider only the stylized facts to explain firm performance in an international context. In fact, it would be misleading if researchers did not include country-specific factors as additional explanatory variables. This study is only a first attempt to evaluate the importance of some universally used corporate governance characteristics in explaining the performance of individual firms across countries. A challenging future task will be to perform empirical tests on a larger data set from many other countries. The recent worldwide interest in the disclosure of company-specific corporate governance data would be a valuable stimulus in this direction.

Notes

1. We are indebted to Marcel Das, Piet Moerland and Theo Nijman, who earlier took part with us in a related research project. We also thank Jana Fidrmucova and Peter Roosenboom for helping us with data collection.
2. An important governance characteristic in Dutch firms is the structured regime. We start with a random selection of 25 Dutch firms with this regime and we locate for each firm a matching firm in the same industry (manufacturing, trade or service) and the smallest difference in total sales. For these 50 Dutch firms, we locate 50 Belgian and 50 UK matched firms based on the same industry/size matching.
3. Shareholdings by individuals include insider shareholdings. In the UK the average insider blockholdings are 3.9 percent and in the Netherlands on average 6.7 percent is held by insiders. In Belgium, no insider shareholdings are reported for our sample of firms.
4. De Jong et al. (2002) show that 60 percent of the Dutch firms have adopted the structured regime. Although, by construction, our sample has a lower percentage, this difference is small. Therefore, it is not likely that the selection will influence our findings.

References

Agrawal, A. and C. Knoeber (1996), 'Firm performance and mechanisms to control agency problems between managers and shareholders', *Journal of Financial and Quantitative Analysis*, **31**: 377–97.

Banerjee, S., B. Leleux and T. Vermaelen (1997), 'Large shareholdings and corporate control: an analysis of stake purchases by French holding companies', *European Financial Management*, **3**: 23–43.

Bethel, J., J. Porter Liebeskind and T. Opler (1998), 'Block share purchases and corporate performance', *Journal of Finance*, **53**: 605–34.

Bolton, P. and E. von Thadden (1998), 'Blocks, liquidity and corporate control', *Journal of Finance*, **53**: 1–25.

Borokhovich, K., R. Parrino and T. Trapani (1996), 'Outside directors and CEO selection', *Journal of Financial and Quantitative Analysis*, **31**: 337–55.

Burkart, M., D. Gromb and F. Pannunzi (1997), 'Large shareholders, monitoring, and the value of the firm', *Quarterly Journal of Economics*, **112**: 693–728.

Cho, M.-H. (1998), 'Ownership structure, investment and the corporate value: an empirical analysis', *Journal of Financial Economics*, **47**: 103–21.

Dahya, J., J. McConnell and N. Travlos (2002), 'The Cadbury committee, corporate performance, and top management turnover', *Journal of Finance*, **57**: 461–83.

de Jong, A., D. Dejong, G. Mertens and C. Wasley (2002), 'The role of self-regulation in corporate governance: evidence from the Netherlands', working paper.

Demsetz, H. and B. Villalonga (2001), 'Ownership structure and corporate performance', *Journal of Corporate Finance*, **7**: 209–33.

Demsetz, H. and K. Lehn (1985), 'The structure of corporate ownership: causes and consequences', *Journal of Political Economy*, **93**: 1155–77.

Denis, D. and D. Denis (1995), 'Performance changes following top management dismissals', *Journal of Finance*, **50**: 1029–57.

Dimson, E., P. Marsh and M. Staunton (2001), 'Millennium book II: 101 years of investment returns', London: ABN-AMRO/London Business School.

Fama, E. and M. Jensen (1983), 'Separation of ownership and control', *Journal of Law and Economics*, **26**: 301–25.

Franks, J. and C. Mayer (1996), 'Hostile takeovers and the correction of managerial failure', *Journal of Financial Economics*, **40**: 163–81.

Franks, J., C. Mayer and L. Renneboog (2001), 'Who disciplines management in poorly performing companies?', *Journal of Financial Intermediation*, **10**: 209–48.

Himmelberg, C., Hubbard, R.G. and D. Palia (1999), 'Understanding the determinants of managerial ownership and the link between ownership and performance', *Journal of Financial Economics*, **53**: 353–84.

Jensen, M. and W. Meckling (1976), 'Theory of the firm: managerial behaviour, agency costs and ownership structure', *Journal of Financial Economics*, **3**: 305–29.

Kabir, R., D. Cantrijn and A. Jeunink (1997), 'Takeover defenses, ownership structure and stock returns in the Netherlands: an empirical investigation', *Strategic Management Journal*, **18**: 97–109.

La Porta, R., F. Lopez-De-Silanes, A. Shleifer and R. Vishny (1998), 'Law and finance', *Journal of Political Economy*, **106**: 1113–55.

Lehman, E. and J. Weigand (2000), 'Does the governed corporation perform better? Governance structures and corporate performance in Germany', *European Finance Review*, **4**: 157–95.

Loderer, C. and K. Martin (1997), 'Executive stock ownership and performance: tracking faint traces', *Journal of Financial Economics*, **45**: 223–55.

McConnell, J. and H. Servaes (1990), 'Additional evidence on equity ownership and corporate value', *Journal of Financial Economics*, **27**: 595–612.

Morck, R., A. Shleifer and R. Vishny (1988), 'Management ownership and market valuation: an empirical analysis', *Journal of Financial Economics*, **20**: 293–315.

Morck, R., A. Shleifer and R. Vishny (1989), 'Alternative mechanisms of corporate control', *American Economic Review*, **79**: 842–52.

Prowse, S. (1995), 'Corporate governance in an international perspective: a survey of corporate control mechanisms among large firms in the US, UK, Japan and Germany', *Financial Markets, Institutions & Instruments*, **4**(1): 1–63.

Renneboog, L. (2000), 'Ownership, managerial control and the corporate governance of companies listed on the Brussels Stock Exchange', *Journal of Banking and Finance*, **24**: 1959–95.

Shleifer, A. and R. Vishny (1997), 'A survey of corporate governance', *Journal of Finance*, **52**: 737–83.

[14]

Corporate governance cycles during transition: theory and evidence from the Baltics

Derek C. Jones and Niels Mygind

I. Introduction

The transition in Eastern Europe has been characterized by development of specific types of ownership structures. These ownership structures have been changing fast not only in relation to privatization, but also in the post-privatization period. The aim of this chapter is to analyze the specific patterns in these ownership dynamics, which is an important part of the development of new enterprise governance structures. In the analysis we focus on ownership identity and concentration; we do not include board representation, management position, compensation and so on.

The theoretical starting point is that the choice of governance structure is determined by enterprise characteristics: size, need of capital, information asymmetries and so on, as well as surrounding institutions, market conditions and the like. The enterprise characteristics change over the life cycle of the firm. Ownership structures are expected to change because different stakeholder groups can contribute in different ways to the development of the company at different times in the firm's development. This means a change in governance structure over the life cycle – a specific governance cycle. However, the surroundings differ between countries, and countries in transition have specific features and specific paths of development. Therefore, a specific governance cycle can be identified during transition. Because of the rapid changing environment, corporate governance patterns established at early stages of transition can be expected to change quite quickly. But the speed of transition, the institutional framework and the needs of capital and other inputs from different stakeholders vary across countries and are expected to produce differences in the nature of the typical life cycle across countries – for example in the speed at which particular ownership changes will occur.

Although the three Baltic countries (Estonia, Latvia and Lithuania) show many similarities in the transition process, there are also important differences in the developments in the institutional environment. Special attention is paid to differences in the privatization process and also to the sophistication of the security of property rights. The speed and the depth of reforms have varied in the three Baltic countries. It is of special interest to examine these similarities and differences and to analyze if these are associated with differences in key dimensions of governance cycles across countries.

To provide simple hypothesis tests, we use new and rich enterprise panel data sets for the three countries. The data enable various measures of ownership to be constructed (including the identity of major owners and ownership concentration). The empirical analysis covers the ownership cycle with emphasis on initial ownership and subsequent changes. Our key method is to assemble a series of transition matrices showing both starting and final ownership configurations for sample enterprises and to simultaneously provide information on changes in concentration for the largest single owner. For Estonia this is supplemented with an analysis of the frequencies of different ownership cycles including intermediary stages of ownership.

The structure of the chapter is as follows. The next section outlines the conceptual framework for governance changes over the life cycle of the company both in general and in relation to the specific conditions in countries in transition. In Section III we describe the differences in the transition process and developments in the institutional environment in the three Baltic countries. Section IV outlines the data, reviews previous work on ownership changes in transition economies, and presents the results of the Baltic analysis in a series of transition matrices that show the start and end of the governance cycles both covering ownership identities and concentration. In a final section we offer conclusions and implications.

II.   Governance Cycles: Conceptual Framework

Since our idea of the governance cycle for firms in transition economies draws on well-established concepts for firms in developed economies, it is useful to begin by highlighting some themes in that literature and also by examining some matters of scope and definition.

In this chapter the type of ownership is connected to the identity of the owners defined in relation to their specific stake in enterprise activities – as pure capital providers, managers, employees and state representatives. We also distinguish between foreign and domestic owners since in economies in transition this is often an important difference. Furthermore, we analyze the concentration of ownership among the largest single stakeholders, defined as an individual, group or legal entity with specific interests in the enterprise – managers, other employees, creditors, external owners, customers, suppliers, central or local government. The governance structure for an enterprise can be defined as the distribution among stakeholders of both the formal rights and the appropriated rights concerning: (1) control, (2) income flow, (3) assets and liabilities, and (4) information about the enterprise (Mygind, 2001). The ownership rights are the residual rights left for the owner when the fixed rights to other stakeholders (such as wages, interest, taxes) have been fulfilled. Thus the identity of the owners is a central part of the governance structure. Other aspects, such as the actual organization of governance in relation to the board structure and the stakeholders' representation on the board, are beyond the scope of this chapter.

The ownership structure in market economies is determined by a combination of institutional, cultural and economic factors. To the extent that there is a possibility for ownership structures to adjust it can be assumed that, given the institutional setting, the type of ownership that gives the highest return to the owners will prevail. The optimal ownership structure can be explained from several perspectives including agency, property rights and the transaction cost approaches. In addition, resource dependence theory analyzes the firm from the point of view of its ability to get access to critical resources (Pfeffer and Salancik, 1978). The importance of these resources varies over the life cycle of the firm. At the start the entrepreneurial skills connected to the initial business idea is the crucial factor, while supply of necessary capital is more important in the following stages. While these different theories emphasize different factors, the following elements are of recurring importance and are likely to be included in an eclectic approach to ownership dynamics. We begin first by considering factors whose main impact is at an individual firm level.

Ownership determinants: technology and market at the company level

The size of the company is connected with higher demands on capital and entails a pressure away from concentrated ownership. The size and capital demands of the company may be very high even in relation to a wealthy owner. Therefore, growth is associated with a more diversified ownership structure, a fall in owner concentration (Jensen and Meckling, 1976; Putterman, 1993; Shleifer and Vishny, 1997). A large size of the company is often used as an explanation for no employee ownership. Alchian and Demsetz (1972) argue that a large group of employees need a central monitor to avoid shirking. The larger the group, the smaller is each employee's share in the ownership rights and the easier it is for a single employee to free-ride. Hansmann (1996) argues that a larger group of employees combined with higher heterogeneity means higher costs for collective decision making.

A second factor is the *need for capital*, which is connected to capital intensity, the size of the company, and the specificity of capital (see below). This means that it is difficult for wealth-constrained insiders to take over the company, and if they own the company it will mean a high concentration of risk. Insiders put all their eggs, jobs and capital, into one basket (Meade, 1972). While for employees this argument is connected with capital intensity, for management ownership it will be linked to the absolute amount of risk capital that is needed. There is a trade-off between single proprietorship by the manager with no governance problem between manager and owners and the possibility of diversification and higher capital supply by external more diversified investors with less control with management (Fama and Jensen, 1983).

The *specificity of the different inputs* constitutes another microeconomic factor. If the fixed assets can be used in many alternative activities it is much easier to finance them by loans instead of by direct risk capital. In these cases banks will play a strong role (Williamson, 1985). However, the sunk cost of specific capital puts the risk on the provider of capital. In turn, the larger the need for direct risk capital, the less likelihood there is that a single provider of capital will emerge to fulfill these needs and more diversified ownership can be expected (Fama and Jensen, 1983; Putterman, 1993). On the other hand, the existence of specific capital means a higher dependence on other links in the value chain. The hold-up problem may lead to a stronger connection to core suppliers or customers with quite concentrated strategic ownership of the company (Grossman and Hart, 1986). A special relation concerns the inputs of human capital. If it is highly specific, the risk is high for the employees. To limit this risk, the employees have an incentive to take direct control and ownership of the enterprise.

Transaction costs for outside investors are also closely connected to the specificity of the assets of the company, information asymmetries, and of the institutional framework (see below). New and as yet unproven business ideas with complex human capital make it very difficult and costly for external investors, including both passive suppliers of capital like banks and active external owners, to get reliable information about the company and to monitor the performance of managers.

The *economic performance* of the firm is another potential influence on the ownership type, with, for example, an economic crisis often implying a shift in ownership. However, this ownership change may take several directions: an outside raider or a strategic investor related to the value chain may take over the company and perform the necessary restructuring. A managerial buy-out may be the result if, based on insider information, the managers estimate the value of the firm to be higher than estimates of external investors (Wright et al., 2001). An economic crisis may induce a defensive take-over by the employees to introduce more flexible wages and to save their jobs and their specific human capital (Ben-Ner and Yun, 1996). However, it can also be argued that high performance increases the value of equity and therefore cash-constrained employees are tempted to sell their shares. In general, high performance means that the company can be sold for a high price, and this will attract strong external investors.

Ownership determinants: economic, institutional and cultural environment for a country

There are also several factors that together constitute the economic, institutional and cultural environment for a country, with differences across countries expected to be associated with differences in ownership dynamics. If economic performance is found to influence the type of ownership, then macroeconomic cycles can also be expected to have an impact on the governance structure, and the governance cycle will be related to the business cycles. Thus it has been estimated that management buy-outs (MBOs) are more frequent in business-cycle troughs because of the general low pricing of assets during dips. This can be seen in relation to tendencies of going private (CMBOR, 2003), while boom periods on the stock market mean that initial public offerings (IPOs) and going public give companies a cheaper possibility to raise external finance. Defensive employee take-overs can be assumed to be more frequent in recessions because of higher threats of closure and lower alternative employment possibilities (Ben-Ner, 1988). However, the focus in this chapter is not the macroeconomic business cycle, but rather the life cycle of the firm.

The institutional setting in relation to legislation may present specific barriers or provide advantages to different forms of ownership. Thus US legislation has limited bank ownership of non-financial companies and Employee Stock Ownership Plan (ESOP) legislation has included tax benefits that favor some elements of employee ownership. In Denmark foundation ownership has been favored by tax benefits (Pedersen and Thomsen, 1997). The degree of protection of minority owners through legislation and the liquidity and development of the stock markets can be determining for the diversification of ownership. Thus concentrated ownership is widespread in countries with a lower degree of minority owner protection and less developed capital markets, while diversified ownership is more frequent in countries such as the USA and the UK with highly developed capital markets and a high degree of protection of minority owners (La Porta et al., 1999; Becht et al., 2002). Also, the development of the banking sector enhances the possibility of financing growth through bank loans, and for the role of the banks as creditors and potential owners in the governance structure of the firm.

Informal social relations and culture, defined as the historical traditions, cultural values, norms and preferences of the stakeholders, can also explain important differences in the governance structure between countries. Thus the optimal ownership structure in Japan is expected to be different from the optimal structure in the USA because stakeholders have different objectives and different relations to each other.

Changes in ownership over the life cycle of the firm

Based on these influences on and determinants of ownership, some trends in the development of a typical ownership structure for a firm can be noted in relation to the typical life cycle of the firm. The stages can be related to specific stages of the development in the ownership structure. Over its life cycle, a company will change technology, markets and relations to the different stakeholders. These shifts will have an impact on the role of different stakeholders including the identity of the dominant owners, which is the part of the corporate governance structure we focus on when examining the governance cycle.[1]

The governance cycle can be developed in relation to the core stages or core events in the company life cycle. Most companies start up as small entities with few employees, low capital and low knowledge about the economic potential of the firm. A high proportion fail in the early stage; but most of the succeeding companies go into a stage of early growth, with demands for higher inputs of capital, knowledge, networks and employees. The need for extra capital may be spread over several growth stages, eventually leading to some diversification of ownership. However, a specific shock in the environment may also lead the company into a stage of crisis, which makes some kind of new inputs necessary. These will often be a new input of capital, which can only be facilitated through an ownership change. During these stages the change in ownership can be related to the different determinants of the ownership structure. Changing conditions from both within and outside the company generate changes in ownership and hence changes in the development of the governance cycle.

The classic entrepreneurial company starts up as a small entity often only based on the entrepreneur and a few close friends or relatives as partners. It is often based on relatively low capital inputs, which can be covered by the entrepreneur, and debt based on personal loans, for example with collateral in the family house. For the newly started firm, information about the core competence, the main business idea, is yet unproven and difficult to transmit to an external investor. The asymmetry in information between the insider and external investor is thus very large and the transaction costs of writing and controlling a contract are very high. High uncertainty and lack of reliable information about the prospects of the new business and its market potential aggravate the problem of asymmetric information and risks to the external investor. Therefore most new companies are started by single proprietors, and they are often owned by the entrepreneur, sometimes with participation of close relatives and friends. The capital needed can in most cases be covered by the founders and by loans with collateral in the entrepreneurs' personal assets.

The exceptions for starting up new entities are capital-intensive projects developed inside large companies or as joint ventures between several companies. When new entities are started by parent companies or venture companies from the start, external ownership, with a separation of ownership and control, exists. However, these types of start-ups (spin-offs) are rare in comparison to the high number of entrepreneurial management start-ups.

Many small entrepreneurial companies close down during the initial stages but eventually, those that survive enter an initial growth stage. The expansion of the company to benefit from economies of scale demands high capital investments, knowledge and network relations to facilitate continued high growth. At the same time, the firms start to gain some reputation and market experience, which can improve the information relevant for potential external investors. It becomes possible to give external investors the necessary information and guarantees based on the assets of the new company. Suppliers of capital can be banks or other financial institutions. In most cases these creditors will not claim direct control, but

Table 14.1   Governance cycles in developed market economies: core stages of change in governance/ownership – classical cycle

---

Start-up stage
Entrepreneur ownership (management, family ownership)

Early growth stage
Change in ownership/governance because of need of supply of external capital, management skills and networks by:

- bank (often rather passive role in relation to management)
- closely related investors, take active part in management
- venture capital, take active part in management

Later growth stage

Change in ownership/governance because of need of supply of external capital, management skills and networks by:

- strategic investor, take full control of the company
- public investors, often diversified ownership

Crisis/restructuring stage
Change in ownership/governance because of take-over by

- bank (bad loans *de facto* transferred to ownership capital)
- venture capital (often specialized in take-overs (often unfriendly))
- strategic investor (use opportunity to take over cheap assets)
- defensive take-over by insiders (to avoid close-down and unemployment)
- close-down (assets transferred to other uses)

---

often they require close monitoring of the collateral behind the loan. In other cases venture capital with a dominating ownership share may supply capital. This happens mostly in the early stages of the life cycle. In some cases the owner tries to attract other owners by issuing extra share capital. Often the new owners are found within a rather closed circle of stakeholders, typically top employees of the company, investors from the local society or close business partners.

At a later more mature growth stage, when the company has developed its potential, it may attract a strategic investor with an interest in including the company in its value chain. Another possibility for attracting capital at a developed stage is to go public. This stage could be connected to the exit of the venture capital, which sells the company after fulfilling its task. The development of going public is also often part of a process of diversification of ownership. Therefore the process of growth is often combined with a lower degree of concentration.

Sooner or later many companies run into a stage of crisis. Diverse internal and external factors, including changes in technology and/or markets or the institutional setting, force the company to adjust to the new conditions. The company faces strong pressures to undertake some restructuring. New external capital and expertise are needed, and banks, venture capital and strategic investors may play an important role. As an alternative to closure, insiders may make a defensive take-over to protect their jobs and their specific human capital. The crisis may also result in an exit of the company and liquidation of the assets, which is then taken over by new investors for other activities.

To a large degree, the institutional setting determines both the extent of external ownership and the timing of when external owners become involved in the life cycle. Particular concerns include the choice between debt and equity, and the involvement of minority shareholders. The protection of minority shareholders depends on the functions of legislation, the transparency of the information about the company, and the functioning of the market for shares (not only in relation to publicly traded, but also for closely held, companies). In countries with developed markets for ownership and strong protection of minority owners we see a more diversified ownership structure (La Porta et al., 1999).

Specific conditions for the governance cycle in transition economies

Returning to the case of transitional economies, we expect that a specific governance cycle exists in firms in those countries. The dynamics of enterprise governance and ownership are quite distinct in transitional economies because enterprises go through a transition in ownership structure, a transition in relation to the changing institutions in the environment, and a transition of the market in relation to prices, costs and competitive structure, with a strong pressure for restructuring of products and production methods. Therefore most enterprises in transition economies start with rapid change of the structure of governance combined with a strong pressure for restructuring production simply to be able to survive. The specific elements in early transition that influence the governance cycle are shown in Table 14.2.

To understand the specific governance cycles appearing in transitional economies, three special conditions should be taken into account. The first of these is the privatization process. The early years of transition created specific conditions for the initial development

Table 14.2   Specific elements in early transition influencing the governance cycle

---

Starting stage determined by privatization method, which may favor managers, other employees, concentrated foreign investors or diversified external ownership.

Most enterprises have a **strong need of restructuring** (inputs, production methods, outputs not adjusted to new market conditions, with a new set of prices and incentives)

The **financial system** not developed:

- external finance from banks limited
- the stock exchange not functioning
- venture capital firms not existing

The **governance institutions** for securing property rights (especially shareholder rights) not fully developed:

- widespread insider ownership
- enterprises have to rely on internal finance
- slow strategic restructuring

---

of private ownership. The different methods favored different types of owners. For example, in some countries employees had a strong political position, resulting in a very high frequency of employee ownership. Also, managers often had a strong position in relation to the political system. On the other hand, voucher privatization could lead to a high degree of domestic external ownership, while direct sale without restrictions for foreign capital gave foreign investors the lead in the change to concentrated external ownership (Mygind, 2001). The privatization process can be seen as a state-governed process where the specific privatization methods creating a specific ownership structure, which would not have developed in a more market-based system for ownership adjustments. It can be argued that path dependency may create a learning process and institutional development, which may lead to specific paths for subsequent developments in the governance structure. Such path dependencies can to a high degree be used to explain persistent differences in the governance structure in the West.[2] On the other hand, it can be expected that there will be post-privatization adjustments bringing the ownership structure back to a more 'normal' equilibrium.

A second condition occurs because, from the start of transition, nearly all state-owned enterprises are confronted with a strong pressure to restructure production, production methods, organizational structure and markets. They are in a situation of crisis with an acute need of capital, new skills and new networks. In the developed market economies this would very often lead to a change in ownership, bringing new investors with the necessary resources for restructuring. In some cases, privatization has delivered the best-fitted investor for this restructuring. In other cases post-privatization dynamics include a take-over to facilitate such restructuring.

However, there is a third and most important feature of transitional economies, which delays this kind of ownership adjustment. This concerns the process of building up a well-functioning market economy and especially developing the necessary institutions required to facilitate the adjustment of governance structures in enterprises. In the early stage of transition, the lack of developed institutions favors special types of ownership arrangements. For example, insiders have an advantage in relation to outside owners because the institutions supporting outside ownership such as credible auditing procedures and transparent stock markets are not developed (Mygind, 2001). The delayed development of the institutional framework combined with stabilization and more developed markets enables other adjustments of the ownership structure to be made.

Hypotheses on the specific governance cycle in transition economies

Based on these three special conditions, some specific hypotheses about the governance cycle in transition can be developed. However, since some conditions can give rise to tendencies whose directions are ambiguous, the final conclusions must be based on empirical analysis.

The first set of hypotheses concerns the scope and resilience of employee ownership. We note that the privatization process in many countries, including the Baltic republics, has led to a high degree of broad employee ownership. However, employees' lack of governance skills, their lack of capital and the risk concentration may lead to a quite rapid tendency to sell to other investors. This movement away from employee ownership could be delayed by various conditions, including: if learning processes give employees higher governance skills; if there are strong defensive arguments for keeping ownership to protect employment; or if the specific company has a high degree of specific human capital which would be threatened by a sale to another investor.

In general, the lack of development of the institutional environment weakens the role of external investors. The lack of transparency and high risk, especially in the early stages of transition, combined with the lack of markets for company shares means that, in general, managers have a strong advantage compared to external investors (Kalmi, 2002). Therefore, it can be expected that managers often take over the shares that the broad group of employee wants to sell. During the early stages of transition in particular there will be a strong tendency for ownership changes from employees to managers. The exceptions are expected to be relatively small enterprises with high human capital.

Some privatization methods provided for a high degree of public offering of shares to diversified external owners. To some extent this was the situation in Lithuania with voucher privatization. Also, in many countries, privatization to former employees in agricultural entities would be registered as sales to external owners. These kinds of sales would often mean overly diversified ownership in relation to the volatility of the markets, the low quality of information to external owners and the lack of development of the institutional framework. At the same time most of these initial small external shareholders were under strong wealth constraints. Therefore, during the early years these companies will be in a process of concentration of ownership. Because of their strong position it is expected that managers will take over companies from diversified external owners. Such management take-overs will be accompanied by an increase in ownership concentration. Also, concentration in the hands of a smaller group of external investors (including foreign) can be part of this process.

When the institutional framework becomes more advanced during the process of transition it can be expected that external investors will be in a stronger position, and we will see shifts from insider to outsider ownership. This tendency will be strengthened if the company, either because of high growth or because of pressure for restructuring, has a strong need for extra capital.

The stock markets in the transitional countries are quite weak, with few companies listed, low capitalization and low turnover, and IPOs are rare (EVCA, 2003). Therefore it is too early to observe the tendency found in the West for more mature firms to diversify ownership to small external investors. Instead we expect a dominating tendency in the direction of higher concentration of ownership when we look at continued external ownership.

The specific ownership development for privatized enterprises can be expected to be quite different from the dynamics for new start-ups. For new firms we expect developments to follow the cycle of Western economies to a much higher degree, with manager-owned start-ups subsequently being taken over by external domestic owners or, for the most successful cases, by foreign investors. However, while new start-ups are not influenced by the special transitional privatization bias, they are still subject to gaps in the institutional environment, thus pushing them in the direction of the specific transition-economy governance cycle.

In many cases foreign companies establish their subsidiary companies directly as new greenfield entities. In these cases we expect a rather stable ownership structure. Also, when foreign investors have taken over companies in the privatization process we expect that these enterprises have reached their final stage of development in the ownership cycle – we expect no further changes of ownership within the relatively short time-horizon of our analysis. However, in cases where the foreign subsidiary has been established as a joint venture in early transition we expect a change to a wholly owned subsidiary when the legislation opens up for this possibility. We summarize the expected governance cycle for a firm in a transition economy in Table 14.3.

However, it should be noted that the analysis has emphasized some general tendencies for the governance cycle in transitional countries in comparison to Western countries. This leads us to expect to find some quite similar tendencies in the three Baltic countries. We also expect that the existence of cross-national differences, especially concerning institutional differences related to the speed and form of transition, may make the starting points and the speed of change between different phases of the cycle slightly different across countries.

Table 14.3   Expected governance cycles in countries in transition

Privatized (starting point depends on privatization method)
employee → **manager** → **outside concentrated (domestic → foreign)**
diversified domestic → **manager** → **outside concentrated (domestic → foreign)**
outside concentrated, foreign stable (very long run more diversified for large listed companies)
New
manager → **outside concentrated (domestic → foreign)**
foreign concentrated (stable)

The dominant form of privatization will determine to what degree the starting point of the cycle for privatized firms will be employee ownership or perhaps foreign ownership (Mygind, 2001). In addition to the specific privatization methods, the advancement of the institutional development and the general economic and political stability will determine the level of foreign investment (Bevan et al., 2004). The speed of change also depends on the transition of institutions. The development of the banking sector and the possibility of debt financing are especially important. The dynamics also depend on the development of the capital market and the possibility of expanding the equity both for listed companies and for trading shares of non-listed companies. In turn this might be expected to produce differences in ownership concentration at particular times.

Hence in the next section we look more closely at specific developments in the three Baltic countries. In turn, we will then develop some hypotheses for how this can be expected to affect the character of corporate governance cycles, especially the starting points and speed of ownership change in these countries.

III. Privatization and Governance Institutions in the Baltic Countries

The results of privatization in the Baltic countries are summarized in Tables 14.4 and 14.5. There have been important differences in starting conditions and in political development. Therefore different paths have been chosen for changing the ownership structure from a planned system to a market system based on private ownership (for a deeper analysis see Mygind, 1997 and 2000). In Estonia the nationalist-oriented policies in relation to the large Russian-speaking minority meant that the period supporting broad employee take-overs of enterprises was very short and, except for a few experiments and some large agricultural enterprises, only covered the privatization of small and medium-sized enterprises. This was also the case in Latvia, but here a large group of small and medium-sized enterprises initially leased by their employees were later formally taken over by employees. Therefore we also have some privatizations to employees later in the process in Latvia. Before independence, employee take-overs implied that control was taken away from central authorities in Moscow to the Baltic republics. When this goal was accomplished in Estonia and Latvia the next goal was both to strengthen the position of the titular population and to find a more efficient ownership structure.

Table 14.4   Overview of privatization

	Private % GDP	Large priv.	Small priv.	Main method	Secondary method	Peak years
Estonia	75	4	4+	Direct sale	Voucher	1994–95
Latvia	70	3	4+	Direct sale	Voucher	1996–97
Lithuania	75	4–	4+	Insider/voucher	Direct sale	1992–94

Note: Based on Mygind (2000) and EBRD (2003), where scores for privatization and governance range from 1 = none to 4+ = full.

Table 14.5   Overview of privatization of enterprises

	Estonia	Latvia	Lithuania
Early	In all three Baltic countries end 1980s: new cooperatives and leasing by worker collective according to Soviet legislation, formally worker owned, but management dominated		
	From 1991 Estonian leasing 200 firms, mostly to managers		1990–91 employee got shares for around 3% of assets
Small	First law 1990 gave insiders advantages, but these were canceled in 1992–93	First law 1991 gave insiders advantages, but these were canceled by 1993	No formal advantages to insiders
Large	Few experiments 1989–91, mostly to employees	1991 experiments to insiders 1992–94 decentral process, 234 firms leased to insiders	1991–95 LIPSP: most shares sold for vouchers; employees could buy 50% of shares for quite low price
	From 1992 direct tender sale (= German *Treuhandanstalt*) Tenders based on price, investment and job guarantees combined with few public offerings for vouchers	From 1994 direct tender sale through Privatization Agency combined with some public offerings for vouchers	From 1996 direct tender sale through Privatization Agency 1998 State Property Fund speeds up tender process

In Lithuania, with a negligible Russian-speaking minority, workers and employees in general had a much stronger political role. The early ideas of insider take-overs were further developed in the early years of transition with the implementation of the 'Program of Initial Privatization', called LIPSP. At the same time, there was strong resistance against selling out Lithuania to foreign investors. Lithuanians feared Russian take-overs. Lithuanian policies were for a long period quite restrictive towards foreign direct investment (FDI). Estonia, on the other hand, implemented very liberal rules for foreign capital, opening up the economy to the inflow of especially Finnish and Swedish capital.

In the former Soviet Union, the first movements in the direction of private enterprises (in the form of new cooperatives, individual firms, leasing and joint ventures) began during the second half of the 1980s (Bim et al., 1993). Similar developments took place in what were to become the Baltic republics, especially in Estonia, which functioned as a laboratory for market reforms in the USSR. The 'small state enterprises' with semi-private spin-offs from state-owned enterprises were part of this development. Also in Latvia, rapid development of new cooperatives made an early start with private entrepreneurship. Most of these firms had a strong element of employee ownership although often they were dominated by managers.

All three countries have had large voucher schemes involving most residents. However, in both Estonia and Latvia the bulk of vouchers were related to the privatization of land and housing. In Lithuania 65 percent of the vouchers were used in enterprise privatization in the LIPSP– in Estonia only 28 percent and in Latvia 42 percent (Mygind, 2000). In Estonia and Latvia most of these vouchers went to broad public offerings of minority holdings after the sale of the majority to a core investor. A core investor could also finance a big share of the down-payment by vouchers in the tender privatizations. In Lithuania, vouchers could only be used in the LIPSP. Often majority share holdings were bought mainly for vouchers. Although the LIPSP resulted in a more diversified ownership structure than the tender privatizations in Estonia and Latvia, in most cases a core group of owners, most often insiders, acquired a majority of shares.

Because of the limited role of vouchers in enterprise privatization in Estonia and Latvia, investment funds were not important. However, in Lithuania 300–400 investment funds were started in relation to the LIPSP. While many funds were used as a mechanism enabling a group of insiders to take control of their companies, some of them developed into more orthodox investment funds representing a high number of investors and with a diversified portfolio in a large number of companies. However, there were severe governance problems, giving the shareholders too little influence on the administrators, resulting in asset stripping of many funds. When the regulation was tightened in 1997, most of the investment funds were dissolved.

The timing of privatization of small enterprises was quite similar for the three countries. The majority of small enterprises were privatized two to three years after the start of transition. However, for the medium and large enterprises there have been marked differences. With the implementation of the LIPSP, Lithuania was at its peak of privatization in 1993 and larger enterprises were privatized by the end of 1994. However, in most companies some shares remained state owned, and especially in some very large companies only around 10 percent of the shares were privatized, so in total only around 50 percent of the capital was privatized in the companies involved. In Estonia privatization had its greatest momentum by 1994 and most large enterprises were privatized by the end of 1995. In Latvia privatization gained momentum in 1995–96 to peak in 1997, and large privatization was nearly accomplished by the end of 1998. Looking at the largest enterprises in utilities and infrastructure, Estonia was fastest, followed by Latvia. While being fastest in the first round, Lithuania was slowest in the last round of privatization although it regained momentum in 1998.

Foreign investors played only a minor role in the privatization of small enterprises. The advantages for insiders crowded out the possibilities for outsiders, especially foreign investors. However, after 1992, foreign investors had some possibilities in Estonia and Latvia. In Lithuania foreigners had a weak position not only in small privatization, but also in the LIPSP. Foreigners, however, were soon given opportunities to start up new firms. Again, this happened somewhat faster in Estonia than in the other Baltic countries.

Estonia was the first country to use privatization to promote foreign investment in relation to large privatization. In the tender process, foreign investors had a strong position because of their access to capital, management skills and international business networks. From 1993 foreigners took over many of the largest enterprises under privatization. By the end of 1998 foreigners had taken over approximately one third of enterprise assets included in large privatization. Latvia started the same process in the autumn of 1994 and the foreign share of purchase was 38 percent for the years 1994–98. In Lithuania the LIPSP allowed very little room for foreigners, and only four enterprises were taken over by foreign investors in 'the privatization for hard currency' of 46 enterprises in the period up to 1995. After LIPSP the pace of privatization stagnated and not until 1998 did foreign capital start to play an important role in privatization in Lithuania.

Table 14.6   Overview of corporate governance institutions

	Estonia		Latvia		Lithuania	
Bankruptcy system	Strict legislation 92, tough enforcement		Strict legislation 96, tighter enforcement		Strict legislation 97, tighter enforcement	
Governance	1995	2002	1995	2002	1995	2002
EBRD governance score	3	3+	2	3–	2	3
Competition regulation	2	3–	2	2+	2	3
Bank market	1995	2002	1995	2002	1995	2002
Number of banks (foreign)	19 (5)	7 (4)	42 (11)	19 (12)	15 (0)	14 (4)
Loans to private, % of GDP	14.0	29.8	7.5	33.4	12.3	14.2
Bad loans, % of total loans	2.4	0.8	19.0	2.1	17.3	5.8
Bank regulation	Strict by 1992		Strict from 1994		Strict from 1995	
EBRD score	3	4	3	4	3	3
Stock market start	May 1996		July 1995		September 1993	
	1996	2002	1996	2002	1996	2002
Listed firms	16	34	34	69	ca. 600	46
Capitalization, % of GDP	21	33.6	3.0	8.0	11.4	9.5
Turnover/capitalization	0.13	0.54	0.08	0.17	0.04	0.07
EBRD score	2	3+	2	3	2	3

Source: EBRD (2003). Capital market data from central banks and stock exchanges.

Table 14.6 gives an overview of developments in the Baltics of the main institutions for the functioning and development of the governance structures at the enterprise level. Although the Baltic countries started their transition two years later than the leading countries in Central Europe (Poland, the Czech Republic and Hungary), they are about to catch up (EBRD, 2003). The legislation on bankruptcy procedures was developed quite early in Estonia – September 1992. The law was strictly enforced so by 1995 more than 1000 bankruptcies had already been implemented. Therefore, takeovers of liquidated assets can be assumed to have an important role in the ownership dynamics in Estonia. In Latvia and Lithuania bankruptcy laws were passed in 1992, but implementation was relatively weak. The legislation was strengthened in Latvia in 1996 and in Lithuania in 1997, and the implementation has been tightened in recent years. However, according to an EBRD survey, the implementation of laws has been somewhat slower in Latvia and Lithuania than in Estonia.

Quite early in the transition process state-owned banks were split into a two-tier system with a central bank and a number of commercial banks to be privatized later in the process. This bank privatization was performed fastest in Estonia, peaking in 1995, in Latvia in 1996, and in Lithuania only in 2001. A large number of new private banks were established in the early years of transition to service some of the large enterprises. Many of these banks had a weak capital base, but the development of the financial sector shows a strong consolidation with a fall in the number of banks and a development of banking activities from simple money transfers to deepening the main activity of channeling savings from the population to lending to companies. However, this development has been quite unstable and most of the countries have been through severe financial crises. The financial system developed relatively fast in Estonia. As early as 1992–93 the system was strengthened after a major financial crisis. In Latvia there was an even more serious banking crisis in 1995 involving the largest commercial bank in Latvia. In Lithuania three of the largest banks were in crisis in 1995–96. In all three countries the largest banks are now owned by Scandinavian banks and the importance of the banks for supplying capital to enterprises has increased a great deal recently.

The Tallinn Stock Exchange opened in May 1996. Before that time some trading of shares had taken place in the over-the-counter market. The privatization through public offerings of minority shares facilitated the development of the exchange, but there has been no strong relation between the privatization process and the development of the stock exchange. The Tallinn Stock Exchange is characterized by a small number of companies and only a few of them are heavily traded. Capitalization and turnover on the Riga Stock Exchange (Latvia) are considerably lower than in Estonia. However, following the acceleration of privatization of large companies and the associated public offerings of shares, the Latvian Stock Exchange has developed quite rapidly in recent years. The National Stock Exchange of Lithuania was established in September 1993, closely connected to the LIPSP process. Although more than 600 enterprises were listed, capitalization in relation to GDP was not higher in Lithuania than in Estonia, and turnover has been low, with thin trading of most companies. The three Baltic stock exchanges have started a common Baltic list of blue-chip stocks. The three exchanges are connected to NOREX, dominated by the stock exchanges in Stockholm and Copenhagen. This integration will probably further accelerate the strengthening of regulation and transparency. Importantly, however, for the overwhelming majority of Baltic enterprises, including those investigated in this chapter, the stock exchanges have no influence on their governance because they are not listed.

The general picture of the transition in the three Baltic countries is that similarities dominate. For all three Baltic countries we expect to see a strong representation of insider ownership, including employee ownership in the early years of transition. Especially for Estonia and Latvia there is a bias towards employee ownership in relation to small and medium firms, while in Lithuania the LIPSP also enables the introduction of employee ownership in quite large and capital-intensive enterprises (Mygind, 2000). Since privatization to foreigners was allowed earlier in Estonia, this would lead us to expect that foreign ownership as a starting point of the governance cycle would be more frequent in Estonia than elsewhere.

Estonia's faster development of the financial sector, early tough bankruptcy legislation and in general the fastest institutional development can be expected to encourage a higher speed of change in the ownership cycle than in the other countries. This is both because the optimal ownership structure will converge to the Western model at an earlier date and because the institutional development means that it will be easier to make the necessary adjustments. For example, managers have better access to capital for take-overs from the more developed banking system. A fast reactive restructuring means that employment is expected to be cut quite fast in the early stages of transition in Estonia. When employee owners leave the company they may keep their shares, and for employee-owned companies this may mean a change in ownership from employees to former employees. Finally, a fast transition process and development of the institutional system improve the business climate and attract foreign investors, facilitating a faster change of ownership structures in the direction of foreign ownership.

IV.   Data and Empirical Analysis

Much literature has examined ownership structures after privatization in transition economies, with considerable attention paid to investigating the relation between ownership and performance (e.g. Estrin and Wright, 1999; Djankov and Murrell, 2002). By contrast, in part because of the inability to access panel data sets, studies that investigate post-privatization ownership dynamics are quite rare and have tended to be concentrated in a few transition countries (e.g. Earle and Estrin, 1996; Blasi et al., 1997; Estrin and Wright, 1999; Filatotchev et al., 1999).[3]

Another body of work in this area is our own for the Baltic republics. In our previous work (e.g. Jones and Mygind, 1999) we analyze the determinants behind the ownership changes after privatization by using panel data for Estonia. We find that high-capital-intensive companies are more likely to be owned by outsiders and that economic performance does not seem to be the key determinant of ownership structure. Outside ownership often develops in stages so that companies with minority outside ownership have a high probability of being taken over by outsiders.[4]

In this chapter we build on our earlier work and provide a comparative empirical analysis of ownership dynamics in all three Baltic countries. Moreover, the analytical focus on the idea of the existence of governance cycle dynamics is novel. Thus we wish to see if there is empirical support for our notion of the governance life cycle and to see if this is equally apparent in all countries. In addition, we progress beyond previous empirical work for the Baltics and include ownership concentration in the analysis. Furthermore, since we have obtained new data for Estonia, our analysis covers both the early years of privatization and also companies privatized in the main rounds through the Estonian Privatization Agency. Also, whereas previous work typically has investigated a single change in ownership, our analysis of governance cycle dynamics examines several steps in ownership changes. Ownership groups are determined according to the widely used 'dominant owners' approach, where the firm is assigned to the ownership group holding more shares than any other group.[5]

For each of the three Baltic countries we have collected data through ownership surveys designed by the authors. In this way we assemble ownership for a panel of firms in all three countries. However, for reasons including varying opportunities for data collection, the nature of the panel data sets varies from country to country.

The Estonian panel is derived from a sample of 500 private enterprises in 1995, stratified by size and industry. Of the original 500 firms, 409 (82 percent) cooperated in the initial ownership survey undertaken in 1995. Respondents were asked to indicate the number of shares held by different groups on 1 January 1995 as well as at the time of privatization. Subsequent ownership surveys were administered annually, with the last survey in 2002. During this process some firms exited the panel because of closure or denial of response.[6] Other groups were added later to give a broad coverage of later stages of the privatization process.[7] The total group of companies included in this unbalanced panel is 800 companies.

The ownership data for Latvia is based on an ownership survey performed by the Statistical Department of Latvia under the authors' direction. The sample for the analysis was chosen from the Statistical Department's financial data sets for Latvian enterprises and was based on the following criteria: availability of financial data; employment of at least 20 for at least one year during 1994–97; and some overrepresentation of enterprises with more than 100 employees. Based on these criteria, the Statistical Department received responses from 1054 enterprises that contained details of ownership structures for 1997, 1998 and 1999. For 730 of these enterprises we also have ownership information for 1995 and 1996 from the surveys administered by the Statistical Department itself, though without the distinction for insiders between employee and manager ownership.

The ownership information for Lithuania is based on a manager survey performed in the spring of 2000. This provides information on ownership at the time of privatization, and for start-up firms in 1993, 1996, 1999 and spring 2000 for 405 respondents. The sample is a stratified random sample and is derived from a database covering 7546 enterprises that provided financial data for 1997. In constructing our sample we applied the following criteria: eliminate firms that were fully state-owned enterprises or were very small (in fact, employed fewer than 20 employees); include all (large) enterprises with more than 100 employees and one third of the smaller firms (employing 20–100). Applying these criteria resulted in 1372 enterprises being identified. Attempts were made to contact all these enterprises, though many were found to have closed and others refused to respond. The 405 responses make up around 30 percent of the initial group.

The first step in our empirical work is to report simple descriptive statistics for initial ownership structure. In Table 14.7 we show the relation between the initial ownership at the time of privatization or start-up as a new private firm and the year of privatization/start-up. From the description of the privatization process it can be expected that employee ownership is most frequent in the early stages of transition. In fact the data reveal that this tendency is most pronounced for Estonia and that it is also evident for Lithuania. However, this phenomenon is not apparent in Latvia, probably because of the high number of leased enterprises that were not formally taken over by the employees until later in the privatization process. For Estonia, privatizations to domestic external owners[8] increase over the observed period, while privatizations to foreign and managers have no clear tendency.[9]

Most of the foreign-dominated enterprises are new firms; this is especially the case in Lithuania. The exception is the Estonian large privatization during 1994–99, when many companies were taken over by foreigners. The relatively low total number of privatized foreign enterprises makes it difficult to see a clear development over time for privatizations to foreigners. Management ownership is dominant for new enterprises, but management has also assumed ownership of a high share of privatized enterprises. Domestic and especially

Table 14.7   The relation between time of privatization/start and initial ownership

		Foreign		Domestic		Manager		Employee		Total	
		No.	%	No.	%	No.	%	No.	%	No.	%
Estonia											
Privatized	To 1992	9	19	10	21	10	21	18	38	47	100
	1992–93	9	25	7	19	13	36	7	19	36	100
	1994–99	33	13	144	56	66	25	16	6	259	100
	Total	51	15	161	47	89	26	41	12	342	100
New firms	To 1992	8*	20	13	32	17	42	3	7	41	100
	1992–93	9	12	27	35	29	38	12	16	77	100
	1994–99	5	11	17	39	17	39	5	11	44	100
	Total	22*	15	57	35	63	38	20	13	162	100
Total		73	15	218	43	152	30	61	12	504	100
Latvia											
Privatized	1991	1	9	4	36	3	27	3	27	11	100
	1992–93	9	4	109	46	40	17	79	33	237	100
	1994–97	14	8	54	32	57	34	43	26	168	100
	Total	24	6	167	40	100	24	125	30	416	100
New firms	1991	10	8	19	16	76	62	17	14	122	100
	1992–93	37	18	45	22	101	50	18	9	201	100
	1994–97	43	28	33	21	66	42	13	8	156	100
	Total	90	19	97	20	243	51	48	10	479	100
Total		114	13	264	29	343	38	173	19	895	100
Lithuania											
Privatized	1991–92	3	4	30	38	13	16	33	42	79	100
	1993–94	3	3	38	41	18	20	33	36	92	100
	1995–98	1	3	19	51	9	24	8	22	37	100
	Total	7	3	87	42	40	19	74	36	208	100
New firms	To 1992	5	19	1	4	17	65	3	12	26	100
	1993–94	16	44	6	17	12	33	2	6	36	100
	1995–96	8	32	6	24	10	40	1	4	25	100
	Total	29	33	13	15	39	45	6	7	87	100
Total		36	12	100	34	79	27	80	27	295	100

Notes:
Only private companies included. We do not have the timing information for all companies. Therefore the number of enterprises is lower than in the total data sets.

*   25 foreign new enterprises established before 1992 are not included in table because they were later added to the initial random sample.

employee ownership is more frequent for privatization than for new start-ups. However, external domestic start-ups vary from 15 percent of the total start-ups in Lithuania to 30 percent in Estonia. The high frequency may be explained by the entrepreneur being backed by closely related external investors or by external investors setting up subsidiaries, for example in trade. The importance of new employee-owned enterprise varies from 7 percent in Lithuania to 12 percent in Estonia. For the early years this can probably be explained by the emergence of new cooperatives and new entities spun off from existing state-owned enterprises.[10]

In the rest of this section we present fresh evidence on ownership dynamics. Before doing so, however, some methodological remarks are in order. The data sets we use are as described, which, for Estonia, spans the time of privatization until 2002, for Latvia from 1995 to 1999, and for Lithuania from 1993 to 1999. The longer observation period for Estonia means that the data can be used to analyze a sequence of up to four ownership changes, rather than the single switch that is customary. To maximize the number of observations we have included companies that have been privatized later in the process, and companies for which we do not have information about the full period.[11] The changes for Latvia and Lithuania are reported as a two-step process for the first and the last observed ownership types. These processes are shown in a series of ownership transition matrices as explained below.

We should note that not all the changes in the nature of the identity of the dominant owner are reported in the tables. If the governance cycle follows a pattern by which dominant ownership reverts to an earlier configuration, for example 'employee manager–domestic manager', then this is considered as a shift from employee to manager ownership. That is, we assume that intermediate changes such as manager–domestic manager are simply temporary adjustments involving relatively few shares.

For all three countries we have information about the concentration of ownership for the largest single owner. For the descriptive ownership analysis we have used this to define ownership of former employees as diversified domestic ownership, with the largest single owner having less than 20 percent of ownership. This definition can be justified because practically no enterprises were privatized to diversified external owners. It is important to distinguish between the groups of domestic external investors and former employees because there are basic differences between the process behind the ownership change to external investors and to employee owners leaving the firm but keeping their ownership.

The transition matrix for Estonia[12] (Table 14.8) shows the change between first ownership type after privatization (or when the firm started as a new entity) until the last year for which information is available.[13] The matrix shows that 114 enterprises, which were foreign owned at the start of privatization (or when they were set up as new firms), were also foreign owned at the last year of record. From the relevant row it can also be seen that ten changed to domestic dominant ownership and nine to manager ownership, while none ended up as employee owned. This means that, as predicted, foreign-owned enterprises have a quite stable ownership structure with a total 'ownership change' rate of only 14 percent. Therefore, as expected, foreign ownership can be placed in the last part of the governance cycle. Firms that became foreign owned can be seen by examining the first column. Such firms emerge mainly from domestic externally owned enterprises, but also from management owned. Only four take the short cut directly from employee ownership. These results fit

Table 14.8   Estonia privatization/start 2002 ownership transition matrix: first year as private by last year recorded

Last year First year	Foreign	Domestic	Manager	Employee	Former employee	Total	Change (%)
Foreign	114	10	9	0	0	133	14.3
Domestic	11	132	37	0	0	180	26.7
Manager	8	22	107	3	0	140	23.6
Employee	6	22	35	28	8	99	71.7
Former empl.	0	4	3	2	15	24	37.5
Total	139	190	191	33	23	576	

Privatized

Last year First year	Foreign	Domestic	Manager	Employee	Former employee	Total	Change (%)
Foreign	45	4	1	0	0	50	10.0
Domestic	8	106	15	0	0	129	17.8
Manager	2	11	56	2	0	71	21.1
Employee	1	12	15	11	3	42	73.8
Former empl.	0	4	2	2	12	20	40.0
Total	56	137	89	15	15	312	

New

Last year First year	Foreign	Domestic	Manager	Employee	Former employee	Total	Change (%)
Foreign	69	6	8	0	0	83	16.9
Domestic	3	26	22	0	0	51	49.0
Manager	6	11	51	1	0	69	26.1
Employee	5	10	20	17	5	57	70.2
Former empl.	0	0	1	0	3	4	25.0
Total	83	53	102	18	8	264	

Notes: Former employee ownership defined as domestic dominant with concentration < 20% 1999. Only those firms with domestic dominant ownership and with information on concentration in 1999 are included; their number fell from 649 to 568. Also including some companies for which we have data only for some years, e.g. 1997–2000.

well with the last stage of the predicted governance cycle: management→external domestic→foreign.

Firms with external domestic ownership from the start have a higher rate of 'ownership change' (26.7 percent). A total of 19.1 percent have changed into management ownership. In

Table 14.9   Estonia – transition matrix and ownership concentration 2000/2002

2000 ╲ 2002	Foreign	Domestic	Manager	Employee	Former employee	Total
Foreign	83	6	2	–	–	91
	77.5/81.1	61.1/74.0	88.0/75.5	–	–	76.7/80.5
Domestic	6	122	13	1	–	142
	63.5/76.6	78.1/79.7	52.1/47.4	14.0/18.0	–	74.5/76.1
Manager	–	9	107	1	–	117
	–	59.5/59.1	61.3/61.7	23.0/27.0	–	60.8/61.1
Employee	–	3	5	18	2	28
	–	27.6/60.7	24.8/63.4	19.6/20.3	5.0/6.5	20.3/31.3
Former empl.	–	5	2	–	15	22
	–	14.6/28.8	11.0/45.0	–	8.5/9.5	10.1/17.5
Total	89	145	129	20	17	400
	76.6/80.8	73.1/75.9	58.6/60.1	19.5/20.5	8.1/9.1	63.8/66.4

five of the reported cases in Table 14.9 the accompanying change in concentration was constant and in another five cases it was increasing, while in three cases ownership concentration fell. However, the fall for these three is quite steep, so that the average development for all 13 enterprises for the period 2000–2002 was a fall in concentration. This is reported in Table 14.9, which only covers the later years when we started to collect concentration data in Estonia.

Of firms that were initially management owned, 23.6 percent have changed ownership type and most of these have changed to outside ownership (15.7 percent to domestic and 5.7 percent to foreign). For the later years reported in Table 14.9 these changes are accompanied by both upward and downward changes in concentration, leaving the average quite constant. Only three (2.1 percent) have changed into employee ownership. However, movement away from employee ownership proceeds at a very high rate, with more than seven in ten cases switching ownership type. In about half of these 71.7 percent the move is to ownership by management. This includes 35.4 percent of the initial group, compared to 28.3 percent to outside ownership and 8.1 percent to former employees. The high rate of change of employee-owned firms confirms the prediction of the high frequency of this specific type of change in transition economies. It is a bit surprising that ownership by former employees is more stable than employee ownership. However, the continuation of ownership by employees leaving the firm can be taken as an indicator of inertia, which also functions as a barrier to further ownership changes. Employee ownership has quite low concentration of ownership on the single largest owner and Table 14.9 shows that the changes away from both employee and former employee ownership is accompanied by quite steep increases in concentration. In general the concentration rate is increasing over the period and the steepest increases happen in parallel with shifts in ownership.

The results on ownership dynamics are robust to shortening the period to 1999 or to including only firms with full information for the period 1995–99. For this restricted group

(N = 373) the rate of change away from foreign ownership is 15 percent, while the corresponding shares are 26 percent from domestic ownership, 22 percent from dominant ownership by managers, 72 percent from employee-owned firms and 29 percent away from firms owned by former employees. These changes are similar to those generated by the larger sample except for the category of 'former employees', where the rate of change is rather lower (by some 8 percent) compared to figures based on the total sample.[14]

Surprisingly, the results are also quite robust to dividing the groups into privatized and new start-ups. Because of the initial disequilibrium in ownership caused by privatization, one might expect a higher rate of change for privatized companies. However, the initial years of transition are very volatile for both privatized and new companies because of rapidly changing markets and institutional environment. In a more stable institutional environment one might expect a higher change rate for new companies compared to more mature companies.

Table 14.10 shows findings derived from the analysis when intermediary changes between the initial and final ownership configurations that are given in the transition matrix are examined.[15] While dominant ownership changes in 171 cases, in 29 instances we observe a second ownership switch while in five cases there is third categorical change.[16] The most frequent initial change is from employee to managerial ownership change and the most frequent three-step change is, as predicted, from employee to manager to outsider (one to foreign and five to domestic). The pattern employee→external domestic→manager is recorded with five cases, but three of these have a fourth step with the firm ending up as foreign owned, and therefore they come close to the predicted employee→manager→outsider. Hence we conclude that this is clearly the most frequent ownership cycle in our sample. Our predictions are also supported by the high frequency of initial ownership changes that are of the type manager→domestic (representing 73 percent of the first changes from manager ownership), as well as the fact that 49 percent of the changes away from employee ownership are from employee to manager. The existence of a frequency of domestic→manager movements that is quite high might reflect the fact that our cases labeled domestic may also include former employee ownership, but with a concentration higher than our limit of 20 percent. It could also be the case when diversified domestic ownership is substituted by more concentrated management ownership, as predicted in the theoretical section.

For Latvia we report transition matrices for both the period 1995–99, for which we cannot distinguish between manager and employee ownership in 1995, and for 1997–99, where the available data do enable us to make the distinction (see Tables 14.11–14.13). If we do not include the broad insider category for the starting point of 1995, we are able to identify ownership cycles with three-steps for only four out of 915 enterprises.[17] Therefore we report ownership dynamics in transition matrices with only two points in time. The combination of insider ownership in 1995 and manager ownership in 1997 is counted as manager ownership for both years. Therefore the switch from employee ownership to manager ownership, which is expected to be the most frequent change, cannot be identified during this period. The change in this direction is in the table only for firms with no data for the first years.[18]

Table 14.11 shows some of the same patterns that we saw for Estonia. Insider ownership is by far the least stable ownership category. The most frequent change is from insider to former employee (38 cases). If we include these cases as employee owned from the start, we end up with a change away from employee ownership of the same magnitude as in Estonia.

Table 14.10   Estonia overview of governance cycle ownership changes (N = 576)

Initial dominant owner after privatization or start as new	First ownership change	Second ownership change
Foreign	8 (42%) to domestic	0
114 (86%) stable	10 (53%) to management	2 to domestic
19 (14%) change	1 (6%) to employees	1 to manager
133 (100%) total	19 (100%) change	3
Domestic	11 (23%) to foreign	0
132 (73%) stable	36 (75%) to management	0
48 (27%) change	1 (2%) to employees	1 to manager
180 (100%) total	48 (100%) change	1
Manager	5 (15%) to foreign	0
107 (76%) stable	24 (73%) to domestic	1 to foreign, 2 to employees*
33 (24%) change	4 (12%) to employee	1 to domestic
140 (100%) total	33 (100%) change	4
Employee	1 (1%) to foreign	1 to domestic
28 (28%) stable	23 (32%) to domestic	3 to foreign, 5 to manager**
71 (72%) change	35 (49%) to manager	1 to foreign***, 5 to domestic
99 (100%) total	12 (17%) to former empl.	4 to manager
	71 (100%) change	19
Former empl.	4 (44%) to domestic	0
15 (63%) stable	1 (11%) to manager	0
9 (37%) change	4 (44%) to employees	2 to manager
24 (100%)	9 (100%)	2
Total 397 stable	171 first changes	29 second changes

Notes: The principles for defining ownership change are as follows: Changes from an initial single dominant owner to situations of co-equal dominant owners are not considered. The ownership sequence employee–employee–manager–domestic–manager–manager is recorded as manager–employee. Five third changes are observed: * one with third change to foreign, ** three with third change to foreign, *** one with third change to domestic.

Except for the 13 cases coming from ownership by former employees, we see very few cases switching over to employee ownership. Many enterprises owned by insiders are also seen to be moving to domestic external ownership.

When we look only at the period 1997–99 (Table 14.12), managerial ownership is surprisingly stable, whereas both ownership by employees and former employee again are the most common changes. As in Estonia, the most frequent changes are from employee to manager ownership and from ownership by former employee to ownership by external

Table 14.11   Latvia 1995–99: ownership transition matrix private firms

All

First year \ Last year	Foreign	Domestic	Manager	Employee	Former employee	Total	Change (%)
Foreign	105	7	6	0	0	118	11.0
Domestic	11	139	20	4	1	175	20.6
Manager	1	9	308	2	1	321	4.0
Employee	1	4	13	118	6	142	16.9
Former empl.	0	10	1	13	39	63	38.1
Insider	6	32	12	8	38	96	79.2
	124	201	360	145	85	915	

Privatized

First year \ Last year	Foreign	Domestic	Manager	Employee	Former employee	Total	Change (%)
Foreign	24	2	1	0	0	24	11.1
Domestic	4	79	9	2	1	95	16.8
Manager	0	1	89	0	1	91	2.2
Employee	1	2	9	83	5	100	17.0
Former empl.	0	8	0	13	34	55	38.2
Insider	5	16	6	7	32	66	80.3
	34	108	114	105	73	434	

New

First year \ Last year	Foreign	Domestic	Manager	Employee	Former employee	Total	Change (%)
Foreign	81	5	5	0	0	91	11.0
Domestic	7	60	11	2	0	80	25.0
Manager	1	8	219	2	0	230	4.8
Employee	0	2	4	35	1	42	16.7
Former empl.	0	2	1	0	5	8	37.5
Insider	1	16	6	1	6	30	76.7
	90	93	246	40	12	481	

Notes: Inside ownership 1995 followed by manager (employee) ownership in 1997 is recorded as manager (employee) ownership for both 1995 and 1997. Firms going from insider to manager had another owner type in between. Former employee ownership is domestic ownership with concentration < 20%.

Table 14.12   Latvia 1997–99: ownership transition matrix private firms

All

1997 \ 1999	Foreign	Domestic	Manager	Employee employee	Former	Total (%)	Change
Foreign	110	8	5	0	0	123	10.6
Domestic	8	161	13	4	2	188	14.4
Manager	2	12	326	2	0	342	4.7
Employee	2	6	15	135	9	167	19.2
Former empl.	0	16	0	6	73	95	23.2
	122	203	359	147	84	915	

Privatized

1997 \ 1999	Foreign	Domestic	Manager	Employee employee	Former	Total (%)	Change
Foreign	26	2	1	0	0	29	10.3
Domestic	5	89	8	3	2	107	16.8
Manager	0	3	95	0	0	98	3.1
Employee	1	2	9	98	9	119	17.6
Former empl.	0	13	0	6	62	81	23.5
	32	109	113	107	73	434	

New

1997 \ 1999	Foreign	Domestic	Manager	Employee employee	Former	Total (%)	Change
Foreign	84	6	4	0	0	94	10.6
Domestic	3	72	5	1	0	81	11.1
Manager	2	9	231	2	0	244	5.3
Employee	1	4	6	37	0	48	22.9
Former empl.	0	3	0	0	11	14	21.4
	90	94	246	40	11	481	

domestic owners. Both these changes are accompanied by steep increases in concentration among the largest single type of owner (Table 14.13). Switches from domestic to managerial ownership and in the other direction from manager to domestic are also quite frequent. In addition, as in Estonia, some changes are accompanied by an increase in concentration. However, it is also worth noting that the level of concentration on average is lower in Latvia than in Estonia. This difference can be only partly explained by the fact

Table 14.13 Latvia – transition matrix and ownership concentration, 1997/1999

1997 \ 1999	Foreign	Domestic	Manager	Employee	Former employee	Total
Foreign	105	8	5	–	–	118
	72.1/74.7	53.9/64.5	89.5/52.9	–	–	71.6/73.1
Domestic	8	152	13	4	2	179
	49.5/56.3	59.3/59.4	45.7/50.1	47.2/33.5	49.7/11.3	57.5/57.4
Manager	2	12	323	2	–	339
	100/100	48.6/47.7	55.8/58.4	33.9/58.5	–	55.6/58.3
Employee	2	6	15	135	9	167
	26.7/38.8	33.1/32.5	35.9/59.8	19.1/20.2	6.7/10.3	20.5/23.9
Former empl.	–	16	–	6	72	94
	–	9.05/34.9	–	6.5/21.2	5.2/6.1	5.9/11.8
Total	117	194	356	147	83	897
	70.2/73.2	53.4/56.1	55.1/58.1	19.6/21.2	6.4/6.72	46.4/48.8

that the Estonian concentration data are observed three years later. Also, switches to managerial ownership from external domestic ownership probably include cases of take-overs from former employees.[19] Finally, when we split the group into new and privatized enterprises, this does not reveal any differences in patterns of ownership dynamics between these two groups.

The last Baltic republic for which we are able to furnish new empirical evidence is Lithuania. There we can follow the change during the period from the time of privatization and the years when data from ownership surveys were collected, namely for 1993, 1996, 1999 and 2000. From all of these cases in only 15 instances was there more than one shift in ownership. Since this group is too small to identify specific tendencies, as in Latvia, ownership dynamics are shown in a matrix that covers only the first and the last recorded private ownership type. The results show the same pattern as we have seen earlier, with employee and former employee-owned enterprises being the least stable. Although the period covered is the same length as in Estonia, the rate of change away from employee ownership is somewhat lower than in Estonia. This is probably due to the slower development of the surrounding governance institutions in Lithuania. The average concentration rate on the largest single owner increases in Lithuania from 41.6 percent to 47.5 percent during the period of observation. While this is around the same level as in Latvia, it is still far less than the level of more than 60 percent observed in Estonia (compare Table 14.9 and Table 14.15). Part of the difference can be explained by a higher proportion of foreign and domestic external ownership and a lower proportion of employee-owned enterprises in the Estonian sample. Nevertheless, Estonia has a higher concentration rate separately for each of these ownership categories. These differences can be interpreted as another manifestation of the more advanced development of institutions in Estonia having facilitated more rapid adjustments of ownership. This adjustment concerns both ownership concentration and owners' identities. At the same time, it is

Table 14.14   Lithuania ownership transition matrix: privatization/start to 2000

All

2000 priv/start	Foreign	Domestic	Manager	Employee	Former employee	Total	Change (%)
Foreign	31	3	2	0	0	36	13.9
Domestic	2	70	6	1	3	82	14.6
Manager	3	5	69	6	0	83	16.9
Employee	6	10	33	41	3	93	55.9
Former empl.	1	11	4	2	18	36	50.0
Total	43	99	114	50	24	330	

Privatized

2000 priv/start	Foreign	Domestic	Manager	Employee	Former employee	Total	Change (%)
Foreign	5	2	0	0	0	7	28.6
Domestic	2	60	5	1	3	71	15.5
Manager	2	3	37	2	0	44	15.9
Employee	5	10	30	39	3	87	55.2
Former empl.	1	11	3	2	17	34	50.0
Total	15	86	75	44	23	243	

New

2000 priv/start	Foreign	Domestic	Manager	Employee	Former employee	Total	Change (%)
Foreign	26	1	2	0	0	29	10.3
Domestic	0	10	1	0	0	11	9.1
Manager	1	2	32	4	0	39	17.9
Employee	1	0	3	2	0	6	66.7
Former empl.	0	0	1	0	1	2	50.0
Total	28	13	39	6	1	87	

expected that it will take several years before the Baltic countries reach the next stage in the development of institutions favoring small diversified external owners in large enterprises.

The most frequent change in Lithuania is clearly from employee to managerial ownership, followed by the change from employee and former employee ownership directly to external domestic ownership. All these changes are accompanied by steep changes in con-

Table 14.15   Lithuania – transition matrix and concentration privatization/start/2000

2000 priv/start	Foreign	Domestic	Manager	Employee	Former employee	Total
Foreign	28	3	2	–	–	33
	68.2/74.3	62.7/69.4	55.0/62.5	–	–	66.9/73.2
Domestic	1	54	5	1	2	63
	67.0/77.3	53.1/52.2	27.4/42.5	47.0/76.0	45.7/17.1	51.0/51.1
Manager	1	4	56	5	–	66
	100/50.0	43.1/54.4	55.8/59.8	77.5/44.3	–	57.3/58.1
Employee	5	9	27	30	2	73
	24.8/69.5	32.1/36.7	19.5/37.6	17.1/20.5	16.2/16.3	20.3/32.1
Former empl.	1	5	4	2	16	28
	1.0/21.1	11.4/42.9	11.5/49.1	12.9/37.2	8.9/12.1	9.8/25.0
Total	36	75	94	38	20	263
	61.2/71.6	47.6/50.5	41.9/52.1	25.5/26.0	13.3/13.0	41.6/47.5

Note: *N* is smaller compared with Table 14.14 because we do not have concentration data for all enterprises for all years.

centration. As in other countries, except for one case, there are no shifts from outside ownership to employee ownership. Foreign-owned companies again are the most stable form of ownership, although here they are not significantly more stable than is domestic outsider ownership. While the number of foreign-owned enterprises is increasing, it remains quite low. The frequency of 11 former employee-owned firms going to outside domestic ownership is quite high. In these firms the concentration on the single largest outside owner has increased from below 20 percent to more than 20 percent or, for the five enterprises included in Table 14.15, from 11.4 percent to 42.9 percent. Finally, as is the case with the two other Baltic countries, there are no significant differences between the dynamics of privatized firms and new firms. Hence, all in all, findings based on the Lithuanian data also fit quite well with the proposed transitional governance cycle of employee→manager→ external domestic→foreign.

V.   Conclusion

We have investigated changes in governance structures and focused on the identity of owners over the life cycle of the company. Based on agency, property rights, transaction cost and resource dependence theory and related to key stages of the life cycle of the firm, we can identify a typical governance cycle for developed market economies, namely: manager→outside investor participation→outside investor take-over. This cycle develops in parallel with a tendency for a change from concentrated to more diversified ownership. Specific governance cycles are also determined by developments in the country's institutional and cultural framework and by specific market developments.

The transitional economies are undergoing fundamental changes in institutions, with emerging and changing markets creating specific transitional conditions for enterprises and their life cycles. Privatization, pressures for restructuring and weak but developing institutions define the conditions for the evolution of ownership structures. Therefore specific transitional governance cycles can be predicted. Most medium and large enterprises have gone through a process of privatization. The specific method used for the change from state to private ownership determines the initial ownership structure of the privatized enterprises. In many countries employees were favored in the privatization process. This was the case for the privatization of small and medium-sized enterprises in Estonia and Latvia and for the privatization of medium and large enterprises in the first half of the 1990s in Lithuania. For these enterprises we predict an ownership cycle of employee→manager→outsider (domestic or foreign). This process is expected to take place in parallel with increasing concentration of ownership. Since the institutional framework (and especially stock markets) are not so developed in transition economies, we do not expect to observe the tendency towards diversification that is observed in developed economies. In some cases diversified outside domestic ownership has been the result of privatization. In such cases we expect to witness a cycle: diversified domestic→manager→outside concentrated ownership. The shifts in owner type are expected to be accompanied by an increase in concentration. In the large privatization in Estonia and later in Latvia and even later in Lithuania, enterprises were sold to a core investor, often a foreign owner. This ownership structure is predicted to be the last stage in transitional economies and we therefore expect that this type will be relatively stable. This does not exclude the possibility for changes in the long run to other foreign investors or to new strong domestic investors. The speed of the adjustment process for ownership types and the accompanying concentration processes are expected to be closely connected to the development of the surrounding governance institutions. Change will be slow when, for example, property rights are uncertain, bankruptcy legislation is weakly enforced, and the financial system is too weak to play an important role in the financing of investments for enterprise restructuring. When institutional reform is successfully implemented, the development over the governance cycles will speed up, and countries with the fastest transition are expected to have most companies reaching the final stages of the specific transitional cycle.

Our empirical work is based on data generated from ownership surveys designed by the authors and administered in all three countries. We undertake two kinds of analyses. The first and more static analyses involve investigating ownership structures at the time of privatization. In these exercises we divide firms into privatized and new enterprises and examine the relation between time of privatization (time of start-up) and the initial ownership structure. The other analyses are more dynamic. Transition matrices that combine information on initial ownership type with ownership at a later stage are used to investigate ownership dynamics. This work is supplemented by a direct analysis of the frequencies of different cycles of ownership changes for the long panel of Estonian enterprises. The change in concentration on the largest owner is directly connected to the analysis of change in ownership identity. While the ownership data go back to the mid-1990s, the concentration data only cover the period from 1997 in Latvia and from 2000 in Estonia.

The static analysis of the initial ownership structure provides support for the predictions derived from our theory of the corporate governance life cycle. Privatization and the specific conditions during early transition lead to a specific private ownership structure. Employee-owned enterprises are found to make up a large share of privatized enterprises in all three countries and they are especially related to early privatizations in both Estonia and Lithuania. For Latvia, employee-owned firms are also frequent during later privatization, when many companies that were initially leased by employees were fully privatized. As predicted, employee ownership is rare among new start-ups – the exception being the new cooperatives started up in the late 1980s or early 1990s. Ownership concentration is lowest in employee-owned enterprises, higher in firms owned by domestic external owners or managers, and highest in firms that are foreign owned. Initial management ownership is both frequent among privatized and new start-ups in all three countries.

The dynamic analysis of ownership changes for each country strongly supports the proposition that employee ownership is expected to be the least stable type of ownership and that the most frequent take-overs will be undertaken by managers. The analysis also supports the next step in the predicted governance cycle for transition economies since managerial ownership mainly changes to outside ownership. Most often this involves a shift to external domestic ownership, but there are also cases of direct shifts to foreign ownership. Changes back to employee-dominated ownership are extraordinary. External domestic ownership shifts quite frequently to foreign ownership. In this way the analysis strongly supports the predicted transitional governance cycle of employee→manager→external domestic→foreign. The detailed analysis based on the long time-span information from Estonia covering 1993–2002 also supports this specific governance cycle. The most frequently observed cycle is in fact the predicted: employee→manager→outsider.

In addition some of our findings were not completely anticipated by our theoretical model of the corporate governance cycle. Quite frequently we observe shifts from external domestic to manager ownership. Especially in Latvia and Lithuania this change is accompanied by an increase in concentration. Thus many of the changes are connected to the predicted concentration process, a move from relatively diversified domestic ownership to more concentrated management ownership. Over time there is a general tendency toward higher concentration. This tendency also applies to enterprises with stable ownership, but it is especially strong for enterprises that change their dominant ownership group. This is particularly the case for shifts away from employee ownership, but it is also quite strong for movements from domestic outsider to foreign ownership and also for shifts from foreign to domestic outsider ownership. The reason behind this strong tendency towards higher concentration is that, initially, privatization, together with slow development of the institutional framework, resulted in an ownership structure that was too diversified. The limited development of the banking sector during early transition meant that reinvestment of profits and extra equity capital from existing or new core owners was the main source for investment for the necessary restructuring. Small diversified shareholders and institutional portfolio investors were rare and they were involved in only a handful of listed companies.

In the analysis of ownership dynamics we separate ownership by former employee from the group of domestic outsider-dominated enterprises. We assume that low concentration or high diversification of external domestic owners can be understood as a situation where employee owners have left the company, but have kept their shares. A substantial part of the changes away from employee ownership can be explained by this process.[20]

Although there have been quite important differences between the three Baltic countries in the privatization processes and the development of different governance institutions, our findings indicate that the similarities are more important. In all three countries the corporate governance cycles follow the expected patterns and are accompanied by a strong tendency for higher concentration. The main differences occur in the speed of the adjustments. The change away from employee ownership was fastest in Estonia, and here also the level of concentration is significantly higher than for Latvia and Lithuania. In general, Estonia had the fastest transition process. The faster development in corporate governance institutions such as the banking system and the implementation of strict bankruptcy procedures probably explain the faster development over the governance cycle of Estonian enterprises compared to firms in Latvia and Lithuania. However, further research on transition countries with more differences in relation to the institutional development can dig deeper into these relations.

In the literature privatization methods that favor insiders and especially those favoring employee ownership have often been criticized for delaying restructuring of the economy.[21] However, performance studies are quite ambiguous on this point.[22] In any event, this study shows that developments away from employee ownership are quite fast and follow certain patterns, with managerial ownership playing a key role. To a large degree the speed of change depends on the development of the institutions for corporate governance, including the development of the financial sector. In other words, there is no reason to worry about unwanted effects of employee privatizations, so long as institutional developments are fast. This was the case in Estonia (and in later years in Latvia and Lithuania) and, under these circumstances, ownership adjusts and runs through the governance cycle. The developments over the transition-specific governance cycle that are documented in this chapter mean that many companies have taken important steps in their restructuring process and also transformed the Baltic economies into more advanced market economies. With further institutional developments, including in banking and capital markets, we would expect the governance cycle in the future to be much more similar to that observed in 'old' developed market economies.[23]

Notes

1. Country differences in relation to macroeconomic development, institutional framework and culture influence the development in the governance structure and, therefore, the governance cycles in transitional countries have some specific elements related to the transitional process. We shall examine these aspects at a later point in the chapter.
2. For example, compare German and Anglo-American systems. See Roe (1990).
3. Most of these studies look at Russia and document the strong position of insiders in the Russian privatization and the tendency for management take-overs of employee-owned enterprises.
4. In a more recent paper Jones et al. (2003) build on that work, again using data for Estonia, documenting the strong tendency away from employee ownership most often to manager owners. Gradual increase in outside ownership is often a process where former employees get a majority (Kalmi, 2002).
5. It turns out that there are no essential differences from the results based on majority owner (for Estonia see Jones and Mygind, 1999). But by using the dominant rather than the majority ownership approach we are able to include firms in our analysis which would otherwise be dropped (the 'no overall majority' group) and thus we avoid issues of censorship and selectivity.

6. The data on the reason for exit do not have enough reliability to be included in the analysis.
7. The panel was supplemented with 25 fully foreign-owned enterprises and 232 state-owned enterprises. Some remained state owned and have been used as comparisons in the statistical analyses; others were closed. Some were later privatized and included in the yearly surveys. In 1999 134 enterprises privatized through the Estonian Privatization Agency were added to the survey.
8. Kalmi (2002) makes a deeper analysis of the initial ownership in relation to the origin of the company for Estonia. He finds that firms emerging from the consumer cooperative sector or construction association were mostly owned by external domestic investors (members of cooperatives or central cooperatives), and successor firms of collective and state farms were taken over by their employees.
9. In Estonia and Lithuania there was a bias in the construction of data so that privatized enterprises were overrepresented compared to new ones. Therefore the high proportion of new companies in the Latvian sample cannot be taken as an indicator of higher entrepreneurship.
10. For spin-offs it is difficult for respondents to choose between the categories new and privatized.
11. We do not have reliable information about whether the reason for exit is in fact close-down or lack of response. However, there are no significant differences between the ownership dynamics of the group with information for the full period and those that have exited the observation.
12. From the 803 Estonian companies in the database we have excluded 154 state-owned for all recorded years and 73 domestic externally owned for which we have no concentration data to distinguish firms with ownership by former employees. This leaves 576 forms for the analysis. Normally we have ownership data for privatized firms from the time of privatization and, for new firms, from the date of start-up until 2002. However, in some cases the data series is abbreviated when companies stopped participating in later waves of data collection.
13. The results follow the same pattern as the matrix (not reported) without estimates of former employee ownership.
14. The total sample covers a longer period, which should give a higher rate of change, but this group also includes drop-outs, and this tends in the opposite direction.
15. In fact, some intermediary changes are excluded, because they are probably only caused by marginal variations.
16. Reported in the notes to the table.
17. Again excluding reversals.
18. The presented results from insider to manager are in fact three-step observations with intermediate outsider ownership.
19. Such cases were initially recorded as outside domestic ownership because the concentration was larger than 20. In fact the 13 cases from domestic to management would fall to only eight if the definition of former employee ownership were increased to less than 30 percent concentration. Half of the cases of former employees going to domestic would fall away if the borderline changed to 30 percent.
20. This is supported by Kalmi (2002) and by case evidence from Estonia (Kalmi and Mygind, 2003).
21. See, for example, Djankov and Murrell (2002).
22. For an analysis of Estonia see Jones and Mygind (2002), and for the Baltics see Jones and Mygind (2000).
23. In this mainly descriptive chapter we have identified the main tendencies among different possible sequences for the governance cycle as well as accompanying concentration tendencies. Deeper analysis of the specific conditions in the life cycle of the company, including investigations of the different directions for ownership changes and ownership concentration, will require multivariate analysis. This will enable diverse issues to be addressed including: what characterizes the employee-owned enterprises that are taken over by the managers? Which enterprises are most likely to take further steps in the transitional governance cycle? The corporate governance cycle theory has a spectrum of predictions and in future work we plan to use our panel data to test key hypotheses.

References

Alchian, Armen and Harold Demsetz (1972), 'Production, information costs, and economic organization', *American Economic Review*, **62**: 777–95.

Becht, M., P. Bolton and A. Roell (2002), 'Corporate governance and control', ECGI Working Paper Series in Finance, www.ecgi.org/wp.

Ben-Ner, Avner (1988), 'The life cycle of worker-owned firms in market economies: a theoretical analysis', *Journal of Economic Behavior and Organization*, **10**: 287–313.

Ben-Ner, Avner and Buyong Yun (1996), 'Employee buyout in a bargaining game with asymmetric information', *American Economic Review*, **86**(3): 502–23.

Bevan, A., S. Estrin and K. Meyer (2004), 'Institution building and the integration of Eastern Europe in international production', *International Business Review*, **13**(1): 43–64.

Bim, Alexander, Derek C. Jones and Tom Weisskopf (1993), 'Hybrid forms of enterprise organization in the former USSR and the Russian Federation', *Comparative Economic Studies*, **35**(1): 1–37.

Blasi, J., M. Kroumova and D. Kruse (1997), *Kremlin Capitalism: The Privatization of the Russian Economy*, Ithaca, NY: ILR Press.

CMBOR (2003), *Public to Private Buy-out Market in 2002, Management Buy-outs*, Nottingham: Centre for Management Buy-out Research, pp. 37–52.

Djankov, S. and P. Murrell (2002), *The Determinants of Enterprise Restructuring in Transition – an Assessment of the Evidence*, Washington, DC: World Bank.

Earle, J.S. and S. Estrin (1996), 'Employee ownership in transition', in Roman Frydman, Cheryl Gray and Andrzej Rapaczynski (eds), *Corporate Governance in Central Europe and Russia, vol. 2: Insiders and the State*, Budapest: CEU Press.

EBRD (2003): *Transition Report*, London: EBRD.

Estrin, Saul and Mike Wright (1999), 'Corporate governance in the former Soviet Union: an overview', *Journal of Comparative Economics*, **27**: 398–421.

EVCA (2003), *Venture Capital and Private Equity in Europe 2002*, Zaventem: European Venture Capital Association.

Fama, E. and M. Jensen (1983), 'Separation of ownership and control', *Journal of Law and Economics*, **26**(2): 301–25.

Filatotchev, I., M. Wright and M. Bleaney (1999), 'Privatization. Insider control and managerial entrenchment in Russia', *Economics of Transition*, **7**: 481–504.

Grossman, S. and O. Hart (1986), 'The costs and benefits of ownership: a theory of vertical and lateral integration', *Journal of Political Economy*, **94**, August: 691–719.

Hansmann, Henry (1996), *The Ownership of Enterprise*, Cambridge, MA: Belknap Press.

Jensen, M.C. and W.H. Meckling (1976), 'Theory of the firm: managerial behavior, agency costs and ownership structure', *Journal of Financial Economics*, **3**(4): 305–60.

Jones, Derek C. and Niels Mygind (1999), 'The nature and determinants of ownership changes after privatization: evidence from Estonia', *Journal of Comparative Economics*, **27**: 422–41.

Jones, Derek C. and Niels Mygind (2000), 'The effects of privatization on productive efficiency: evidence from the Baltic republics', *Annals of Public and Cooperative Economics*, **71**(3): 415–39.

Jones, Derek C. and Niels Mygind (2002), 'Ownership and productive efficiency: evidence from Estonia', *Review of Development Economics*, **6**(2): 284–301.

Jones, Derek C., Panu Kalmi and Niels Mygind (2003), 'Choice of ownership structure and firm performance: Evidence from Estonia', William Davidson Working Paper, no. 560.

Kalmi, Panu (2002), *On the (In)stability of Employee Ownership, Ph.D serie 10.2002*, Copenhagen Business School.

Kalmi, Panu and Niels Mygind (2003), 'Privatization and evolution of ownership and corporate governance in Estonia – 12 cases', mimeo, Center for East European Studies, Copenhagen Business School.

La Porta, R., F. Lopez-De-Silanes and A. Shleifer (1999), 'Corporate ownership around the World', *Journal of Finance*, **54**(2): 471–517.

Meade, J.E. (1972), 'The theory of labor-managed firms and of profit-sharing', *Economic Journal*, **82**: 402–28.

Mygind, Niels (1997), 'A comparative analysis of the economic transition in the Baltic countries', in T. Haavisto; *The Transition to a Market Economy – Transformation and Reform in the Baltic States*, Cheltenham, UK and Northampton, USA: Edward Elgar, pp. 17–65.

Mygind, Niels (2000), 'Privatization. Governance and restructuring of enterprises in the Baltics', OECD working paper CCNM/BALT. 6, pp. 1–83.

Mygind, Niels (2001), 'Enterprise governance in transition: a stakeholder perspective', *Acta Oeconomica*, **51**(3): 315–42.

Pedersen, T. and S. Thomsen (1997), 'European patterns of corporate ownership: a Twelve Country Study', *Journal of International Business Studies*, **28**(4): 759–78.

Pfeffer, J. and G.R. Salancik (1978), *The External Control of Organizations: A Resource-Dependence Perspective*, New York: Harper & Row.

Putterman L. (1993), 'Ownership and the nature of the firm', *Journal of Comparative Economics*, **17**: 243–63.

Roe, M. (1990), 'Political and legal restraints on ownership and control of public companies', *Journal of Financial Economics*, **27**: 7–41.

Shleifer, A. and R.W. Vishny (1997), 'A survey of corporate governance', *Journal of Finance*, **52**(2): 737–83.

Williamson, O. (1985), *The Economic Institutions of Capitalism: Firms, Markets, Relational Contracting*, New York: The Free Press.

Wright, Mike, Robert E. Hoskinsson, Lowell W. Busenitz and Jay Dial (2001), 'Finance and management buyouts: agency versus entrepreneurship perspectives', *Venture Capital*, **3**(3): 239–61.

Index